I HAVE PUT MY HOPE IN YOUR WORD!

- Psalm 119:4?

QUIET TIME//

**ONE-YEAR DAILY
DEVOTIONAL WITH
COMMENTARY**

QUIET TIME//

ONE YEAR DAILY DEVOTIONAL WITH COMMENTARY

Word of Life Local Church Ministries
A division of Word of Life Fellowship, Inc.
Don Lough – Executive Director
Jack Wyrtzen & Harry Bollback - Founders
Ric Garland – VP of Local Church Ministries

USA	**Canada**
P.O. Box 600	RR#8/Owen Sound
Schroon Lake, NY 12870	ON, Canada N4K 5W4
talk@wol.org	LCM@wol.ca
1-888-932-5827	1-800-461-3503

Web Address: www.wol.org

Publisher's Acknowledgements
Writers and Contributors:

Dr. Tom Davis	1 & 2 Thessalonians, Deuteronomy, 2 Peter & Jude, Joel
Dr. Paul Enns	Colossians
Gary Ingersoll	Proverbs, Galatians, Jeremiah
Don Kelso	Psalms
Dr. Chuck Scheide	Habk. & Zeph., 1, 2, 3, John, 1 Timothy, Daniel
Dr. Marshall Wicks	Acts, Job

Editor: Dr. Tom Davis
Associate Editor: Gary Ingersoll
Curriculum Manager: Don Reichard
Cover and page design: David Choate

ISBN - 978-1-935475-24-8

Printed in the United States of America

The purpose of this Quiet Time is to meet the needs of spiritual growth in the life of the Christian in such a way that they learn the art of conducting their own personal investigation into the Bible.
Consider the following helpful hints:

1 Give priority in choosing your quiet time. This will vary with each individual in accordance with his own circumstances.
The time you choose must:
- have top priority over everything else
- be the quietest time possible.
- be a convenient time of the day or night.
- be consistently observed each day.

2 Give attention to the procedure suggested for you to follow.
Include the following items.
- Read God's Word.
- Mark your Bible as you read. Here are some suggestions that might be helpful:
  - a. After you read the passage put an exclamation mark next to the verses you completely understand.
  - b. Put a question mark next to verses you do not understand.
  - c. Put an arrow pointing upward next to encouraging verses.
  - d. Put an arrow pointing downward next to verses which challenge you spiritually.
  - e. Put a star next to verses containing important truths or major points.
- Meditate on what you have read (In one sentence, write the main thought). Here are some suggestions as guidelines for meditating on God's Word:

a. Look at the selected passage from God's point of view.
b. Though we encourage quiet time in the morning, some people arrange to have their quiet time at the end of their day. God emphasizes that we need to go to sleep meditating on His Word. "My soul shall be satisfied and my mouth shall praise thee with joyful lips: when I remember thee upon my bed, and meditating on thee in the night watches" (Psalm 63:5,6).
c. Deuteronomy 6:7 lists routine things you do each day during which you should concentrate on the portion of Scripture for that day:
   — when you sit in your house (meals and relaxation)
   — when you walk in the way (to and from school or work)
   — when you lie down (before going to sleep at night)
   — when you rise up (getting ready for the day)

■ Apply some truth to your life. (Use first person pronouns I, me, my, mine). If you have difficulty in finding an application for your life, think of yourself as a Bible SPECTator and ask yourself the following questions:

S – Is there any SIN for me to forsake?

P – Is there any PROMISE for me to claim?

E – Is there any EXAMPLE for me to follow?

C – Is there any COMMAND for me to obey?

T – Is there a TRUTH for me to embrace?

■ Pray for specific things (Use the prayer sheets found in the My Prayer Journal section).

3 Be sure to fill out your quiet time sheets. This will really help you remember the things the Lord brings to your mind.

4 Purpose to share with someone else each day something you gained from your quiet time. This can be a real blessing for them as well as for you.

MY PERSONAL

PRAYER
JOURNAL

DAILY PRAYER LIST

DATE | REQUEST   **DATE | ANSWER**

DAILY PRAYER LIST

DATE | REQUEST

DATE | ANSWER

DAILY PRAYER LIST

DATE | REQUEST   **DATE | ANSWER**

DAILY PRAYER LIST

DATE | REQUEST   **DATE | ANSWER**

SUNDAY

FAMILY

DATE | REQUEST   DATE | ANSWER

CHRISTIAN FRIENDS

DATE | REQUEST   DATE | ANSWER

SUNDAY

FAMILY

DATE | REQUEST   **DATE | ANSWER**

CHRISTIAN FRIENDS

DATE | REQUEST   **DATE | ANSWER**

MONDAY

FAMILY

DATE | REQUEST

DATE | ANSWER

CHRISTIAN FRIENDS

DATE | REQUEST

DATE | ANSWER

FAMILY

DATE | **REQUEST** DATE | **ANSWER**

CHRISTIAN FRIENDS

DATE | **REQUEST** DATE | **ANSWER**

TUESDAY

FAMILY

DATE	REQUEST	DATE	ANSWER

CHRISTIAN FRIENDS

DATE	REQUEST	DATE	ANSWER

TUESDAY

FAMILY

DATE | **REQUEST**   DATE | **ANSWER**

CHRISTIAN FRIENDS

DATE | **REQUEST**   DATE | **ANSWER**

WEDNESDAY

FAMILY

DATE | REQUEST   DATE | ANSWER

CHRISTIAN FRIENDS

DATE | REQUEST   DATE | ANSWER

WEDNESDAY

FAMILY

DATE | **REQUEST**

DATE | **ANSWER**

CHRISTIAN FRIENDS

DATE | **REQUEST**

DATE | **ANSWER**

THURSDAY

FAMILY

DATE | REQUEST   DATE | ANSWER

CHRISTIAN FRIENDS

DATE | REQUEST   DATE | ANSWER

THURSDAY

FAMILY

DATE | **REQUEST**   DATE | **ANSWER**

CHRISTIAN FRIENDS

DATE | **REQUEST**   DATE | **ANSWER**

FRIDAY

FAMILY

DATE | REQUEST   DATE | ANSWER

CHRISTIAN FRIENDS

DATE | REQUEST   DATE | ANSWER

FRIDAY

FAMILY

DATE	REQUEST	DATE	ANSWER

CHRISTIAN FRIENDS

DATE	REQUEST	DATE	ANSWER

SATURDAY

FAMILY

DATE | REQUEST   DATE | ANSWER

CHRISTIAN FRIENDS

DATE | REQUEST   DATE | ANSWER

SATURDAY

FAMILY

DATE	REQUEST	DATE	ANSWER

CHRISTIAN FRIENDS

DATE	REQUEST	DATE	ANSWER

DAILY PRAISE LIST

DATE | I'M PRAISING GOD FOR...

DAILY PRAISE LIST

DATE | I'M PRAISING GOD FOR...

DAILY PRAISE LIST

DATE | I'M PRAISING GOD FOR...

SOMETHING FOR EVERYONE

Some people just can't get enough! That is why we have several dimensions in the Word of Life Quiet Time. Along with the daily reading, content and application questions for each day, two reading programs are given to help you understand the Bible better. Choose one or both.

Reading Through the New Testament Four Times In One Year

Turn the page and discover a schedule that takes you through the New Testament four times in one year. This is a great method to help you see the correlation of the Gospels and other New Testament books.

Reading Through the Whole Bible In One Year

Turn another page and find a program of several pages that will guide you through a chronological reading of the entire Bible. Follow this schedule and you will move from Genesis through Revelation in one year.

The Choice is Up to You

Whether you have a short quiet time, a quiet time with more scripture reading or one with a mini-Bible study each day, we trust your time with God will draw you closer to Him in every area of your life.

Read through the New Testament four times in one year

Weeks 1-13

- ☐ Matthew 1-3
- ☐ Matthew 4-6
- ☐ Matthew 7-9
- ☐ Matt. 10-12
- ☐ Matt. 13-15
- ☐ Matt. 16-18
- ☐ Matt. 19-21
- ☐ Matt. 22-24
- ☐ Matt. 25-26
- ☐ Matt. 27-28
- ☐ Mark 1-3
- ☐ Mark 4-5
- ☐ Mark 6-8
- ☐ Mark 9-11
- ☐ Mark 12-14
- ☐ Mark 15-16
- ☐ Luke 1-2
- ☐ Luke 3-5
- ☐ Luke 6-7
- ☐ Luke 8-9
- ☐ Luke 10-11
- ☐ Luke 12-14
- ☐ Luke 15-17
- ☐ Luke 18-20
- ☐ Luke 21-22
- ☐ Luke 23-24
- ☐ John 1-3
- ☐ John 4-5
- ☐ John 6-7
- ☐ John 8-10
- ☐ John 11-12
- ☐ John 13-15
- ☐ John 16-18
- ☐ John 19-21
- ☐ Acts 1-3
- ☐ Acts 4-6
- ☐ Acts 7-8
- ☐ Acts 9-11
- ☐ Acts 12-15
- ☐ Acts 16-18
- ☐ Acts 19-21
- ☐ Acts 22-24
- ☐ Acts 25-26
- ☐ Acts 27-28
- ☐ Romans 1-3

- ☐ Romans 4-6
- ☐ Romans 7-9
- ☐ Romans 10-12
- ☐ Romans 13-16
- ☐ 1 Cor. 1-4
- ☐ 1 Cor. 5-9
- ☐ 1 Cor. 10-12
- ☐ 1 Cor. 13-16
- ☐ 2 Cor. 1-4
- ☐ 2 Cor. 5-8
- ☐ 2 Cor. 9-13
- ☐ Galatians 1-3
- ☐ Galatians 4-6
- ☐ Ephesians 1-3
- ☐ Ephesians 4-6
- ☐ Philippians 1-4
- ☐ Colossians 1-4
- ☐ 1 Thes. 1-3
- ☐ 1 Thes. 4-5
- ☐ 2 Thes. 1-3
- ☐ 1 Timothy 1-3
- ☐ 1 Timothy 4-6
- ☐ 2 Timothy 1-4
- ☐ Titus 1-3
- ☐ Philemon
- ☐ Hebrews 1
- ☐ Hebrews 2-4
- ☐ Hebrews 5-7
- ☐ Hebrews 8-10
- ☐ Hebrews 11-13
- ☐ James 1-3
- ☐ James 4-5
- ☐ 1 Peter 1-3
- ☐ 1 Peter 4-5
- ☐ 2 Peter 1-3
- ☐ 1 John 1-3
- ☐ 1 John 4-5
- ☐ 2 Jn, 3 Jn, Jude
- ☐ Revelation 1-3
- ☐ Revelation 4-6
- ☐ Revelation 7-9
- ☐ Rev. 10-12
- ☐ Rev. 13-15
- ☐ Rev. 16-18
- ☐ Rev. 19-22

Weeks 14-26

- ☐ Matthew 1-3
- ☐ Matthew 4-6
- ☐ Matthew 7-9
- ☐ Matt. 10-12
- ☐ Matt. 13-15
- ☐ Matt. 16-18
- ☐ Matt. 19-21
- ☐ Matt. 22-24
- ☐ Matt. 25-26
- ☐ Matt. 27-28
- ☐ Mark 1-3
- ☐ Mark 4-5
- ☐ Mark 6-8
- ☐ Mark 9-11
- ☐ Mark 12-14
- ☐ Mark 15-16
- ☐ Luke 1-2
- ☐ Luke 3-5
- ☐ Luke 6-7
- ☐ Luke 8-9
- ☐ Luke 10-11
- ☐ Luke 12-14
- ☐ Luke 15-17
- ☐ Luke 18-20
- ☐ Luke 21-22
- ☐ Luke 23-24
- ☐ John 1-3
- ☐ John 4-5
- ☐ John 6-7
- ☐ John 8-10
- ☐ John 11-12
- ☐ John 13-15
- ☐ John 16-18
- ☐ John 19-21
- ☐ Acts 1-3
- ☐ Acts 4-6
- ☐ Acts 7-8
- ☐ Acts 9-11
- ☐ Acts 12-15
- ☐ Acts 16-18
- ☐ Acts 19-21
- ☐ Acts 22-24
- ☐ Acts 25-26
- ☐ Acts 27-28
- ☐ Romans 1-3

- ☐ Romans 4-6
- ☐ Romans 7-9
- ☐ Romans 10-12
- ☐ Romans 13-16
- ☐ 1 Cor. 1-4
- ☐ 1 Cor. 5-9
- ☐ 1 Cor. 10-12
- ☐ 1 Cor. 13-16
- ☐ 2 Cor. 1-4
- ☐ 2 Cor. 5-8
- ☐ 2 Cor. 9-13
- ☐ Galatians 1-3
- ☐ Galatians 4-6
- ☐ Ephesians 1-3
- ☐ Ephesians 4-6
- ☐ Philippians 1-4
- ☐ Colossians 1-4
- ☐ 1 Thes. 1-3
- ☐ 1 Thes. 4-5
- ☐ 2 Thes. 1-3
- ☐ 1 Timothy 1-3
- ☐ 1 Timothy 4-6
- ☐ 2 Timothy 1-4
- ☐ Titus 1-3
- ☐ Philemon
- ☐ Hebrews 1
- ☐ Hebrews 2-4
- ☐ Hebrews 5-7
- ☐ Hebrews 8-10
- ☐ Hebrews 11-13
- ☐ James 1-3
- ☐ James 4-5
- ☐ 1 Peter 1-3
- ☐ 1 Peter 4-5
- ☐ 2 Peter 1-3
- ☐ 1 John 1-3
- ☐ 1 John 4-5
- ☐ 2 Jn, 3 Jn, Jude
- ☐ Revelation 1-3
- ☐ Revelation 4-6
- ☐ Revelation 7-9
- ☐ Rev. 10-12
- ☐ Rev. 13-15
- ☐ Rev. 16-18
- ☐ Rev. 19-22

Read through the New Testament four times in one year

Weeks 27-39

- ☐ Matthew 1-3
- ☐ Matthew 4-6
- ☐ Matthew 7-9
- ☐ Matt. 10-12
- ☐ Matt. 13-15
- ☐ Matt. 16-18
- ☐ Matt. 19-21
- ☐ Matt. 22-24
- ☐ Matt. 25-26
- ☐ Matt. 27-28
- ☐ Mark 1-3
- ☐ Mark 4-5
- ☐ Mark 6-8
- ☐ Mark 9-11
- ☐ Mark 12-14
- ☐ Mark 15-16
- ☐ Luke 1-2
- ☐ Luke 3-5
- ☐ Luke 6-7
- ☐ Luke 8-9
- ☐ Luke 10-11
- ☐ Luke 12-14
- ☐ Luke 15-17
- ☐ Luke 18-20
- ☐ Luke 21-22
- ☐ Luke 23-24
- ☐ John 1-3
- ☐ John 4-5
- ☐ John 6-7
- ☐ John 8-10
- ☐ John 11-12
- ☐ John 13-15
- ☐ John 16-18
- ☐ John 19-21
- ☐ Acts 1-3
- ☐ Acts 4-6
- ☐ Acts 7-8
- ☐ Acts 9-11
- ☐ Acts 12-15
- ☐ Acts 16-18
- ☐ Acts 19-21
- ☐ Acts 22-24
- ☐ Acts 25-26
- ☐ Acts 27-28
- ☐ Romans 1-3

- ☐ Romans 4-6
- ☐ Romans 7-9
- ☐ Romans 10-12
- ☐ Romans 13-16
- ☐ 1 Cor. 1-4
- ☐ 1 Cor. 5-9
- ☐ 1 Cor. 10-12
- ☐ 1 Cor. 13-16
- ☐ 2 Cor. 1-4
- ☐ 2 Cor. 5-8
- ☐ 2 Cor. 9-13
- ☐ Galatians 1-3
- ☐ Galatians 4-6
- ☐ Ephesians 1-3
- ☐ Ephesians 4-6
- ☐ Phil. 1-4
- ☐ Colossians 1-4
- ☐ 1 Thes. 1-3
- ☐ 1 Thes. 4-5
- ☐ 2 Thes. 1-3
- ☐ 1 Timothy 1-3
- ☐ 1 Timothy 4-6
- ☐ 2 Timothy 1-4
- ☐ Titus 1-3
- ☐ Philemon
- ☐ Hebrews 1
- ☐ Hebrews 2-4
- ☐ Hebrews 5-7
- ☐ Hebrews 8-10
- ☐ Hebrews 11-13
- ☐ James 1-3
- ☐ James 4-5
- ☐ 1 Peter 1-3
- ☐ 1 Peter 4-5
- ☐ 2 Peter 1-3
- ☐ 1 John 1-3
- ☐ 1 John 4-5
- ☐ 2 Jn, 3 Jn, Jude
- ☐ Revelation 1-3
- ☐ Revelation 4-6
- ☐ Revelation 7-9
- ☐ Rev. 10-12
- ☐ Rev. 13-15
- ☐ Rev. 16-18
- ☐ Rev. 19-22

Weeks 40-52

- ☐ Matthew 1-3
- ☐ Matthew 4-6
- ☐ Matthew 7-9
- ☐ Matt. 10-12
- ☐ Matt. 13-15
- ☐ Matt. 16-18
- ☐ Matt. 19-21
- ☐ Matt. 22-24
- ☐ Matt. 25-26
- ☐ Matt. 27-28
- ☐ Mark 1-3
- ☐ Mark 4-5
- ☐ Mark 6-8
- ☐ Mark 9-11
- ☐ Mark 12-14
- ☐ Mark 15-16
- ☐ Luke 1-2
- ☐ Luke 3-5
- ☐ Luke 6-7
- ☐ Luke 8-9
- ☐ Luke 10-11
- ☐ Luke 12-14
- ☐ Luke 15-17
- ☐ Luke 18-20
- ☐ Luke 21-22
- ☐ Luke 23-24
- ☐ John 1-3
- ☐ John 4-5
- ☐ John 6-7
- ☐ John 8-10
- ☐ John 11-12
- ☐ John 13-15
- ☐ John 16-18
- ☐ John 19-21
- ☐ Acts 1-3
- ☐ Acts 4-6
- ☐ Acts 7-8
- ☐ Acts 9-11
- ☐ Acts 12-15
- ☐ Acts 16-18
- ☐ Acts 19-21
- ☐ Acts 22-24
- ☐ Acts 25-26
- ☐ Acts 27-28
- ☐ Romans 1-3

- ☐ Romans 4-6
- ☐ Romans 7-9
- ☐ Romans 10-12
- ☐ Romans 13-16
- ☐ 1 Cor. 1-4
- ☐ 1 Cor. 5-9
- ☐ 1 Cor. 10-12
- ☐ 1 Cor. 13-16
- ☐ 2 Cor. 1-4
- ☐ 2 Cor. 5-8
- ☐ 2 Cor. 9-13
- ☐ Galatians 1-3
- ☐ Galatians 4-6
- ☐ Ephesians 1-3
- ☐ Ephesians 4-6
- ☐ Phil. 1-4
- ☐ Colossians 1-4
- ☐ 1 Thes. 1-3
- ☐ 1 Thes. 4-5
- ☐ 2 Thes. 1-3
- ☐ 1 Timothy 1-3
- ☐ 1 Timothy 4-6
- ☐ 2 Timothy 1-4
- ☐ Titus 1-3
- ☐ Philemon
- ☐ Hebrews 1
- ☐ Hebrews 2-4
- ☐ Hebrews 5-7
- ☐ Hebrews 8-10
- ☐ Hebrews 11-13
- ☐ James 1-3
- ☐ James 4-5
- ☐ 1 Peter 1-3
- ☐ 1 Peter 4-5
- ☐ 2 Peter 1-3
- ☐ 1 John 1-3
- ☐ 1 John 4-5
- ☐ 2 Jn, 3 Jn, Jude
- ☐ Revelation 1-3
- ☐ Revelation 4-6
- ☐ Revelation 7-9
- ☐ Rev. 10-12
- ☐ Rev. 13-15
- ☐ Rev. 16-18
- ☐ Rev. 19-22

Bible reading schedule

Read through the Bible in one year! As you complete each daily reading, simply place a check in the appropriate box.

☐ 1 Genesis 1-3
☐ 2 Genesis 4:1-6:8
☐ 3 Genesis 6:9-9:29
☐ 4 Genesis 10-11
☐ 5 Genesis 12-14
☐ 6 Genesis 15-17
☐ 7 Genesis 18-19
☐ 8 Genesis 20-22
☐ 9 Genesis 23-24
☐ 10 Genesis 25-26
☐ 11 Genesis 27-28
☐ 12 Genesis 29-30
☐ 13 Genesis 31-32
☐ 14 Genesis 33-35
☐ 15 Genesis 36-37
☐ 16 Genesis 38-40
☐ 17 Genesis 41-42
☐ 18 Genesis 43-45
☐ 19 Genesis 46-47
☐ 20 Genesis 48-50
☐ 21 Job 1-3
☐ 22 Job 4-7
☐ 23 Job 8-11
☐ 24 Job 12-15
☐ 25 Job 16-19
☐ 26 Job 20-22
☐ 27 Job 23-28
☐ 28 Job 29-31
☐ 29 Job 32-34
☐ 30 Job 35-37
☐ 31 Job 38-42
☐ 32 Exodus 1-4
☐ 33 Exodus 5-8
☐ 34 Exodus 9-11
☐ 35 Exodus 12-13
☐ 36 Exodus 14-15
☐ 37 Exodus 16-18
☐ 38 Exodus 19-21
☐ 39 Exodus 22-24
☐ 40 Exodus 25-27
☐ 41 Exodus 28-29
☐ 42 Exodus 30-31
☐ 43 Exodus 32-34
☐ 44 Exodus 35-36
☐ 45 Exodus 37-38
☐ 46 Exodus 39-40
☐ 47 Leviticus 1:1-5:13
☐ 48 Leviticus 5:14-7:38
☐ 49 Leviticus 8-10
☐ 50 Leviticus 11-12
☐ 51 Leviticus 13-14
☐ 52 Leviticus 15-17

☐ 53 Leviticus 18-20
☐ 54 Leviticus 21-23
☐ 55 Leviticus 24-25
☐ 56 Leviticus 26-27
☐ 57 Numbers 1-2
☐ 58 Numbers 3-4
☐ 59 Numbers 5-6
☐ 60 Numbers 7
☐ 61 Numbers 8-10
☐ 62 Numbers 11-13
☐ 63 Numbers 14-15
☐ 64 Numbers 16-18
☐ 65 Numbers 19-21
☐ 66 Numbers 22-24
☐ 67 Numbers 25-26
☐ 68 Numbers 27-29
☐ 69 Numbers 30-31
☐ 70 Numbers 32-33
☐ 71 Numbers 34-36
☐ 72 Deuteronomy 1-2
☐ 73 Deuteronomy 3-4
☐ 74 Deuteronomy 5-7
☐ 75 Deuteronomy 8-10
☐ 76 Deuteronomy 11-13
☐ 77 Deuteronomy 14-17
☐ 78 Deuteronomy 18-21
☐ 79 Deuteronomy 22-25
☐ 80 Deuteronomy 26-28
☐ 81 Deuteronomy 29:1-31:29
☐ 82 Deuteronomy 31:30-34:12
☐ 83 Joshua 1-4
☐ 84 Joshua 5-8
☐ 85 Joshua 9-11
☐ 86 Joshua 12-14
☐ 87 Joshua 15-17
☐ 88 Joshua 18-19
☐ 89 Joshua 20-22
☐ 90 Joshua 23 - Judges 1
☐ 91 Judges 2-5
☐ 92 Judges 6-8
☐ 93 Judges 9
☐ 94 Judges 10-12
☐ 95 Judges 13-16
☐ 96 Judges 17-19
☐ 97 Judges 20-21
☐ 98 Ruth
☐ 99 1 Samuel 1-3
☐ 100 1 Samuel 4-7
☐ 101 1 Samuel 8-10
☐ 102 1 Samuel 11-13
☐ 103 1 Samuel 14-15
☐ 104 1 Samuel 16-17

Bible reading schedule

Day 105 - 199

- [ ] 105 1 Samuel 18-19; Psalm 59
- [ ] 106 1 Samuel 20-21; Psalm 56; 34
- [ ] 107 1 Samuel 22-23; 1 Chronicles 12:8-18; Psalm 52; 54; 63; 142
- [ ] 108 1 Samuel 24; Psalm 57; 1 Samuel 25
- [ ] 109 1 Samuel 26-29; 1 Chronicles 12:1-7, 19-22
- [ ] 110 1 Samuel 30-31; 1 Chronicles 10; 2 Samuel 1
- [ ] 111 2 Samuel 2-4
- [ ] 112 2 Samuel 5:1-6:11; 1 Chronicles 11:1-9; 2:23-40; 13:1-14:17
- [ ] 113 2 Samuel 22; Psalm 18
- [ ] 114 1 Chronicles 15-16; 2 Samuel 6:12-23; Psalm 96
- [ ] 115 Psalm 105; 2 Samuel 7; 1 Chronicles 17
- [ ] 116 2 Samuel 8-10; 1 Chronicles 18-19; Psalm 60
- [ ] 117 2 Samuel 11-12; 1 Chronicles 20:1-3; Psalm 51
- [ ] 118 2 Samuel 13-14
- [ ] 119 2 Samuel 15-17
- [ ] 120 Psalm 3; 2 Samuel 18-19
- [ ] 121 2 Samuel 20-21; 23:8-23; 1 Chronicles 20:4-8; 11:10-25
- [ ] 122 2 Samuel 23:24-24:25;
- [ ] 123 1 Chronicles 11:26-47; 21:1-30, 1 Chronicles 22-24
- [ ] 124 Psalm 30; 1 Chronicles 25-26
- [ ] 125 1 Chronicles 27-29
- [ ] 126 Psalms 5-7; 10; 11; 13; 17
- [ ] 127 Psalms 23; 26; 28; 31; 35
- [ ] 128 Psalms 41; 43; 46; 55; 61; 62; 64
- [ ] 129 Psalms 69-71; 77
- [ ] 130 Psalms 83; 86; 88; 91; 95
- [ ] 131 Psalms 108-9; 120-21; 140; 143-44
- [ ] 132 Psalms 1; 14-15; 36-37; 39
- [ ] 133 Psalms 40; 49-50; 73
- [ ] 134 Psalms 76; 82; 84; 90; 92; 112; 115
- [ ] 135 Psalms 8-9; 16; 19; 21; 24; 29
- [ ] 136 Psalms 33; 65-68
- [ ] 137 Psalms 75; 93-94; 97-100
- [ ] 138 Psalms 103-4; 113-14; 117
- [ ] 139 Psalm 119:1-88
- [ ] 140 Psalm 119:89-176
- [ ] 141 Psalms 122; 124; 133-36
- [ ] 142 Psalms 138-39; 145; 148; 150
- [ ] 143 Psalms 4; 12; 20; 25; 32; 38
- [ ] 144 Psalms 42; 53; 58; 81; 101; 111; 130-31;141;146
- [ ] 145 Psalms 2; 22; 27
- [ ] 146 Psalms 45; 47-48; 87; 110
- [ ] 147 1 Kings 1:1-2:12; 2 Samuel 23:1-7
- [ ] 148 1 Kings 2:13-3:28; 2 Chronicles 1:1-13
- [ ] 149 1 Kings 5-6; 2 Chronicles 2-3
- [ ] 150 1 Kings 7; 2 Chronicles 4
- [ ] 151 1 Kings 8; 2 Chronicles 5:1-7:10
- [ ] 152 1 Kings 9:1-10:13; 2 Chronicles 7:11-9:12
- [ ] 153 1 Kings 4; 10:14-29; 2 Chronicles 1:14-17; 9:13-28; Psalm 72
- [ ] 154 Proverbs 1-3
- [ ] 155 Proverbs 4-6
- [ ] 156 Proverbs 7-9
- [ ] 157 Proverbs 10-12
- [ ] 158 Proverbs 13-15
- [ ] 159 Proverbs 16-18
- [ ] 160 Proverbs 19-21
- [ ] 161 Proverbs 22-24
- [ ] 162 Proverbs 25-27
- [ ] 163 Proverbs 28-29
- [ ] 164 Proverbs 30-31; Psalm 127
- [ ] 165 Song of Solomon
- [ ] 166 1 Kings 11:1-40; Ecclesiastes 1-2
- [ ] 167 Ecclesiastes 3-7
- [ ] 168 Ecclesiastes 8-12; 1 Kings 11:41-43; 2 Chronicles 9:29-31
- [ ] 169 1 Kings 12; 2 Chronicles 10:1-11:17
- [ ] 170 1 Kings 13-14; 2 Chronicles 11:18-12:16
- [ ] 171 1 Kings 15:1-24; 2 Chronicles 13-16
- [ ] 172 1 Kings 15:25-16:34; 2 Chronicles 17; 1 Kings 17
- [ ] 173 1 Kings 18-19
- [ ] 174 1 Kings 20-21
- [ ] 175 1 Kings 22:1-40; 2 Chronicles 18
- [ ] 176 1 Kings 22:41-53; 2 Kings 1; 2 Chronicles 19:1-21:3
- [ ] 177 2 Kings 2-4
- [ ] 178 2 Kings 5-7
- [ ] 179 2 Kings 8-9; 2 Chronicles 21:4-22:9
- [ ] 180 2 Kings 10-11; 2 Chronicles 22:10-23:21
- [ ] 181 Joel
- [ ] 182 2 Kings 12-13; 2 Chronicles 24
- [ ] 183 2 Kings 14; 2 Chronicles 25; Jonah
- [ ] 184 Hosea 1-7
- [ ] 185 Hosea 8-14
- [ ] 186 2 Kings 15:1-7; 2 Chronicles 26; Amos 1-4
- [ ] 187 Amos 5-9; 2 Kings 15:8-18
- [ ] 188 Isaiah 1-4
- [ ] 189 2 Kings 15:19-38; 2 Chronicles 27; Isaiah 5-6
- [ ] 190 Micah
- [ ] 191 2 Kings 16; 2 Chronicles 28; Isaiah 7-8
- [ ] 192 Isaiah 9-12
- [ ] 193 Isaiah 13-16
- [ ] 194 Isaiah 17-22
- [ ] 195 Isaiah 23-27
- [ ] 196 Isaiah 28-30
- [ ] 197 Isaiah 31-35
- [ ] 198 2 Kings 18:1-8; 2 Chronicles 29-31
- [ ] 199 2 Kings 17; 18:9-37; 2 Chronicles 32:1-19; Isaiah 36

Bible reading schedule

Day 200 - 288

- [ ] 200 2 Kings 19; 2 Chronicles 32:20-23; Isaiah 37
- [ ] 201 2 Kings 20; 2 Chronicles 32:24-33; Isaiah 38-39
- [ ] 202 2 Kings 21:1-18; 2 Chronicles 33:1-20; Isaiah 40
- [ ] 203 Isaiah 41-43
- [ ] 204 Isaiah 44-47
- [ ] 205 Isaiah 48-51
- [ ] 206 Isaiah 52-57
- [ ] 207 Isaiah 58-62
- [ ] 208 Isaiah 63-66
- [ ] 209 2 Kings 21:19-26; 2 Chronicles 33:21-34:7; Zephaniah
- [ ] 210 Jeremiah 1-3
- [ ] 211 Jeremiah 4-6
- [ ] 212 Jeremiah 7-9
- [ ] 213 Jeremiah 10-13
- [ ] 214 Jeremiah 14-16
- [ ] 215 Jeremiah 17-20
- [ ] 216 2 Kings 22:1-23:28; 2 Chronicles 34:8-35:19
- [ ] 217 Nahum; 2 Kings 23:29-37;
- [ ] 2 Chronicles 35:20-36:5; Jeremiah 22:10-17
- [ ] 218 Jeremiah 26; Habakkuk
- [ ] 219 Jeremiah 46-47; 2 Kings 24:1-4, 7; 2 Chronicles 36:6-7; Jeremiah 25, 35
- [ ] 220 Jeremiah 36, 45, 48
- [ ] 221 Jeremiah 49:1-33; Daniel 1-2
- [ ] 222 Jeremiah 22:18-30; 2 Kings 24:5-20; 2 Chronicles 36:8-12; Jeremiah 37:1-2; 52:1-3; 24; 29
- [ ] 223 Jeremiah 27-28, 23
- [ ] 224 Jeremiah 50-51
- [ ] 225 Jeremiah 49:34-39; 34:1-22; Ezekiel 1-3
- [ ] 226 Ezekiel 4-7
- [ ] 227 Ezekiel 8-11
- [ ] 228 Ezekiel 12-14
- [ ] 229 Ezekiel 15-17
- [ ] 230 Ezekiel 18-20
- [ ] 231 Ezekiel 21-23
- [ ] 232 2 Kings 25:1; 2 Chronicles 36:13-16; Jeremiah 39:1; 52:4; Ezekiel 24; Jeremiah 21:1-22:9; 32:1-44
- [ ] 233 Jeremiah 30-31, 33
- [ ] 234 Ezekiel 25; 29:1-16; 30; 31
- [ ] 235 Ezekiel 26-28
- [ ] 236 Jeremiah 37:3-39:10; 52:5-30; 2 Kings 25:2-21; 2 Chronicles 36:17-21
- [ ] 237 2 Kings 25:22; Jeremiah 39:11-40:6; Lamentations 1-3
- [ ] 238 Lamentations 4-5; Obadiah
- [ ] 239 Jeremiah 40:7-44:30; 2 Kings 25:23-26
- [ ] 240 Ezekiel 33:21-36:38
- [ ] 241 Ezekiel 37-39
- [ ] 242 Ezekiel 32:1-33:20; Daniel 3
- [ ] 243 Ezekiel 40-42
- [ ] 244 Ezekiel 43-45
- [ ] 245 Ezekiel 46-48
- [ ] 246 Ezekiel 29:17-21; Daniel 4; Jeremiah 52:31-34; 2 Kings 25:27-30; Psalm 44
- [ ] 247 Psalms 74; 79-80; 89
- [ ] 248 Psalms 85; 102; 106; 123; 137
- [ ] 249 Daniel 7-8; 5
- [ ] 250 Daniel 9; 6
- [ ] 251 2 Chronicles 36:22-23; Ezra 1:1-4:5
- [ ] 252 Daniel 10-12
- [ ] 253 Ezra 4:6-6:13; Haggai
- [ ] 254 Zechariah 1-6
- [ ] 255 Zechariah 7-8; Ezra 6:14-22; Psalm 78
- [ ] 256 Psalms 107; 116; 118
- [ ] 257 Psalms 125-26; 128-29; 132; 147; 149
- [ ] 258 Zechariah 9-14
- [ ] 259 Esther 1-4
- [ ] 260 Esther 5-10
- [ ] 261 Ezra 7-8
- [ ] 262 Ezra 9-10
- [ ] 263 Nehemiah 1-5
- [ ] 264 Nehemiah 6-7
- [ ] 265 Nehemiah 8-10
- [ ] 266 Nehemiah 11-13
- [ ] 267 Malachi
- [ ] 268 1 Chronicles 1-2
- [ ] 269 1 Chronicles 3-5
- [ ] 270 1 Chronicles 6
- [ ] 271 1 Chronicles 7:1-8:27
- [ ] 272 1 Chronicles 8:28-9:44
- [ ] 273 John 1:1-18; Mark 1:1; Luke 1:1-4; 3:23-38; Matthew 1:1-17
- [ ] 274 Luke 1:5-80
- [ ] 275 Matthew 1:18-2:23; Luke 2
- [ ] 276 Matthew 3:1-4:11; Mark 1:2-13; Luke 3:1-23; 4:1-13; John 1:19-34
- [ ] 277 John 1:35-3:36
- [ ] 278 John 4; Matthew 4:12-17; Mark 1:14-15; Luke 4:14-30
- [ ] 279 Mark 1:16-45; Matthew 4:18-25; 8:2-4, 14-17; Luke 4:31-5:16
- [ ] 280 Matthew 9:1-17; Mark 2:1-22; Luke 5:17-39
- [ ] 281 John 5; Matthew 12:1-21; Mark 2:23-3:12; Luke 6:1-11
- [ ] 282 Matthew 5; Mark 3:13-19; Luke 6:12-36
- [ ] 283 Matthew 6-7; Luke 6:37-49
- [ ] 284 Luke 7; Matthew 8:1, 5-13; 11:2-30
- [ ] 285 Matthew 12:22-50; Mark 3:20-35; Luke 8:1-21
- [ ] 286 Mark 4:1-34; Matthew 13:1-53
- [ ] 287 Mark 4:35-5:43; Matthew 8:18, 23-34; 9:18-34; Luke 8:22-56
- [ ] 288 Mark 6:1-30; Matthew 13:54-58; 9:35-11:1; 14:1-12; Luke 9:1-10

Bible reading schedule

Day 289 - 365

- [ ] 289 Matthew 14:13-36; Mark 6:31-56; Luke 9:11-17; John 6:1-21
- [ ] 290 John 6:22-7:1; Matthew 15:1-20; Mark 7:1-23
- [ ] 291 Matthew 15:21-16:20; Mark 7:24-8:30; Luke 9:18-21
- [ ] 292 Matthew 16:21-17:27; Mark 8:31-9:32; Luke 9:22-45
- [ ] 293 Matthew 18; 8:19-22; Mark 9:33-50; Luke 9:46-62; John 7:2-10
- [ ] 294 John 7:11-8:59
- [ ] 295 Luke 10:1-11:36
- [ ] 296 Luke 11:37-13:21
- [ ] 297 John 9-10
- [ ] 298 Luke 13:22-15:32
- [ ] 299 Luke 16:1-17:10; John 11:1-54
- [ ] 300 Luke 17:11-18:17; Matthew 19:1-15; Mark 10:1-16
- [ ] 301 Matthew 19:16-20:28; Mark 10:17-45; Luke 18:18-34
- [ ] 302 Matthew 20:29-34; 26:6-13; Mark 10:46-52; 14:3-9; Luke 18:35-19:28; John 11:55-12:11
- [ ] 303 Matthew 21:1-22; Mark 11:1-26; Luke 19:29-48; John 12:12-50
- [ ] 304 Matthew 21:23-22:14; Mark 11:27-12:12; Luke 20:1-19
- [ ] 305 Matthew 22:15-46; Mark 12:13-37; Luke 20:20-44
- [ ] 306 Matthew 23; Mark 12:38-44; Luke 20:45-21:4
- [ ] 307 Matthew 24:1-31; Mark 13:1-27; Luke 21:5-27
- [ ] 308 Matthew 24:32-26:5, 14-16; Mark 13:28-14:2, 10-11; Luke 21:28-22:6
- [ ] 309 Matthew 26:17-29; Mark 14:12-25; Luke 22:7-38; John 13
- [ ] 310 John 14-16
- [ ] 311 John 17:1-18:1; Matthew 26:30-46; Mark 14:26-42; Luke 22:39-46
- [ ] 312 Matthew 26:47-75; Mark 14:43-72; Luke 22:47-65; John 18:2-27
- [ ] 313 Matthew 27:1-26; Mark 15:1-15; Luke 22:66-23:25; John 18:28-19:16
- [ ] 314 Matthew 27:27-56; Mark 15:16-41; Luke 23:26-49; John 19:17-30
- [ ] 315 Matthew 27:57-28:8; Mark 15:42-16:8; Luke 23:50-24:12; John 19:31-20:10
- [ ] 316 Matthew 28:9-20; Mark 16:9-20; Luke 24:13-53; John 20:11-21:25
- [ ] 317 Acts 1-2
- [ ] 318 Acts 3-5
- [ ] 319 Acts 6:1-8:1
- [ ] 320 Acts 8:2-9:43
- [ ] 321 Acts 10-11
- [ ] 322 Acts 12-13
- [ ] 323 Acts 14-15
- [ ] 324 Galatians 1-3
- [ ] 325 Galatians 4-6
- [ ] 326 James
- [ ] 327 Acts 16:1-18:11
- [ ] 328 1 Thessalonians
- [ ] 329 2 Thessalonians; Acts 18:12-19:22
- [ ] 330 1 Corinthians 1-4
- [ ] 331 1 Corinthians 5-8
- [ ] 332 1 Corinthians 9-11
- [ ] 333 1 Corinthians 12-14
- [ ] 334 1 Corinthians 15-16
- [ ] 335 Acts 19:23-20:1; 2 Corinthians 1-4
- [ ] 336 2 Corinthians 5-9
- [ ] 337 2 Corinthians 10-13
- [ ] 338 Romans 1-3
- [ ] 339 Romans 4-6
- [ ] 340 Romans 7-8
- [ ] 341 Romans 9-11
- [ ] 342 Romans 12-15
- [ ] 343 Romans 16; Acts 20:2-21:16
- [ ] 344 Acts 21:17-23:35
- [ ] 345 Acts 24-26
- [ ] 346 Acts 27-28
- [ ] 347 Ephesians 1-3
- [ ] 348 Ephesians 4-6
- [ ] 349 Colossians
- [ ] 350 Philippians
- [ ] 351 Philemon; 1 Timothy 1-3
- [ ] 352 1 Timothy 4-6; Titus
- [ ] 353 2 Timothy
- [ ] 354 1 Peter
- [ ] 355 Jude; 2 Peter
- [ ] 356 Hebrews 1:1-5:10
- [ ] 357 Hebrews 5:11-9:28
- [ ] 358 Hebrews 10-11
- [ ] 359 Hebrews 12-13; 2 John; 3 John
- [ ] 360 1 John
- [ ] 361 Revelation 1-3
- [ ] 362 Revelation 4-9
- [ ] 363 Revelation 10-14
- [ ] 364 Revelation 15-18
- [ ] 365 Revelation 19-22

Our English word "Psalms" is derived from a Greek word denoting poems sung to the accompaniment of string instruments. The English translation of the Hebrew title is "Book of Praises." The book of the Psalms is actually an artistic arrangement of five collections of psalms – each collection ending with a doxology Psalm (or, a Psalm of Praise). The superscriptions in the Hebrew text ascribe authorship of seventy-three Psalms to David and twenty-seven to various other writers. Fifty Psalms are anonymous. However, New Testament references and textual content indicate that some of the fifty were authored by David. Truly, David was "raised up on high, the anointed of the God of Jacob" not only to be king, but also as "the sweet psalmist of Israel" (2 Samuel 23:1).

The Psalms contain praise, petition, prophecy, and perspective on the past history of God's people. A number of them are songs about Creation, glorifying the Creator. Others extol the veracity and power of God's Word. The prophetic Psalms are especially intriguing. Sixteen of these are designated Messianic because, in whole or in part, they foretell events concerning either the first or the second coming of the Messiah (Greek for "the Christ"). The words of the risen Christ Himself in Luke 24:27 and Luke 24:44 should alert us to search for our Lord in many of the Psalms.

Several Scriptures let us know that the human authors of the Psalms, as well as other Old Testament books, were aware that they were writing under the power and in the wisdom of a Divine Author. See 2 Samuel 23:2, Psalm 102:18, and 1 Peter 1:10-12. If you'll find time to meditate on the words of the Psalms, here are some promises for you. You will be fruitful and prosperous in all that you do (1:2-3). You will sleep well (4:4, 8). Your soul will be satisfied (63:5-6). You will be glad in the Lord (104:34). You will not sin against your God (119:11) but will have respect unto His ways (119:15). You will be wiser than your enemies and understand more than your teachers and elders (119:97-100).

Please note that each year, in the Word of Life Quiet Time, we cover a different portion of the Psalms. In six years you will work your way through all 150 Psalms!

SUNDAY 1

Psalm 120:1-7

What is the writer saying?

How can I apply this to my life?

PRAY For fellow church members working in the secular world to exhibit humble, holy living that creates a thirst in others to know Christ.

Today we begin a distinct collection of fifteen *Pilgrim Psalms,* 120-134. Each is entitled "A Song of degrees" which indicates *choruses sung while ascending* up to Jerusalem for an annual Feast. It seems that these psalms were brought together as a chorus book after Judah's exile and return when Jews would make pilgrimages to the Temple for worship. Each psalm reflects thoughts on a single subject, hope, or feeling.

This psalm, while personal in character, is anonymous and without any circumstances as to its origins. The best explanation for it is that the psalm is a *statement of collective experience* [thus, all are saying "I" and "my" together] of the many scattered Israelites who had been subject to persecution, slander, and even false charges in courts. These were gathering together as they fellowshipped on their journey to Jerusalem.

Our psalm can be outlined in three simple parts:
• Verses 1-2, Distress caused by slander. Deliverance will be found in God.
• Verses 3-4, A Question asked of the deceitful tongue:
  What will be done to you?
  An Answer is given:
  Sharp arrows and hot coals of judgment will be coming!
• Verses 5-7, Disheartened by "long" living with harsh, hate-filled people.
  Yet Determined to do nothing to enflame "war."

Mesech and *Kedar* (v. 5) are distant, heathen peoples living near the Black Sea and eastern Syria. Since two distant, unrelated places are mentioned here, we would understand that the *collective "I"* is speaking of the distant and barbaric places from where they all journeyed.

LIFE STEP If we, as Christians, find ourselves living or working with slanderous, deceitful, harsh, fighting people what should our conduct be like? Ask the Lord how you should proceed. Perhaps you need to (1) leave the situation, (2) ask for His guidance so as to not further irritate the strife, (3) seek the Lord's enablement so that you may bear it patiently, or (4) look for a present, personal peace in knowing that your reward is in the peace of Heaven to come.

MONDAY 1

Psalm 121:1-8

What is the writer saying?

How can I apply this to my life?

PRAY Angola – For the establishment of a righteous government to heal the despair caused by war, famine, and religious persecution.

While nothing is known of the occasion for the writing of this psalm, it has the broadest possible application for all conceivable situations of life and it is available to be claimed by any traveler along life's often dangerous paths as he places his own trust in the LORD as his Keeper!

Likely for this very reason it was adopted as one of the fifteen "songs of ascent (degrees)" as Jews looked up ahead to see the hills of Jerusalem come into view. At the top of those hills was the Temple of the LORD their Keeper! However, a godly traveler's *eye of faith* would see beyond the physical mountains to behold the Maker (v. 2) of those mountains.

This psalm was likely intended to be an antiphonal dialogue, with questions asked and answers given. Notice how it starts with "I" and "my" then changes to "you" and "your." Next, let us notice that <u>six times</u> in the answers we have the words

"*keep*," "*keeper*," and "*preserve*" [from the same Hebrew word] which mean *to guard, to watch, to protect, to care for*. These imply *paying close attention to* a person so as *to continue to care for*. We note:

- Verse 2, God has the power to "help" since He *created* all!
- Verses 3-4, Since God never "slumbers" [thus always *paying attention*], He will not even allow your "foot" to slip in dangerous places.
- Verses 5-6, God protects you by providing "shade" [a picture of His general, providential care]. He is like a bodyguard at your "right hand."
- Verses 7-8, The concept of *God's protection* is now broadened; God guards from (1) <u>all</u> that is bad, (2) <u>all</u> that is dangerous to your "soul," (3) during <u>all</u> your goings and comings, and (4) for <u>all</u> time.

LIFE STEP God had more than one purpose for preserving these ancient writings through all these centuries. Romans 15:4 points out that they are for our learning, comfort, and hope. The principle purpose is that we be aware that God is worthy of constant praise, adoration, and glorification. "By him therefore let us offer the sacrifice of praise to God continually, that is, the fruit of our lips giving thanks to his name" (Hebrews 13:15).

TUESDAY 1

Psalm 122:1-9

What is the writer saying?

How can I apply this to my life?

PRAY France – For believers to be evangelizing to the 150,000 known French Muslims.

The psalmist writes from the viewpoint of a worshipper of the Lord who is joyously anticipating his pilgrimage to Jerusalem. The men of Israel were required to assemble before the presence of the Lord three times a year (Exodus 23:14-17). Usually entire families went to one of these, the Feast of Tabernacles, dwelling in booths around Jerusalem.

Notice [even better, make a note in your Bible's margin!] that the psalm begins and ends with a reminder that the "house of the LORD," that is, the Temple, was the focus of Israel's *gladness* and *goodness* (vv. 1, 9). Then notice that the center of the psalm (v. 5) mentions the "house of David," that is, the king's palace, as another focal point of God's blessing upon Israel due to His promises to King David. Thirdly, notice that the call to prayer encourages people to "pray for the peace of Jerusalem" (v. 6), by those who love God and are committed to keeping the laws and statutes of the LORD (vv. 4-5). So then we see that the advice given here goes something like this — If you will pray for God's continued blessing upon this special place, you may well "prosper" (vv. 6 - 7, *to be in a state of peace, security, and safety*, conditions needed to prosper in business) and *be fruitful* (the intent of KJV's "thy good," v. 9)

Hundreds of years after the psalmist's call for prayer for the peace of Jerusalem, Jesus Christ came, bringing peace from Heaven (Luke 19:38). He wept over the city of Jerusalem because His reign of righteousness and peace was rejected (Luke 19:41-42). Two thousand years after that rejection, the faithful are still praying the psalmist's prayer of verses 7-9. It will be answered! The time will come when, not only the tribes of Israel, but all the nations of the world will come to the Prince of Peace at Jerusalem to worship Him (Zechariah 8:20-23).

LIFE STEP When praying for peace, remember that peace is the end-product of living for righteousness. "The work of righteousness shall be peace; and the effect of righteousness, quietness and assurance forever" (Isaiah 32:17). Do you want *prosperity* and *fruitfulness* (vv. 7-9) in your life? Then begin now praying for righteousness and peace in your heart.

WEDNESDAY 1

Psalm 123:1-4

What is the writer saying?

How can I apply this to my life?

PRAY Papua New Guinea - has a very high crime rate. Please pray for those youth who are engaged in criminal activities.

An understanding of this little psalm centers upon seeing the contrast between three things: (1) Our eyes focused upon the Lord, (2) our situation of being scorned and under contempt by the world, and (3) the Lord's faithfulness to extend His "mercy upon us."

Due to past sins and the wayward hearts of the people of Israel, the Lord had brought judgment upon them scattering them far from Jerusalem, with no opportunity for the repentant believers to go up to Jerusalem to worship the Lord. Therefore, the LORD supplied this psalm for His people who would experience times of "contempt" (v. 3, powerful people *expressing disrespect by means of mocking and belittling*) and "scorn" (v. 4, *to speak against with ridicule and disdain*).

The psalmist begins by declaring "mine eyes" are fixed upon the One enthroned in the Heavens. In verse 2b, he includes all servants of the LORD, "our eyes wait upon the LORD." He compares their attention to the things of God with "eyes" of men "servants" and "maidens" (v. 2a) that look only to their earthly masters in expectant eager service. In the ancient world a servant was expected to watch for a *hand* signal from his master to begin some activity, perhaps the serving of a meal.

Notice the contrast of the psalm; in spite being "exceedingly filled" with contempt and scorn by the rich and powerful people around him, the life-focus of the psalmist was to watch for the LORD's smallest hand signal indicating what the servant of the LORD was to do next!

Because of their distress and in recognition of their entire dependence upon Him, the psalmist beseeches the Lord to deliver them. The psalmist understood that his only hope was found in God's "mercy" which causes Him to supply the needs of His people. The word "mercy" (vv. 2-3) means *gracious acts toward someone in need.*

LIFE STEP Every dedicated servant of the Lord will be the object of scorn and contempt in this world (John 15:20). Here is the answer for this dilemma! Keep your eyes upon Jesus to serve Him faithfully and pray for God's mercy to enable you to be godly in conduct during exceedingly hard times. How can you keep your eyes on Him?

THURSDAY 1

Psalm 124:1-8

What is the writer saying?

How can I apply this to my life?

PRAY Hungary – For new workers to have a burden for Hungary and the funds to support them.

Today's psalm sounds like someone gasping in amazement as he finds himself in a safe place after a harrowing escape from an impossible situation. So real is the writer's amazement that he begins with a parade of unfinished sentences, "If it had not been the LORD ... If it had not been the LORD ... Then ... Then ... Then ..." (vv. 1-5)! While we are given only a hint as to the writer's predicament, that is, "when men rose up against us" (v. 2b), the writer does illustrate his dire situation with a series of four images:

1. Escape from a ground-opening <u>earthquake</u>! (v. 3, like the earthquake in the wilderness, Numbers 16:30.)

2. Escape from an overwhelming <u>flood</u>! (vv. 4-5, like the Hebrews coming up from Red Sea, Exodus 14:29.)

3. Escape from the <u>teeth</u> of a ravenous predator seeking to devour! (v. 6, like the lion and bear which David slew, 1 Samuel 17:34-36.)

4. Escape like a bird from out of the <u>snare</u> of the fowler! (v. 7, like King Hezekiah's miraculous deliverance from the Assyrians who boasted in their records that they held Hezekiah as a bird in a cage, 2 Kings 19:35.)

Verse 8 draws the psalm to a close with a major theme of the Old Testament; true help is only found in the LORD – Our confidence in the LORD's help is based upon His <u>consistent reputation</u> and <u>eternal power</u> which He has demonstrated to all since the days of Creation!

"Help" refers to *aid* or *assistance* that is given. Often "help" referred to *military assistance*. While the LORD was Israel's military Helper, He was also the Helper of the poor, the fatherless, the ill, the oppressed, and the troubled in times of great personal distress (Psalm 37:40; 86:17).

The lesson of this psalm applies to Christians today! We also have overwhelming situations come upon us. And we have those who would *tear* at us with their words and set *traps* against us with evil cunning.

LIFE STEP Perhaps you are now experiencing some overwhelming personal distress. Take a few moments and write out the reasons why you know the Lord is there to help you in all your troubles! Afterwards express your confidence in the Lord in a prayer that begins with the words, "Lord, I know you are my Helper."

FRIDAY 1

Psalm 125:1-5

What is the writer saying?

How can I apply this to my life?

PRAY Austria – Austria has some of the highest suicide, abortion and alcoholism rates in Europe. Pray that people will turn to Jesus to meet their deepest needs.

Today's short psalm has three parts; (a) a proclamation of trust in God's protection (vv. 1-3) and (b) a prayer for God to do good to the upright who seek to follow Him (v. 4) and (c) a warning to those who turn away unto "crooked ways" (v. 5).

Our psalm begins with a double image. The believer who trusts in the LORD is like a mountain (v. 1) surrounded by mountains (v. 2)! For the pilgrims traveling up to Jerusalem, they could see that Jerusalem was a mountain surrounded by mountains. The majority of the city has elevations from 2300 to 2333 feet. The present-day Temple Mount area in Jerusalem is 2440 feet (the original Mt. Zion), the highest point in the city. To the <u>north</u> of Jerusalem is *Mt. Moriah* at 2540 feet. To the <u>east</u> is the *Mt. of Olives*, at 2700 feet. To the <u>south</u> is the *Hill of Evil Counsel*, at 2349 feet. To the <u>west</u> is *Western Hill*, at 2552 feet. This psalm is declaring that God establishes His people and then surrounds His people,

protecting them from danger from any direction.

The reason for this double proclamation is explained in verse 3; the godly believers were suffering under the "rod," or scepter [an ornate baton that symbolized political power and control], of wicked foreign rulers. Yet even here the psalm declares confidence in the LORD who would not allow them to be troubled beyond their ability to endure.

Our psalm now moves on to a short prayer, "Do good, O LORD, unto those who are good" (v. 4a)! While some were "turning aside" to follow "crooked ways" (v. 5a), others were "upright in their hearts" (v. 4b). Ethically, uprightness is a manner of life or a quality of heart that strives to be blameless, seeks to discern "what is right and good in the sight of the LORD" (Deuteronomy 6:18), and strives to walk on *right paths* that are *straight* and not "crooked."

LIFE STEP Christian friend, how about a couple of minutes of self-evaluation? Is your daily conduct on a right and good path? Are there inner thoughts, ethical choices, or daily practices confronting your Christian life that are *crooked in the sight of the LORD*?

SATURDAY 1

Psalm 126:1-6

What is the writer saying?

How can I apply this to my life?

PRAY   Venezuela – For the defeat of any legal proposal to end or restrict evangelism in any way.

The psalmist recounts the singing and thanksgiving joyfully expressed by the remnant who returned to Jerusalem after the seventy years of captivity in Babylon. At the completion of the laying of the foundation of the restored Temple, there was singing, praising, giving thanks, and shouting (v. 2, Ezra 3:11). When worship was restored at the completion of the temple they "kept the feast of unleavened bread seven days with joy" (Ezra 6:22). At the celebration of the completion of the walls of Jerusalem, they rejoiced "with great joy: the wives also and the children rejoiced: so that the joy of Jerusalem was heard even afar off" (Nehemiah 12:43).

Today's psalm reflects their singing and rejoicing with a 4-part outline:

Verse 1 – Having *returned* home from exile and servitude, the freed Jews were emotionally overwhelmed by these wonderful events.

Verses 2-3 – Their *reaction* was one of singing and laughter as they testified concerning the "great things" the "LORD hath done."

Verse 4 – Next they turned to the LORD with a prayer *request*, "restore our fortunes, O LORD." Remember, the farmlands and the cities had all been destroyed, so they were praying for God to bless their land again.

Verses 5-6 – The LORD's *response* was a promise to multiply their agonizing efforts ["weeping," v. 6] to "sow" again the "seed" of a revived nation.

It is apparent that more than a bountiful wheat crop is in view. This is an agricultural metaphor of the LORD's larger goal for His people. First of all, He wanted them to rebuild their nation. But more importantly, they were to be involved in a spiritual *farming* with a harvest of people who have come to faith in God (per Jesus in Matthew 13:1-8, 18, 23).

 LIFE STEP The seed is the word of God" (Luke 8:11). In His parable of the sower of the seed, Jesus applies the truth of vv. 5 and 6. In what agonizing work of *seed sowing* are you involved? God's response is clear; as we sow spiritual seed for Christ, God will bountifully multiply our efforts! So then, what *faith seeds* are you going to plant today?

SUNDAY 2

Psalm 127:1-5

What is the writer saying?

How can I apply this to my life?

PRAY   Costa Rica – For believers to avoid denominational rivalries that turn people away from the gospel.

Psalm 127 is one of two in the Book of Psalms ascribed to Solomon. Today's psalm uses words and imagery that reflect other writings of Solomon; verses 1-2 echoing the language of Ecclesiastes and verses 3-5 stressing children and the family, an important theme of Proverbs.

A. The Subject of this psalm concerns three areas of human interaction and, as a result, of potential personal "sorrows" (v. 2):
1. The House, v. 1a
2. The City, v. 1b
3. The Family, vv. 3-5

B. The Thesis of the psalm is that the LORD alone is the sure foundation for all aspects of life:
1. V. 1a – The home (expressing the idea of "home-business") must be built by the LORD. *Houses* (or businesses), no matter how well built, eventually are destroyed by fire, wind, flood, adversary, or time. Therefore rely upon the Lord!

2. V. 1b – The city (expressing the idea of society) must be protected by the Lord. *Cities*, no matter how well fortified, fall by disaster or conquest, and therefore we must rely upon the Lord's preservation!

3. VV. 3-5 – Even our children (expressing the idea of family) are a gift from the LORD as His reward. Children bring purpose and stability into the earthly life of parents. They are the only assets of this life parents can enjoy eternally.

C. The Lesson of the psalm is that it is "vain" (vv. 1-2) for the head of the home, by his own efforts, to anxiously seek to work for the safety and success of his business, society, and family.

So then, this psalm is an examination of the statement, "The LORD has done great things for us!" (Psalm 126:3), reminding us that rest and security are gifts from the Lord (Psalm 3:5), available by appropriation through faith.

LIFE STEP   Christian, do not vainly seek to advance your business, culture, and family by your own extraordinary efforts! Learn to cooperate with the Lord in all your endeavors as you do your part and trust the Lord to do His part! What aspect of your life needs God's attention?

MONDAY 2

Psalm 128:1-6

What is the writer saying?

How can I apply this to my life?

PRAY Taiwan – For an end to the misconception that Christianity is for intellectuals and the wealthy.

Our psalm today is laying down an often-repeated Bible principle that those who seek to live truly holy lives will also live truly happy lives.

Notice that our psalm uses the words "blessed" and "happy" four times (vv. 1-2, 4-5). The first two occurrences ("blessed" &"happy" in KJV) are the Hebrew word, *hᐧ'-shᐧr*, meaning *having a joyful mind as a result of receiving favorable circumstances*, and has to do with a person's own mental state of being. The latter occurrences ("blessed" & "shall bless") are from a different Hebrew word, *baw-rak*, meaning *having received favorable circumstances from God*, and has to do with the deeds of God to enrich one's life. So then I can be personally "blessed" (a state of mind, i.e. "happy") as a result of blessings received from God.

Our psalm also points out that two requirements are needed for such a double-blessed life. First, we must have a *fear of the LORD* (v. 1b, Proverbs 9:10; 19:23), which in turn leads to the second requirement, *walking in His ways* (v. 1c). First, we must develop a heart that reverences the Lord and then we must strive for a lifestyle (walk) that conforms to His prescribed lifestyle "ways."

The two Hebrew words for "walk" and "ways" both picture *walking on a path*. The first deals with how *I choose to move down a path*. The second deals with *the path that God has pointed out* as an obedient and righteous lifestyle. Thus we learn that I must choose to make God's *appointed lifestyle* my *daily lifestyle* if I expect a double-blessed life!

The psalm also presents a series of rewards that may be expected by those who walk in His "ways":

- Prosperity (v. 2); they enjoy the fruits of their labors.
- Family (vv. 3, 6); wife, children, and grandchildren will be the greatest joy of life.
- Longevity (v. 6); their lives will tend to be long and peaceful.

LIFE STEP We Christians enjoy the additional blessing of having the Holy Spirit of God to guide us in our ways (Romans 8:14), through His illumination of the Scriptures (John 16:13). How is He guiding you to walk in God's ways?

TUESDAY 2

Psalm 129:1-8

What is the writer saying?

How can I apply this to my life?

This psalm is teaching the followers of the LORD that events of their past (vv.1-4) show the way to face both present and future threats (vv. 5-8).

The psalm looks back upon hundreds of years of oppression by conquering nations, who used savage methods of repression (v. 3). Its purpose is to remind Israel that their enemies "have not prevailed" (v. 2) because "the LORD is righteous" (v. 4).

Thus Israel has a solid basis for hope! The Lord is both righteous and sovereign (v. 4) and His "blessing" would continue to be upon Israel (v. 8). The LORD would "cut asunder the cords of the wicked" (v. 4). Extending the agricultural imagery of the plowman from the previous verse (v. 3), verse 4 is picturing the LORD cutting the harness of the plowman so that the plowman can no longer control his oxen, thus saying that Israel was like cruelly treated oxen that will be set free from their wicked masters!

The psalm closes with a prayer that is also a prophecy. Three things are said of Israel's enemies:

V. 5 – These oppressors will be "confounded" (meaning *frustrated in purpose* and *disgraced by their methods*).

VV. 6-7 – Their efforts will be temporary and abortive (v. 6). They are like grass growing on a sod roof, being of no value since it quickly withers away. The oppressors will be destroyed by the heat of God's judgment.

V. 8 – Also, the oppressors will be without friends and excluded from God's blessings. They will never have the joy of singing "Blessed is he that cometh in the name of the LORD" (Luke 13:35; Psalm 118:26).

The perseverance of Israel has now lasted for more than thirty-four hundred years, yet the desire of surrounding nations even today is to destroy Israel. Their desire is still unfulfilled; Israel still prevails. One of the sure proofs of Bible authenticity is the durability and resiliency of the nation of Israel.

LIFE STEP The Lord promised Israel, "the LORD thy God, he it is that doth go with thee; he will not fail thee, nor forsake thee" (Deuteronomy 31:6, 8). Jesus promised His followers, "Lo, I am with you always, even unto the end of the world. Amen" (Matthew 28:20). Take some time to reflect upon the Lord's continuing care and defense of you!

Psalms 130:1–131:3

What is the writer saying?

How can I apply this to my life?

It is good to study these psalms together because 131 completes 130. Note that while the grammar of both psalms is that of an individual's personal prayer of repentance to God, the psalms were sung by large groups of Jewish pilgrims while ascending to Jerusalem to worship the LORD. Thus they sought to express their common conviction of sin and common need of God's "mercy" and "redemption" (vv. 7-8).

Two names for God are interwoven in Psalm 130. The first used is Jehovah (used 5 times, translated "LORD"). It is used to express a cry up to God as the omnipotent One who supplies sinful men with redemption. The second used is Adonai (used 3 times, translated "Lord"). It expresses God's personal relationship to the petitioner as his *Master* and *Father*.

Psalm 130 demonstrates how anyone can appropriate the LORD's "forgiveness" (v. 4) and "redemption" (v. 7). "Forgiveness" means *to be freed or released from something, to spare, to forgive*; the verb's subject is always God! "Redemption" means *to ransom, to transfer ownership through payment of a price or giving an equivalent substitute*. To appropriate the Lord's forgiveness and redemption one must call upon the true God (v. 1). He trusts that the Lord hears him (v. 2). He confesses his utter inability to solve his own sin problem (v. 3). He believes the God upon whom he calls is both able and willing to forgive (v. 4) and redeem (v. 7). He now has assurance of redemption because he has gained a holy regard for the God who saved him (v. 4), and looks only to His Word in expectant hope (vv. 5-6). The evidence that he possesses redemption is that he exhorts others to come to the Lord of mercy for redemption (vv. 7-8).

LIFE STEP In delivering the message of redemption, we have a great advantage over the psalmist. The power is in the Gospel of Christ (Romans 1:16). We deliver that which we received, "that Christ died for our sins according to the scriptures; And that he was buried, and that he rose again the third day according to the scriptures: and that he was seen…" (1 Corinthians 15:3-8).

THURSDAY 2

Psalm 132:1-9

What is the writer saying?

How can I apply this to my life?

PRAY Spain – For godly men to write, develop, and produce more Christian literature in the Basque language.

Today's psalm, the thirteenth of fifteen *Psalms of Ascent*, is longer than the others and does not employ the rhetorical repetition or rhythmic measure that is common in this collection. These last three *Psalms of Ascent* were sung upon arrival at the Temple in Jerusalem. This psalm is also commonly grouped with the Royal Psalms and the Messianic Psalms. Christians in the past used this psalm as a Christmas or Easter celebration song (e.g., the horn of David has budded (v. 17), the "crown" of the Son of David, Jesus the Christ, now flourishes (v. 18), and we Christians have been "clothed with salvation" (v. 16)!

The setting of our psalm is from a time when the Jews had returned to Israel after their exile. Perhaps our psalm was first used at the dedication of the rebuilt Temple in 516 B.C. Perhaps by Nehemiah's time, 430 B.C., it was being used as one of the *Psalms of Ascent*.

The first half of this psalm is a prayer (vv. 1-10) that calls on the LORD to be faithful to His ancient promises to forever establish the house of David (vv. 11, 14, a covenant made six hundred years earlier with David). Thus, it begins with a call to the LORD to "remember David" (v. 1) since it was David who vowed to bring the ark of the covenant to Jerusalem where the Temple was to be built (vv. 1-5; 1 Chronicles 13:5). Verse 7 refers to David's desire to build a Temple as a suitable "house of rest for the ark of the covenant of the LORD, and for the footstool of our God" (1 Chronicles 28:2). The psalm then quotes from Solomon's dedication of that first Temple (vv. 8-9, 16; 2 Chronicles 6:40-42).

LIFE STEP

The psalmist was very zealous for the proper worship of the Lord. As an example of dedication, he presents David's complete absorption by the task of establishing proper worship for his people. He faced great difficulties and ridicule in his endeavor. (The story is in 2 Samuel 6). We should be asking ourselves about our own dedication to worshipping the Lord (John 4:24).

46

FRIDAY 2

Psalm 132:10-18

What is the writer saying?

How can I apply this to my life?

PRAY Canada – Effective ministry among the Innu People (First Nations) in Northern Quebec.

In the Davidic Covenant (2 Samuel 7:12-16), the Lord unconditionally promised to establish David's throne forever. He also promised that every king anointed to sit upon that throne would be of David's seed and of his house, that is, his descendant. In Psalm 132:10-12, a later anointed son of David reminds the Lord of His promises made to David.

We deduce that the author of this psalm was King Hezekiah. Thus the second half of the psalm is the LORD's answer (vv. 11-18) to Hezekiah's prayer in the first half of the psalm (vv. 1-10). It is basically a poetic restatement of God's covenant with King David in 2 Samuel 7:4-17.

- Vv. 11-12 are a poetic reiteration of God's promise that David's descendants would sit on his throne forever (2 Samuel 7:12).
- Then (vv. 13-14) the LORD reaffirms that Mount Zion (the hill at Jerusalem upon which the Temple sat) would continue to be the LORD's place of earthly habitation.

- Next, the LORD declares that Mount Zion will be a place of abundant blessing (vv. 15-16), provisions, bread, salvation and joy.
- Finally, (vv. 17-18), the LORD promises that from amongst David's descendants would the LORD's Anointed One arise, the Messiah. This Anointed One would be a horn that buds, a picture of a powerful, victorious ruler. He would also have a crown that flourishes, a picture of the Anointed One's government that would continue to grow in honor and power (not fade like a flower).

Verses 14-18 look forward to the future reign of the greatest son of David, the Messiah. He is the "horn of David" prophesied in the prayer of Hannah to "give strength unto his king, and exalt the horn of his anointed" (1 Samuel 2:10). So we have God's promise that David's dynasty would never be snuffed out, verse 17, "I have ordained a lamp for mine anointed" (1 Kings 11:36; 15:4).

LIFE STEP Since the coming of Jesus, God's place of habitation has changed. The heart of each Christian is now God's dwelling place; "In whom ye also are builded together for an *habitation of God* through the Spirit" (Ephesians 2:22). How is God at work making your heart "*a spiritual house ... acceptable to God by Jesus Christ*" (1 Peter 2:5)?

SATURDAY 2

Psalms 133:1-134:3

What is the writer saying?

How can I apply this to my life?

PRAY Poland – Young people and students are skeptical of traditional religion but are open to the Good News of Jesus - pray that many would give their lives to Him.

Psalm 133 speaks of the blessedness of brethren dwelling in unity. Psalm 134 is a call to worship in unity. These psalms apparently are a response to some gathering of godly pilgrims, likely near the Temple, when some expression of mutual brotherly love is beheld (133:1).

Both psalms begin with an exclamation, "behold" – *don't miss this*. It is followed by an observation (133:1b), then two illustrations (133:2-3a), and concludes with a promise (133:3b).

- The Observation: "Brethren" refers to all those who gathered together out of a common desire to "forevermore" live in the LORD's "blessings" (v. 3b). The words "in unity" emphasize *an inclusion of everyone in harmony, leaving no one out*. Such a condition for God's people is "good" and "pleasant." "Good" refers to being *beneficial as to function* and "pleasant" refers to being *delightful and causing joy*.

- The First Illustration: Brotherly unity is compared with the sacred oil with which Aaron was anointed (Exodus 30:22-30). This fragrant oil, when poured onto Aaron's head, would flow down across his chest where he bore the names of the twelve tribes of Israel, thus symbolizing the diffusion of God's Spirit upon all God's people.

- The Second Illustration: The brotherly unity of 133:3 is also compared with the "dew" which would flow down from the snow-clad heights of Mt. Hermon. In the arid climate of Israel that did not see rain for months each year, the copious amounts of dew coming down from Mt. Hermon each morning were essential to the growth of crops, vegetation, and animal life. So, too, were the lifegiving, refreshing effects of unity flowing down upon all of God's people.

- The Concluding Promise: The LORD will "forevermore" (v. 3b) cause His life-sustaining "blessings" to flow down upon His people!

LIFE STEP The unity of believers is also important for Christians. Ephesians 4:2-3 tells us that the "unity of the Spirit in the bond of peace" comes "with all lowliness and meekness, with longsuffering, forbearing one another in love." Is there some source of disunity between you and other Christians? How can you help to bring "unity" to the situation?

SUNDAY 3

Psalm 135:1-12

What is the writer saying?

How can I apply this to my life?

PRAY Argentina – For full-time workers to make the development of future leadership a major priority.

This song of praise was evidently used as an antiphonally-sung worship hymn in Temple services. The psalmist has crafted quotes from other Scriptures and allusions to events in Israel's history to form a mosaic of adoration to the One worthy of our praise. The psalm opens with a call to all the "servants of the LORD" to praise Him. The psalm then goes on to furnish us with a list of reasons why it is proper for us to respond to God with praise:

- V. 3 – The fact that the LORD is always good; that is, kind, benevolent, and abundant in blessings.
- V. 3 – The fact that the LORD is always pleasant; God displays an attitude that is delightful (*sweet, melodious*) for others to enjoy!
- V. 4 – The fact that the LORD had "chosen" Israel to be His own unique possession (KJV — "peculiar treasure"). Note that Israel was unique in calling, character, and responsibility amongst all the nations of the ancient world. This word is also used in 1 Peter 2:9 when Peter applies its truth to Christians, another "peculiar people."

- V. 5a – The fact that the LORD is great; this word considers God's importance, power, and limitlessness.
- V. 5b – The fact that the LORD is "above all gods"; the psalm will later expand on this, contrasting what the true God can do (vv. 6-12) with what the idols (false gods) of the nations can't do (vv. 15-18).
- VV. 6-7 – The fact that the LORD is the God of the whole world who does "whatever the LORD pleases," for example, with clouds, lightning, rain, wind.
- VV. 8-12 – The fact that the LORD has brought His judgments upon the enemies of God's people while at the same time fulfilling His promised blessings upon Israel (v. 12). Four examples of His judgments are Pharaoh of Egypt, the Canaanites, Sihon, king of the Amorites, and Og, king of Bashan.

LIFE STEP Psalm 135 teaches that worship is the act of attributing worthiness to God. True worship wells up from a heart of love and gratitude and "giving thanks to his name" (Hebrews 13:15). What evidence is there in your life that God is also worthy of your praise?

MONDAY 3

Psalm 135:13-21

What is the writer saying?

How can I apply this to my life?

PRAY India – Evangelization of children; 70 million child laborers, 13 million homeless, and two million orphaned.

In verses 4 to 12 we saw that the Lord, as Creator of all, is able to do His good pleasure in heaven and earth. This included choosing and redeeming a special nation and then providing for them. Because the Lord is eternal, He is able to preserve and perpetuate His people in the time of judgment. (Verse 14 is a direct quote from Deuteronomy 32:36; its context helps us to understand today's verse).

On the other hand, the idols of the nations, the work of men's hands, have no power to choose, redeem, or provide for those who worship them. They cannot speak, see, or hear. (Verses 15-18 are a shorter version of Psalm 115:4-8, which says also they cannot smell, handle, or walk). Since they have no life and are temporal, they cannot save from judgment unto damnation. For other satirical denunciations of idols see Isaiah 44:9-20 and Jeremiah 10:2-11. The psalm began with four exhortations to praise the Lord. It ends with four calls to bless the Lord. In praising and blessing we are voicing our understanding of all that the Lord is and we are gratefully acknowledging all that He has done for us. We fulfill our desire to praise when we gather together and speak amongst ourselves "in psalms and hymns and spiritual songs, singing and making melody in our heart to the Lord; Giving thanks always for all things unto God and the Father in the name of our Lord Jesus Christ" (Ephesians 5:19-20).

LIFE STEP A good time to bless the LORD is during our daily quiet time. Out of a grateful heart, we tell Him how much we appreciate all that He is and all that He has done. We express our trust in His promises. It blesses His heart to hear our thoughts about His greatness and goodness and of our love for Him. How about making up your own list of four praises of the Lord Jesus and then texting these to a friend!

TUESDAY 3

Psalm 136:1-9

What is the writer saying?

How can I apply this to my life?

PRAY Honduras – Continued economic success for the Christian bookstores that provide resource materials.

Today's psalm is unique. The refrain, the second half of all twenty five verses, is always the same! It was structured for antiphonal singing with a choir proclaiming the first line and the people responding with the refrain.

Its structure makes a point! All the marvelous aspects of God's character spring from one truth, God's steadfast love will remain the same forever!! In response we must ask, what value is it to us if, only in the past, God was good (v. 1), exalted (vv. 2-3), the Creator (vv. 4-9), the Maker of history (vv. 10-26), and the guardian of His people (vv. 11-14, 21-22)? Is He not also steadfast forever in His love for us today? Certainly we, too, can anticipate His loving-kindness towards us!

The psalm begins (vv. 1-3) and ends (v. 26) with thanksgiving. "Thanks" is directed to the LORD (*Yahweh*, v. 1), to God (*Elohim*, v. 2, 26), and to the Lord (*Adonai*, v. 3). These are the three most prominent Old Testament names for God.

While Psalm 135 enjoins us to praise the LORD, here we are instructed to "give thanks" to Him. This Hebrew word means *to publicly acknowledge what is true about God, His attributes, and His deeds.*

So then verse 4 begins a giving of thanks by means of a recital of the "great wonders" of the LORD. First, God's works in Creation are reviewed (vv. 5-9); His creating the Heavens, stretching out the earth, and then giving us the "great lights" of our sky, the sun, moon, and stars. Although these works of creation had been done far in the past, they were still the source of "great wonder." Thus the psalmist adds to his praise a note that the great work of creating the heavens was accompanied by great "wisdom" (v. 5, NASB uses "with skill," ESV uses "by understanding"). Clearly the psalmist understood that deep insight had to accompany the raw power necessary for creation!

The psalm continues with a recital of God's great works relating to Israel's redemption, which are considered in tomorrow's study (vv. 10-25).

LIFE STEP Since we know that God from the beginning of time has been steadfast in His love for His people, how should this influence how you look at your life situations? How can you anticipate God's steadfast love towards you today?

WEDNESDAY 3

Psalm 136:10-26

What is the writer saying?

How can I apply this to my life?

PRAY Bulgaria – Freedom from legal restrictions aimed at believers caused by the slanderous Orthodox media.

Special attention must be given to the words of the refrain, not only because it is repeated twenty six times, but because it is a "Hebraism" for which there is no adequate English equivalent! Young's Literal Translation suggests for the refrain, "... for to-the-age is His kindness."

Where Young used "kindness," KJV uses "mercy." Actually, the Hebrew word has a larger concept than either! It includes several ideas; kindness, goodness, justice, faithfulness, and love. "Mercy" in Psalm 136 denotes the several outward manifestations of God's attribute of love.

The KJV uses "endureth for ever" to get at the idea of "to-the-age" (note "endureth" in KJV and "is" in Young's are both in italics to point out that a verb is supplied that was assumed, but absent, in the Hebrew phrase). For the Hebrews, "to-the-age" indicated *a continuance of a condition until some far-distant time in the future.* A related word means "eternity." Thus

we would suggest an interpretation of the psalm's refrain as follows, "God's kindness will continue to the end of eternity!"

Verses 10 to 15 recount God's manifestations of kindness to Israel by the performance of great wonders in their deliverance from bondage in Egypt, as recorded in Exodus 12-14. Verses 16-22 refer to the great wonders the LORD performed in guiding, providing, and protecting after leaving Egypt until they acquired their promised land.

Verses 23 and 24 reflect upon all the great wonders the LORD performed for Israel in faithfully manifesting His steadfast love for them in the face of their disloyalty to Him. Verse 25 looks forward to God's provision for all people. "For the bread of God is he which cometh down from heaven, and giveth life unto the world" (John 6:33). "And Jesus said unto them, I am the bread of life: he that cometh to me shall never hunger ..." (John 6:35).

LIFE STEP So then, God's kindness was first demonstrated at the beginning of time in God's work of Creation. It continued to be demonstrated in His redemption of Israel throughout the Old Testament, and it will continue on until the end of time in eternity! How might you anticipate what God will do to express his steadfast love?

THURSDAY 3

Psalm 137:1-9

What is the writer saying?

How can I apply this to my life?

PRAY Indonesia – For Indonesian pilots to be trained so the missionary work can continue.

We deduce that this psalm was written by a Temple musician taken captive by the Babylonians when they destroyed Jerusalem in 586 B.C. In verses 1 to 4, the psalmist is reflecting upon the early days of his captivity. By hanging his harp on a tree, he is demonstrating to his captors that the worshipful songs of Zion can only be sung in Zion (the name of the hill upon which Jerusalem and the Temple were built). The tears conveyed the intense sorrow of the situation.

In verses 5 and 6, the psalmist vows never to forget to exalt Jerusalem, that special city dedicated to the worship of the one true God.

When Jerusalem was taken by Babylon, the Edomites rejoiced (v. 7, a small neighboring country next to Judah), blocking the way of escaping Jews and delivering them to the Babylonians. Then they ransacked Jerusalem (Obadiah 10-14). Ezekiel 25:12-14 lets us know the LORD would answer the psalmist's prayer (v 7); the Edomites would be judged.

In verses 8 and 9, the psalmist is invoking the prophecy the LORD made against Babylon two hundred years previously (Isaiah 13:16). The LORD also said concerning Babylon, "I will recompense them according to their deeds and according to the works of their own hands" (Jeremiah 25:14). (See also Jeremiah 51:24). The one who recompenses Babylon is God's chosen instrument, Persia, who would bring God's retribution. The word "happy" in verses 8 and 9 is translated "blessed" in Psalm 1:1 and elsewhere. It means to be *blessed with prosperity*. When the LORD brings judgment upon Babylon, then the Israelites could return to their own land. The psalmist longed for that "happy" day.

LIFE STEP Since Jesus came and conquered Satan (John 12:31, Hebrews 2:14), we do not concern ourselves with retribution. We leave that to the Lord (Hebrews 10:30). Instead we should concern ourselves with that which the Lord has given us to do; to reach a lost world with the saving Gospel message! Is there some revenge you want to bring upon a person who has wronged you? How can you turn that revenge over to the Lord?

FRIDAY 3

Psalm 138:1-8

What is the writer saying?

How can I apply this to my life?

PRAY — Australia – For young people and children to have a desire to attend Sunday School and share the Gospel.

Today's psalm is by an unknown Jewish believer who had faced undefined "trouble" and "wrath" (v. 7) by his enemies yet he had also experienced multiple provisions, again undefined, from the LORD (vv. 3, 7-8). And so he writes to praise God for *stretching forth His helping hand*.

The psalm was likely authored by a Jewish exile, someone like Daniel, who prayed to the LORD while bowing "towards God's holy Temple" (v. 2, Daniel 6:10). Daniel's situation of being exiled in a city filled with temples to the many Babylonian idols would also explain the comment of singing praises to the LORD before "the gods" (v. 1b).

The subjects of the three strophes (poetic paragraphs) of the psalm also fit a situation like Daniel's, an exile who continued to trust in God:

VV. 1-3 – Adoration of the LORD for His loving-kindness and faithfulness in answering the psalmist's previous prayers.

VV. 4-6 – Anticipation of the LORD soon being praised by the "kings of the earth" (likely, some of these "proud" rulers were the present "enemies" of the psalmist!).

VV. 7-8 – Expectation of the psalmist of seeing God's "hand" continuing to help and perfect his life.

A key aspect of God's character is the subject of verse 6; while God is "high" ("exalted" above all men), yet God constantly observes both the "lowly" and "proud." He does not over look the lowly but he respects them by bringing kindnesses to them. Similarly, no distance can hide the proud from His eye and judgment upon their sin (Psalm 97:7-11).

A second key aspect of God is in verse 8a, "The LORD will perfect …me," which is saying, *The LORD will not fail to bring to completion His purpose for me*. This is followed by a prayer (v. 8b); "LORD, do not fail to carry forward to completion the works You have undertaken to do for Israel." Philippians 1:6 gives the New Testament application of verse 8 to Christians, "he which hath begun a good work in you will perform it."

LIFE STEP — How can you express adoration to the Lord for His kindness and faithfulness to you? What are your expectations concerning God's continuing work of bringing your life to completion? What could be the Lord's next step in His refining of your life?

SATURDAY 3

Psalm 139:1-12

What is the writer saying?

How can I apply this to my life?

PRAY Kosovo – For healing from past wars, for missionaries working there, and for new believers threatened due to converting from Islam.

Psalm 139, authored by King David, is arguably the preeminent statement in the Old Testament of a believer's personal faith in God. The psalm presents, in four stanzas of six verses each, four meditations upon God's perfect knowledge of each of us! We outline it as follows:

W. 1-6 – The Lord's Omniscience; God's complete knowledge of me.

W. 7-12 – The Lord's Omnipresence; God is with me in every place.

W. 13-18 – The Lord's Omnipotence; God is directing my life.

W. 19-24 – The Lord's Omni-righteousness; God's will is that I be holy!

The first stanza (vv. 1-6) is about a very personal, omniscient God and His interaction with me. God knows all about <u>what we do</u> (vv. 1-3). God knows all about <u>what we think</u> (v. 2). God knows <u>all we say</u> (v. 4). Of greatest importance to our spiritual walk is the understanding that God, who knows everything about each of us, has placed His "hand" upon our shoulder to comfort and guide us (vv. 5-6). He has an intimate awareness of our thoughts, our walk, our ways, and our words. Yet even David recognized that such knowledge was beyond the reach his understanding!

The second stanza (vv. 7-12) presents another poetic portrait. It pictures the omnipresence of God and how that affects His interaction with me. Again, the first four verses of the stanza paint a picture, and the last two are personal meditations upon its truth. The stanza offers two rhetorical questions (v. 7), two hypothetical examples (v. 8), and two alternate life-styles, flying at the speed of dawn's light or living on the far east side of the Mediterranean Sea (v. 9), so that David could poetically declare his conviction that there was absolutely no place to escape from God's presence (Jeremiah 23:24).

LIFE STEP Jesus said, "I will not leave you comfortless: I will come to you" (John 14:18). "Lo, I am with you always, even unto the end of the world. Amen" (Matthew 28:20). "For He hath said, I will never leave thee nor forsake thee. So that we may boldly say, the Lord is my helper, and I will not fear what man shall do unto me" (Hebrews 13:5-6).

SUNDAY 4

Psalm 139:13-24

What is the writer saying?

How can I apply this to my life?

PRAY Slovakia – For an attitude of spiritual optimism and activism to explode among Slovakian youth.

Yesterday we started our look at this psalm beginning with stanza 1 (vv. 1-6), The *Omniscient God* and stanza 2 (vv. 7-12), The *Omnipresent God*. Today we continue our study with stanzas 3 and 4.

In stanza 3 (vv. 13-18), The Omnipotent God, the psalmist paints a word picture of the *All-Powerful One's* interaction with me! When I was hidden away from human eyes in my mother's womb, the Creator of all things carefully crafted every element of my being (v. 13). He watched over every intricate detail of the formation of that which He had planned for me before the world was. He thought it all through to its completion.

God has *many thoughts* (vv. 17-18). His thoughts are very deep (Psalm 92:5). They are also much higher than mine (Isaiah 55:9). He has heart thoughts about the generation in which I live (Psalm 33:11). His thoughts are in our direction. Marvel

of marvels, "the Lord thinketh upon me" (Psalm 40:17). His thoughts towards me are good thoughts (Jeremiah 29:11). Therefore, His thoughts are precious to me.

Stanza 4 (vv. 19-24) is about the Omni-righteous One's interaction with me! God defines the wicked (v. 19) as those who speak against Him, blaspheme His holy name (v. 20), and rise up against Him (v. 21). The psalmist then declares that he would take a righteous stand with the LORD against these wicked ones (vv. 20-21). Yet the psalmist knew he was less than righteous himself, so he asks the LORD to examine his heart to see what evil ways needed to be purged out of his life (the effect of God's "trying" his life, v. 23). "Wicked way" refers to any harmful habit or manner that would cause an offense against God (this word is closely related to the word *idol*).

LIFE STEP Have you declared yourself to be on God's side and against evil? If so, you must also ask the Lord, "Search me, dear Lord; I beseech you to reveal to me the wicked thoughts of my heart. When You see wickedness there, please show me" (Jeremiah 17:9-10). How can you begin to think like God so that you can also begin to walk in His ways; "O Lord, I know that the way of man is not in himself: it is not in man …to direct his steps" (Jeremiah 10:23)?

MONDAY 4

Psalm 140:1-13

What is the writer saying?

How can I apply this to my life?

This psalm has been attributed to David and there is no compelling reason to doubt this tradition. There are a number of situations in 1 and 2 Samuel that could cause David to write Psalm 140. He petitions the LORD to deliver him and then keep him from the devices of evil enemies.

The psalm can be outlined in five parts with "Selah" dividing the first four:

VV. 1-3 – David's prayer for deliverance from the tongues of evil men. In Romans 3:12-18 the apostle cites verse 3 along with several other Scriptures in describing the depravity of the human heart

VV. 4-5 – David's prayer for deliverance from the hands of the wicked. Notice that David asks the LORD to "keep me," meaning God was to guard by *looking closely after* him as a shepherd does his sheep.

VV. 6-8 – David's confident prayer for the LORD's strength and covering. Note that David used all three of the prominent names for God: LORD (Jehovah, the proper name for God denoting His eternality and work of redemption), God (Elohim, here the short form, El, is used, which means *thou art my hero*), and Lord (Adonai, which points to God's supreme authority or power).

VV. 9-11 – David's prayer for the overthrow of evil and violent men. Here David implores the LORD to judge evil (note the repeated use of "let").

VV. 12-13 – David's prayer that the Lord would maintain the poor and afflicted who were righteous and upright. David closes by expressing assurance that God will vindicate the afflicted, and so they will render thankful praise as they dwell in His presence.

The greatest lesson to be learned from this psalm is that when we face evil, violent, wicked, proud men we can also confidently pray to the LORD as did David, "Thou art my God" (v. 6), who is "the strength of my salvation" (v. 7), who will "maintain the cause of the afflicted" (v. 12). This same righteous *LORD* will cover you in your "day of battle" (v. 7)!

LIFE STEP When we petition God, it is good for us to call Him "our God," to speak of past deliverance, and declare our present trust in Him. Are there wicked people seeking to "overthrow your goings"? How can you pray to your God so that He would be your shield and keeper?

TUESDAY 4

Psalm 141:1-10

What is the writer saying?

How can I apply this to my life?

This prayer by David is similar to Psalm 140. He is again in a perilous situation but this time he faced critical ethical choices as well. So, he urgently beseeches the LORD to give immediate and active attention to his situation. While the actual situation being referred to is not known to us, the psalm does give us several of the circumstances:

- David and unknown associates are at "the grave's mouth" (v. 7); they were in a *deadly* situation!
- Snares and lures have been set to trap David (v. 9).
- David was in a situation where he could have lied or given some evil testimony. Doing so would have brought about his escape from peril. It would have also brought to him the same *delicacies* the evil men were enjoying (vv. 3-4). Apparently, David was tempted to speak in this dishonest manner when he prays for the LORD keep his mouth closed

and keep his heart "inclined" towards righteousness.

- Apparently David was also receiving counsel from sincere and normally honest men (v. 5) who thought that the circumstances justified his yielding to their advice to somehow speak rashly or falsely so as to side with the wicked men.
- Even though he has been tempted give in to their advice, he commits himself to keep his heart away from anything dishonorable or wicked. David chose not to do anything that would give him a worldly advantage to follow.

As a result of these inner, ethical struggles, David ends his prayer by declaring that he looks to the Lord as the only one who could be trusted to direct David to the upright path. At the same time, David also asks the Lord to guard him from his enemy's traps while at the same time causing his enemies to fall into their own traps!

LIFE STEP Sometimes it is hard to determine the right course to take, especially when trusted advisors support you following a path that is not honest or upright! Are there *traps* being placed to ensnare you? How can the Lord help you choose the right path? Will you follow it even when doing so means you will be denied access to the *delicacies* of evil men?

WEDNESDAY 4

Psalm 142:1-7

What is the writer saying?

How can I apply this to my life?

The setting for Psalm 142 finds David completely overwhelmed by his circumstances. He had fled alone from King Saul who was set upon killing him. Refuge was denied him by the king of Gath (1 Samuel 21:10-15) and he was now hiding in a cave (1 Samuel 22:1).

From the glorious days of being anointed Israel's next king by Samuel and then being acclaimed as a national hero by the country, David had been reduced to hiding in a dark cave, pursued and rejected. Soon David came to the depths of personal despair and he pours out his heart in prayer to the LORD. This is the subject of David's opening prayer (vv. 1-4); an abundance of foes (vv. 1-3) and an absence of friends (v. 4).

It is evident that the LORD heard David's plea for in the second half of the psalm (vv. 5-7) David is again on top of his circumstances. To gain his victory over his own despair, David says he had to realize four things:

- V. 5a – God truly was David's refuge.
- V. 5b – God truly was David's "portion" (i.e., inheritance), that is, God's friendship was really what David wanted out of life.
- V. 6 – God truly was David's only source of strength against powerful enemies.
- VV. 6-7 – God truly was David's Deliverer. God had rescued David out of the "prison" of his despair.

Be sure to see how trusting prayer brought David from despair to victory over circumstances. Complaining to the LORD about his troubles (v. 2) changes by means of further reflection in prayer before God (often this is the quiet, listening aspect of one's prayer!) to praising God's name (v. 7). Notice the contrasts in David's outlook: "Refuge failed me" (v. 4) becomes "Thou are my refuge" (v. 5). "No man cared for my soul" (v. 4) becomes "for thou shalt deal bountifully with me" (v. 7).

LIFE STEP David's prayer didn't motivate God to immediate action. Instead, David's prayer changed David's thinking; despair became victorious hope as David remembered who God truly was! Have the hard things of life brought you to despair your situation? Take time to consider that God is your refuge, portion, strength, and Deliverer!

THURSDAY 4

Psalm 143:1-12

What is the writer saying?

How can I apply this to my life?

PRAY Jamaica – For churches to model compassion to the poor, who receive minimal exposure to the gospel.

David, who years before (v. 5) had been anointed by God to serve as king over Israel, finds himself "persecuted" (v. 3a, *pursued*), "smitten to the ground" (v. 3b, *beaten down*), "dwelling in darkness" (v. 3c), "overwhelmed" (v. 4a, *paralyzed with fear*), and "desolate" (v. 4b, *to come to a wasted and ruined state*). In this crushing plight, he petitions the LORD on the basis of the LORD's faithfulness and righteousness (v. 1).

David had spent time meditating upon how the LORD had helped him in the past (v. 5). Now David is wasting away, yearning to have his thirst quenched by God (v. 6). He is saying, "Please hurry; save me for I am perishing; let me again experience your loving-kindness (v. 11); I'm trusting in you" (v. 12). Notice the reasons David uses in his request:

V. 2 – David starts with the negative (v. 2): Don't save me because of my own righteousness. No man is justified by his own merit!

V. 1 – Save me due to Your own faithfulness and righteousness.

V. 5 – Save me as I have previously seen you save others! David remembers God's willingness to deliver in the past.

V. 6 – Save me because I am reaching out my hands to You. David had a great spiritual thirst for the LORD.

V. 9 – Save me because I have fled to You knowing You will hide me.

V. 10 – Save me because I have declared You as my God.

V. 11 – Save me for the sake of Your righteous name.

In this psalm, David declares God to be faithful, righteous, just, loving, kind, good, and merciful. All of these characteristics are assumed to be included in the meaning of His "name," LORD (v. 11). Thus it is for the LORD's "name's sake" that David asks to be brought back from the brink of death to a life of productive service ("I am your servant," v. 12).

LIFE STEP When you are feeling like David, persecuted, beaten down, overwhelmed, or ruined, you too need to invest some time in your own two-way-communication prayer to the Lord ("Lord, hear me," v. 7, and "cause me to hear," v. 8). Through your hard situations, how can you learn to walk in uprightness and to follow the will of the Lord (v. 8)? What does God want to teach you and how will He lead you (v. 9)?

FRIDAY 4

Psalm 144:1-15

What is the writer saying?

How can I apply this to my life?

PRAY   Romania - Pray that schools in Romania will be open to religious teaching.

Today's psalm is a composite psalm; formed almost entirely as a musical patchwork of quotes from other verses of Scripture (e.g., Psalms 8, 18, 33, 39, & 104). First, note that David uses "I," "me," and "my" eleven times in verses 1-11. Then note that verses 12-15 seem to be a kind of congregational response (seven times the plural pronoun "our" is used here) by the "people" (v. 15) to the song leader's recital of the LORD's many blessings (v. 1)

While the psalm does not tell us the historical situation which prompted the initial arranging of its pieces, a good possibility is David's and the army of Israel's remarkable victory over Goliath and the army of the Philistines; 1 Samuel 17:47, "And all this assembly shall know that the LORD saves not with sword and spear: for the battle *is* the LORD'S."

Let's focus on the nine titles given in verses 1-2 to the LORD as David declares his blessing (*a verbal salute of adoration*) upon God:

- God is my Strength, literally "Rock," symbol of stability, dependability.
- God is my Teacher; God instructs, imparts what I need to know.
- God is my Goodness; or we could say *my loving-kind-good Master.*
- God is my Fortress; God is like having my own defensive position high in the inaccessible rocks of a mountain.
- God is my High Tower; God is like a high and safe watchtower that is out of range of an enemy's arrows.
- God is my Deliverer; God is the One who continues to help me escape from "great waters" (v. 7) that threaten my life.
- God is my Shield; God is my source of protection from dangerous "arrows" that godless people shoot at me.
- God is my Refuge; God is like my shade tree where I can find protection from a dangerous desert sun.
- God is my Conqueror; God will give me complete victory.

LIFE STEP   Since verses 12-15 were likely Israel's congregational response to David's adoration of God, why don't you in a similar way write your own personal response to David? Like ancient Israel, what do you personally anticipate as future blessings from God that will be experienced in your life? How will He be your strength and refuge?

Psalm 145:1-9

What is the writer saying?

How can I apply this to my life?

This "most exquisite psalm" (Graham Scroggie) is the only psalm which bears the Hebrew title *Tehillah* ("a praise"), from which the name of the whole Book of Psalms is derived *Tehillim* ("praises"). Clearly, it was David's opinion that this was the *crown jewel of praise* amongst all psalms! A simple outline that captures the majesty of the Psalm is:

VV. 1-6 – I will praise God for His Might Acts.

VV. 7-9 – I will praise God for His Gracious Character.

VV. 10-16 – I will praise God for His Glorious and Universal Kingdom.

VV. 17-21 – I will praise God for His Care of His Own.

Let's consider the personal resolve of the six "I will's" in the psalm to "every day" and "forever and ever" praise God's name (vv. 1-2).

- V. 1 – "I will extol thee," that is, I will <u>lift up</u> God with my highest praise.

- V. 1 – "I will bless thy name forever," that is, I will <u>bend-my-knee</u> to You as long as there is life within me – and even into eternity!

- V. 2 – "Every day will I bless thee," that is, since I am daily dependent upon your care, I will not fail to <u>daily extend</u> my thanks to You.

- V. 2 – "I will praise Your name forever"; literally, I will <u>shine-like-a-star</u> as I seek to <u>radiate</u> in life and speech to declare Your "*name*" (the summation of God's revealed character). I will <u>boast</u> of You.

- V. 5 – "I will speak of the glorious honor of Thy majesty," that is I will <u>publicly make known</u> Your care of and blessings upon me!

- V. 6 – "I will declare Your greatness," literally, I will <u>make a list in a book</u> that gives a recounting of Your great deeds. Thus it is saying, I will point out to others a listing of all Your greatnesses.

 LIFE STEP Christian friend, what is your personal resolve in this matter of *radiating* in your life and speech so that you might make known to others God's care and goodness towards you? Take a few minutes and write out your own list of "I will" declarations concerning how you will daily express your walk with and for God.

SUNDAY 5

Psalm 145:10-21

What is the writer saying?

How can I apply this to my life?

PRAY South Africa – For churches to commit financial aid to those seeking to attend Bible school.

This is the last of the nine acrostic psalms. The first verse begins with *Aleph*, the first letter of the Hebrew alphabet. The second begins with *Beth*, and so on through the twenty two letters. However, the verse for the fourteenth letter, *Nun*, is missing. That is why the psalm has twenty one verses instead of twenty two. One ancient manuscript supplied "Faithful is the LORD in his words and holy in all his works" as verse 14. Translators deduced it to be a scribe's attempt to fix the problem until the discovery of the Dead Sea Scrolls that caused many to accept the verse as authentic.

This most noble of Psalms has several unique features:

- Its trait of rapid transitions to the many aspects of God's greatness reveals a meditative heart reflecting on the rich fullness of God.

- It has an *eternal outlook*, beginning and ending with "ever and ever" (vv. 1, 21). In between it declares the LORD's kingdom is "everlasting" and "throughout all generations" (v. 13).

- It has a messianic hope in verses 10-13 that looks forward to the future messianic kingdom of the Lord Jesus when all the LORD's works will be universally praised for "the glorious majesty of his kingdom."

- Its most striking feature is a desire to express God's universal goodness to all His creation (e.g., "all" and "every" occur 16 times). While the psalm opens with a collective "I will extol Thee" (in effect saying, *We all, who trust in God, exalt You*), it anticipates a widening of praise to all the "sons of men" and all "flesh" (vv. 12, 21).

Because of all that is said in this psalm about His greatness (v. 3), His majesty (vv. 5, 12), His wondrous works (v. 5), His goodness (vv. 7, 9), His righteousness (vv. 7, 17), His graciousness, compassion and mercy (v. 8), and His glory and power (v. 11) the psalmist concludes with the words, "Let all flesh bless His holy name" (v. 21)!

LIFE STEP When we read the promise of verse 18, we are thankful that "in Christ Jesus, ye (*we*) who sometimes were far off are made nigh by the blood of Christ" (Ephesians 2:13). Since you, as a believer in Jesus Christ, are now included in the "all" of this psalm, what need is there in your life for which you can personally claim the promise, "The LORD preserveth all them that love Him" (v. 20)?

Psalm 146:1-10

What is the writer saying?

How can I apply this to my life?

PRAY Venezuela – For missionaries to overcome the obstacles that make obtaining a visa a difficult process.

Today's psalm is a study of <u>whom we should praise</u> based upon <u>whom we can trust</u>. The psalmist presents both positive and negative counsel: a contrast between God's Reliability (vv. 1-2, 10) and Man's Fallibility (vv. 3-4, that is, *liable to miss, deceive, or fail*).

The psalmist begins by warning us not to put our trust in rulers and other powerful people (v. 3a). In fact, it is foolish to trust in any person regardless of their rank or power (v. 3b). The reason given goes to the core of the issue; people are one breath from death (v. 4a) and when they die their promises, plans, and intentions die with them (v. 4b).

In contrast, note the psalmist's reasons for trusting in God alone:

V. 5 – God has always been Israel's *help* and *hope*. For us Christians, God has become an even "better hope" (Hebrews 7:19; 6:11, 18-19)!

V. 6 – God, who is the all-powerful and eternal Creator, is the only one who "keeps" His promises! He alone can be relied upon.

V. 7 – God, the Just One, is compassionate towards the needy and overrides the injustices of wicked men.

V. 8 – God gives spiritual sight to the "blind" (Psalm 119:18) and renewed hope to those who are "bowed down."

V. 9 – God gives special protection to defenseless people, like strangers and the fatherless. In a similar way, God "turns upside down" the evil plans of the wicked; their schemes will be *bent to the side* and fail.

Note the two catalogues presented in this psalm. First, there is a list of troubled people: the oppressed, hungry, prisoners, blind, bowed down, strangers, fatherless, and widows. Then there is a list of the loving-care of God: God helps, protects, nourishes, liberates, illuminates, renews hope, keeps, sustains and, at the same time, bends away the evil plans of the wicked. Truly, the LORD is worthy of our praise.

LIFE STEP Is your life "happy" (v. 5a, *in a joyful state of mind*)? The key to happiness is found here, that is, trusting only in the LORD (v. 3a)! Consider the greatest source of trouble in your life. Rather than trusting in people and plans to overcome this trouble, how can you trust in the Lord? How can God be your helper, teacher, or defender?

TUESDAY 5

Psalm 147:1-11

What is the writer saying?

How can I apply this to my life?

PRAY Aruba – For outreach among those who have immigrated from Latin America, the Caribbean and Asia.

The psalmist begins with a call to sing praises unto our God because it is "good" (*proper and pleasing*, also 92:1), "pleasant" (God is *a joy to be with*, 135:3), and "comely" (*appropriate* 33:1). He continues by presenting five categories worthy of our singing praises unto our God:

- Because of His great abilities: God has wisdom beyond all (v. 4), He has great power beyond all (v. 5), He has infinite understanding. (The word includes ideas of *insight, reasoning, intelligence, and judgment that distinguishes right from wrong*.)
- Because of His wonderful works for Israel: He rebuilds Jerusalem (v. 2), brings back the exiles (v. 2b), sends peace to the nations (vv. 13-14), and gives His Law to Israel (vv. 19-20).
- Because of His blessing upon all nations: He sends rain to all so the grass will grow (v. 8), He feeds the wild animals (vv. 9-10), He controls the weather (vv. 15-18).
- Because of His glorious works in the heavens: He alone counts and names the stars (v. 4, thus He knows the character of each!) and He has absolute power over the heavens (v. 5).
- Because of His care for the redeemed: He heals the broken in heart and binds up their wounds (v. 3), He sustains and holds up the meek (v. 6a) while bringing low the wicked (v. 6b), and He delights in those who honor Him and hope in his unfailing love (vv. 10-11)

Verse 7 exhorts us to include thanksgiving in singing His praises and to use musical instruments to enhance the singing. Notice that the singing is "unto our God." It is not for the aggrandizement of the performer or the hilarity of the human audience!

LIFE STEP We have so many things to praise God for!! Go pick up a hymnbook or chorus book and pick out a song you can quietly sing throughout your day! Also, as one of the LORD's redeemed, what could you do today that would cause God to delight in you?

WEDNESDAY 5

Psalm 147:12-20

What is the writer saying?

How can I apply this to my life?

PRAY Poland – For God to protect missionaries and ministry equipment from criminal activity.

Considering verses 12-14 together with verse 2, we conclude that this psalm was written soon after the rebuilding of the walls of Jerusalem in 443 B.C. This was 143 years after the destruction of Jerusalem by the Babylonians in 586 B.C. It was also seventy two years after the completion of the rebuilt Temple (Ezra 6:15). All during this time the returned Jews faced fierce opposition from those who were against their return to their land.

Today's portion, verses 12-20, continues to build upon the climax of the first half of the psalm, namely "The LORD taketh pleasure in them that fear Him, in those that hope in his mercy" (v. 11) which is to say, God delights in His people who reverently and confidently trust in and wait for God to act upon His continuing love for His own.

We must not miss the six-fold emphasis here that the confident hope of these believers was based upon God's "word" (vv. 15, 18, 19; along with synonyms;

commandment, v. 15, *statutes*, v. 19, and *judgments*, v. 19). The psalmist poetically illustrates the effective agency of God's word by declaring that God through His word controls the earth, snow, frost, ice, cold, seasons, wind, and water (vv. 15-18). This poetic illustration lays a foundation for the more important subject — the application of God's Word to the hearts of His people (v. 19a),which was above and beyond all physical blessing given to Israel. God's Word had been given exclusively to Israel (v. 20) as a great blessing to her, for by it Israel knew God's *statutes* and *judgments* (v. 19b), which taught them how to walk in God's ways in their daily conduct. The Apostle Paul comments upon this greatest privilege of Israel in Romans 3:1-2, namely, the greatest "advantage" of the Jewish people was that God had *committed* His *oracles* unto them!

LIFE STEP Since God's distinguishing blessing to Israel was giving them His Word, how much more should we Christians treasure and study our now-completed Word of God! To demonstrate your own thankfulness to God for His Word, is there a time each day you could commit to reading a chapter of a book about the Bible?

THURSDAY 5

Psalm 148:1-14

What is the writer saying?

How can I apply this to my life?

PRAY France – That evangelical churches would be purged of liberal theology and political correctness.

In this antiphonal song of praise, the psalmist calls upon the whole of creation in its two Hebrew divisions, heaven and earth, to praise Jehovah, the eternal One who created everything else (Exodus 3:14).

Praise ye the LORD from the Heavens (vv. 1-6).

What do the angelic hosts say when they praise the LORD? They say "Glory to God in the highest" (Luke 2:13-14). They say, "Holy, holy, holy, Lord God Almighty, which was, and is, and is to come" (Revelation 4:8). They say with a loud voice, "Worthy is the Lamb that was slain to receive power, and riches, and wisdom, and strength, and honor, and glory, and blessing" (Revelation 5:12).

How do the sun, moon, and stars praise Him? By showing His handiwork, they speak of His knowledge day and night in every language "to the end of the world" (Psalm 19:1-4). They do it because "he commanded, and they were created" (v. 5). They perform according to His decree and do not digress from it.

Praise ye the LORD from the Earth (vv. 7-12).

How do the creatures of the sea and the elements of the weather fulfill His word? They do His bidding, even when it is against their nature (Jonah 2:10; Mark 4:39). Mountains quake at His presence (Psalm 68:8). Animals speak at His behest (Numbers 22:28). Birds perform His work (Genesis 8:8; 1 Kings 17:4), according to His command. The time will come when the kings of the earth will worship Him (Isaiah 49:7; 60:3).

When rulers and the redeemed of every kind (v. 11) join the angels in praising the LORD, what will they say? They will all say "Amen: Blessing, and glory, and wisdom, and thanksgiving, and honor, and power, and might, be unto our God for ever and ever. Amen" (Revelation 7:12).

LIFE STEP How should we praise our Lord? "…be filled with the Spirit; Speaking to yourselves in psalms and hymns and spiritual songs, singing and making melody in your heart to the Lord; Giving thanks always for all things unto God and the Father in the name of our Lord Jesus Christ" (Ephesians 5:18-20). How can you today join this great chorus of praise?

Psalm 149:1-9

What is the writer saying?

How can I apply this to my life?

PRAY Germany – For godly public officials who will use their influence for the furtherance of the Gospel.

Our psalm is written to the "congregation of the saints" (vv. 1, 5), which means *the assembly of those* faithful followers (145:10) who exercise a loyalty in their walk before God and in kindness to other men. The LORD is to be praised for the salvation that beautifies His saints (v 2-5) and for the hope He has given of future triumphs over hostile, heathen nations (vv. 6-9) that will be subjugated to the Lord Jesus during His messianic kingdom known as the Millennium (Psalm 2:8).

Every generation must renew this call for a new song unto the LORD. The psalm gives us several reasons for renewed singing to the Lord:

- We sing because our Lord "takes pleasure" in us, His people (v. 4a). The words "takes pleasure" means God has an attitude of fondness and pleasure towards us. It implies a relationship between the two parties, as a father takes pleasure in his children.
- We sing because He beautifies our lives with meekness, a fruit of His *salvation*

(v. 4b, *meekness* is one of the fruits of the Spirit in Galatians 5:22-23). The Lord beautifies us by *adorning so as to make beautiful*. God is transforming our broken, sinful lives so that we, by the work of His Spirit, become lovely, pleasing, an object of wonder!

- We sing because our Lord will surely punish our enemies (vv. 6-9).
- We sing because our Lord is the source of all our "honor" (*glory*, v. 9). This word is used all through the Old Testament to describe the best qualities of God (e.g., 1 Chronicles 16:27); His glorious appearance, splendor, and majesty that instill awe in us.

We note that our psalm calls upon us to dance as a part of our praise to God. We would add a cause that proper scriptural dancing is an outward expression of joy before the LORD. It is always by groups (Exodus 15:20: 1 Samuel 21:11) or individuals (2 Samuel 6:14) but never by couples. It is never for displaying one's talents before an audience.

LIFE STEP How can you express your own joy in God's work of beautifying your life? How has He adorned you with transforming qualities that cause others to wonder at the changes in your character?

SATURDAY 5

Psalm 150:1-6

What is the writer saying?

How can I apply this to my life?

PRAY Philippines – Evangelistic discernment for Filipinos working abroad in countries hostile to the Gospel.

If the Book of Psalms were a river of praise, then it flows into a flood of praise in Psalms 146-149, culminating into a final cascade of praise in Psalm 150. After the "Praise ye the LORD" of each of the final five psalms, this psalm exhorts unto praise twice in each verse. It tells to whom, where, why, with what, and by whom praise should be offered.

Under the old covenant, God's sanctuary (v. 1) on earth, first the Tabernacle and then the Temple, was that place He set apart for communion with His people (Exodus 25:8, 22). The term "firmament" (v. 1b) can mean the first heaven (Genesis 1:15-17). "The firmament of His power" may as well extend the term to include God's heavenly abode. Thus God is to be praised everywhere, in heaven or on earth. "His mighty acts" (v. 2a) arise from "His excellent greatness" (v. 2b). We are encouraged to praise God in recognition of both His inherent power and for the various mighty acts He does by His power. The psalms regularly suggest that we praise God for His work of creation, for His ongoing providential care of His creation, and for His special interest in bringing to us His redemption.

Next the psalm encourages us to worship God with all kinds of musical instruments (vv. 3-5); in fact, nine kinds of musical instruments are mentioned. While the design and distinctive features of each is now lost to us, the intent of these verses is not; we are to use all resources available to us in our exaltation of the great name of God.

The psalm closes (v. 6) with a final call for all things that breathe to praise the Lord; that is man and animals together. "Breath" for the Hebrews included the idea of one's whole life, thus our verse is saying, "Let the *whole life* of each of us be dedicated to speaking forth our thankfulness!"

LIFE STEP What resources do you possess and can employ in your own personal worship of the Lord? How can you join with one or more other believers today to create your combined orchestra of praise? How can your whole life today speak forth your thankfulness to God's powerful and timely care in your life?

First Timothy is one of three books (the others: 2 Timothy and Titus) written by the Apostle Paul to two younger men, Timothy and Titus, who were pastors. Paul wants to tell them how to *behave* themselves "in the house of God, which is the Church of the living God" (1 Timothy 3:15). Due to their similar purpose and content, these three books have come to be known as the *Pastoral Epistles.*

To understand 1 Timothy, we need to know the background of all three books and all three men. Paul is approaching the end of his life and ministry. Timothy and Titus are anticipating many years of ministry still ahead. Both of them have been greatly influenced by Paul, beginning first with their salvation. He addresses each of them as his "own son" in the faith, using the Greek word *teknon*, which literally means, *a born one*, and is used to speak of *a little child*. Paul also attaches "in the faith" in his address to Timothy, and "after the common faith" to Titus, implying that he is their spiritual father.

Timothy had a Greek father and a Jewish mother (Acts 16:1). Timothy's salvation apparently took place in his hometown of Lystra, in the Roman province of Galatia (in modern Turkey). He soon became one of Paul's most trusted aides, ministering with him in such places as Philippi, Thessalonica, Berea, Corinth and Ephesus. Timothy is left on his own in Ephesus, becoming the *senior pastor* of the Ephesian church. There he receives this first of the Pastoral Epistles. The relationship between Paul and Timothy is a father-son relationship.

Titus is a Greek believer converted from paganism. Some traditions state that he was the younger brother of Luke. In 2 Corinthians 2:13 he is a member of Paul's ministering team. Both Titus and Timothy are ministering in exceedingly difficult places when Paul writes to them. For Timothy, in Ephesus he has the challenge of the famous Temple of Diana. All sorts of violent and immoral acts take place there in the name of worship. It is a city famous for sorcery, superstition and sexual wickedness. Paul ministered there successfully for three years. Yet he warns that after his departure "shall grievous wolves enter in... not sparing the flock" (Acts 20:29). Timothy is sent to this work and to these conditions.

Titus fares no better. His assignment is to the island of Crete. The people there, by their own admission, are "liars, evil beasts, slow bellies (lazy gluttons)" (Titus 1:12).

Paul is the great champion of the Christian faith. At one time he was a "blasphemer, and a persecutor" of those who claimed the name of Christ (1 Timothy 1:13). Then on the Damascus Road (Acts 9), he became a believer, and the change in his life became a pattern for others to follow (1 Timothy 1:16).

While these three books are written to individuals, Paul identifies himself as "an apostle of Jesus Christ." Surely neither Timothy nor Titus needs such identification, but they need the weight of Paul's title behind them in their ministry. They faced challenges because of their youth and inexperience. Paul gives them a hammer – the hammer of his apostleship.

Three themes are obvious in all three books: (1) Church Organization; (2) Sound Doctrine; and (3) Consistent Christian Living. Even so, each book has its particular emphasis. The three themes are in logical order as placed in the Bible even though Titus was written before 2 Timothy.

- 1 Timothy emphasizes *Church Organization;*
- 2 Timothy emphasizes *Sound Doctrine;*
- Titus emphasizes *Consistent Christian Living.*

Charles Erdman explains: "Church government is not an end in itself; it is of value only as it secures sound doctrine: and doctrine is of value only as it issues in life."

SUNDAY 6

1 Timothy 1:1-11

What is the writer saying?

How can I apply this to my life?

PRAY Uganda – For believing Ugandans living abroad to be called back to minister among their people.

Paul introduces himself as an Apostle of Jesus Christ. He is writing to Timothy, his "son in the faith" (v. 2). He refers to Christ in three tenses:

- He is "Our Savior" – *the past*, looking back to redemption;
- He is "Our Lord" – *the present*, looking at present responsibility;
- He is "Our hope" – *the future*, looking to His future return.

To Timothy (*he who honors God*) he extends the salutation "Grace, mercy, and peace" (v. 2). Grace: God's assistance is extended; Mercy: God's judgment is withheld; Peace: harmony with God.

He identifies his purpose: Timothy is to rebuke false doctrine (v. 3). Paul exhorts him to *hang in there* ("abide still"), as he challenges false teachers. They were teaching that obeying the Law of Moses was required for salvation, implying that Christ's work on the cross was only a partial payment for sin.

Paul introduces a basic Gospel principle: True "faith" (vv. 2, 5) results in love (v. 5, "charity"), which comes from (1) a pure heart, (2) a good conscience (see v. 19), and (3) a sincere faith. These characteristics are not found in the false teachers who are marked by "vain jangling" (*purposeless talk*) (vv. 5-6) and do not understand the purpose of the Law (v. 7), which is to show Israel her need of faith in God's grace!

"Sound doctrine" (v. 10) means *healthy teaching* or *teaching that promotes spiritual health*. The Greek word translated "sound" gives us our English word, *hygiene*. Later Paul pictures false teaching as the opposite, a canker (*gangrene*, 2 Timothy 2:17). Only sound doctrine can successfully combat the disease of false teaching!

LIFE STEP If you have true faith in Jesus Christ as your Savior, then that should be apparent in your love for the things of God and for other people. Consider your own heart. Is it "pure" before God? Likewise, do you serve others well?

MONDAY 6

1 Timothy 1:12-20

What is the writer saying?

How can I apply this to my life?

PRAY Angola – For the financial support and godly staff needed to train future church leadership.

Paul's tone changes here in verse 12. The emphasis is on praise and thanksgiving, an attitude prompted by his mentioning his call to the gospel ministry (see v. 11). He thanks God for: (1) empowerment — strength to fulfill his calling; (2) trust — God counts him faithful; (3) calling — God puts him into the ministry (v. 12). He then reviews his past, "a blasphemer... persecutor...injurious..." Nevertheless, he received mercy, and the thought of that mercy results in praise.

Paul next lists the three motivating forces in his life: (1) grace — providing salvation; (2) faith — appropriating it; and (3) love — applying it (v. 14). He then offers the first of five "faithful sayings" (see 3:1; 4:9; 2 Timothy 2:11; Titus 3:8). These are probably well-known doctrinal pronouncements from the earliest days in church history. Here, "Christ Jesus came in to the world to save sinners" (v. 15). Paul refers to himself as the "chief" of sinners, an indication that he never forgot the extra grace God extended to him.

His life becomes a "pattern" (v. 16) for others: turn to Christ (v. 16), experience salvation, return praise to God (v. 17) and serve Him (v. 18).

Paul then returns to the charge he has begun in verse 3. He uses military language: a "charge" (*An order that gives instructions for the coming battle*) to "war a good warfare" (v. 18). The war is to be waged on two fronts, doctrinal and moral, and to be fought using two weapons, *faith* and a *good conscience* (v. 19). Paul then mentions two men whose false words were blasphemous. These are judged by excommunication with an intended purpose, "that they may learn not to blaspheme" (v. 20).

LIFE STEP Paul's life provides a pattern for us to follow: turn to Christ, experience salvation, praise God and serve Him. As a member of the army of God, are you *warring a good spiritual warfare*? How can you praise and serve the Captain of the Army of God, the Lord Jesus?

1 Timothy 2:1-7

What is the writer saying?

How can I apply this to my life?

PRAY Paraguay – For the maturity of new believers among the Lengua, Angaite, Chorote, and Toba Indians.

Paul now moves from "sound doctrine" to prayer. The ministry of the Word and the ministry of prayer are the main pastoral responsibilities (see Acts 6:4). The words "first of all" (v. 1) emphasize prayer's place of priority in the church. The four *Ingredients of Prayer* are: (1) "supplications" — asking for one's own spiritual needs; (2) "prayers" — probably devotion and adoration of God; (3) "intercessions" — the coming near to God on behalf of others; and (4) "giving of thanks" — appreciation for what He has done.

In verses 2-7 we see the *Aims of Prayer*: (1) to maintain peace in society. Through prayer "for kings, and for all that are in authority," God protects His church, making possible "a quiet and peaceable life" (v. 2); (2) to please God. Prayer is good in God's sight (v. 3). If we pray only to have needs met, we have a low view of God; and (3) the salvation of the lost (vv. 4-7). Christ died for all and wants all to be saved.

Also we find a *Basic Rule of Prayer*. Prayer is offered *only* to God the Father through the *only* "mediator" possible, the Lord Jesus (v. 5). He is the *only* go-between, between God and men (Hebrews 4:14-16). His willingness to be a "ransom" for man made salvation possible (v. 6).

This passage provides a great salvation message outline as well. Verses 3 & 4 present God the Father's desire that all men come to Him (ultimate truth!!). Verses 5 & 6 present God the Son's death for the salvation of all men. Verse 7 presents God the Holy Spirit's commissioning of men to preach this good news.

LIFE STEP How's your prayer life? Ask yourself the following: (1) What are my own spiritual needs? (2) How can I express my devotion to God? (3) How can I pray on behalf of others in need of God's help? (4) What has God already done that needs to be on my "giving of thanks" list?

WEDNESDAY 6

1 Timothy 2:8-15

What is the writer saying?

How can I apply this to my life?

PRAY Pray for the faithfulness of those who evangelize and minister to those in your local prisons.

Praying in the Church is to be: (1) "without wrath"– prayer is a work of love in the church (v. 8); (2) "lifting up holy hands" – indicating a condition of a pure heart and cleansed life (v. 8); and (3) "without … doubting" – doubting is the opposite of faith; faith believes that God hears (v. 8)!

Paul deals with the dress (vv. 9-10), behavior (vv. 11-12) and role (vv. 13-14) of women in the church. Godly women are attractive because of their "good works" (v. 10). In verse 11, Paul speaks on the subject of the woman's behavior in the church. While Paul's ministry includes female co-workers (1 Corinthians 11:5; Philippians 4:1-3), he makes it clear that their role is one of subordination to male leadership. A woman is not "to teach, nor to usurp authority over the man" (v. 12). He supports his teaching from God's activity (Adam was created first and had precedence over Eve), and human history (Satan found the woman easier to deceive, verse 14). To accept such a role of subordination demonstrates Christ-like humility, for Christ, though equal with the Father, subordinated His will to the Father's will. Verse 15 needs to be interpreted in its context, that of the Garden of Eden. At issue is not *soul* salvation, but *societal* salvation. Adam's purpose in life was to be found in the "sweat of thy face"; his "sweat" providing for their needs (Genesis 3:19). Eve's salvation was to be found in childbirth; that is, accepting God's ordained role of subjection to her husband and bearing children. (Note: the "they" of v. 15 refers to both husband and wife.)

LIFE STEP Paul has given us a *woman's guide to attractive living*. Everything about her draws attention to her walk in godliness! Dear lady, does your outer appearance (apparel, hair, jewelry) draw attention to an inner *well-balanced* walk that pleases God?

1 Timothy 3:1-7

What is the writer saying?

How can I apply this to my life?

Verses 1-13 give the primary qualifications for church "office" (v. 1): the pastor (vv. 1-7) and the deacon (vv. 8-13). The title of *pastor* does not appear here. Instead we have the term *bishop*. A number of New Testament passages make it clear that those two terms, plus *elder*, are used interchangeably. All refer to the same individual and provide a job description for his ministry: (1) as elder, he provides authority; (2) as bishop, administrative oversight; (3) as pastor, he feeds the congregation as a shepherd does his sheep (see Acts 20:17,28; 1 Peter 5:1-2.).

To be worthy of the office of the elder/pastor/bishop one must meet certain qualifications. A total of sixteen items are found here. These fall into three categories.

(1) PERSONAL QUALIFICATIONS, verses 2-3. Some thirteen are listed, beginning with being "blameless" (*irreproachable*). Nothing is in his life that would discredit his witness. It continues down through "not covetous;" he consistently puts Christ and his church first in his life.

(2) FAMILY QUALIFICATIONS, verses 4-5. He, not his wife, is the leader in his home. He is to be in control. After all, if he cannot rule his own house, how shall he take care of the house of God?

(3) CHURCH QUALIFICATIONS, verses 6-7. He cannot be a novice. Leadership demands experience and wisdom; serious decisions must be made. A novice could be in danger of the sin of pride. Finally, he must have a "good report" with those outside the church. The bottom line? The men who serve as pastors must be of unquestioned character.

LIFE STEP Church leaders should take care that they measure up to their biblical qualifications. Put your pastor(s) and deacons on your prayer list and pray for them regularly that they might lead your church successfully.

FRIDAY 6

1 Timothy 3:8-16

What is the writer saying?

How can I apply this to my life?

PRAY Ecuador – Pray for an end to anti-missionary sentiment promoted by those with financial agendas.

Here we have the qualifications of a deacon; many are similar to those of a pastor. The English word "deacon" is transliterated from the Greek word, *diakonos*. It is often translated elsewhere as "minister" or "servant." "Servant" is the key idea. Collectively the term "deacons" is a reference to a class of helpers chosen to serve the church under leadership. The first deacons (Acts 6) were selected to meet the needs of church members (there had been a dispute over two groups of widows). This responsibility continues today.

As with the pastor, the emphasis of his qualifications is on character (vv. 8-10, 12). Again, there is a need for a proven reputation (v. 10), marital example and parental control (v. 12). The pastor's requirement, "apt to teach," is not repeated. The deacon who serves "well" gains the respect of those served, allowing him to function with "great boldness" (v. 13).

In the middle of Paul's list of qualifications are some for the deacon's wife (v. 11). Hers are similar to his. There must be a spiritual maturity on the part of ministry wives.

Paul goes on to describe the church and its ministry. It is the household of God and "the pillar and ground of the truth" (v. 15). This is architectural language. It stresses the church's responsibility of faithfully preserving, preaching and practicing the "truth" (the Word of God). Verse 15 summarizes the purpose behind Paul's writing — to give to Timothy instructions as to how to act in church.

Verse 16 is probably an early Christian hymn, beginning with "the mystery of godliness." It speaks of God's special program to bring about godliness through Jesus Christ who has come into the world.

LIFE STEP Do you desire to be involved in the ministry of the church? Then, what is the quality of your personal conduct?

SATURDAY 6

1 Timothy 4:1-8

What is the writer saying?

How can I apply this to my life?

PRAY Japan – For an end to the resurgence of nationalistic Shintoism, which threatens religious freedom.

Earlier Paul warned the Ephesians about the coming of false doctrine (Acts 20:29-30). Here he predicts that a falling away from the truth is imminent, in fact, is already present (see 2 Thessalonians 2). Its cause: the satanic influence of demons (v.1). The marks of these teachers of false doctrines are: *first*, they are hypocritical liars, with "seared" (*without feeling*) consciences; *second*, they teach a false piety/asceticism, forbidding marriage and certain foods. This asceticism reflects pagan gnostic teaching that all matter [or *flesh*] is evil and only what is *spirit* is good. Abstinence is seen as denying the *flesh* and thus increasing one's *spirit* or holiness.

Paul's answer to the danger of verses 1-3 is found in verses 4-6, "the word of God and prayer" (v. 5). God has declared all foods clean (Genesis 1:29-31; Mark 7:14-23; 1 Corinthians 10:23-26; Acts 10). Genesis 9:3 points out that God has provided man with meat and plant life for nourishment. Through prayer, the believer thanks God and dedicates his food to His glory (1 Corinthians 10:31). The pastor who is "nourished up in the words of faith and of good doctrine," and points out these truths to his people, is judged to be "a good minister" (v. 6).

In verses 7-8 Paul instructs Timothy to "refuse profane and old wives' fables," since these are never helpful (a contrast with "sound doctrine," 1:10). Paul exhorts Timothy to emphasize spiritual discipline over physical discipline. This is not to ignore genuine healthy habits, but *exercising godliness is profitable eternally* (paraphrase of v. 8).

LIFE STEP Do you have a pastor who fits the "good minister" definition of verse 6 and the "exercise" in godliness of verse 7? Then would you take a minute and write him a note, telling him that you have noticed his good service and will be praying for him to continue on his path of godliness?

SUNDAY 7

1 Timothy 4:9-16

What is the writer saying?

How can I apply this to my life?

PRAY — Costa Rica – For continued growth in missionary outreach, which has doubled over the last 10 years.

Paul once again uses a "faithful saying" (v. 9, see 1:15) to drive home the truth of verse 10, which is "we trust in the living God, who is the Saviour of all men, specially of those that believe." The bottom line? Jesus Christ is the only Savior of people lost in sin, and His work on the cross provided an offer of salvation for all (1 John 2:2).

This prompts Paul to state that he is giving his ministry his best efforts. "We both labour and suffer reproach," provides a backdrop for his instructions concerning Timothy's ministry. He begins, "Let no man despise thy youth" (v. 12). Most likely, some older believers (Timothy is thirty to thirty five years old) are disregarding Timothy since he is not yet forty (apparently they didn't trust anyone under 40). The best way to deal with the fears that follow such accusations is to demonstrate such a maturity in godly living that his life would be a pattern for all others.

In verse 13 Paul emphasizes the public reading of the Word of God. It is to be read, then explained – "doctrine," a ministry of teaching; and applied – "exhortation," a ministry of encouraging. Timothy's gifting has been recognized by the church (v. 14 with 2 Timothy 1:6) and would be noticed by others, therefore he should "neglect not" to fulfill his calling.

Paul then challenges Timothy to "meditate" on these truths. Putting Paul's instructions into action wholeheartedly removes any opportunity for others to look down on Timothy (v. 15). Paul closes with a reminder: "Take heed unto thyself, and unto the doctrine" (v. 16). Be sure to care for your own spiritual welfare while carrying out ministry responsibilities. Proper care will result in the salvation, or *protecting*, of one's ministry.

LIFE STEP — Check through the list of qualities that Timothy needs in his life and then evaluate your own character against them. What item in particular do you need God's help to reproduce in your life?

MONDAY 7

1 Timothy 5:1-8

What is the writer saying?

How can I apply this to my life?

PRAY   Kenya – Believers willing to meet the spiritual and physical needs of the 2,100,000 living with AIDS and the 730,000 AIDS orphans.

In chapters 5 and 6, Paul details various categories of people the church must include in ministry. Age relationships are dealt with first. Paul encourages the establishment of a family mentality within the church. Older men and women are to be treated like parents; younger men and women like brothers and sisters. Added caution is to be exercised in relationships with young women: treat them "with all purity" (v. 2). The minister's dealings with females must be above reproach.

Verse 3 begins an extended treatment of ministry to widows. The early church cared for widows (Acts 6:1-6; James 1:27), giving them "honour" (v. 3). This would include financial assistance. To protect the process, some guidelines are put in place. Four classes are mentioned: (a) <u>real widows</u>, (vv. 3, 5, 9-10); (b) <u>widows with relatives</u>, (vv. 4,

8, 16); (c) <u>widows living in pleasure</u>, (vv. 6-7); (d) <u>young widows</u>, (vv. 11-15). A *real widow* (a "widow indeed") is truly destitute, without family, and having no means of support. These widows (vv. 5-10) are to be church supported, with the church becoming her family. For *widows with family*, the "first" responsibility for her care belongs to her family (v. 4). *Widows living in pleasure* (v. 6), having chosen a decidedly unchristian path, have placed themselves outside the church's responsibility. For *young widows* (v. 11) Paul instructs that they are to remarry.

Paul instructs Timothy to pass this "charge" to the church (v. 7). When they carried out their responsibilities they would be "blameless."

LIFE STEP   Are there "real widows" in your church? What can you do as their son or daughter in the faith to help them this week?

1 Timothy 5:9-16

What is the writer saying?

How can I apply this to my life?

PRAY Argentina – Increased scholarship funding to enable foreign students to attend Bible colleges.

Paul continues the qualifications necessary to be included on the *widow's support list*. No family support is not reason enough. One's lifestyle and age must be considered (v. 9; minimum sixty years). Paul lists ten qualifications in verses 5-10. Paul includes an unblemished married life (v. 10). They should have a good testimony earned by: (a) raising of children, if so blessed; (b) hospitality, "lodged strangers"; and (c) humility, having "washed the saints' feet," a demonstration of her willingness to accept even menial tasks.

Younger widows (v. 9) are not to be included (vv. 11-16). The reason is they might pledge faithfulness to serve Christ and the church early in their widowhood, but in time turn away and be consumed by a desire to be remarried. As a result, they grow "wanton" (*to feel the impulses of romantic desire*) and grow cold spiritually. They stop serving others ("they learn to be idle," v. 13) and become "tattlers also and busy-bodies" (v. 13), bringing reproach upon the name of Christ. Since they lacked the wisdom of age and experience, they tend to fall prey to their own romantic desires (v. 11).

Paul then gives instructions: a young widow should (a) remarry, (b) bear children, and (c) guide the household. In carrying out these duties she will "give none occasion [*no base of operations*] to the adversary to speak reproachfully" (v. 14), as some have already done (v. 15).

Paul then summarizes his instructions. Responsibility for the care of widows falls first as an obligation on her family. This allows the church to be free to care for the genuinely destitute (v. 16).

LIFE STEP Widows who sow a godly lifestyle reap positive consequences. Observing their godly lifestyle, let us give them proper "honour"! How can you, like those in the early church, be actively involved in relieving the needs (v.16) of others who are genuinely in need of help?

1 Timothy 5:17-25

What is the writer saying?

How can I apply this to my life?

PRAY Korea – Complete renewing of the mind for South Koreans saved out of Buddhism and Confucianism.

Paul now deals with two issues concerning the treatment of church leaders: (1) How they are to be paid, and (2) How to treat them when they sin. Elders who "rule well" [literally, *having taken the lead well*] are "worthy of double honour" ("honour" is also used in the matter of financial care for widows, 5:3). The qualifying word is "well." If that is the case, he is to receive *double pay*, or at the very least, *ample* or *generous pay*. "The ox that treadeth out the corn" is not muzzled, nor should the one be who labors in the Word and doctrine (v. 18, quoting Deuteronomy 25:4; Luke 10:7). As Jesus Christ has already said, he is worthy of his reward.

When a church leader sins, how is the church to respond? Paul's answer:

(a) Get the facts. Accusations must be supported by two or three witnesses (v. 19)!

(b) Give the matter honest, non-partial appraisal (v. 21).

(c) Rebuke him publicly if proven guilty (v. 20).

Such a procedure would deter others from falling into sin (v. 20).

Verses 22, 24-25 warns not to promote a young believer too quickly. It takes time for an individual's true colors to emerge. Hasty actions lead to the placing of unworthy men in leadership, whether in the first or twenty first century!

In verse 23 Paul inserts a personal bit of medical advice to Timothy. Timothy has stomach problems, probably from drinking polluted and unsafe water. His advice is, "Drink no longer water [only], but use a little wine." Paul is offering Timothy a water purification method – the placing of a little wine in a much larger portion of water, a common procedure in that day.

LIFE STEP Leaders must understand that sin in a *public* leader's life merits *public* rebuke. Church members must remember that hasty action in selecting their leaders can cause great damage. Pray now for your church leaders.

THURSDAY 7

1 Timothy 6:1-8

What is the writer saying?

How can I apply this to my life?

In the Roman Empire, slaves made up about fifty percent of the population. Slaves are valued with cattle (both being agricultural commodities). Many slaves believed in Christ. Christian slaves were prone to take on a false superiority because of their new spiritual freedom in Christ, tempting them not to give their best service. Paul cautions against this, for such an attitude would cause others to blaspheme God (v. 1). Paul's desire is that a slave's actions would cause his master to see the true character and teachings of God.

Slaves with "believing masters" are tempted to take advantage of their spiritual oneness. They are to understand that such behavior would be unacceptable. They are to serve them well ("do them service") because of their faith in Christ (v. 2; See also Ephesians 6:5; Colossians 3:22).

Verses 3-5 warn about false teachers who "consent not to wholesome words," especially on matters concerning the doctrines of Christ and "godliness" (v. 3). These teachers are "proud," ignorant, have an abnormal interest in disputes (KJV, "doting"), and are argumentative (v. 4). Their behavior is disruptive and their "disputings" are "destitute of the truth" (v. 5). They are "supposing" that they gain "godliness" by their disputings about religion. The believer is not to keep their company (v. 5).

Conversely, "godliness, with contentment, is great gain" (v. 6). The point is, physical possessions are temporary. Contentment and godliness are eternal possessions that go with us when we depart. All else will be left behind (vv. 6-7). Thus, having food and raiment, let us be content (v. 8).

LIFE STEP Your boss is the "master" of your work day. God says you owe him your best service. Do your actions cause him to praise the true God of heaven or does he "blaspheme" (*speak against*) the things of God because of your poor example?

FRIDAY 7

1 Timothy 6:9-16

What is the writer saying?

How can I apply this to my life?

PRAY — Mexico – Believers to realize their responsibility to contribute to the support of ministers of the Gospel.

Paul moves from the positive ("godliness with contentment") to the negative (greed). In verse 9, his warning is to those whose goal in life is to become rich. Focused on gaining wealth, they are "foolish," they "fall," and then "drown" (v. 9). Paul warns them (v. 10), "The love of money is the root of all evil." Those "that will be rich" are likened to a bowman who *shoots himself* through with many arrows of sorrow!

Verses 11-16 are a summary of Paul's challenges to Timothy. He calls him a "man of God," a mature Christian – surely a great encouragement to Timothy. Paul's "charge" to Timothy is four-fold.

(a) FLEE: pride, covetousness, false teaching (v. 10 and 11a). Sometimes the wisest thing a believer can do is run (see also 2 Timothy 2:22)!

(b) FOLLOW: righteousness, godliness, faith, love, patience, meekness. These are six virtues that should be obvious in the life of a man of God (v. 11b).

(c) FIGHT "the good fight of faith," (a picture taken from the Olympics, where the contestant keeps on until attaining the prize or goal). "Fight" is a word meaning to *contend for a prize.*

(d) FOCUS on eternal life as found in Jesus Christ (1 John 5:11-13). Eternal life is both a *present possession* and *future expectation.*

Verses 15-16 are a doxology to the "King of kings and Lord of lords," a title Paul uses nowhere else. He focuses on the Lord's sovereignty and His immortality.

LIFE STEP — Paul's four-fold "charge" to Timothy is one that we can apply personally. Take a look at the little list and ask yourself, how am I doing? There are things for you to *flee* and things to *follow.* There is a *good fight* that is a part of your life of faith, and there is an *eternal focus* to maintain. What areas of your life need to change so you can stop *shooting yourself*?

SATURDAY 7

1 Timothy 6:17-21

What is the writer saying?

How can I apply this to my life?

In verses 17-19 Paul returns to the subject of *riches*. This time he addresses not those who wish to be rich (vv. 9-10), but those who are rich. He instructs them as to how to use wealth for the glory of God.

(a) BE HUMBLE ("not highminded") – recognizing that all the wealth a person has is a gift from God. Focus on the *Giver*, not the *gift*!

(b) BE TRUSTING– riches present a danger of trusting in one's own money, which can only bring uncertainty, rather than trusting in God!

(c) BE APPRECIATIVE – it has been given to be enjoyed. The danger is that money can also buy much evil. Use the money for good things.

(c) BE USEFUL – it has been given not just for enjoyment. Be sure that riches are employed to "do good." Be generous and willing to share.

(d) BE VISIONARY – or forward-looking. Invest the earthly riches in eternal treasures, "laying…a good foundation against the time to come." This is what Christ calls "treasures in heaven" (Matthew 6:20).

Paul closes the letter by challenging Timothy to remember his calling and to avoid the "profane and vain babblings" of false teachers. He is to "keep" (*to place a guard around*, see also v. 14) that which has been committed (*entrusted to his care*) to his trust (*deposited into his bank account*). Paul is using a banking term, referring to that which has been placed on deposit and which, when demanded, is to be returned in its entirety. What has been deposited with Timothy is the Gospel message, which has earlier been committed to Paul (1:11), and which Timothy would later commit in trust to others (2 Timothy 2:2).

LIFE STEP The Gospel message came from God to Paul, and then from Paul to Timothy. He is to pass it on to others. Those others are to pass the trust on to other faithful men also (2 Timothy 2:2). And so it has continued. Now it is your turn. How are you *keeping* the Gospel message that has been *trusted* to your *account*?

In Bible usage, the word **proverb** denotes a *terse saying* of practical wisdom and often conveys moral direction. The name of the book comes from the Hebrew word for a proverb, *mashal,* which is from a root word meaning *to reign*, *rule* or *to be like, represent.* Thus, *mashal* came to mean a pointed, compact, and wise saying that is intended to *rule*, that is *regulate* or *govern*, one's conduct and life. The Book of Proverbs includes not only practical sayings but also other types of instructional literature, such as parables, poems, and oracles.

Ancient proverbs were designed principally for oral transmission. They were structured in couplets [poetic pairs of ideas] to impact the hearer and to be easy to remember.

- A frequent form of this teaching device was the contrasting couplet, "A fool uttereth all his mind; but a wise man keepeth it in till afterwards" (Proverbs 29:11).
- "Commit thy works unto the LORD, and thy thoughts shall be established" (16:3) is an example of a completive couplet.
- Whereas "Better is a little with righteousness than great revenues without right" (16:8) is a comparative couplet.

Proverbs 1:1, 10:1, and 25:1 tell us that King Solomon authored the Book of Proverbs. It is interesting that 1 Kings 4:32-34 says that Solomon composed three thousand proverbs and 1005 songs. Thus the Book of Proverbs is only a portion of all his proverbial writings.

The Book of Proverbs has an unusual feature of having been enlarged some 250 years after Solomon's original "release" of the book! Proverbs 25:1 tells us that the next section of the book (chaps. 25-29) was added to the original text as the result of the compiling work of known proverbs of Solomon by a committee appointed by King Hezekiah. Another feature of Proverbs is that the last two chapters of Proverbs are attributed to two unknown persons, Agur and King Lemuel (30:1; 31:1). It has been suggested that these may have been family names or "nicknames" for Solomon, which would also imply that the name "Solomon" was then an official or royal court name given to Solomon. This would be like the practice of European kings and popes in our own time.

The story of how Solomon acquired such wisdom is found in 1 Kings 3:5-13. 1 Kings 4:31 says Solomon was wiser than all men. That statement, of course, was no longer true once Christ became a man, for in Him are hidden all the treasures of wisdom and knowledge (Colossians 2:3).

Some of the virtues commended in Proverbs are the pursuit of wisdom, respect for parents, liberality, marital fidelity, honesty, humility, and piety. Vices condemned include lust, drunkenness, lying, cheating, laziness, strife, greed, pride, folly, gluttony, and vengeance.

The principle theme of the book is wisdom. The words wise and wisdom occur more than 118 times in the text. Since proverbs were often constructed as comparative thoughts, it is not surprising that another key family of words in Proverbs is "fool, fools, foolish, and folly" which are used ninety four times in the text.

As we consider various passages in the Book of Proverbs, we must remember *"truth"* in the book of Proverbs is different from the *absolute* and *unchangeable truth* spoken of elsewhere in the Bible. For instance, throughout the rest of the Bible we are taught the *absolute* and *unchangeable truth* that God is holy --- for this truth there are definitely no exceptions! Yet, in the Book of Proverbs, a proverb states what is *generally true* and not what is *invariably true (invariably = without variation, consistently, uniformly)*. A present day proverb, "like father, like son," serves as an example. This is a common observation that is generally true yet you can find variations from this observation that do not hold true; some sons are nothing like their fathers! Similarly, the proverb "a soft answer turns away wrath" (15:1) is often true, yet you will encounter exceptions or variations to this general rule. Perhaps the guy to whom you speak softly will still get angry with you!

Finally, we must touch upon one final feature of the Book of Proverbs. We observe that the main subjects of the book of Proverbs are touched upon again and again in an unassociated manner throughout the book (e.g. "Pride": 6:17; 11:2; 13:10; 15:25; 16:18, 19; 18:12; 21:4,24; 29:23; 30:13). This is unlike our modern methods of education where all that is to be taught on a single topic will typically be presented in a single chapter of a book with following chapters moving on to concentrations on different topics.

Proverbs is using a different method of teaching; it is deliberately presenting an unstructured procession of devotional thoughts on multiple topics. The idea was for someone to daily read or copy out the next couple of proverbs so that they could consider and meditate upon these throughout the day. A different aspect of a given topic could again be considered several days later. The intent was for a person's character, little by little, to be adjusted in multiple ways over time.

A final note on this year's selected passages from the Book of Proverbs; since this is the sixth year of the Quiet Time Diary's 6-year cycle, we begin at Chapter 26 and continue through to the end of the book. Be patient, next year we begin again at Chapter One!

Proverbs 26:1-16

What is the writer saying?

How can I apply this to my life?

In today's passage, we have the Bible's highest concentrated use of the terms "*fool*" (used eleven times) and "*slothful/ sluggard*" (both are from same Hebrew word, used four times). Solomon in verses 1-12 gives varying advice on dealing with fools. He then moves on in verses 12-16 to examine the conduct of the lazy person. The best definition of a "*fool*" is *one who has eyes but unable to see*! The idea of the Bible term is not mental deficiency but is close to *impudence* and *obstinacy* (respectively, *a haughty disregard for advice*; an *unwillingness to learn wisdom from his mistakes* and *a stubborn determination to have one's own way while resisting advice, and reason*). Notice that verses 5 and12 are saying that *conceit* is a serious component of foolishness; "*conceit*" has to do with one's eyes and is used figuratively here to mean *seeing in others that which results in an opinion of contempt, undersized evaluation, and lack of respect*.

"*Slothful*" and "*sluggard*" are the Old English terms for *lazy*. These all mean *to take no initiative; not inclined to action or labor; indolence, a dislike and avoidance of work*. A slothful man will make the most bizarre excuses (v. 13). He will always delay starting work (v. 14). Similarly, he will hide from work but not from pleasures (v. 15). Yet, in his own eyes (KJV = "*conceit*"), he is smarter the seven men who work (v. 16)! In verses 4 and 5 we have a contradiction intending to offer different advice for similar situations. In verse 4 we are told not to answer a fool. In verse 5 we are told to answer a fool. Thus there are times we *should not answer* so as to become like the fool; that is, don't answer in an arrogant, scoffing manner. On the other hand, there are times when we *should answer* a fool, lest he think he won the argument and think he is wise! When we do answer our goal should be to expose his shallowness, to humble his pride, and to show him his need to further study a subject.

LIFE STEP   How do you usually respond to advice? Is your first tendency an *unwillingness* to listen, a *determination* to resist, or a *conceit* that you are better than the one giving you advice? Take time now to ask God for the wisdom and humility needed to make your heart ready to listen to and seek to apply advice given to you today!

MONDAY 8

Proverbs 26:17-28

What is the writer saying?

How can I apply this to my life?

PRAY Netherlands Antilles – For a well-staffed body of believers on each of the five islands.

Today's passage presents a collection of proverbs that mostly deal with the misuse of words by troublemakers or talebearers who can cause great hurt. We are cautioned that conversations may look like *pure silver* but are really deceptive, like pottery painted with "*silver dross*" (v. 23). Sadly, a trusting person can get wounded with word-arrows! Warnings are given in several areas regarding the misused words:

- Strife and Quarrels, (vv. 17, 20-21): Have you ever stepped in to help settle an argument, only to have both sides turn on you, or bite you like a dog (v. 17)? Similarly, if you get into the fiery argument of others don't be guilty of adding "wood" to their hot fire (v. 20).
- Deception and Deceit, (vv. 18-19, 24-26): We are warned of the *wicked* (v. 26) practice of shooting a *neighbor* with *fiery word-arrows* (v. 18) and then adding to the mischief by claiming we were only *joking* (v. 19). Such people are being *deceitful* (vv. 19, 24, 26) and seeking to

disguise (v. 24, KJV "dissembles") their deep-cutting word-arrows!
- Talebearers and Gossips, (vv. 20-22): People love to pass on rumors, and so we are told that the best way to stop a rumor is not to pass it on. Rumors are like fires that easily stay hot and spread. They *go out* only if we are careful not to allow fuel to be added to the rumor-fires. Similarly, don't be the one who *rekindles* an earlier strife-fire by stirring the hot coals so they again become a lively, hot flame (v. 21b).
- Lying Lips and Flattering Mouths, (vv. 23, 28): Another way the tongue can be misused is by giving false, flattering remarks to people. Such people will mask the *hate* (vv. 24, 28) in their *hearts* (v. 25) behind kind words. Be sure to notice that Solomon warns that this kind of evil will come back to *roll over* (v. 27b) the person who used it. Such a person is *working his own ruin* (v. 28b), and will *fall into his own pit* (v. 27).

LIFE STEP In your interactions with people today, how can you now seek the Lord's help so that you will not misuse words so as to harm others? Write out your commitment not to be the *shooter of fiery word-arrows* or the *kindlier of rumor-fires* that harm others. When you encounter a rumor later today, how can you be ready to assist in putting out its fire?

TUESDAY 8

Proverbs 27:1-9

What is the writer saying?

How can I apply this to my life?

PRAY — Czech Republic – For godly public school teachers who will use their religious freedom to evangelize.

What is a *true friend* like? What kind of person would make a true friend? What kind of person must you be to become a true friend? We have some wonderful guidelines in today's passage. Notice that concepts of *friendship* occur sixteen times in the twenty seven proverbs of this chapter.

Let us consider some characteristics that make a good friend:

- In verses 1 and 2, we see that a good friend is humble. A humble person does not *boast* about what they are going to accomplish (v. 1) and they don't praise themselves. If they do accomplish some noteworthy exploit they let someone else speak of it (v. 2).

- In verses 5 and 6, we see an important quality of a true friend; a friend will demonstrate his love by courageously rebuking his friend's fault. By speaking the truth, he may cause pain but he does so for his friend's good. One who keeps *secret* his observation of a fault (often because of a fear of offending) is being deceitful and leaves his friend exposed to greater harm than the *wound* of the *rebuke*.

- Verse 6 also makes the contrasting observation concerning a deceitful friend. It is easier many times not to correct someone when they are doing wrong. So a *deceitful* person will just give his friend a welcoming *kiss* as if all is well and no *rebuke* is necessary. Ultimately, such a person is really an *enemy*, for he leaves his friend exposed to the dangers of the fault.

- Verse 9 comes back to the topic of being a true friend. It reminds us how to respond to a friend's *hearty* [*sincere, from the soul*] counsel; honest, heartfelt counsel is like an ointment that heals or a perfume that honors a guest. Remember it is a *sweet* thing to receive honest advice.

LIFE STEP

Are you a good friend? Do you have the qualities needed to be a true friend? What aspect of your *friendliness* needs refining by our Lord Jesus? Ask the Lord to build your friendship qualities today by first showing you an opportunity for being a true friend and then by giving you the wisdom and courage to act like a true neighbor!

WEDNESDAY 8

Proverbs 27:10-18

What is the writer saying?

How can I apply this to my life?

PRAY New Zealand – Bold and vibrant witness of those ministering in secondary schools and universities.

Solomon begins this passage with the words, "My son, be wise" (v. 11) as he presents several contrasts between the conduct of a fool with that of a wise person. Note how to *Become Wise, my son!*

Verse 12: A fool does not have the foresight to be able to see the results of sinful behavior and so he is "punished."

A wise person sees the consequences of the sinful behavior of others. So he wisely avoids joining in the behavior. He also knows to turn to the Lord for protection as his "hiding place" (Psalm 32:7).

Verse 14: A fool, when trying to do a good thing (like giving deeply felt thanks, i.e., bless), will fail to consider the *proper manner* and *timing* for his good deed! So, instead of being honored for his efforts, he is *cursed*, which is to say he gains only *ill will.*

A wise person will not express deeply-felt thanks in a loud, verbose manner and he will consider a proper time to present his *blessing* so that his efforts are gladly received.

Verses 15-16: A fool makes a terrible wife, in part because such a woman will continually complain about the troubles of life. It is easier to "hideth the wind" (v. 16a) or to *grab oil in your hand* (v. 16b) than it is to stop a foolish woman from complaining!

Verse17: A wise person will be like one piece of iron that sharpens another piece of iron by means of the whetting interaction between them; that is, a wise man will influence the appearance, behavior, habits, and language of those with whom he interacts.

Verse 18: Just as a wise farmer will tend and cultivate his fig trees so that he might in due time eat their fruit, so the wise person will consider how to best care for those who are his authority in human affairs ("his master"). Thus, be careful to make sure your boss succeeds in his responsibilities; after all, he is the one who will be signing your check!

LIFE STEP How can you be the wise person who considers how you will do true and praiseworthy service for our Heavenly Master? What can you do today for the Lord Jesus so that He could say to you, "Well done, thou good and faithful servant..." (Matthew 25:21)?

THURSDAY 8

Proverbs 27:19-27

What is the writer saying?

How can I apply this to my life?

PRAY Portugal – For information technologists to utilize the Internet for evangelization and discipleship.

Today's passage reflects on aspects of wise business conduct.

Three negatives are presented:

Verse 20: A problem many face is not being satisfied with enough. We always seem to want a little more. John Rockefeller, one of the richest men of his day, was asked how much money was enough. His reply was, "Just a little bit more." Similarly, we also stumble over greed!

Verse 24: Riches can be lost and elevated positions are temporary. So be careful to use riches and positions of power to influence for eternity!

Verse 22: A hardened fool will not allow the *braying* (a pounding, grinding action in a mortar by a pestle) of life to remove the worthless *husks* (corrupting qualities) that cover a valuable *kernel* of character within.

Three positive pieces of advice are also given:

Verse 19 is a Hebraism which is saying, *Just as still water will reflect a person's face so words from the heart will reflect a person's character.*

Verse 21: As the fiery crucible brings impurities to the surface leaving purified gold, so praise can be an effective crucible to refine a person; gloating, arrogance, and conceit are *impurities* to be burned off, and modesty, humility, and thankfulness are valuable *metals* to obtain.

Verses 23-27 are a single lyrical poem illustrating rural industry as a guideline for wise conduct applicable to many areas of life beyond the farm.

- Be diligent! Just as watchful care is needed by both shepherds (v. 23) and farmers (v. 25), so a ruler or businessman must have constant vigilance for his country or business to thrive.
- Work a careful plan! Just as a farmer takes the *long view* on commerce so should all professions. A plan for harvesting hay can bring a second cutting (v. 25). Careful planning also gives extra lambs' wool for clothing (v. 26a) or selling of male goats for money (v. 26b).

LIFE STEP What are you seeking to accomplish with your life? Ask God to plant in your heart His dreams for your life's harvest. Don't make life-directing decisions based on how much money you will make. How can you work a plan of life so that you gain a great harvest of service and souls for the Lord Jesus?

FRIDAY 8

Proverbs 28:1-14

What is the writer saying?

How can I apply this to my life?

PRAY Pray for the salvation and protection of the emergency service workers in your community.

This chapter gives us a concentration of proverbs that deal with two topics: the righteous and wicked (vv. 1, 4, 10, 12, 13, 16, 18, 28) and the rich and poor (vv. 3, 6, 8, 11, 19, 20, 22, 25, 27). Today, let us look at the first topic. Note that the chapter deals with *righteousness, justice, integrity,* and *uprightness* (16 times) and with *wickedness, wrong, perversity,* and *sin* (17 times). So what, then, are the characteristics of an upright person?

- A righteous person is able to *boldly* face the issues of life since he knows the law is on his side; he has no reason to "flee" (v. 1).
- Additionally, he is generally a "happy" person since he "feareth" God and allows the laws God has given to guide his heart (v. 14).
- A righteous person desires to keep the law and as a result must "contend with" the wicked (v. 4)! "Contend" means *to initiate an action* thus taking steps to oppose what is wicked and evil.
- A righteous person has not had evil blind his mind to true justice (v. 5a), but rather he has had his mind purified so that he can understand true justice and, in fact, "all things" with a God-intended clarity (v. 5b).
- A righteous person seeks to choose what is *upright* (a condition of blamelessness and complete integrity) and seeks to avoid all that is "perverse" (morally or socially crooked or deceitful). He will maintain this standard even if it costs his great riches, leaving him "poor" (v. 6).
- A righteous person will cause others to follow upright ways (intended insight from the opposite of the evil man of v. 10a). As a result, the life of the righteous will tend to be enriched by "good things" (v. 10b)!
- While he will seek to do what is right, a righteous person is not a perfect or sinless person! Indeed, a key insight into the heart of a righteous person is his own recognition of his sins and failures (his spirit is acted upon by the Spirit of God) which lead him to confessing and forsaking his sin (v. 13b; e.g., David, Psalm 51:1-12).

LIFE STEP Take a minute and consider this list of qualities of the righteous person. Is there one characteristic weak or lacking from your life? First, take some time asking the Lord to help you in this area. Then formulate a plan to put into practice that characteristic in your life today!

Proverbs 28:15-28

What is the writer saying?

How can I apply this to my life?

As noted, this chapter has two topics: the righteous and wicked and the rich and poor. Today we will look at advice about riches.

- Verse 18a: An interesting piece of advice, *The only way to be safe in business is to be an honest person of blameless integrity.*
- Verse 18b: Yet, if a person seeks to advance his career by "perverse" means (*pretending to be of honest conduct while taking crooked paths*) then God will work things out so that he will "suddenly fall."
- Verse 19: If a person works hard, he will have "plenty of bread," but if he just chases after fantasies, he will have "poverty enough."
- Verse 20a: Notice that the abundant life is not always measured in money! If you are faithful, that is, honest, steady, and dependable, you will have all of the blessings from God that you need in life.
- Verse 20b: Yet, many wrongly believe money is the door to abundant life so they "maketh haste to be rich." Sadly, such "haste" usually involves the use of unscrupulous means, without regard for what is right.
- Verse 25a: Proud persons tend to *stir up strife* as they grab for power, self-exaltation, and personal pleasures. They are never quiet, never satisfied and always quarreling and contentious with others.
- Verse 25b: In contrast, the humble person places his "trust in the LORD." He seeks a peaceable life with others. He will find true prosperity for the Lord will cause him to "be made fat" by God's abundant care.
- Verse 27: Since the humble, trusting person of v. 25b views all his money and possessions as belonging to God, he will also have an easier time giving what he has to others who "lack." He will give to the poor knowing that God will continue to meet his personal needs. He will not *hide his eyes* from seeing the needs of others.

LIFE STEP Are you truly a person who "trusts in the Lord" for an abundant life? If so, pick one of the following as a personal task: 1. How can you today practice being an honest person of integrity? 2. How can you be the steady and dependable person others need? 3. How can you be peaceable to others and content in your heart? 4. How can you *see* the *lack* of others and do something about it?

SUNDAY 9

Proverbs 29:1-14

What is the writer saying?

How can I apply this to my life?

PRAY Turkey - 60% of the population are under the age of 24. Youth workers are needed to share Christ with these young people.

Today's passage has several comparisons between the righteous and the fool. Let's look at several Aims of the Righteous Leaders.

Verse 2: We begin by noting that when righteous individuals are placed in power, in general the people rejoice under his leadership. The verse is pointing out that the personal *goodness* of leaders gives immense advantage to a nation's growth and development.

Verse 4: Similarly, a leader's righteous conduct in his "judgment" "establishes" a land. That is, he *makes strong and sustains* his country by his practices, regulations, and justice.

Verse 7: Next, we notice that the righteous leader takes up the "cause of the poor." The word "cause" usually has to do with a legal situation. Thus a righteous leader will insure that those people who are limited in resources are fairly defended and not just overpowered.

Verse 14: Similarly, a righteous leader, who comes to the defense and judges fairly and equitably the poor under his jurisdiction, has fulfilled his greatest responsibilities and thus will be favored by God.

Verse 8: Rather than stirring up flaming anger in a city by arrogant talk and evil conduct, a "wise" leader will guide a city into God's blessing by steering the city away from sin that brings God's "wrath."

Verse 10: "Bloodthirsty" men hate an "upright" leader, for such a leader would restrain, punish, or seek to reform such people. Yet a truly righteous leader does not "hate" the evildoers he seeks to restrain! Rather, he will be found praying for the *souls* of such wicked men!

Verse 11: It is a good thing for a "wise" leader to control his words. Unlike the "fool" who immediately blurts out everything that comes into his mind on a topic, the wise man will take some time to consider what would be the best response and even seek counsel before saying what he thinks about a controversial topic.

LIFE STEP While you don't have as much responsibility as a king, you certainly have some responsibilities! In your areas of responsibility, how can you personally conduct yourself with godly goodness? How can you come to the defense of those for whom you are responsible, especially those with limited resources? How can you control your words?

Proverbs 29:15-27

What is the writer saying?

How can I apply this to my life?

Today's passage gives us much to think about as it lists several proverbs about various Sources of Trouble in a Person's Life.

Verses 15, 17: Parents must not indulge bad behavior in their children! Rather, they must utilize the rod and correction; two companion strategies: *physical punishment* [13:24; 22:15; 23:14] accompanied by *verbal rebuke* that explains why an action was wrong.

Verse 18: Since God's Word gives people a "vision" for right living, then a lack of knowledge of God's Word leads to unrestrained, evil lifestyles that come under God's judgment.

Verse 20: A "hasty" verbal response, before thought is given as to the best way to respond, will commonly result in *gushing* [15:2, 28] out thoughtless, insensitive remarks that lead to conflicts with others. There are times in our lives when we need to speak out, but we should first be sure to think deeply and pick our words carefully.

Verse 22: Literally, "a nose full of fury"; thus an uncontrolled temper always leads to conflicts with others and sin against God.

Verse 23: Pride in oneself will surely result in a response from God that will "bring him low." Conversely, God will work things out so that the person who is meek and humble in attitude will be honored.

Verse 24: Being in partnership with a thief brings a person ruinous troubles. His complicity with the thief will even cause him to abandon his moral standards so that when called upon to testify in court against the thief he will not speak the truth but seek to conceal the wicked deeds of the thief!

Verse 25: When the fear of people is allowed to take precedence over trusting in the LORD, a person is·falling into a trap! The real reason we are often afraid to speak out against some wrong is that we fear what others might say or think of us. At such times we need to trust the Lord that if we say what we should, He will protect us.

LIFE STEP Ask God to have the Holy Spirit bring to your personal attention one of the *sources of trouble* listed above. In what do you need His help to make you to become of a wise and righteous follower of the Lord?

TUESDAY 9

Proverbs 30:1-10

What is the writer saying?

How can I apply this to my life?

PRAY Canada – For more missionaries to be called to this vast country (second largest country in the world).

This chapter considers the words of Agur, who's identity is now lost to us. Perhaps this is a *title* of the *one who gathered (perhaps a scribe)* the verses of the chapter. This view explains verses 2-3, where *Agur* says he himself did not have the *understanding, wisdom*, or *knowledge* from God to have *authored* these things but rather is but a *gatherer*, like a scribe who *records* the wisdom received from others.

Agur's opening *proverb* (v. 4) is a string of five unanswered questions! All five can receive but one <u>assumed answer</u>, "*Only God*!" Agur is declaring the wisdom presented had been received from the One who is all-wise! After all, the five questions declare God's *Omnipresence, Omnipotence, All-Control, Sovereignty*, and His *unchangeable name* [a Hebraism for a *good character* that never changes or fails to live up to expectations].

In verses 5-6, we see *Agur's* source of wisdom. He says the *Word of God* is *pure*, that is, like silver that has been tested and proven pure, Psalm 12:6. Thus "*pure*" is declaring *when tested, the Word of God will prove to be true and flawless in its guidance*. As a result, nothing is to be added to God's Word (Deuteronomy 4:2, Revelation 22:18).

In verses 7 to 9 we have a double prayer request from Agur. His prayer reflects back upon his lack of wisdom and knowledge that leaves him vulnerable to falling into sin (vv. 2-3). Thus his first request is for the LORD to remove from him, until his death (v. 7), *vanity* and *lies* (v. 8a, e.g., idolatry, delusion, pride, and temptation).

Secondly, he asks not to be given *poverty* or *riches*, due to the temptations either would set before him. If Agur became *rich*, he feared he would grow self-indulgent and forget the overruling care of God (v. 9a)! Likewise, if he became *poor* he would be tempted with dishonesty and then perjury to prevent detection and punishment. Such perjury would ultimately lead to lying oaths made in the "name of my God" (v. 9b).

LIFE STEP Ask the Lord to give you the kind of lifestyle that will keep you *humble* and always trusting in Him. Also, ask the Lord to teach you the truth of the *purity* of the Word of God. How can you learn that the Word of God, when tested, will prove to be true and flawless in its guidance?

WEDNESDAY 9

Proverbs 30:11-20

What is the writer saying?

How can I apply this to my life?

We now repeatedly encounter a *proverbial* construction (vv. 11, 15, 18, 21, 24, 29), "There are three ... yea four ...." Each collection of fours was likely an answer from Agur to Ithiel and Ucal (v.1). It is suggesting that Agur's lists of four are not necessary complete; perhaps others items could be added but these four are a sufficient answer. The first set of fours (vv . 11-14) all begin with "*generation*" suggesting these undesirable behaviors are found in every generation. Included in the list of detestable qualities are (1) disrespectful children who wish their parents dead rather than repaying the parent's investment in their children. (2) Hypocritical people who imagine themselves to be holy before God but are yet full of *filthy* practices of sin. (3) Proud people who are full of their own self-importance which is openly and arrogantly declared in facial expressions and open contempt for others. (4) Cruel peoples who devour the *poor* and *needy* to increase their own wealth.

The next set of fours are all like the "leech" (vv. 15-16), never satisfied and always greedy for more. The *grave* always wants to take in more dead. The *barren womb* always desires to give birth. *Farm lands* always want more water. And *fire* always seeks to consume more. A warning follows (v. 17) which says that the arrogant "*eye*" of a child is like a leech; it is always finding fault and always despises its parents.

The third set of fours present wonderful, amazing things (vv. 18-19): An *eagle* soaring in the air, a *snake* moving across a rock, a *ship* navigating out on the ocean and a *man* affectionately courting a woman. All are untraceable, all have mastered seemingly impossible skills, and all have variations in their art to accomplish the same goal. A warning then follows concerning an adulterous woman (v. 20). An adulterous woman is like a person who wipes his mouth after eating to remove all evidence of his eating. The adulterous woman can live in her sin and yet can hide all guilt while saying, "I have done no wickedness!"

LIFE STEP Are you being affected by today's generation of undesirable behaviors? Ask God to give you the power to *affect* this generation, not *reflect* it! How can you avoid the greed for the things of this world and instead find satisfaction in God?

Proverbs 30:21-33

What is the writer saying?

How can I apply this to my life?

Agur was very perceptive as he observed life around him. He looked at life with a view toward God's control and love. He seems to have been in constant awe of the creative genius of the Lord. In verses 21 to 23 there are four things Agur observes. All four bring disorder in God's creation. They are *a servant* who becomes a king, *a fool* when he is well fed, *a woman* who is hateful being married, and *a maidservant* who succeeds her mistress. All of these are out of place and as a result they cause havoc in the world.

The next four things (vv. 24-28) that he observes are little things, but they teach big lessons if we are willing to learn. The *ants teach* us the importance of planning for the future. The *rock-rabbits teach* us the importance of building safe places to live. The *locusts teach* us the importance of teamwork and the *gecko teaches* us the importance of working skillfully.

The next four principles Agur points out in verses 29 to 31 concern lessons about how to present oneself. It seems in today's culture that people think it is fine to present yourself in any way you desire, but that is not the case. We are always representing the Lord Jesus and it is vital to do that in a way that accurately shows His glory to the world around us. Even in the animal kingdom you see that they present themselves in a stately way, not in a sloppy way. That does not mean that we are to be proud and pompous, for in verse 32 we see that we are not to exalt ourselves, for if we do we are being foolish.

LIFE STEP Do you find yourself in awe of the creation around you? The Bible says that the heavens declare the glory of God. Ask God to give you eyes to see His glory in the world around you. As you see it, thank God for the wonders of His creative power!

Proverbs 31:1-9

What is the writer saying?

How can I apply this to my life?

This last chapter of Proverbs is written by King Lemuel about whom we know nothing! He presents the words taught to him by his mother, thus she was the real author here and Lemuel later published her advice. Some have speculated that Lemuel was the family name for Solomon. She told her son she had made a covenant with the Lord (v. 2c) concerning what she would teach her son. Apparently she observed that he gave attention to shameless women (v. 3), this would *destroy* a king who was responsible for *judgment* (v. 5) and *righteousness* (v. 9). Thus his mother taught him not to give his "*strength*" to women, meaning he should not spend his time on women who did not warrant his attention. This word "strength" meant his influence as king, or his virtuous character that allowed him to rule with righteousness authority.

Similarly, he was taught to be sober (vv. 4-7), for alcohol would hinder his ability to make decisions. As Christians we are wise if we are like Lemuel and do not even touch this kind of drink. In verse 5 we see that decision-making is skewed by drinking. The issue of drinking in verse 6 is most likely medicinal. We must remember that wine was used as a medicine in this culture, and was used for people who were in agony and needed some relief. Today people would be given medication for relief. This is not teaching that we should drink when we are sad. Notice, we are to give it to those who are perishing, or literally dying (v. 6).

Lemuel was taught by his mother to be just in how he dealt with people (vv. 8-9). Especially, Lemuel was to *speak up* on the behalf of (1) those who were unable to speak, or (2) those, because they were poor, were suffering oppression, or (3) the needy, those who are defenseless and helpless. Thus, the most powerful people were to be the defenders of the weakest. Wise persons were to be *righteous*, that is ethically just, in their dealings with all people.

LIFE STEP   How do you treat those around you? Do you treat some people differently than others? How do you treat the less popular person? As a representative of Jesus, how can you be wise in your conduct as you *speak up* on behalf of others?

What is the writer saying?

How can I apply this to my life?

PRAY   Fiji – For pastors to confront believers influenced by alcohol and the worship of ancestral spirits.

Today we have an acrostic poem composed by Lemuel's mother as she directed him to choose a "*virtuous*" wife [one who has *strength of character*]. It starts with a question that points out that such a woman, while rare and of great value, will be the joy of the heart of her husband! Note that this passage points out the important social and economic role women played in Bible times.

- Her Worth: She is more precious than *rubies* (v. 10). She is clothed with *strength* (v. 17) and *dignity* (v. 25) beyond other noble women (v. 29).
- Her Works: Her priority is her *husband* and family; providing clothing (vv. 13, 21), preparing a wide-range of foods (vv. 14-15), purchasing products and making many goods herself for her family (vv. 17-19). As a result she and her family are richly clothed (vv. 21-22).
- Her Wisdom with Money: She buys and sells property (v. 16), she plants *vineyards* with her earnings (v. 16), and she makes and sells quality garments to *merchants* (v. 24). She also finds time to extend a helping *hand* to the *poor* and *needy* (v. 20).
- Her Wise Words: She controls her *tongue* so that her *words* are always *kind* and full of *wisdom* (v. 26).
- Her Worship: While she may be *graceful* and *beautiful*, she realizes these are vanity and so instead she fears the LORD [i.e., a profound, reverent respect for God, her true Master] (v. 30).
- Her Admirers: Above all others, she is admired by her *husband*! He trusts her completely (v. 11) knowing she will always seek to do him *good* (v. 12). He owes much of his success to her quiet, persistent care (v. 23). And so he will go out of his way to praise her (v. 28b). Likewise, her children bless her (v. 28a) and her community praises her works (v. 31).

LIFE STEP   *Ladies*, how can you be such a woman of great worth? Which of the above could you ask the Lord to help you put into practice this week? *Men*, have you been looking for a charming and beautiful woman instead of a noble and virtuous wife? *Husbands*, how can you today go out of your way to praise your wife's persistent care for you?

GALATIANS

The Book of Galatians is generally recognized as Paul's earliest epistle. It is written to the group of churches that Paul founded on his first missionary journey. These would include Iconium, Lystra, Derbe and Antioch. Paul's visit to these cities is recounted in Acts 13 and 14. He revisits them briefly on his second journey (Acts 16:1-6) and some of the northern cities on his third missionary journey (Acts 18:23). Because the Epistle to the Galatians references a number of historical events, we are able to place the date of writing with some certainty. Paul mentions his trip to Jerusalem to meet with Peter (1:18). This probably corresponds to Acts 9:26. In Galatians 2:1 Paul speaks of a visit fourteen years later. This is most likely the *famine visit* of Acts 11:27-30 as opposed to the Jerusalem Council visit referenced in Acts 15. The fact that Paul does not refer to the Council of Jerusalem in Galatians indicates that he wrote Galatians before the Council. Therefore, the letter is most likely written in 49 A.D. just prior to the Jerusalem Council.

The purpose for this letter is very clear. A theological battle has been brewing in Galatia ever since Paul's first visit to those cities. Certain Jewish religious leaders claiming the support of both the apostles and the church leaders in Jerusalem have begun to teach a *hybrid* gospel. This gospel tries to maintain a *by grace* salvation coupled with a *by law* sanctification (growth as a Christian). This way they are able to enslave Church Age believers to the Mosaic Law. They teach that circumcision is absolutely necessary for keeping oneself saved.

This short epistle may have ignited the flames of controversy that ultimately led to the council in Jerusalem the following year. These false teachers, generally called Judaizers, would follow and plague the ministry of Paul throughout his whole life. The following is a brief outline for the book:

1. Introduction (1:1-9)
2. Paul Defends His Authority – Autobiographical (1:10–2:21)
3. Paul Explains His Theology – Doctrinal (3:1–4:31)
4. Paul Exhorts Proper Christian Living (5:1–6:10)
5. Conclusion (6:11-18)

SUNDAY 10

Galatians 1:1-9

What is the writer saying?

How can I apply this to my life?

The normal opening found in Paul's other letters would be: (a) introduce himself with a salutation, (b) pray for those being addressed, (c) offer thanksgiving to God for the spiritual progress of his readers, and, finally, (d) move on to the main subject of his letter. Here, there is no thanksgiving to God; they are not progressing! Rather there is a criticism based on the charges that the Galatians were moving away from their faith in the *grace of Christ* (1:6).

Paul selects a form of the Greek word for *removed* (v. 6) to express two charges against the Galatians. (1) The present tense of *are removed* (such as in "I am making a cake," not past tense, "I made a cake") is used to indicate that the Galatians are in the process of defecting from the truth although they have not yet completed the process. Paul is writing with the intent of turning around this process (5:1). (2) The word *removed* is also in the middle voice There are the three possible "voices" of a Greek verb: active voice (for example, John *hit* Tom), passive voice (John *was hit* by Tom) and middle voice (John *hit himself*). Paul is saying that, while there are others present who are teaching a false gospel (vv. 7-9), the Galatians are responsible for *removing themselves* from the true Gospel. This word is used in the Greek world of someone who has *deserted* one army for another. An example would be Benedict Arnold who, during the American Revolutionary War, *removed* himself from the American army to join himself to the opposing army of the British.

LIFE STEP Loyal follower or deserter? What influences from "this present evil world" (v. 4) will you face today that will encourage you to *remove yourself* from your walk of faith with the Lord? How must you prepare yourself to respond to those influences so that you may "stand fast" (5:1) in your walk of faith? What are three or four things that you can be doing today to keep yourself *loyal* to the Lord?

Galatians 1:10-17

What is the writer saying?

How can I apply this to my life?

PRAY Bermuda – For teens to mature and develop godly leadership skills through Bible clubs.

Paul opens this section with a series of questions. These questions reflect the accusations being used to discredit Paul and his Gospel message (namely, salvation is only by faith in Christ's death on the cross, "Who gave himself for our sins," v. 4). The word "now" (v. 10) is key to understanding the accusations. *Now* implies an antecedent of *back then*. The false teachers are saying that back then, Paul sought to "persuade" (to win over) Jews by observing the Law and by presenting a message that would please the Jews. But "*now*" Paul is seeking to please Gentiles by saying they do not need to keep the Law, and by altering his message to conform to the current situation.

In response, Paul contends that his Gospel is not obtained from other men (vv. 10-11) or other apostles (vv. 16-17). Nor is it obtained through the labors of studying in school (the intent of "neither was I taught it," v. 12). Rather, Paul received his message by the "revelation of Jesus Christ." "Revelation" literally means *to remove a cover*. It gives us a picture of Christ giving a gift box to Paul that contains the true Gospel message, which Paul then *unwraps* for us in his letters.

To further establish his claim that his Gospel is from Christ, Paul reminds them that they knew of his life before he was saved (v. 13, "ye have heard"). They knew he had been zealous in pursuing the "traditions of my fathers" (v. 14, i.e., trusting in the rites and ceremonies of Judaism). They knew he had persecuted Christians (v. 13). Yet they also know he had been called of God (v. 15) to a new life based upon God's grace and not Paul's former zealous works to earn righteousness.

LIFE STEP Notice how Paul points to his own life history as a support for his gospel message. How can you live today so that your life *endorses* the truth of the Gospel of Christ that is the basis of your salvation?

What is the writer saying?

How can I apply this to my life?

Paul continues his defense against those who claim that he has changed his message. They charge Paul with being a manipulative preacher. To defend his former activities, Paul uses the forceful courtroom terminology, "before God, I lie not" (v. 20, equivalent to our *Do you solemnly swear to tell the truth?*). The Galatians would have understood that Paul is willing to go to court to defend the truthfulness of his past actions.

Apparently, the false teachers are implying that Peter held their position, at least in practice, yet they conveniently overlook the fact that Paul corrected Peter's lack of consistency and that the matter has been resolved. In Galatians 2, Peter is the one who changes his teachings! Paul's purpose in today's passage is to support his claim that his Gospel message is by revelation of Jesus Christ (v. 12). This is best seen by Paul's choice of words "to see Peter" (v. 18). The Greek word translated, "to see," is used only here in the New Testament. It means to *come to know by personal enquiry*, thus, *visiting someone to get acquainted*. It is used of one who visits a famous place, thus, it is the basis for the English word *history*. The Galatians would have understood that this word *did not* permit a suggestion of Paul being taught by Peter during Paul's short visit to Jerusalem. Rather, Paul has been directly taught by Christ Jesus. Thus Paul's Gospel message is genuine; a man is justified by faith in Jesus Christ alone (2:16).

LIFE STEP

Notice the implied warning for us today: Our beliefs must be based upon the *revelation of Jesus Christ*! Take a minute and list the different ways you are regularly taught about God. Do these avenues of teaching use the Bible as their only foundation for instruction? Are they, like Paul, directing your focus back to the *revelation of Jesus Christ*? Similarly, are you able to trace your foundational beliefs back to the Word of God?

What is the writer saying?

How can I apply this to my life?

PRAY Ghana – That the young people who come to Christ will play a crucial role in future national affairs.

Today's passage continues to support the claims of the first chapter, namely, that Paul, from the beginning, has declared the same message and has had the same mission. Both come directly from God.

First, notice that Paul is directed "by revelation" (by God's leading, not by Peter's command) to go to Jerusalem. Paul desires to *communicate* to the apostles at Jerusalem (*to lay before* for the apostles' consideration) what he preached. He does not want his efforts to be *rendered useless* ("in vain," v. 2) because of a misunderstanding between the ministry of Paul and Barnabas to Gentiles, and the ministry of Peter and James to Jews.

Next, notice that the apostles, who are men of importance to the church at Jerusalem (v. 2), added nothing (v. 6) to Paul's message. This means they (1) agree with the gospel message that Paul *laid before them*, and they (2) have nothing new to add to Paul's teachings. *Third*, notice Paul says, "That gospel which I preach" (v. 2). The Greek form of the verb "I preach" asserts the fact of continuous action from the past to the present. Today he would have to say, "This is the gospel that I have, in the past, always preached and, now, continue to preach!" Again, Paul declares he has consistently preached the same gospel message; a person is saved by faith in Jesus alone.

Finally, notice that Titus, a Greek, also comes to Jerusalem (vv. 1, 3). Titus is Paul's proof that his message has been consistently the same, that is, salvation for Jews and Gentiles is by faith alone and does not require the keeping of the additional religious rituals of the Jews.

LIFE STEP Consistency in life and ministry is the trademark of Paul's defense. How about you and your life and ministry? While it may not be a *flashy* lifestyle, what elements of your life will be noticed by others so that they will say, "There is a person who seeks 'God's leading' in his life!" Also, consider if there is an area of your life that needs more consistency!

Galatians 2:7-14

What is the writer saying?

How can I apply this to my life?

PRAY Czech Republic – For the organization and funding needed to start a national Christian radio network.

Paul now turns his defense to those who seemed (three times in vv. 6, 9) to be pillars (v. 9) in the church (i.e., those who were the *supports* of the church). The idea here is that Peter, James and John are men who are recognized by all as leaders of the church at Jerusalem and, thus, those to whom the "gospel of the circumcision" (v. 7, to the Jews) is committed. Paul says these three saw (v. 7) that the "gospel of the uncircumcision" (to the Greeks and other Gentiles) has been committed by God to Paul.

There are different Greek words for "see" in the Bible. Here the word for "see" (*eido*) means, *to take a long look with the mind*, which is to say, *to observe something so that the mind becomes aware of the significance of it.* Here we must ask, what happens to cause them to see something of significance in the ministry of Paul and Barnabas (likewise with "perceived," v. 9)? The answer centers on an understanding of the words "wrought effectually" and "mighty" (v. 8).

"Wrought effectually" and "mighty" are different forms of the Greek verb, *energeo*. It means *to be instrumental in a work* or, as we might say, *the power source that produces a work.* Our word *energy* comes from this Greek word. It is used throughout the Greek Old Testament to describe God's mighty works. Peter, James, and John saw that the same mighty power that *energized* God's great works in the Old Testament and that *energized* their own ministries was now *energizing* the ministry of Paul and Barnabas. For this reason they have extended to Paul and Barnabas the "right hands of fellowship" (v. 9), as they recognize Paul as a co-equal apostle to themselves.

LIFE STEP God has been and wants to continue being the energy source behind your life and spiritual ministry! What is an area of your life that needs to hook up to God's "mighty" battery charger?

FRIDAY 10

Galatians 2:15-21

What is the writer saying?

How can I apply this to my life?

PRAY Pray for God to show your church leaders creative ways to minister to and meet the needs of your community.

The Judaizers claim that the ways of the Jews are, by nature (v. 15), superior. Paul says, no, your only advantage is the revelation given to you in Scripture. The word "knowing" (v.16) picks up on this idea. Here the Greek form of "knowing" is saying, *We Jews, above all people, came to know in the past and continue to know now that the observance of religious rituals will not justify us.* Paul then answers the question, how do we Jews come to know that we were not justified "by the works of the law?" He quotes David from Psalm 143:2, "And enter not into judgment with thy servant: for in thy sight shall no man living be justified." David is saying *do not judge me by Thy Law* since no man has kept the whole Law and thus no man could be justified by the Law. So Paul is reminding us that David was relying upon his faith, not his works, to be justified before God. Notice that "justify" is used four times (vv. 16-17) and "righteousness" is used in v. 21. "Justify" is the verb form and "righteousness" is the noun form of the same Greek word, *dikaios*. It is a common legal term meaning, *to declare a person to be righteous who had been found guilty.* In the secular courts of that day, a person guilty of an offense could be declared righteous by a judge after the person *worked off* the debt of his offense. Paul makes it clear that the Old Testament teaches that no man, Jew or Gentile, is able to *work off* his spiritual debt to God for his sin. Rather, Paul declares that we are declared right before God only by faith in Christ who paid for our violations by His crucifixion and resurrection (v. 20).

LIFE STEP Are you seeking justification by your own works or by the work of Christ? Are you trying to work off the debt of your own sin ("works of the law," v. 16)? Or have you "believed in Jesus Christ" (v. 16) as the One who *worked off* your debt?

SATURDAY 10

Galatians 3:1-9

What is the writer saying?

How can I apply this to my life?

PRAY Brazil – Pray that Christians in high profile positions would keep a moral and ethical testimony.

Paul has finished his defense and is now moving on to teach the Galatians the true basis of being justified (v. 8, also "righteousness," v. 6) before God. Paul begins by rebuking them since they were foolish (v. 1, 3) in not perceiving the significance of the evidence that has been set before their eyes (v. 1).

"Foolish" literally means *not applying the mind*. Also, he says they have been "bewitched," a word that draws from the superstitions of the day. It was a commonly held fear that staring into the eyes of an evil person could result in the evil person gaining control over them so that he might draw them into great harm (like a modern magician saying, "look into my eyes"). It is used figuratively here to express that the false teachers are drawing them into evil doctrines. Paul is telling the Galatians to use their minds and *see* the truth before their eyes.

Now notice that "faith" (a noun), "believed" (a verb) and "faithful" (an adjective) are used seven times in vv. 2-9. All three words come from the same Greek root word, *pistis*, which means, *to have a firm persuasion or conviction*. What is Paul's doctrine of justification by faith?

- V. 6 – Abraham "believed" and that belief was the basis of his righteousness.
- V. 7 – All who are of "faith" are in Abraham's spiritual family.
- V. 8 – The Old Testament Scriptures (Genesis 12:3) foretold of the Gentiles coming to God by the same "faith" as exercised by Abraham.
- V. 9 – All those of "faith" will be blessed (to cause to prosper) by God, just like faithful Abraham was blessed.

LIFE STEP Think back to that time period just before you were saved. How did God cause your mind to *see* the truth about Christ so that you were *firmly persuaded* of your need to trust in Christ as your means of justification before God? How has God blessed your life since you believed?

109

SUNDAY 11

Galatians 3:10-16

What is the writer saying?

How can I apply this to my life?

PRAY North Korea – For opportunities to be given to godly Chinese businessmen so they may use their easy access to North Korea to share the Gospel.

Yesterday, we looked at the blessings (v. 9) that come upon the Galatians when they, by faith, are *justified* before God. Today, Paul argues from the opposite view, that is, if one seeks to be *justified* by "the works of the law," he is under the "curse" of the Law (v. 10). The word "cursed" (*to call down wrath upon*) is an Old Testament term found especially in Deuteronomy when Moses is giving the Law. The "blessings" and "cursings" are included to warn the people concerning their response to the Law (Deuteronomy 30:19, "I have set before you ... blessing and cursing").

The curse of the Law signifies being handed over to the judgment and wrath of God. From our judicial system, we have a similar picture of a convicted criminal being delivered to the electric chair for justice to be carried out. This is a serious thing made worse by being linked here with the word "under." Rather than merely facing the possibility of a future punishment, "under" emphasizes that the follower of the Law is already subject to the wrath of God upon sin.

Paul closes with the declaration that Christ redeemed us from this hopelessly bleak situation of being under the curse of God. In the New Testament world, a person could be redeemed from slavery when someone paid the slave's debt, thus buying the slave's deliverance. This image is applied here to Christ's death on the cross (v. 13, "hangeth on a tree"). His death is the price paid to deliver us (v. 13) who have placed our faith in Him from our slavery to the curse of the Law.

LIFE STEP Think of it! Redeemed from slavery to the curse of the Law and receiving the blessings that "come on the Gentiles through Jesus Christ" (v. 14). Take a minute and write a note to Jesus, thanking Him for paying the price that freed you from your hopeless situation.

What is the writer saying?

How can I apply this to my life?

PRAY Slovakia – For a clear expounding of God's Word that results in obedience to His authority.

Again, we have a key word that is central to Paul's next point in his ongoing line of argument which is, a person is saved by faith in the death of Christ. "Promise" is used eight times in this chapter, which is the greatest concentration of that word in the New Testament. In the Greek world, "promises" (with the definition of *notification of an agreement*) are made between parties after pledges are negotiated in a contract.

A second definition is also used for "promise," that is, *to announce an intention*. This definition is used when Greeks pledged to give a *freewill* offering (no two-way contract implied) to one of the Greek gods. It is significant that Greek gods are never said to give *freewill* promises to men. In contrast, the very character of the Old Testament is built around the *freewill* promises of God! The first promise of God is to Eve, found early in Genesis (3:15). Late in Old Testament history, when Israel's sins against God are at their worst, God gives His most revealing promises concerning the coming Messiah (such as in Isaiah and Daniel).

Foremost in Paul's thinking is God's promise to Abraham in Genesis 12:3 ("in thee shall all families of the earth be blessed") which Paul quotes in Galatians 3:8. In 3:17 and 18, Paul points out that God's covenant and promises to Abraham are separate from the Law. The two are separated by both a great time period and by purpose. The Law is added (3:19) later because of sin. The Law does not disannul (*to render cancelled*, v. 17) the promises. Rather, the Law is "added ... till the seed should come" (v.19), since the seed (which is Christ, v. 16) is the thing promised to them that believe (v. 22).

LIFE STEP Since God is faithful to His promises concerning both our initial salvation and our ongoing Christian walk, which promises will you claim today?

Galatians 3:23-29

What is the writer saying?

How can I apply this to my life?

PRAY Angola – For medical missionaries laboring in a nation where landmines outnumber people.

Paul now gives an illustration of how the Law is to assist the Old Testament believers. The illustration centers on the words "schoolmaster" (vv. 24, 25) and "children" (v. 26) and refers to a Roman household of a wealthy person. The lord of the household would acquire a slave trained as a "schoolmaster," literally *a child-leader*. This *child* (Greek, *pais*) refers to a seven to fourteen-year-old boy. A pais has no privileges and is considered just a member of the household, the same as any other slave. The schoolmaster's primary responsibility is to guard the children under his care against temptations and danger. He is responsible for their moral and physical well-being, which includes disciplining the children. While he teaches the children informally, he is not their teacher; rather, he is responsible to take his charges to school. It is important to note that Jesus is commonly recognized in this role as the *teacher* (same as *master*). Thus, the role of the Law, in the household of God, is to bring those under the Law to the true Teacher, Jesus Christ.

The word "children" in 3:26 is a different Greek word, *huios*, which is used of a man over twenty-five who is a legal heir. A *huios* could be either the natural offspring or an adopted son. An adult son is released from the schoolmaster (v. 25) and is granted the legal privileges as the recognized heir of the lord of the household. Paul says that by faith (v. 26) we have become the *acknowledged sons* in the household of God. This is a new concept for believers since the Jews only viewed themselves as the *pais* of God; little children in God's great household. Thus, Christians now have a better relationship with God!

LIFE STEP You have been adopted into God's family and have been recognized as an adult-son in the household of God! What are some of the privileges granted to you? What are some of the responsibilities extended to you?

WEDNESDAY 11

Galatians 4:1-7

What is the writer saying?

How can I apply this to my life?

PRAY   Japan – Praise the Lord for the new openness caused by economic, social, and natural disasters.

Today's key word, "heir" (4:1), picks up where yesterday's "heirs" left off (3:29). The word "heir" comes from a family of Greek words that deal with inheritances. The Bible's idea of inheritance is a very rich study. First, an inheritance is a reminder that man is neither an independent, self-sufficient being, nor is he an isolated being. It is a reminder that a person receives what has been passed on to him from God's workings in past history. Second, it is a reminder and a comfort that a person of faith receives even greater blessings as he looks forward to the future.

Paul reminds us that an heir, while he is still a minor, is treated as a household slave. He would one day be lord of all (v. 1) the property, yet as a minor he is required to obey the tutors (*guardians who sanctioned* and limited a child's activities, v. 2) and the governors (*one who serves as trustee of all the inheritance*) until the child becomes an adult. The illustration teaches that mankind is like a minor in God's household-world. Mankind is under the control of external laws and demands of the world (v. 3). But, when Christ came, He redeemed (*paid the slave's debt and set him free*, v. 5a) those under the Law and He caused us to "receive the adoption of sons" (*we who were homeless outsiders become heirs to the household-heaven of God*, v. 5b).

Just like the father orders that a special ring be given to the prodigal son upon his return (Luke 15:22), we are given the Spirit. The ring is a token that shows the father has recognized the prodigal as his son and has granted the son full identity, privilege and authority as his son. The presence of the Spirit in our hearts (v. 6) is our special ring from God.

LIFE STEP   As an "heir of God through Christ" (v. 7), how has your identity changed? What privileges has He given you? How will men see the Spirit in you?

Galatians 4:8-18

What is the writer saying?

How can I apply this to my life?

PRAY Chile – For the Chilean church to overcome its spiritual isolation and develop a missionary zeal.

Previously, Paul has been arguing against the Jews who are seeking to add the Jewish religious rituals to the Gentile churches of Galatia. Now Paul appeals to these Gentiles with the following four points:

- Verse 8, Pre-salvation bondage: Because the Gentiles are ignorant of the true God, they "did service unto them," all the "no-gods" (idols, demons, and other men who exalted themselves).

- Verse 9a, Post-salvation liberty: *Knowing God* is a summary phrase for all that happens when a person is saved: freedom from their bondage to sin to become partakers in the blessings of the new life in Christ. Being "known of God" includes an acknowledgement that God has sought them out to save them. It also gives the idea of being welcomed into God's family as a son and heir.

- Verse 9b, Interim turn again to bondage: "Weak" means *without-strength*, thus one who is feeble or sick. "Beggarly" literally means *poor and unable to work*, like a crippled beggar. Thus, the Galatians have become sick and crippled as they turn to the false belief of Jewish ritualism. This new bondage is powerless to justify them before God. It could not work to enrich their walk with God.

- Verses 12-13, Final return to their first liberty: Paul's words, "be as I am," are like saying, "When you heard the graciousness of my Gospel you begged to hear more. Now I beg you to return to that attitude of admiring the graciousness of God's plan of salvation."

LIFE STEP Which will it be: Liberty in Christ or bondage by the works required of religious rituals? What influences from the world zealously affect you (v. 17a)? How can you avoid those things that seek after you, desiring to exclude (*lock out*) the blessing of God from your life (v. 17b)?

FRIDAY 11

Galatians 4:19-26

What is the writer saying?

How can I apply this to my life?

PRAY Panama – For discipleship that encompasses family dynamics, as over 70% of births are illegitimate.

Paul desires "to change my voice" (v. 20) towards the Galatians for he has been speaking with a harsh voice of rebuke. Since he loves the wayward Galatians, he prefers to speak with the voice of a loving mother to her newborn (v. 19). Yet his harsh words are necessary because the false teachers are placing them in bondage under the Law (v. 21). Since the Judaizers claim to understand the Law of Moses, but they actually pervert the Law by claiming that salvation is faith-plus-law observance, Paul chooses to draw an analogy from the Books of Moses.

The analogy is from the life of Abraham (Gen. 16, 17, 21) and it looks at an event where Abraham seeks to *work* at fulfilling the promises of God rather than by merely *trusting* God to fulfill His own promises. Abraham feels he needs to *add something* to his simple trust in God's promise (Gen 12:2-3; 15:4) lest he *miss out* on the fulfillment of God's promise. Likewise, the pagan Galatians have become Christians through simple faith in the promise that they could trust in the death of Christ. Now they were *seeking after* the false teachers who are saying the Galatians need to *add something* to their simple trust in God's promise or they too would *miss out* on God's promise to them.

It is important to note that this story of Abraham ends with God demonstrating that Abraham's additional work to fulfill God's promise failed to *help out* God. In fact, Abraham's works were ultimately harmful to his children (v. 29).

LIFE STEP Learn from Abraham's mistakes! When faced with uncertainties, do you patiently wait for God? When you question whether faith in Christ's death is enough for your salvation, do you remind yourself that God, Who is always faithful, has declared you to be a "child of promise" (v. 28)? Take a minute and write out a "Declaration of Faith" in God's promises.

Galatians 4:27–5:1

What is the writer saying?

How can I apply this to my life?

PRAY India – For God to save and call to homeland missions many of the 22 million Indians living abroad.

Paul is building on his contrast between *freedom* and *bondage*. Paul's argument is that just as Isaac was the *child of promise* to Abraham and Sarah, so those who trust in Christ by faith are also the children of promise. As such all (4:26) people of faith are (a) free from bondage to paganism (4:8), (b) free from bondage to Jewish legalism (4:5) and (c) free from any other teaching that seeks to draw those of faith back into the "yoke" of works (5:1) to earn salvation.

Today's passage rolls over into chapter 5 to complete the word-contrast between *freedom* and *bondage*. First, note that the Greek word for "liberty" (5:1) is the noun form of the word *free*, which is used later in this verse and is used several times in Chapter 4. Verse 5:1 extends the word-contrast with two Greek imperatives (*a word form that gives a strong command*), "stand fast" and "entangled."

"Stand fast" gives the positive command, *be standing up straight with feet fixed*, and suggests the negatives, *don't be pushed over* and *don't be driven away*. The word is illustrated by a line of soldiers standing with weapons ready and with feet fixed as they are prepared to meet an on-rushing enemy. The opposite form of the word is used in 5:12, "trouble," where it means *to cause one to flee his station*.

"Entangle" literally commands *don't be held in* and is illustrated by a bird caught in a net with its wings being held in. It is coupled here with the picture of a slave who is forced to bend over because of the straps that bind him into a yoke.

LIFE STEP Which of these illustrations better fits your spiritual life?
(1) A soldier courageously standing, facing his enemies.
(2) An eagle soaring "free" with outstretched wings.
(3) A soldier fleeing his post when enemies "trouble" him.
(4) Or perhaps, a bird snagged in a net unable to fly.

SUNDAY 12

Galatians 5:2-6

What is the writer saying?

How can I apply this to my life?

PRAY Austria – Pray for more godly Austrian men to respond to the call to full-time Christian service.

Paul here uses a form of the verb "circumcised" (v. 2) to express a *continuous idea* beyond the normal physical circumcision. Thus, continuing circumcision refers to an ongoing keeping of all the Jewish religious ceremonies and practices, physical circumcision being just the first step. The Galatians are being taught that these are needed to maintain an additional layer of acceptance before God. Paul emphatically states that there can be no *double foundation* upon which a person's salvation rests. Righteousness must either be obtained by faith in Christ or the keeping of all (3:10) the practices of the Law. By adding the Jewish rituals to their faith, the Gentiles of Galatia are in danger of making their walk (not their salvation) with Christ of no effect (v. 4). "Of no effect" means *cut off from*, thus, ceasing to be connected with the grace of Christ needed for daily living ("fallen from grace," v. 4b).

In contrast with v. 4, Paul presents the true basis for salvation (v. 5): (a) "we through the Spirit" (b) "wait for the hope of righteousness" (c) "by faith."

- "Through the Spirit" acknowledges that it is the Spirit Who works in us, drawing us to Christ and then imputes the righteousness of Christ to us.
- "Wait for the hope of righteousness" refers to the fact that, at salvation, a believer is declared righteous but some of the benefits promised to a believer are not received until he gets to Heaven.
- "By faith" in Christ, without any mixing with personal works, is the means by which people receive acceptance before God.

LIFE STEP Are you seeking acceptance by God through a mixture of trusting in Christ *and* trusting in the religious deeds you may have done to *earn* salvation? If you are trusting in Christ alone for your salvation, then think back through the *work* the Holy Spirit did to bring you to Christ!

Galatians 5:7-15

What is the writer saying?

How can I apply this to my life?

Today's passage could be entitled, "Running or Hindered?" The phrase "Ye did run well" (v. 7a) refers to the Greek stadiums where foot races were conducted. "Well" means *with excellence* and here refers to the character of the runner and his *excellent* conduct in the race.

The next phrase, "who did hinder you...," continues the metaphor of running a race. The Greek word "hinder" literally means *to cut into*, referring to a retreating army that would cut into (break up) a road to make it temporarily impassable, thus delaying their enemy. Later, it is used with the idea of *to cut short, to check*, as in checking the course of a ship (turning to stop forward motion). It is also used of a runner who comes across the line to jostle an opposing runner, causing him to stumble and fall out of the race. Paul uses it here to picture the false teachers who are building up spiritual obstacles in front of the Galatians and deliberately *pushing* the beliefs of the Galatians. They are seeking to hinder the Galatians' faith in God and to *check* their walk with the Lord.

Next, Paul says, "I have confidence in you through the Lord" (v. 10). In what is Paul confident? Paul expects the Galatians to again "run well" as they had before. Paul then goes on to define what he has in mind for their renewed run. The Galatians are (a) to serve one another (v. 13), (b) to love thy neighbor (v. 14), (c) to take heed of their conduct (v. 15), (d) to walk (v. 16) and live (v. 25) in the Spirit (tomorrow's study) and (e) to desire humility (v. 26).

LIFE STEP Are you running well? Which of the above areas of spiritual running do you need to practice so that your game can become excellent? Which area needs you to ask for some help from God?

TUESDAY 12

Galatians 5:16-21

What is the writer saying?

How can I apply this to my life?

PRAY Portugal – To see lasting changes in the hearts and lives of those attending Christian camps.

"Walk in the Spirit" (v. 16) is the focus today. First notice the little word "in." Let us picture the subjects of today's passage in relation to the boundary of a marathon race course. The Holy Spirit has provided the markers that define the boundaries *within* which we can run free (v. 7) and live free (v. 25). Also notice that failing to walk (v. 16) *inside* the Holy Spirit's boundaries results in our always failing to do the things we want to do (v. 17)! Now notice that Paul gives two lists. One list of seventeen items, "the works of the flesh" (vv. 19-21), is the out-of-bounds area. The other list of nine items, "the fruit of the Spirit" (vv. 22-23), is *in*-bounds and is tomorrow's passage. So let's look at the first list:

- *Adultery, fornication, uncleanness,* and *lasciviousness* all involve sexual impurity that abandons godly morals.
- *Idolatry,* worshipping idols, also anything taking God's rightful place.
- *Witchcraft* is the use of drugs (potions) in sorcery, enchantments.
- *Hatred,* a personal quarrel with others leading to a desire to murder.
- *Variance* means arguments and strife resulting from selfishness.
- *Emulations* are jealousies that make war on the good in another.
- *Wrath,* an outburst of uncontrolled anger due to a lack of self-control.
- *Strife & seditions,* taking sides by selfishness that destroys harmony.
- *Heresies,* divisive and destructive views on doctrinal beliefs.
- *Envyings* are active and often treacherous desires to get even.
- *Murders,* intentional killing, the destroying of another's character.
- *Drunkenness & revellings* are unrestrained carousing and partying.

LIFE STEP Does your life, at times, run *out-of-bounds*? For example, do you find yourself wanting to get even for some wrong done to you? Well, that is out-of-bounds! How can you keep from going out-of-bounds? How can you work together with the Holy Spirit, your *race Referee,* to stay inside the Spirit's boundaries for your life's race for God?

WEDNESDAY 12

Galatians 5:22-26

What is the writer saying?

How can I apply this to my life?

PRAY Canada – For outreach into the Asian, Indian, Chinese, and Arabic-speaking immigrant communities.

Today we get the good list, the *in-bounds areas* that allow us to run well (v. 7). Let's begin by noting that there are no laws (v. 23) like our speed limits or construction zone restrictions that require us to drive slowly when using today's list. Remember, Paul has been arguing against those who wanted to install the Old Testament Law into the churches of Galatia. Here, Paul is also pointing out that neither the Old Testament Law, nor any other set of religious rules, can give a person love, joy, peace, etc. These are only obtained when a person places himself under the Holy Spirit and thereby removes himself from being under religious rules and rites.

The nine "fruit of the Spirit" (v. 22) are the crops that the Spirit *grows* in our lives. These are the expected *harvest* of the Spirit's working in the *soil* of your life as a Christian. Let's look at His crops:

- *Love*, (Greek: *agape*), a self-giving devotion that does what is best for the other person regardless of what that person does in return.
- *Joy*, a cheerful attitude, delighting in God, regardless of situation.
- *Peace*, a quiet calmness of heart, knowing my life is in God's hands.
- *Longsuffering*, to suffer long; endurance when wrongly treated.
- *Gentleness*, showing kindness, conveying consideration, patience.
- *Goodness*, good in character, demonstrated by generosity.
- *Faith*, faithfulness in conduct due to a complete confidence in God.
- *Meekness*, an inward submission to God's dealings in one's life, resulting in an outward balance in the expressions of one's strength.
- *Temperance*, having the mastery of self-control over fleshly desires; the right use of the powers given to a man by God.

LIFE STEP Since these are *growing* crops or fruit, which of the above do you need to concentrate on producing in your life? How can the Spirit help you? How can you *fertilize* these spiritual crops?

THURSDAY 12

Galatians 6:1-5

What is the writer saying?

How can I apply this to my life?

PRAY Kenya – Continued growth for Kenya, which has the highest percentage of believers in all of Africa.

Today's passage picks up on the second of two extremes facing Christians in their life of liberty in Christ. The first extreme is the danger of losing one's liberty by coming again under the law (5:18) of legalism. Paul already noted that the second extreme is allowing one's liberty to become a license to sin (5:13). Liberty in Christ does not mean lawlessness. Rather, it is every believer's responsibility to "fulfill the law of Christ" (v. 2) which is a law of "love" (5:13) and is accomplished by applying the fruit of the Spirit (5:22-23) to the situations of life.

Paul gives an example of this in a brother "being overtaken in a fault" (v. 1). "Overtaken" means *drawn into a trap and taken*. It is coupled with "fault" (*to misplace one's step; to slip and fall*). Thus, Paul gives a picture of a brother who falls into the mud of sin because he was careless, not having considered his steps that led him into the trap. A spiritual Christian (*one being led by the Spirit*) cannot say, "Well, it is his own fault, let him suffer! Maybe next time he will be more careful."

While such a comment may be true, it is not loving. Love demands that the spiritual one come to the aid of the one overtaken and restore him (v. 1, literally, *to set a broken bone, allowing it to heal*). The spiritual one must use care ("meekness," v. 1) since broken lives, like broken bones, are very painful. Meekness demands the precision and gentleness of a spiritual doctor who brings health to his patient. Finally, Paul reminds us that people with broken lives, like those with broken bones, often need others to carry ("bear," v. 2) their burdens for a time.

LIFE STEP As in the Parable of the Good Samaritan, what spiritually injured person has God placed in your path so that God might teach you how to become "spiritual" through the use of the qualities listed as the fruit of the Spirit? Ask God to show you how you might be able to bear up that friend of yours who needs you to carry him along for a while.

FRIDAY 12

Galatians 6:6-10

What is the writer saying?

How can I apply this to my life?

PRAY Argentina – Pray that the Church will have a vision to impact their communities and do more to address the enormous poverty in cities.

Paul shows the functioning of the fruit of the Spirit (5:22-23) in the believer's daily life by giving two applications to the model of "bear ye one another's burdens" (v.2). The first is in yesterday's passage and dealt with serving as a *spiritual doctor* to those who have been overtaken by the troubles of life.

Today we look at the second application. Lehman Strauss, in his commentary on Galatians, puts it this way, "The word 'communicate' (v.6) conveys the idea of sharing, of having things in common. The teacher passes on the great truths of God's word which are the fruit of his labor; the one taught acknowledges this by communicating to him 'in all good things' (v.6b)." Paul is implying that the members of the churches of Galatia are neglecting their spiritual leaders ("him that teacheth," v.6) whose work was the sowing (v. 8) of the word (v. 6).

The law of sowing and reaping (vv. 7-8) teaches all men that only a fool thinks he can break God's Law and escape the consequences (v. 7). Paul is urging the ones who are being taught (v.6) not to faint (v. 9b) or become weary in well doing (v. 9a) in their temporal support (salary, housing, food, and other needs) of their spiritual teachers.

Yes, the teacher who ministers in the Spirit, with the fruit of the Spirit, will reap a great harvest of God's blessing. But, notice here that Paul is emphasizing the reaping of the ones *being* taught, that is, the member in the pew. These also will reap a great harvest of God's blessing by faithfully supporting the work of the ministry with the temporal seeds that they have opportunity (v.10) to sow upon the work of the church.

LIFE STEP What "opportunity" seeds has God given you to plant in the garden of your life? Don't become weary at working your garden! Take a moment and remind yourself of the great harvest you are going to reap.

What is the writer saying?

How can I apply this to my life?

PRAY Nigeria – For the HIV/AIDS epidemic in Nigeria. If the epidemic continues, by the year 2020, 60% of Nigerians will have HIV/AIDS.

To stress its importance, Paul takes the pen from his scribe and writes with bold letters this last paragraph. The three sections of the conclusion correspond, in reverse order, to the three sections of the letter.

First, he warns that the false teachers, who constrain (v. 12b) the Galatians to be circumcised, are not interested in the spiritual welfare of the Galatians. Rather, they are being self-serving by seeking (a) to obtain a "fair shew" (v. 12a, *win favor with their religious superiors*), (b) to avoid persecution (v. 12c) by staying in good standing with the Jews and (c) to "glory in your flesh" (v. 13) by making a display of the number of Gentiles they had won to the Jewish ritual.

Second, Paul makes a final defense of his own credentials. Notice the contrast given by the repeating of the word "glory" (vv. 13-14, *basis for boasting*). Paul rightly boasts in the "cross of our Lord Jesus Christ" (v. 14). Paul has in mind more than just the cross upon which Christ died. He is emphasizing all that was accomplished by the complete work of Christ. Paul points out two aspects: (a) Paul is now *dead* to the world (v. 14, "crucified") and (b) he is now *alive* to Christ (v. 15, "a new creature").

Third, Paul says he has marks (v. 17b) on his body to prove that his arguments in this letter are true. The word "marks" refers to the scars on his body. The marks declare that Christ owns Paul. There are three classes of people in the ancient world who were branded: soldiers, slaves and devotees. The religious devotees would voluntarily accept branding to announce that they belonged to a certain God.

LIFE STEP What *proof of ownership* can be found from your conduct during the past week? In what will you seek glory: self-serving things that give you a "fair shew" or self-sacrificing things that *show Christ* in you?

Daniel is called a prophet by our Lord (Matthew 24:15). He is called a "greatly beloved" man (Daniel 9:23; 10:11,19). His name means *God is my judge*. He was a statesman in the courts of a succession of heathen monarchs. The book of Daniel is often referred to as *The Apocalypse of the Old Testament* since it contains some of the most detailed and far-reaching prophecies of the Word of God. These include:

- The four great world powers of Gentile dominion.
- The coming of the time of trouble upon the earth.
- The coming of a man to head up the last world power before the coming of Christ.
- The coming of Christ and the establishment of the kingdom.
- The time of the seventy weeks of Israel that sets the stage for the time period of the great tribulation (time of trouble coming upon the world), and the resurrection of the righteous of the nation of Israel.

Dr. Merrill Unger says this book is the key to all biblical prophecy. Without the information in this book, the remaining prophetic portions of the Word of God cannot be understood. Jesus' great Olivet discourse (Matthew 24-25; Mark 13; Luke 21), 2 Thessalonians 2, and the entire Book of the Revelation are unlocked only through an understanding of the prophecies of Daniel. The great themes of New Testament prophecy are all treated in Daniel.

The Book of Daniel has great prophetic information and Daniel himself is a great example of personal holiness. His life was marked by constant prayer (chaps. 2, 6, 9, 10); he was guided by a study of God's Word (9:1-2); he had a testimony of life (chap. 6) and lip (chaps. 2, 4, 5); and he was dedicated to keeping himself pure for God (1:8). Daniel's example is worth studying and following.

The Book of Daniel presents that time when Jerusalem is under Gentile control ("the times of the Gentiles" – Luke 21:24) and when Israel is not in its proper place before God. Daniel shows that this time started in the third year of the reign of Jehoiakim. It is marked by the rise and fall of four great Gentile powers. Three of these great world powers are named as Babylon, Medo-Persia and Greece. The fourth is strongly implied to be Rome, the power that follows Greece. This period will come to a close after the leader of the last world power (the man over it is totally against God and against the people of Israel) is destroyed by God Himself. God's kingdom will then be established on the earth, never to be given to another people or nation.

The Book of Daniel is usually divided into two main sections, the first being *events* and *experiences* that show the times of the Gentiles, and the second being *prophecies* or *visions* given to Daniel reviewing this same period.

Outline of the Book of Daniel

I. Experiences (Events) and the Time (chaps. 1-6)

  A. The Beginning, 1
Daniel and his friends deported. They remain faithful and are rewarded with wisdom and knowledge.

  B. The Dream of the Image, 2
Daniel interprets Nebuchadnezzar's dream of a great image. It illustrates how God would sovereignly elevate and then depose four successive Gentile empires, with Messiah's kingdom bringing to a close "the times of the Gentiles."

  C. The Fiery Furnace, 3
God's power is demonstrated through the preservation of His servants in the fire. When the heat is turned up, God is still there for His children.

  D. The Dream of the Tree, 4
The tree pictures Nebuchadnezzar and his kingdom. His pride results in his humbling, his recognition of God's supremacy, and his eventual conversion.

  E. The Feast of Belshazzar, 5
This arrogantly defiant ruler defies God, places his trust in man-made protection, and loses both his kingdom and his life.

  F. The Lion's Den, 6
Daniel's faith demonstrated through devout worship is rewarded. Darius the king learns of the power of Daniel's God.

II. Visions (Prophecies) and the Time (chaps. 7-12)

  A. The Four Beasts, 7
Daniel's vision of the four beasts supplements and parallels Nebuchadnezzar's image dream of chapter 2. Once again God's sovereignty is displayed, the Gentile kingdoms are deposed, and "the saints of the Most High shall take the kingdom" (v.18).

  B. The Two Beasts, 8
Here the focus is narrowed and we find Israel under the Medo-Persian and Grecian empires, the Ram and Goat respectively.

  C. The Seventy Weeks, 9
Here in chronological sequence is God's perfect plan for the redemption and deliverance of Israel, a chronology given to Daniel after his prayer of repentance for his people.

  D. The Last Days, 10-12
The book concludes with one final vision, giving the details of Israel's future history. Though more persecution still awaits, Daniel's people will be saved out of tribulation and resurrected to everlasting life.

SUNDAY 13

Daniel 1:1-8

What is the writer saying?

How can I apply this to my life?

PRAY Peru – A God-honoring end to animosity and division between Quechua and Spanish-speaking believers.

The book begins with the commitment of the book's author, Daniel (v. 8), and subsequently his three friends, to be faithful to their God. The time period is during the reign of Jehoiakim, King of Judah, and the setting is the first of three attacks the Babylonians made on Jerusalem (605 B.C.). Later attacks will see Ezekiel deported (597 B.C.) and Jerusalem destroyed (586 B.C.). In this attack Jehoiakim was taken captive along with some of Israel's finest young men, probably in their late teens. Their deportation was to break the spirit of the Jews while at the same time provide the Babylonians with new young leaders for the king's court.

Historians often give Nebuchadnezzar credit for Israel's demise. In reality it was God (v. 2) who used the Babylonians to accomplish His sovereign will. God is always in control of the circumstances, both in nations and in individuals. Israel's captivity was the result of her idolatry and failure to keep the sabbatical year for the land (2 Chronicles 36:14-21). Babylon was God's tool to punish her.

Among the deportees were four committed young Jewish boys named Daniel, Hananiah, Mishael, and Azariah. All four were names that identified them as worshipers of Jehovah. The Babylonians gave them pagan names (v. 7) designed to discourage them from continuing in the faith of their fathers. But, while their names were changed, their commitment to their God was not. That commitment, forged in their growing-up years in Israel, caused them to purpose in their hearts not to be defiled with the king's meat which had been offered to idols and was ceremonially unclean. The account that follows demonstrates how God honors faithfulness in the lives of His children.

LIFE STEP Circumstances will sometimes place believers in situations over which they have no control. But a clear commitment to a sovereign God will demonstrate the truth of Romans 8:28. We will see that truth fleshed out in Daniel's life. Can it be seen in yours?

MONDAY 13

Daniel 1:9-21

What is the writer saying?

How can I apply this to my life?

PRAY Canada – Pray for continued growth in the French-speaking missionary outreach.

The commitment of Daniel and his three friends now becomes action. Having found favor with the king's delegated leadership, Daniel, as the spokesman, tactfully requests that an exception be made. He proposes a ten-day test during which time they would be placed on a vegetarian diet (since vegetables were not offered to idols they were not ceremonially defiling). At the end of the ten days they would be compared with those who ate from the king's menu. If the test did not validate their vegetarian diet, they were probably ready to accept the king's food, for Jews could legitimately ignore ceremonial regulations under extreme circumstances (cf. Ezekiel 4:12-15). The king's overseer, Melzar (vv. 10-14), no doubt thinking that no great harm could come to the young men in ten days, agreed to the test. At the end of the ten days he could tell simply by looking at them (v. 15) that they had passed the test. Therefore, he placed them permanently on the vegetarian diet (v. 16). This was the beginning of a three-year program.

Their commitment did not go unnoticed or unrewarded, for in verse 17 we read that "God gave them knowledge and skill in all learning and wisdom." Just as Moses was educated in the knowledge of the Egyptians, so Daniel and his friends were educated in the knowledge of the Chaldeans. Plus Daniel had the added advantage of being gifted of God prophetically. The record (vv. 19-20) goes on to tell us that at the end of the three years, Daniel and his friends graduated at the top of their class. In fact, they were found to be ten times better than all the others in the kingdom. As for Daniel, the passing of the test led him to be counselor to the king until the very end of the Babylonian empire (v. 21).

LIFE STEP Daniel's experience illustrates how important it is to make right choices. His unwillingness (along with that of his three friends) to go along with the crowd resulted in great blessing. May it be so in your life as well.

Daniel 2:1-13

What is the writer saying?

How can I apply this to my life?

In the second year of his reign, Nebuchadnezzar was troubled by a recurring dream, one he perceived as being so significant that he could not continue to sleep. He called upon his wise men, men who professed to be able to tell the future, to provide an interpretation. He further insisted that they first tell him the dream. They protested that the assignment was an impossible one, even noting that only the gods could comply (v.11). In effect they admitted that their previous interpretations were inaccurate and deceptive.

Some English texts appear to suggest that the king had forgotten the content of his dream. However, other texts indicate that he knew what he had dreamed and was putting his advisors to the test. Surely they who had supernatural wisdom to interpret should be able to use the same power to tell what had been dreamed. Like all tests, there were consequences. To pass the test would result in great honor (v. 6); to fail, death ("cut in pieces" v. 5).

The wise men repeated their request to be told the dream (v. 7). The king charged them with stalling for time (v. 8), and reminded them of the penalty for failure (v. 9). He felt that only by first revealing his dream to him could they legitimately demonstrate their trustworthiness. If they failed to do so, he could conclude that they were lying and corrupt. Their admission of being unable to comply with his request (v. 11) resulted in furious anger on the king's part (cf. 3:13, 19). He issued an executive order, "Destroy all the wise men of Babylon," an order that would include Daniel and his friends, all of whom were, at that time (v. 1), in training for future service as wise men in the king's court.

LIFE STEP The wise men of Babylon proved to be less than advertised. They were unable to perform in a manner acceptable to the king. May similar charges not be leveled against us for we are ambassadors of Jesus Christ (2 Corinthians 5:20). May our service be pleasing to Him.

What is the writer saying?

How can I apply this to my life?

PRAY Ukraine – Christian camps. For God to give youth a passion to live for Him and reach their land.

The events of the early verses of this chapter were unknown to Daniel. When informed that he was under a sentence of death, he went to Arioch, the captain of the king's guard (chief of the executioners), and tactfully ("with counsel and wisdom," v.14), asked the reason why. Arioch's explanation caused Daniel, with great boldness, to go to see the king. "The righteous are bold as a lion" (Proverbs 28:1). For reasons unexplained, the king clearly held Daniel in high regard. Not only did he receive him, but he granted him his request; a stay of execution so that he could interpret his dream. This was a clear step of faith for at that moment he had no more information than the other wise men, who earlier made a similar request that was denied.

In these verses we find the key to Daniel's effective, lifelong ministry. He knew the importance of prayer in the life of a believer. He sought out his three friends, told them what had transpired, initiated a prayer meeting, and looked to the God of heaven for wisdom (cf. James 1:5). Their prayer was specific for the answer was in response to "what we desired of thee" (v. 23). They wanted to know Nebuchadnezzar's dream and its interpretation, which they referred to as a "secret" (or "mystery") for it could not be comprehended without divine assistance. The Lord answered their request and Daniel, in spite of the stress of the situation and the hour, immediately took the time to thank God and to praise Him for His revelation. In verse 20 Daniel notes that wisdom and might belong to God. In verse 23 he thanks God for providing him with those two attributes.

LIFE STEP Daniel, though an Old Testament saint, practiced a New Testament principle, "Where two or three are gathered together in my name, there am I in the midst of them" (Matthew 18:20). May our lives be marked by similar practice. It was effective then; it will be effective now.

THURSDAY 13

Daniel 2:24-30

What is the writer saying?

How can I apply this to my life?

PRAY   Let us come before His presence with thanksgiving; let us shout joyfully to Him with psalms (Psalm 95:2).

Armed with the knowledge of Nebuchadnezzar's dream and its interpretation, Daniel returned to Arioch and instructed him not to destroy the wise men. He also requested an audience with the king, for he was now ready to follow through on his commitment made a day earlier (v. 24). Knowing the urgency of the hour, Arioch, "in haste" (v. 25), brought Daniel into the king's presence. In a somewhat deceptive and self-serving manner he implied to Nebuchadnezzar that after a diligent search he had found a man who could meet the king's request. Arioch's readiness to take unearned credit for finding this dream interpreter, for Daniel had actually presented himself to Arioch, is in marked contrast to Daniel's constant desire to give glory to God (vv. 23, 28, 30).

As he faced the king, and in response to the king's questions as to his ability to tell him his dream and its interpretation, Daniel quickly responded that what he had requested was humanly impossible (v. 27). "But," Daniel continued, "There is a God in heaven" who can (v. 28). Then he proceeded to do so. The dream, said Daniel, was in answer to the king's meditations (v. 29) concerning events that would happen in the future. It had to do with the latter days (v. 28), that time period known as "the times of the Gentiles" (Luke 21:24). With Nebuchadnezzar being the first of many Gentile rulers, it was appropriate he should be the dream's recipient. Before spelling out the dream's details, Daniel made sure to disclaim any natural or magical ability, but credited the Lord with the dream's interpretation (vv. 27-30).

LIFE STEP   God has always used men and women to accomplish His purposes and to deliver His message. To be so chosen should be seen as a great honor. In the carrying out of the assignment, the humility that marked Daniel's life should be the hallmark of today's Christian servants. Can that be said of you?

Daniel 2:31-43

What is the writer saying?

How can I apply this to my life?

"Thou, O king, sawest, and behold a great image (v. 31)." With those words Daniel began to tell and interpret Nebuchadnezzar's dream. This image or statue was large and of extraordinary splendor. It was composed of five different materials: gold (head), silver (chest and arms), bronze (belly and thighs), iron (legs), and iron and clay (feet). As the king looked on, the statue was struck in the feet by a stone not of human origin ("cut out without hands," v. 34). With that blow the image was shattered and turned into a chaff-like substance and blown away by the wind. The stone then increased in size and became a great mountain (often a metaphor for a kingdom), and filled the whole earth (vv. 34-35).

Having told the dream, Daniel gave its interpretation. Each portion of the image depicted a different world kingdom, kingdoms that would rule over all the earth (v. 39). The head of gold is *Babylon*: then follows *Medo-Persia* (silver breast and arms), *Greece* (bronze belly and thighs), and finally *Rome* (first iron legs and then iron and clay feet). The stone cut out without hands is Christ, who is pictured in Scripture as the rejected stone, the chief cornerstone, and the smiting stone (cf. Matthew 21:42). This chapter records the fulfillment of Psalm 2:9. The image, from a human perspective including that of Nebuchadnezzar, portrays a very pessimistic picture of world history. The various materials, representing successive world kingdoms, decrease in weight, value, and strength (from gold to clay) as the end of human history approaches. Each new kingdom is inferior (v. 39) to its predecessor.

LIFE STEP The world faces the future pessimistically. Not the believer. The God who used Daniel to interpret the king's dream has a purpose for you as well. You can trust him with your life and with the world.

SATURDAY 13

Daniel 2:44-49

What is the writer saying?

How can I apply this to my life?

PRAY Nicaragua – For gifted Bible teachers committed to the development of future church leaders.

If our last passage ended on a negative note, this passage begins on a positive one. Nebuchadnezzar's image presents the earth as a single, united image. There are no breaks between the kingdoms and as a result when the stone struck the feet of the image, the whole thing was destroyed. The stone, symbolic of Christ and His kingdom, at first a smiting stone, immediately became a mountain that filled the whole earth (2:35). It is the prophecy of a literal kingdom to be ushered in by the Lord Jesus Christ at His second coming when He returns to conquer the nations (Revelation 19:11). It is a kingdom which shall stand forever (v. 44). The dream underscored and asserted the sovereignty of God in the affairs of men and His superiority over the gods of the pagans.

Nebuchadnezzar did not miss the point and he delivered on his promise (2: 6) to reward the one that could tell and interpret the dream. Four things took place. First, the king prostrated himself before Daniel and ordered an offering to be made to him (an honor normally reserved for pagan gods), though Daniel earlier made it clear that his wisdom came from his God (vv. 27-28, 30). Second, the king, while remaining a polytheist, recognized Daniel's God, as a "God of gods...Lord of kings...revealer of secrets" (v. 47). Third, Daniel was elevated to a position of prominence and power among the unbelieving Babylonians (v. 48), and his new position greatly increased his influence in Nebuchadnezzar's court. Finally, Daniel demonstrated his loyalty to his praying friends (2:17-18) and saw to it that they shared his honors (v. 49).

LIFE STEP Daniel, throughout his life, demonstrated great character. So far he has purposed in his heart to remain pure. He has shown great trust in his Lord. He has demonstrated loyalty to his friends. May our lives be marked by similar character.

Daniel 3:1-7

What is the writer saying?

How can I apply this to my life?

PRAY Brazil – For many to accept Christ through the ministry of Christian concerts and musical dramas.

Here we see a demonstration of commitment to God that parallels the events of chapter 1. There Daniel and his three friends, Shadrach, Meshach, and Abednego, purposed in their hearts not to be defiled with the king's meat. God rewarded their stand. The latter three (with Daniel apparently away on the king's business) once again demonstrated their faithfulness to their God by refusing to bow to the king's image.

The events under consideration took place fifteen to twenty years following chapter 2, a chapter that ended with Nebuchadnezzar praising Daniel's God. Now it appears he had forgotten God's greatness and had reverted to idolatrous self-worship. Perhaps remembering his earlier dream, the king attempted to duplicate it in material form with a huge image (90 feet high by 9 feet wide). Rather than simply a head of gold (as the image of chapter 2), the entire image was of gold (probably wood overlaid with gold as the gold altar of Exodus 37). The king's actions were no doubt an expression of rebellion against God's revelation, and through the image of all gold (no changing of metals) he was saying, *My kingdom will never be replaced by another kingdom. It will rule forever!*

Once erected, he ordered all of the officers of his kingdom to attend the official dedication and, on signal; everyone was to bow before it. To fail to do so would be counted as treason, the penalty of which was death by being thrown into a fiery furnace. These three Jewish youths faced a dilemma. If they worshipped the image they would violate the first two of God's Ten Commandments.

LIFE STEP There is always a danger of failing to remember lessons that had been taught earlier (2 Peter 1:12). That was Nebuchadnezzar's problem. It wasn't so with Shadrach, Meshach, and Abednego (they knew Exodus 20). May our lives follow the pattern they demonstrated.

MONDAY 14

Daniel 3:8-18

What is the writer saying?

How can I apply this to my life?

Nebuchadnezzar's image of gold, and his command to bow before it, presented a problem for Daniel's three friends. As Jews they could not prostrate themselves, as pagans could, in such idolatrous worship. It was strictly forbidden by the Mosaic Law (Exodus 20:3-5). But to stand while all others bowed exposed them to possible execution. Their disobedience was reported (vv. 8-12) in a malicious, anti-Semitic, biased fashion. The implication was that these Jews, as non-Chaldeans, could not be trusted, a charge clearly inconsistent with their previous record (cf. 1:18-20).

While their behavior enraged the king (v. 13), to his credit he did not demand their immediate execution. Instead he summoned them, perhaps suspecting that the accusers were jealous of the position of these three Jews in the kingdom. He asked if the charges were accurate. Had they intentionally refused to bow down? Then, no doubt to the dismay of the accusers, he proposed to give them another opportunity to prove their loyalty. To refuse the offer would result in execution (v. 15), and "who is that God that shall deliver you out of my hands?" With no disrespect to the king and his position, their answer was, "O Nebuchadnezzar, we are not careful to answer thee in this matter." In other words, *There is no need of our putting you to any further trouble. We have made up our minds. Our answer is ready. We will not serve your gods. If God should choose to deliver us, He can. But even if He doesn't, we will not displease Him by obeying the command to bow before the idol* (vv. 16-18).

LIFE STEP For these three young men the final outcome paled in light of their commitment to the Lord. They served regardless of the cost. May such faith characterize our lives.

Daniel 3:19-30

What is the writer saying?

How can I apply this to my life?

PRAY Indonesia – For the unity and continued growth of churches in the midst of intense persecution.

The calm confidence of these three men infuriated Nebuchadnezzar. He was so angry his facial expression was visibly altered, and he ordered the flames heated seven times as hot as usual (probably by adding oil or petroleum to the normal charcoal). He then ordered his strongest men to bind them and cast them into the burning fiery furnace (v. 20). Bound, unable to walk, and clothed in flammable clothing, there could be no escape. The soldiers carried out their orders. The executioners moved close to the furnace, tossed the prisoners in, and in the process dropped lifeless in their tracks, victims of the intense heat.

Nebuchadnezzar had a ringside seat. What he saw brought him up short. Instead of three men in the furnace there were four. No longer bound, the prisoners were walking around undamaged by the fire or its heat and the fourth one in the fire looked like the Son of God (v. 25). Many scholars say that this was a theophany, a preincarnate appearance of Christ. Realizing that he has been defeated by one much greater than he, the king calls the three Hebrew youths to come forth, calling them servants of the Most High God (v. 26). Upon examination (v. 27), there was no evidence that their lives had ever been in jeopardy. Though still a pagan, in the face of the evidence, the king was constrained to acknowledge that the God of the Hebrews was greater than the gods of the Babylonians (v. 28). His declaration, "There is no other god that can deliver after this sort." He follows his declaration by promoting Shadrach, Meshach, and Abednego in the province of Babylon (v. 30).

LIFE STEP The principle here is that even when the heat gets turned up, God never deserts His children. What a wonderful truth when facing tough times!

Daniel 4:1-18

What is the writer saying?

How can I apply this to my life?

PRAY China – Outreach among the 500 million youth to whom it is illegal to teach religion.

This chapter contains the marvelous story of King Nebuchadnezzar's conversion, written by the king himself. He penned it seven years after its actual occurrence. In verses 1 to 3 and 37 he shares what God has done in and for him. He testifies to God's great and mighty signs and wonders, and acknowledges His everlasting kingdom and dominion.

In verse 4 Nebuchadnezzar begins to tell the story of a dream he had. He called in his wise men, told them the dream and asked for an interpretation. As with his earlier dream (chap. 2), they were unable to provide an answer. Finally ("at the last," v. 8), Daniel was called in, for though the king at this point was a polytheist (believed in many gods), he recognized that in Daniel was a spirit of the holy gods (he didn't realize yet that there is only one God). Daniel had earlier demonstrated that he had contact with that God (cf. 2:47).

Nebuchadnezzar shared his dream with Daniel. He saw a great spreading tree that reached unto heaven. It could be seen over the whole earth, symbolic of a great empire with worldwide fame. Under it many kingdoms and people gathered for rest and security, and its fruit supplied their needs. Then a "watcher" (angel) came down from heaven (v. 13) and commanded it be cut down, scattering those who had been sheltered. Only a bound stump was left and its heart was changed for a period of seven years from that of a man to a beast, making it obvious that the tree was symbolic of a person.

Then, with limited spiritual understanding, Nebuchadnezzar tried to explain the heavenly authority behind his vision (vv. 17-18) and places his confidence in Daniel for an explanation.

LIFE STEP The point of the passage is that God determines who is in charge. This is a lesson Nebuchadnezzar was being taught and may we learn it as well.

THURSDAY 14

Daniel 4:19-27

What is the writer saying?

How can I apply this to my life?

In these verses we have the interpretation of the king's dream. While he no doubt would have preferred an immediate interpretation, Daniel was so disturbed by what it meant he could not speak. He was reluctant to announce judgment upon a man he had grown to love. But, as the chief of the governors over all the wise men of Babylon (2:48), Daniel had a difficult task to perform, and his loyalty to the Most High God compelled him, after a momentary pause, to tell the truth.

The tree, he said, represented Nebuchadnezzar and his kingdom (cf. Judges 9:7-15; Ezekiel 31:12-14). Just as the tree grew to great size and strength, so the king's influence and power had spread throughout the world of his day. And just as the tree was cut down, so Nebuchadnezzar would be driven from his throne (v. 25). He would become insane, eat grass like an ox, and his hair would be matted down from the dew. This madness would last for seven years (vv. 16, 32), until Nebuchadnezzar would acknowledge the fact that "the most High ruleth in the kingdom of men, and giveth it to whomsoever he will" (v. 17). The Lord was teaching this man, who in his image dream (of chap. 2) was pictured as the head of gold and who had made an entire image of gold to elicit worship to himself (in chap. 3), a major lesson in humility.

The positive side of the lesson, however, is this: Nebuchadnezzar learned the lesson that the tree (Nebuchadnezzar), while cut down for a time, would not be uprooted and still had a future. New growth would spring from the stump that remained giving rise to a new tree, and a lengthening of his prosperity (v. 27). Having delivered his message, Daniel, as a messenger of God should do, left the king with a challenge to change his ways.

LIFE STEP Lessons learned can result in blessing. Is there something God is endeavoring to teach you at the present? Be a good student. Learn it well and God will bless.

FRIDAY 14

Daniel 4:28-37

What is the writer saying?

How can I apply this to my life?

PRAY   Mexico – Effective ministry to youth through Christian camping, outreach activities, and social aid.

Here Nebuchadnezzar concludes his personal testimony of how God had worked in his life. His dream (vv. 4-18) had been interpreted by Daniel (vv. 19-27). His message of warning was clear. A failure on the king's part to change and a continuance in his prideful ways would bring judgment. The king paid no immediate attention to Daniel's warning, and so twelve months later, while on the rooftop of his palace overlooking the city, he voiced his enormous personal pride, "Is not this great Babylon, that I have built…by the might of my power, and for the honor of my majesty?" (v. 30). With those words judgment fell. A voice from heaven announced, "O King Nebuchadnezzar, to thee it is spoken; The kingdom is departed from thee" (v. 31).

All the promised judgment of God took place. He lost all reason and was driven from his palace to live like an animal. His true beastly nature was revealed for all to see. "His body was wet with the dew of heaven, till his hairs were grown like eagles' feathers, and his nails like bird's claws" (v. 33). Nebuchadnezzar's symptoms were similar to lycanthropy, a mental condition in which a person thinks he is a wolf. And then, like the prodigal son of Luke 15, he came to himself. He lifted his eyes to heaven (signaling his return to sanity) and his understanding returned. In his recognition of God, he blessed, praised, and honored the Most High. He acknowledged His eternality and everlasting kingdom (v. 34). With his sanity restored he was returned to power. The throne had been vacant during his years of insanity. The pride that once controlled him was replaced by true repentance and an awareness of the true and living God as Savior of the universe.

LIFE STEP   Don't learn Nebuchadnezzar's lesson the hard way. God exalts those who humble themselves before Him (James 4:10). We must recognize His authority and depend upon Him completely as we serve Him.

SATURDAY 14

Daniel 5:1-16

What is the writer saying?

How can I apply this to my life?

Between chapters 4 and 5, some twenty years have passed. Nebuchadnezzar's long reign has been over for some time, and Nabonidus is now on the throne. For various reasons, however, he was often absent from Babylon (one time for fourteen years!). This is one of those times, and he has left his son, Belshazzar, in charge.

Belshazzar's character was less than admirable. One writer describes him as a spoiled brat. This chapter supplies the evidence. Even with the enemy at the gates of the city this irresponsible leader holds a great feast for one thousand of his lords, wives, and concubines (vv. 1-3) in honor of the gods of Babylon (v. 4). The feast turned into an orgy, and before the evening's abrupt end, the revelers were found drinking wine from the gold and silver vessels Nebuchadnezzar had brought from Jerusalem (1:2). Belshazzar's actions

were 1) a demonstration of his trust in man-made protection, that is, the great wall of Babylon, and 2) a clear act of defiance of God Himself (v. 4).

It is against this defiant act that God intervenes. On the wall of the banquet hall a hand appears (v. 5), and what that hand wrote brought great fear to the king's heart (vv. 5-6). He looked to his wise men for answers but none were forthcoming (vv. 7-9). Then the queen (probably Nebuchadnezzar's widow) suggests that Daniel, apparently in retirement, be called in. She recounts his history. Belshazzar takes her advice. Daniel is called, and is promised a reward of being third in the kingdom for a proper interpretation of the writing on the wall.

LIFE STEP As the story continues, the sovereignty of God will become clear. Man's trust is not to be in self, and a failure to understand man's necessary dependence upon God will always end in disaster. May we learn the lessons Belshazzar failed to learn.

SUNDAY 15

Daniel 5:17-31

What is the writer saying?

How can I apply this to my life?

PRAY   Netherlands Antilles – Openness to the Gospel in a land where religious freedom has yielded little fruit.

Belshazzar's offer of third ruler in the kingdom, after Nabonidus and Belshazzar himself (v.16), meant nothing to Daniel, so he rejected it. He does read and explain the writing without obligation on the king's part, but only after delivering a message of rebuke to the rattled king. He recounted the painful experience of the great Nebuchadnezzar when God taught him a lesson in humility (vv. 18-21). God had humbled him until he acknowledged that God was sovereign over the kingdom of men, and that He appoints over it whomsoever He will (v. 21).

Belshazzar should have learned this lesson from Nebuchadnezzar's experience for he knew all about it (v. 22). It was a lesson he would never learn, even the hard way, for his time had run out.

With the rebuke delivered, Daniel offers the interpretation. The words were *MENE*, *MENE*, *TEKEL*, and *UPHARSIN* (v. 25). *Mene* means numbered or reckoned. *Tekel* means weighed. *Upharsin* (or *peres*, the root word) means broken or divided. When they are placed together and directed at Belshazzar they meant, God has numbered your kingdom and finished it; you have been weighed in the balances and found wanting; your kingdom is about to be divided and given to the Medes and Persians (vv. 26-28). Belshazzar followed through on his earlier commitment of making Daniel the kingdom's third ruler indicating that he accepted the interpretation (v. 29).

That very night the prophecy was fulfilled. By diverting the river which flowed under Babylon's walls, the enemy marched into the city via the riverbed, killed Belshazzar, and the Babylonian empire was no more.

LIFE STEP   Philosopher George Santayana wrote, "Those who do not learn from history are doomed to repeat it." That was true of Belshazzar. Don't let it be said of you. Learn the Book, and live by it.

MONDAY 15

Daniel 6:1-15

What is the writer saying?

How can I apply this to my life?

PRAY Bahrain – Pray that Christians would be able to have the courage and sensitively to share the love of Christ with others despite rules against evangelism.

This is the last extended story about Daniel's life. The chapters that follow detail the prophecies Daniel received while serving the foreign kings of Babylon and Medo-Persia. Remember that chapter 5 concluded with Belshazzar's promotion of Daniel. The new government, under Darius the Mede, did not completely purge the old. Daniel's excellent spirit caught Darius's attention and favor, and he planned to place him second in command, above all others (vv. 1-3). This action caused great jealousy among the other leaders and they set about to remove him from the picture, paving the way for their own promotion.

Using flattery and lies (as Satan did in Genesis 3:4-5), and knowing that nothing in Daniel's long life of service would disqualify him, they decided to use his faithfulness to God to bring about his downfall (vv. 4-5). They proposed to Darius that he offer a decree that for thirty days all petitions be made only to him. Failure would result in being cast into the den of lions (v. 7). They claimed that all his leaders were in agreement, a lie, since Daniel certainly wasn't (v. 7). Darius was flattered and complied. He signed the proposal into law, which like all of the laws of the Medes and Persians, could not be repealed, even by the king (see Esther 1:19; 8:5, 11).

Daniel, of course, could not and would not comply. He still offered his petitions to God (vv. 10-11). His actions were reported to the king (vv. 12-13). Darius realized he had been duped by his supposedly loyal followers but was bound by the law. He had no choice but to follow through with the legal punishment (vv. 14-15).

LIFE STEP As a teenager (chap. 1) Daniel was faithful to his God and to his convictions. Now as an old man, nothing has changed. From beginning to end, and regardless of circumstances, his faithfulness to the Lord never wavered. Can the same be said of us?

TUESDAY 15

Daniel 6:16-28

What is the writer saying?

How can I apply this to my life?

PRAY New Zealand – For alienated Maori citizens to seek their significance in Christ and not society.

Because the laws of the Medes and Persians could not be rescinded, Darius was compelled to throw Daniel into the lions' den. As he does, he expresses hope in Daniel's God with these words, "Thy God, whom thou servest continually, he will deliver thee" (v.16). The den was a large pit in the ground, too deep for the beasts to escape, but viewable by spectators. There was also a side entrance through which the lions were fed. It was closed by a stone, and sealed so Daniel could not escape (in this case, two seals were used, the king's and Daniel's accusers', v. 17). This sealing would assure that neither party could remove the stone without the other's knowledge; either to remove Daniel or to agitate the animals to action.

We don't know how Daniel spent the night. The king, however, experienced a night of misery. He couldn't eat or sleep, and refused all entertainment (v. 18).

At daybreak Darius rushed to the den, and in a troubled voice mixed with both hope and fear, called out to Daniel to see whether or not the God he had entrusted Daniel to had delivered him. Daniel responded with respect (v. 21) and informed the king that his God, knowing of his innocence, shut the mouths of the lions so they did not hurt him.

The king was delighted at Daniel's deliverance. He responded by 1) removing Daniel from the pit, 2) replacing him with his hypocritical accusers and their families (a pagan practice to insure no one would be left for revenge), and 3) issuing a decree to his subjects to reverence the God of Daniel, a God who is living and whose kingdom shall never be destroyed (v. 26).

LIFE STEP Daniel's faith delivered him (6:23; Hebrews 11:33). His constant faithfulness to God throughout his life fed his faith. When we're faced with a *lions' den* experience, may our faith be equal to the task.

Daniel 7:1-14

What is the writer saying?

How can I apply this to my life?

PRAY Poland – For the salvation of many who are taking English classes taught by missionaries.

Here begins the second half of the book. From here on out it becomes heavily prophetic. In chapters 1 to 6 Daniel wrote in the third person as he recorded his actions. Now he writes in the first person as he interprets his own dreams and not those of others (chap. 2).

Daniel's dream in this chapter has many similarities, as well as contrasts, to Nebuchadnezzar's dream in chapter 2. Both provide a *4 plus 1* system of prophecy. Nebuchadnezzar's dream was of an image of gold (Babylon), silver (Medo-Persia), bronze (Greece) and iron (Rome). They are followed by a fifth and final kingdom, the *stone* (the Kingdom of Christ) that smashes the image. Daniel's vision follows the same pattern, but is pictured by animals, not metals.

The magnificent image of a man in chapter 2 is how man would look at the four empires of the world, something to be admired and appreciated. Here, however, that same four-fold empire of man is seen from God's perspective as a pack of ferocious, snarling wild hearts, bent on one another's destruction. A further contrast is seen in the ten-fold aspect of the fourth kingdom. It represents Rome with its ten kingdoms (ten toes, ten horns). In Daniel's vision, however, an eleventh horn appears on the scene, a horn which turns out to be the final Antichrist, appearing just before the stone crushes it into smithereens (destroyed by Jesus Christ at His second coming, Daniel 2:41-45).

Then, without notice, the scene moves to the third heaven (v. 9). There the Ancient of Days (God the Father) exercises His role as the Sovereign Judge of the Universe (Isaiah 57:15). He sends His Son (vv. 13-14, the first reference to Christ as the Messiah) to judge the beast, destroy his kingdom, and set up His own (cf. Matthew 24:30).

LIFE STEP The God of the universe is always in control. What a lesson for God's children to learn. Never should we despair when injustice and wrong seem to prevail. The day is coming when righteousness will reign. That's a promise, believe it!

Daniel 7:15-28

What is the writer saying?

How can I apply this to my life?

PRAY Aruba – Praise God for the growth in the evangelical witness and that the growth will only increase.

In chapter 2 Daniel was able to interpret Nebuchadnezzar's dream; in chapter 5, Belshazzar's wall writing. But here in chapter 7 he is unable to interpret his own dream. Not wishing to guess, he is grieved in his spirit (v. 15). He asked one of the angels for an explanation. The answer is that the four beasts were four kings (v. 17) and pictured the four great world empires (Babylon, Medo-Persia, Greece, and Rome), followed by the unending reign of Christ and His saints, the redeemed of all the ages (v. 18).

Daniel understood the overall thrust of his vision, but pressed the angel for more details concerning the fourth beast and its ultimate destruction. He was told that it represented the fourth world kingdom (v. 23), Rome, which was so ferocious and terrifying that no living animal could represent it. It had disruptive power crushing everything in its way. It was a clear description of the Roman Empire at its peak (v. 23). Unlike the first three, it did not quickly pass off the scene, continuing in power for several centuries. Nor was it to pass off of the scene permanently as the first three, for Rome still has a future known as the Revived Roman Empire. That future is depicted (v. 24) by the ten horns of the beast (representing ten kings). Soon after this future ten-king confederacy is in place, an eleventh king will arise. Designated the *little horn*, he will overthrow three existing horns (kings) and dominate the other seven. This all takes place during the tribulation period (v. 24).

This *little horn* represents the Antichrist. He will speak against God and wear down the saints (v. 25). He is given dominion for three and a half years, but his destruction is certain (v. 26, cf. vv.10-11; Revelation 19:19-21). The saints he has persecuted will prevail (v. 27). His desired kingdom, earthly and political, will be given to the saints of the Most High, and is everlasting in duration (v. 27).

LIFE STEP The God of the universe is always in control. Since God always delivers on His promises, this passage should remind us that we are, in the words of Jack Wyrtzen, "On the Victory Side." Thank God that it is so.

FRIDAY 15

Daniel 8:1-14

What is the writer saying?

How can I apply this to my life?

PRAY North Korea – For the abandoned children on the streets to find a place of refuge.

Two years after Daniel had his vision of the four world empires which would rule his people for centuries to come (chap. 7), God gave him further revelation concerning two of those empires. This vision of the ram and the he-goat is an amplification of 7:6, and explains how Greece, the third empire would be able to conquer Medo-Persia, the second empire. So accurately was the vision fulfilled that liberal theologians have tried to argue that it was written after the events, not before. In this passage the Lord was warning His people of the impending persecution while also assuring them that it would end on His timetable.

Daniel 2 recorded the course and characteristics of Gentile world power. Daniel 7 revealed the final form of that power, its relation to God, and its development under the leadership of the Antichrist. Daniel 8 describes the rise of a power that would unleash its hatred on the Jews. The chronological sequence is as follows: 1) A *ram*, representing Medo-Persia appears, butting its way over everything in sight (vv. 3-4); 2) then comes a he-goat, representing Greece, who attacks the ram, breaks his two horns, and becomes great himself (vv. 5-8, a picture of Greece's victory over Medo-Persia under Alexander the Great); 3) the great horn is then broken (Alexander's death) with his kingdom divided among four horns (Alexander's four generals); 4) a *little horn* (though not the *little horn* of the tribulation period, 7:8) comes out of the four horns. This is Antiochus Epiphanes, who conquers Egypt (south) and Persia (east) and then invades Palestine, (v. 9). In the process he plunders the temple, desecrating it by offering a pig on the altar. Trying to destroy the Jews' faith in God, he stopped their daily sacrifices, and set up the transgression of desolation (v. 13), which was to last for 2,300 days; and then 5) the sanctuary shall be cleansed (v. 14).

LIFE STEP No matter how hot the persecution, God will never forsake His children. The transgression of desolation will come to an end. Jehovah God still has a plan for His people Israel. Let us *pray for the peace of Jerusalem* which will come on the timetable already established by God.

SATURDAY 15

Daniel 8:15-27

What is the writer saying?

How can I apply this to my life?

PRAY Germany – For the salvation of those in key areas of leadership so that they can influence public policy.

The events of chapter 8 were still future when Daniel saw them in his vision. Perplexed, he sought for answers (v. 15), and in response God sends His messenger, the angel Gabriel (9:21; Luke 1:11, 19, 26) to provide the answers. Gabriel, whose presence originally frightened Daniel (vv.15-18), calms him down, and tells him that the sacrilege described in verses 13 to 14 would occur at the final period of the indignation, for it pertains to the appointed time of the end (v. 19). The indignation is God's wrath against His people's idolatry and

VISION	EXPLANATION
vv. 3-4	v. 20
v. 5	v. 21
vv. 6-7	–
v. 8	v. 22
v. 9	v. 23
v. 10	v. 24
vv. 11-12	v. 25
vv. 13-14	v. 26

unfaithfulness. It began with the Assyrian and Babylonian captivities and will conclude with the future Great Tribulation. Gabriel, in the verses that follow, goes on to spell out the details of the vision (see chart), and makes it clear, that while the vision will be illustrated by Antiochus Epiphanes, it foreshadows the end of time, the closing years of Jewish history. Antiochus was only a type of the Antichrist, who will someday desecrate the rebuilt temple and persecute the Jews unmercifully after covenanting to protect them (Daniel 9:27). He breaks the covenant, sets himself up as world ruler, and forces the world to worship him. His destruction, however, is inevitable. That was true of Antiochus, and will also be true of Antichrist, who will be broken without hand (v. 25), by the Prince of Princes, the Lord Jesus Christ (Revelation 19:16-19). With the vision interpreted, Daniel faints, gets sick, but then rises up to do King Belshazzar's business, though not fully comprehending the vision.

LIFE STEP The prophetic program is beginning to take shape. Daniel's reaction demonstrates his concern for what his people would someday face. Let us be similarly concerned for the lost of today.

Daniel 9:1-10

What is the writer saying?

How can I apply this to my life?

PRAY Costa Rica – For spiritual and cultural barriers to be broken down so churches can multiply.

Daniel's final four chapters (9-12) contain some of Scripture's most detailed prophecies, many already fulfilled. This chapter's prophecy centers on God's timetable for the nation of Israel. Daniel is now approximately eighty five years of age, and has been in captivity some sixty seven or sixty eight years. Ten years earlier (8:27) Daniel had received a vision he had not fully understood. Now the Lord is going to provide him with the information necessary to clear up his confusion.

This additional information was provided, not in a vision or in a dream, but through Daniel's study of already existent revelation, namely the Book of Jeremiah (25:1-14). As he studied, he became aware that the end of the predicted seventy year captivity and the time for the return home was fast approaching (v. 2). Daniel's comprehension of Jeremiah's prophecy drove him to his knees (vv. 3-4). In it Jeremiah had predicted Israel's Babylonian captivity and Babylon's subsequent punishment (Jeremiah 25:11-12). Both had now taken place and Daniel had experienced them firsthand. Jeremiah had also written of a repentant attitude on the part of the Jewish people prior to their return (29:12-14). Daniel, in response, began a lengthy (vv. 3-19) prayer of confession for the nation. He included himself in that confession saying *we* have sinned against thee (vv. 5, 8).

Daniel's repentant attitude on behalf of his people was genuine (vv. 3-4), not ignoring their sins nor their conscious departure from God's clear instructions (v. 5). Later (v. 14) he will note that Israel's punishment was just, for our God is righteous in all His works and we obeyed not His voice.

LIFE STEP This is a heavily prophetic, but very practical portion. When you are perplexed and a bit in the dark, Daniel's procedure will serve you well. See what the Book has to say. It is "profitable for doctrine, for reproof, for correction, for instruction in righteousness" (2 Timothy 3:16).

Daniel 9:11-19

What is the writer saying?

How can I apply this to my life?

PRAY Panama – For the increased quality and impact of Panama's Christian television and radio broadcasts.

Daniel's prayer of confession continues. In it he associates himself with the sins of the people thirty two times. Though Daniel had not participated in Israel's sins, this was not false humility on his part. The closer one lives to the Lord, the more aware he becomes of his own failures. This was true of Daniel. Furthermore, his love for his people was so great that he was willing to be identified with them and to share in their shame (v. 8). Paul and Christ felt the same way (Romans 9:3; Hebrews 2:14-16).

Having confessed the nation's sins (vv. 5-10), Daniel notes that in judging Israel, God had acted righteously (v. 14). "All Israel have transgressed thy law… therefore the curse is poured upon us" (v. 11). And that curse, the result of ignoring the clear warnings God had given (vv. 12-13), was deportation from the land, the most devastating consequence imaginable (see Leviticus 26:33-39; Deuteronomy 28:36-68). Daniel then used the greatest redemptive event in Israel's history, the Exodus, to request a repeat performance.

His prayer does not stop with confession, it continues with supplication (vv. 16-19). He pleads with God to forgive His people and to restore them, the city of Jerusalem, and the temple to pre-captivity condition. Failing to do so would seem to Israel's pagan onlookers that their gods were more powerful than the God of Israel. Restoration was not requested because Israel deserved it, but because the reputation of the God of mercy was at stake (v. 17-18). Daniel's prayer was also recognition of Jeremiah's prophecy (29:10-14), that the captivity would end only after repentance. In his prayer, Daniel began to do the very thing that would bring an end to the captivity.

LIFE STEP

Sin always has its consequences, and yet God never ceases being a God of mercy. Perhaps this would be a good time to pause and ask God to bring back to fellowship some wandering acquaintance of yours.

TUESDAY 16

Daniel 9:20-27

What is the writer saying?

How can I apply this to my life?

PRAY Austria – Each student receives their own free copy of the Bible at school. Pray that they would study it and accept its truths.

While Daniel was still in prayer, his confession and supplication was interrupted by a messenger from God with the answer to his prayer (see Isaiah 65:24). As in chapter 8, the messenger was Gabriel. What he said about Jeremiah's prophecy is not recorded. What he did was to deliver a revelation about another time period, not of seventy years, but of seventy times seven years. This period of 490 years was decreed for "thy people" (the Jews) and "thy holy city" (Jerusalem). There is no basis to apply this time measurement to any other people or place. During the 490 years God has specific purposes to fulfill including the removal of sin and the bringing in of righteousness (six things are mentioned in v. 24). The final result is the return of Jesus Christ to reign from His Temple in Jerusalem.

The seventy "weeks" (actually "sevens" and therefore we conclude that years are meant) will begin with the commandment to restore and to rebuild Jerusalem in verse 25. That decree, made in 445 B.C., is recorded in Nehemiah 2:3-8. The weeks are divided into three units: 1) seven weeks, 2) sixty two weeks, and 3) one week. *Unit 1* would end when the building of the city of Jerusalem was complete (v. 25). *Unit 2*, sixty two weeks plus the first seven weeks (or sixty nine weeks total), following which the Messiah shall be cut off (v. 26), a reference to the crucifixion of Christ. In that same verse Daniel records that the city and the sanctuary would be destroyed following week sixty nine. Those prophecies were fulfilled in A.D. 70. *Unit 3*, the seventieth week, is still future (v. 27), and is known as the Tribulation Period. It begins with the prince that shall come (the Antichrist) entering into a seven-year treaty with Israel, promising peace and security, a treaty he breaks after three and a half years. He sets himself up as the ruler of the world, desecrates the temple, and demands worship for himself.

LIFE STEP Between weeks sixty nine and seventy (the death of Christ and the signing of the treaty) is the entire Church Age. Let's rejoice in the special relationship we have with Christ, while remembering God still has a plan for Israel.

WEDNESDAY 16

Daniel 10:1-9

What is the writer saying?

How can I apply this to my life?

PRAY   Papua New Guinea – Effectiveness of literacy ministries that enable nationals to study God's Word.

God's earlier revelations to Daniel prepared him for this final vision (chaps. 10-12). It was so overwhelming that Daniel felt compelled to emphasize its truthfulness (v. 1), for it contained much that was hard to believe. It concerned God's rule over Israel, both near and far. God fills in the details of world events already revealed in earlier visions. This vision occurred in the third year of Cyrus's rule over Babylon. Daniel would now be in his seventieth year of captivity, eighty five to ninety years of age. He is in prayer; mourning, fasting, and not anointing himself with perfumed oil (oil signified joy, 2 Samuel 12:20; 14:2). This self-denial indicates his deep concern for his nation. His demeanor prompted God to send a messenger whose appearance was breathtaking (vv. 5-6). He is similar to John's description of the glorified Christ (Revelation 1:13-17; 2:18). Since he was delayed for twenty one days by a demon he was probably an angel who needed a more powerful angel, Michael, to come and help him (v.13). Gabriel would be a good candidate since he appeared earlier to Daniel. Only Daniel saw the vision. His companions, however, were aware something unique was happening and they fled (v. 7). It was so unsettling to Daniel, that while he did not flee, this sudden confrontation with the messenger, and hearing the voice of his words, caused him to turn deathly pale and he fell unconscious (vv. 8-9).

LIFE STEP   Daniel's reaction was that of a believer in the presence of God. How much more overpowering would it be to a non-believer? (see 2 Thessalonians 1:7-8). Let us recommit ourselves to reaching them.

Daniel 10:10-21

What is the writer saying?

How can I apply this to my life?

A messenger is sent to revive the passed out Daniel (v. 9). He answers Daniel's question before it is asked: "Knowest thou wherefore I come unto thee?" (v. 20). Because thou art a man greatly beloved, one who God loves in an unusual way (cf. 1 Samuel 13:14; John 13:23). Setting Daniel upright (v. 11), he delivers his message, a message in answer to Daniel's prayer earlier in the chapter. God had heard it the day it was prayed (vv. 1-3), but the answer was delayed due to Satanic opposition (v. 13).

Just as God sends His holy angels on behalf of His redeemed children, so Satan sends his demons to do his bidding (Revelation 13:7). The battle here was between the prince of Persia (v. 13) and this messenger. It lasted for twenty one days, the same length of time as Daniel's prayer. This prince of Persia's goal was to oppose God's plan for the nations, and to prevent Daniel from learning the plan's details (vv.12, 14). Michael, the defender of Israel, comes to give this holy messenger assistance (v. 13). The message being delivered concerns Israel (v. 14), and that which will happen to her in the latter days (to be revealed in chap. 11), those days surrounding Christ's second coming (cf. 2:28; Genesis 49:1). The messenger's words shocked Daniel into silence (v. 15). Once again he is supernaturally comforted (v. 16) as will happen a third time (v. 18). The first touch was to pick him up, the second was to speak, and the third was to carry on a conversation (v. 19). The message was that the prince of Persia will be overcome, and that the conflict with the prince of Greece will then begin (v. 20). This succession of world powers follows the pattern of Daniel's second vision (8:20-22).

LIFE STEP Spiritual warfare continues in full force today. Defeat can be avoided by following Paul's directives in Ephesians 6:11-17 to "put on the whole armor of God" which is done by "putting on" Jesus Christ (Romans 13:14). This will prepare you for battle.

FRIDAY 16

Daniel 11:36–12:3

What is the writer saying?

How can I apply this to my life?

PRAY Nigeria – For Nigerian missionaries in West Africa to receive their financial support unhampered.

Daniel 11:1-35 contains amazing predictions including what would happen to Alexander the Great's kingdom after his death. The historic fulfillment of these prophecies gives us confidence that the rest will be fulfilled as well! In today's passage the Tribulation is in view with details relative to the Antichrist, his activities, and destruction. He is the willful king of verse 36. He does as he pleases, and has no regard for the gods (*elohim* can refer to the true God or to gods, plural) of his fathers (a reference to Roman gods), nor for the desire of women (in Old Testament times Jewish women longed to be the mother of the Messiah), a reference to Christ (vv. 36-37).

Question: Will the Antichrist be Jewish? Answer: Perhaps, since it appears that the Jewish people eventually accept him as their Messiah (cf. Deuteronomy 18:15, 18; 2 Samuel 7:12). However, since he comes "out of the sea" (Gentile nations, Revelation 13:1) he would be a Jew raised in a Gentile nation with pagan notions. Herod the Great is a perfect example of such a man. While the Antichrist is atheistic, he still has a *religion*. His god is a god of force, and he devotes his treasure to that god (v. 38). With his god, a military machine, he moves against his enemies. Nothing can stop him. He parcels out land and gives positions of leadership to those who honor him (v. 39). Two cautions concerning the ethnic identity of the Antichrist: 1) the illustration of the Antichrist in Scripture (Antiochus Epiphanes) was not Jewish and 2) if the Antichrist is Jewish, his sin does not reflect on the Jewish people in general.

As the Tribulation moves to a close (vv. 40-45), he is attacked from both North and South (v. 40). He meets these attackers in Palestine, stops them, makes Palestine his base (v. 41), and then sweeps down to control Egypt (vv. 42-43). He hears rumors (apparently of the armies of Revelation 9:13-21). Their threatening tone causes him to return to Palestine where he deals with the threat and establishes his headquarters on Mt. Zion. There he remains until he comes to his end at the hand of the returning Messiah (v. 45, Revelation 19:11-21). This period of time is such as never was, a horrific time (12:1), and only those whose names are found written in the book of life will be delivered (Luke 10:20; Revelation 20:12).

LIFE STEP The book of life! What a glorious thought! Is your name written down? If it is, why not take a moment to reflect upon when it took place, and thank Him for such marvelous grace.

SATURDAY 16

Daniel 12:4-13

What is the writer saying?

How can I apply this to my life?

Here we have some final instructions and questions. After the glorious messenger finishes giving the new revelation of chapters 10 and 11 to Daniel, the instruction given is to preserve (shut up) the words of this book until the time of the end (v. 4). This did not mean it was to be left unexplained, but in those end days, when many would run to and fro in an effort to understand the future, the answers would be available in God's Word (here in the Book of Daniel).

As the conversation continued, Daniel saw two men, one on either side of the river (vv. 6-7). One asked how long Antichrist will be able to persecute the Jews (v. 6). The answer from the man clothed in linen was "a time, times, and an half" (or 3 1/2 years, Revelation 12:14). This is the second half of the Tribulation (the seventieth week of Daniel 9:27). It is also when Israel's stubborn rebellion will end and they will place their faith in Christ as opposed to trusting in themselves.

The explanation prompted Daniel to ask a follow-up question, for he still didn't understand, "What shall be the end of these things?" (v. 8) Daniel does not receive a direct answer, but is told that what he wanted to know did not concern him. It was for those Jews who would be saved during the Tribulation (many shall be purified), they would understand, but none of the wicked shall understand (v. 10).

Two time extensions are added to the last half of the Tribulation which begins with the breaking of the seven-year covenant. They are not found elsewhere in Scripture. One is for thirty days (perhaps to judge Israel and the Gentile nations, Ezekiel 20:34-38 and Matthew 25:31-46). The other is for forty five days (perhaps to give time to set up the governmental structure of the millennial kingdom).

LIFE STEP The Tribulation saints will have God's Word (including the book of Daniel) to give them answers. We have it today. It includes all we need to know for effective service and victorious living. Thank God for this wonderful provision!

The Apostle Peter writes to Christians in Asia Minor (modern Turkey) towards the end of his earthly life (A.D. 67) from a Roman prison (the "Babylon" of 1 Peter 5:13). It is Peter's *Last Will and Testament*.

Impetuous Peter is a beloved character because we can identify with his shortcomings and admire his zeal for the Lord. After his dismal denial of the Lord at His initial interrogations by the high priest, Peter is given three opportunities to publicly proclaim his love for his Lord (John 21). Peter is the key leader in the early chapters of Acts, but as the Jews continue to reject the preaching of the kingdom, the Book of Acts transitions to the ministry of Paul among the receptive Gentiles. Peter and Paul agree that Peter should concentrate on the Jews and Paul the Gentiles (Galatians 2:7-9). The last time Peter is mentioned by name in the Book of Acts is in his miraculous release from prison (chapter 12). Paul rebukes him in an undated encounter at Antioch (Galatians 2) that must have transpired before the issue (Mosaic Law observance) is settled by the Council of Jerusalem in Acts 15 (about A.D. 50).

The believers Peter writes to are a mixture of Jewish and Gentile converts. Peter draws heavily on Old Testament Scripture and analogies. Asia Minor is Paul's territory, so it very well could be that Peter is writing to people influenced by Paul. Peter also demonstrates knowledge of Paul's writings, including Ephesians (compare 1 Peter 1:1-3 and 3:1-6 with Ephesians 1:1-3 and 5:22-24). The "Babylon" of 1 Peter 5:13 could refer to the actual city in Mesopotamia where a large Jewish population would benefit from Peter's ministry. It could also be a cryptic reference to *Rome* as the current enemy of God. Trustworthy tradition places Peter's death in Rome during the persecutions of Nero (reigned A.D. 54-68). Peter supposedly was crucified (as a non-Roman) but requested to be hung upside down, feeling unworthy to die in the exact manner as his Lord.

In 1 Peter, Peter reminds the believers of the grace of God, developing the concepts of the believer's salvation (1:1-22); sanctification (1:23–2:12); submission (2:13–3:12); servitude (3:13–4:11) and suffering (4:12–5:14). The Greek grammar of 1 Peter is much better than that in 2 Peter, indicating that his associate, Silvanus, edited the letter for him as he wrote it (cf. 5:12). 1 Peter concerns itself with the *External Pressures of Suffering*, whereas 2 Peter is concerned with the *Internal Pressures of False Teachers*, a theme also echoed by Jude. Peter calls upon his readers to remember correct doctrine ("know" occurs sixteen times in the three chapters).

Chapter 1 discusses the *Development of the Faith*. Chapter 2 contains the *Denouncement of False Teachers*. Chapter 3 presents the *Design for the Future*. Key features of 2 Peter include: the impact of the Transfiguration (1:16); the inspiration of Scriptures (1:21); a warning that false teachers deny Christ's deity, redemption, and second coming (2:1, 3:4); and that false teachers are intellectual (2:18), antinomian (oppose the law) (2:19), and uniformitarian (and therefore likely to be sympathetic to atheistic evolution) (3:4-7). Peter's comments in 1 and 2 Peter are similar in style to his messages in the Book of Acts.

INTRODUCTION TO JUDE

Jude is identified as the half-brother of the Lord Jesus Christ and the full brother of James, the leader of the church in Jerusalem and the author of the Book of James (Matthew 13:55). His name means, *Praised*. It is an abbreviation of *Judas* which comes from *Judah*.

Like Peter in the Book of 2 Peter, Jude is concerned about the inroads false teachers are making in the early church. In his short epistle, the size of one piece of ancient papyrus paper, Jude gives his urgent warning. Verses 1-16 proclaim the ever-present danger of false teachers. In verses 17-23 Jude exhorts the believers to due diligence. It appears that the type of false teaching Jude is attacking is a form of Gnosticism that allowed for immoral living.

Gnosticism comes from the word *to know*. Adherents claim to have secret knowledge (see Colossians 2:18). They deny the Deity of Jesus, suggesting that He is just one of many *emanations* from the one true God. They teach that God did not create the world, since He is too holy to be involved with the carnality of physical existence. The job was done by one of the emanations (analogous to angels). Gnostics do not respect physical existence, and as a result either have no morals (you can't help yourself – eat, drink and be merry for tomorrow you die) or go to the other extreme of severe asceticism (which Paul confronts in Colossians).

In Revelation 2:6 Christ condemns the "deeds of the Nicolaitans," who apparently excused immorality and compromise with pagans. The "deeds of the Nicolaitans" becomes "the doctrine of the Nicolaitans" by Revelation 2:15. In Revelation 2:24, the Gnostic thought can be paraphrased as: *In order to defeat Satan you have to experience evil deeply*. This is Satan's approach with Eve in the Garden of Eden.

Gnosticism is also reminiscent of the so-called *New Age* movement (actually *Old Age* paganism and 1960's-style flower-child philosophy). Notice the frequency with which New Age practitioners make contact with *highly evolved extraterrestrials* and the demonic teachings that are *channeled* from these spirit beings (demons), such as *you are gods*, and *there is no damnation to fear*.

SUNDAY 17

2 Peter 1:1-4

What is the writer saying?

How can I apply this to my life?

PRAY Nicaragua – Outreach to youth in a land where broken homes, poverty, and secularism are the norm.

"Simon" is the Greek equivalent of Simeon, one of the twelve tribes of Israel. It means *hearing*. "Peter" is from *petros*, *a rock*. Elsewhere we are told his father's name so we could give him the modern name: Rock Johnson (*Peter son of Jonas*). Peter, like Paul, refers to himself as both a servant and an apostle. The bondservant is an individual who volunteers to serve a master. A ceremony is mentioned in Exodus 21:6 in which the individual's ear is pierced as a mark of this decision. "Apostle" is *one sent with a message*. In that sense, we are all *apostles*, but the New Testament also uses the word in a specialized sense to refer to the early leaders of the church who had seen Jesus and witnessed His resurrection. They are the ones commissioned by God to give us the books of the New Testament. Every book is written by or under the authority of an apostle. Peter argues that it is Christ's righteousness, not our own, that saves us (v. 1). The theological word *justification* refers to Christ's righteousness being applied to our account. Only by following God's plan can humans hope to have "Grace and peace" (the typical Greek and Hebrew greetings of the day, respectively). Everything we need for life and godly living has been provided by God. We can access that power by getting to know Him and His Word. God calls us to enjoy His glory (both now and in eternity) and practice His virtue. "Precious" (v. 4) is a great adjective for the salvation Christ has given us. It means *costly* and comes from the word for *honor*. This world system promises us fun and happiness, but it so often leads to ruined lives and tragedy. Follow God and escape the destructive influences of this world.

LIFE STEP

We are all fools. That is not the question. The question is, whose fools are we going to be, Satan's or Christ's?

MONDAY 17

2 Peter 1:5-9

What is the writer saying?

How can I apply this to my life?

PRAY Hungary – Evangelistic boldness for believers who struggle with feelings of inferiority and timidity.

In verses 1-4 Peter challenges us to conform ourselves to God's image (see Romans 12:1-2). He now rattles off a list of eight items that detail the lifestyle of one made in the image of God. We are to do this with "diligence," which involves an expenditure of effort and is done with haste. "Faith" apparently sums up verses 1-4 as a synonym for salvation (saving faith). It would also refer to our daily walk as we are not only saved by faith (past tense), but we are being saved by faith (present tense). The entire Christian life is a *faith walk*. To our constant trusting in God's care for us, we are challenged to add "virtue." Virtue is a word that describes intrinsic excellence. Not only do we do good works but we look and act like someone who would be expected to do good works. To this we are to add "knowledge." It is the word for *intimate, experiential knowledge*, such as in marriage. We can't just know God theoretically or superficially. We must know Him deeply and intimately in order to be conduits of His blessings. "Temperance" refers to the ability to respond to situations as though we really are convinced that God is in control. It literally means *in strength*, referring to self-discipline. "Patience" means *to abide under*, similar to our concept of someone *holding up well under pressure*. "Godliness" does not have the word "God" in it in the Greek language. The Greek concept is: *good + to be devout*. It speaks of the character of one devoted to a holy God. Such a one loves the brethren (those of his own family – *Philadelphia*). That is not the highest love, *agape* love is. It is self-sacrificing – not demanding anything in return. "Abound," not just meeting the minimum standards, is stipulated.

LIFE STEP The *what* of the Christian life is easy, the *how* is the challenge.

TUESDAY 17

2 Peter 1:10-14

What is the writer saying?

How can I apply this to my life?

PRAY Argentina – Praise the Lord for the thousands saved through prison ministries. Pray for their maturity.

One of the puzzles of the Christian life is that many verses indicate we can do nothing to merit or keep our salvation. It is a work of God from the start to the finish. We condemn those branches of Christianity that teach we can earn the right to go to heaven by our good works. On the other hand, there are many challenges for us to put forth effort in our walk with the Lord. The balance is that we cannot do this on our own any more than we can merit our salvation on our own. Therefore, both the initial salvation event and the ongoing Christian life (*sanctification*) require our faith, asking God to supply the power to obey His commands. The *effort*, then, is directed, not at being a good person, but in studying what God defines as a good person, what promises He offers to help us be a good person, and then asking Him to give us the wisdom, insight, and power to practice what we have learned.

In verse 10, Peter says that since we are sons of the King then we ought to act like it. Our entrance into heaven is not in doubt. We can, however, have a glorious entry by harnessing all the power and accomplishing all the tasks that God has offered us. Fully aware of the weakness of the human nature, Peter says he wants to constantly remind his readers of these things. He knows they know these things, but it is his duty to make sure they are always thinking this way. He is also mindful of his soon departure and wants the most important things to be emphasized and remembered. "Established" comes from the word for *prop* and therefore, means *to fix firmly in place*. Back in Luke 22:32, Peter is commanded by our Lord to establish his brethren. Peter is faithfully doing what the Lord commanded right to the very end.

LIFE STEP If the Lord told us when we would die, how would that change our lives? Do we always live with eternity's values in view?

WEDNESDAY 17

2 Peter 1:15-21

What is the writer saying?

How can I apply this to my life?

PRAY Kenya – For believers to forsake previous ethnic religious practices and be unified by biblical truth.

Significant events in life become memory markers. Peter uses his death as such a marker, hoping to fix in their minds the importance of his words. The word for "remembrance" here is the word *memory*. Literally he says, *to make a memory*, so that once he is gone the memory lingers. Peter seems to anticipate that his written words will be kept for future reference. In verses 20 and 21 he refers to the process of inspiration in the Old Testament. Whether he realizes it or not, the same process is at work to produce the New Testament Scriptures, including this epistle. When evaluating the probability that the New Testament authors are telling the truth, we must consider their psychological condition at the various points of the story, as well as the potential for successful fabrication of the account. It is clear that they become neither wealthy nor famous as apostles.

They also faced death for their beliefs. Is it reasonable to think that men would suffer deprivation or death for what they know to be a lie? Peter, James and John are eyewitnesses of Christ's glory on the Mount of Transfiguration (Matthew 17). But notice verse 19. In both the King James translation and the Greek text, Peter is saying that the written Word of God is even *more* convincing than the miracle they beheld. Verse 19 certainly refers to the light of spiritual insight and may include even the light of Christ's presence in this sin-darkened world at His second coming. Verses 20 and 21 are classic statements on the process of inspiration. The Bible is both a human and a divine product (as is the Living Word of God, Jesus Christ). "Moved" is used in Acts 27:15 of a ship that is driven by the wind. Likewise, the Holy Spirit drives the prophets and apostles to write the Bible.

LIFE STEP Our Quiet Time can be a visit with Christ on the Mount of Transfiguration! The Holy Spirit within us is given to make Jesus *real* to us just like the man Jesus made God *real* to the disciples.

2 Peter 2:1-9

What is the writer saying?

How can I apply this to my life?

Peter now warns them of the apostles of Satan who are busy promoting his kingdom. This is not something new, as there were false prophets even in Old Testament times. "Privily" refers to their deceptive practices. Their poison is not clearly labeled. "Damnable" means that the heresies are destructive (not that they came from Hell, but that is also true). Notice that Peter says Christ died for even these false teachers. Christ, as an infinite person, offers infinite forgiveness for infinite guilt. Only those who respond in faith receive the benefit of Christ's work on the cross. "Swift" does not mean that it is coming soon (some false teachers live a long life of error), but rather that judgment is imminent (can come at any time), and when it falls it will be decisive and permanent. They will not escape. Notice the characteristics of false teachers. Their sinful lifestyles ("pernicious" =

immoral) give Christianity a bad name. They manipulate scriptural teaching to extract as much money as possible from their followers. To many unsaved, preachers are just con men looking for a quick buck and a good time. Exactly which particular group of sinning angels is not specified. It can't be all fallen angels because we are told elsewhere that they are active. If you believe that Genesis 6 describes angels having sexual relations with humans, it could be that group of angels. Or, perhaps there is a limit to what God tolerates among the fallen angels, and when they cross the line, they are incarcerated (see Matthew 8:29). It doesn't matter that we know specifically. The point is that God does judge, as He did with the world of Noah's day, and with Sodom and Gomorrah. Notice the compliment for Lot who really does not appear that *godly* in the Genesis account.

LIFE STEP   God's payday is coming some day. Make sure you are on the right side. We can take comfort in the fact that truth will prevail in the end.

2 Peter 2:10-16

What is the writer saying?

How can I apply this to my life?

PRAY Canada – For the 2,300 reservations of Canadian indigenous people without an ongoing witness.

False teachers are motivated by fleshly desires. They resent authority. They are a law unto themselves. They are stubborn. They arrogantly condemn other leaders (human and angelic). They are not like the holy angels who demonstrate true meekness, which is power under control. They are true to their unsaved sin nature and behave like animals. Their end is beastly. This is not annihilation, but rather the loss of contact with God for all eternity, the only thing that makes existence worthwhile. Their sin is particularly heinous because it is done under the guise of religion, preys on the weak and gullible, and draws people away from a satisfying life with God. Peter likens them to Balaam, who, in Numbers 22-24, pretends to be a *prophet of Jehovah*, but clearly is really a *prophet for hire*. He is willing to try to influence any of the gods for his human clients. Balak, King of Moab, hires him to curse the Israelites as they are attempting to cross from Egypt through Moab to the Promised Land. At first, God tells Balaam he is not allowed to go to attempt to curse Israel. Then God agrees to allow him to go, but only if he would say whatever God tells him to say. Balaam agrees, but God wants to make sure. Along the way God challenges him. Initially only his donkey sees the angel, and that amazing conversation takes place between Balaam and his donkey. When Balaam arrives he gladly takes Balak's money. Every time he opened his mouth to curse the Israelites, out came a blessing. Since Balak is getting mad and Balaam is in danger of losing his paycheck, Balaam says, *I can't curse them but here's what you should do. Send your women to them to entice them to intermarry and worship your gods. Then God Himself will curse them.*

LIFE STEP Love of money is the root of every kind of evil. Use it but don't be used by it.

SATURDAY 17

2 Peter 2:17-22

What is the writer saying?

How can I apply this to my life?

The Middle East is a dry area of the world and water is a vital issue. Whole armies were lost in antiquity by dry wells in the wilderness. After the long, hot summer, puffy clouds would blow up from the Mediterranean, but they would drop their water before they arrived at Jerusalem. This is Peter's description of the false teachers. Useless mist they have offered, and useless mist will be their abode for eternity. "Wantonness" refers to sexual immorality. Apparently they are teaching the Gnostic heresy that a believer could indulge the flesh and still consider his spirit to be pure and acceptable to God. This is doubly tragic because the ones they are enticing have just recently escaped from that polluted lifestyle (v. 18). The false teachers consider this open-minded approach to be liberating, but it really is bondage. Free love is neither *free* nor is it *love*. Those who follow after righteousness are looking forward to the day when sinners are exposed as fools, as in the fable, *The Emperor's New Clothes*. Verses 20-22 could be used to argue that salvation can be lost, as it appears that these false teachers at one-time knew the truth and then willfully left the truth and now are under God's damnation. Other clear passages in Scripture will not permit that conclusion. Since salvation is neither won nor kept by works, then a person cannot *lose salvation* by bad works. These individuals tasted salvation, and were attracted to the teachings of Christ ("the Lord" not *their Lord*); but before they made a true commitment, they were led away by their sinful flesh. Their current behavior proves that they never possessed saving faith. Their condition is now worse because they will be less likely to consider the claims of Christ a second time.

LIFE STEP The price of freedom is constant vigilance. Every waking day we must report in for our marching orders and instructions in the ongoing battle.

SUNDAY 18

2 Peter 3:1-6

What is the writer saying?

How can I apply this to my life?

PRAY

Praise God for sending "Emmanuel," God with us, to be our precious Savior (Matthew 1:23).

Peter transitions from a condemnation of false teachers to a warning of the troubles that lie ahead because of the world's opposition to Christians. "Stir up" is a phrase used for waking someone from a dead sleep. Peter is not saying that they are spiritually asleep. He is talking about his own enthusiasm for the topic. The word "pure" is the Greek word *sun tested*. It apparently has the same historical background as our English word sincere (*without wax*). In the ancient alabaster trade, if one of these valuable stone vases is cracked, they would smear wax into the crack to hide it. A *sun tested* vase would determine if the vase was *without wax* and therefore, worth the shopkeeper's asking price. Verse 2 takes in the entire Bible (Old Testament and New Testament authors). The "last days" in the New Testament actually take in everything from the ascension of Christ (Acts 1) until His second coming (Revelation 19). Logically, the further we go in the *Last Days*, the more evident these deteriorating conditions are. The word "scoffers" is derived from *to act like a child*. Consider how cruel children can be to each other. It is hard to argue against a snicker. The world gleefully derides our blessed hope of Christ's return. In fact, verse 4 implies that they do not consider Jesus to have been the Christ in His time on earth (they're still looking for the first coming of Messiah). Verse 4 is also describing uniformitarianism, the philosophical basis of the theory of evolution. Peter argues for cataclysm in verses 5 and 6. The laws of physics sometimes are suddenly violated for the greater plan of God.

LIFE STEP

"For when they shall say, Peace and safety; then sudden destruction cometh upon them, as travail upon a woman with child; and they shall not escape." (1 Thessalonians 5:3) Notice how politicians constantly promise "peace and safety." Only in Christ can we truly be secure.

MONDAY 18

2 Peter 3:7-12

What is the writer saying?

How can I apply this to my life?

For Peter, Noah's flood is not only a historical fact, it is a universal (global) flood. Denying the historicity of the Book of Genesis does not solve the theological problem for a theistic evolutionist or those who deny a universal flood. God promises that He would never again destroy the whole world with a watery flood. However, Peter envisions a fiery destruction of the habitat of sinful man. "Perdition" means *destruction*, not to go out of existence, but rather to be ruined – not loss of being, but rather loss of well-being. Verse 8 quotes Psalm 90:4. God's way of reckoning time is not our way. Haggai 2:6-7 says that in a "little while" Messiah will come. Haggai lived five hundred years before Christ, but five hundred years is a "little while" for God. The Bible clearly warns against setting dates for the Lord's return. We do not know the actual date for the creation of the world. Perhaps God plans for six thousand years of human history followed by the one thousand years of the Messianic Era (a *Sabbath Rest*). Genesis 2:17 says that *in the day* that Adam ate of the forbidden fruit he would *die*. This may refer to spiritual death (separation from God) or that he began to die physically. We could also argue that he didn't live the normal human lifespan of one thousand years. He died at 930. If a "day is with the Lord as a thousand years" then he died within that *day*. Peter goes on to argue that God's *delay* is for the sake of those who are yet to be born, and also to have an opportunity for them to hear the Gospel and repent. Peter telescopes end-time events into one fiery cataclysm. This does not mean that other Scriptures which talk about a seven-year tribulation, a one thousand year reign, and then a destruction of the current heavens and earth are in error. Telescopic summary is a valid form of writing. Finally, Peter is an unsophisticated fisherman. How would he know that elements (for example, uranium) could melt?

LIFE STEP Even so come Lord Jesus; even so come today! We may be frustrated waiting for the return of Christ but remember, one generation of humans already enjoyed His First Coming after centuries of waiting!

2 Peter 3:13-18

What is the writer saying?

How can I apply this to my life?

The righteous look forward to and long for a return to the Garden of Eden. Initially, this will be on the millennial earth. Righteousness will be exalted in the beginning because every person entering the messianic kingdom will be saved, and Christ will rule with a rod of iron. In these one thousand years (Revelation 20) babies will be born. They will have the choice to accept or reject Christ as their Savior. Outward rebellion will not be tolerated, but unfortunately, some will be *Secret Service Unbelievers*. At the end of this period, Satan will be released to attempt one final revolt (Revelation 20), but it will fail. At that point, the current heavens and earth will be destroyed and new heavens and earth will be created. Never again will sin spoil the Garden of Eden (see Milton's *Paradise Regained*). Peter does not doubt God's promise, even as he faces his own imminent death. How should we then live? Not stained by sin, but at peace with God, ourselves and others. "Longsuffering" means *to go a long time before boiling over*. God's patience is not a delay but an opportunity for more people to come to Christ. Peter's reference to Paul shows his respect and demonstrates the cooperation among the apostles in the early church. The fisherman agrees that the rabbi is learned but does not excuse people for misunderstanding him. Study is hard work. Notice how often Peter refers to his audience as "beloved." The word for "steadfastness" (v. 17) is the opposite of the word "unstable" in verse 16. The root idea is that of both a strong and a wide base upon which one can safely stand without toppling over or breaking through. Growth must continue. The opposite is not stagnation but death. Our growth is found by getting to know a person better.

LIFE STEP We can fellowship with the greatest personality in the universe. Do we understand that He is more to us than our favorite sports hero, movie star, family member or admired historical personality?

WEDNESDAY 18

Jude 1-7

What is the writer saying?

How can I apply this to my life?

PRAY Brazil – Outreach to youth as over 9,000,0000 children work the streets to earn a living.

Jude, like Peter and Paul, refers to himself as a "servant." He is the brother of James and half-brother of Jesus. He writes to believers. The Greek text behind the King James calls them "sanctified" while the text behind the New American Standard has the word *beloved*. The difference in spelling between these two words is slight, hence the potential for scribal change (*hegiasmenois* versus *egapemenois*). Theologically, both concepts are accurate. They are *preserved*. This Greek word is in the perfect tense which refers to a past activity with ongoing consequences into the present. While it is true that Christ is our sphere of blessing and preservation, the grammar of the sentence probably means that believers are being preserved until the coming of Jesus Christ for them (*kept for Jesus Christ*). Saints are "called" which is the root of the word for *church*. Instead of grace, Jude uses "mercy" (God withholding the punishment we deserve). "Multiplied" comes from the same root as that vivid word, *plethora*. Jude says he had started to write about salvation, but switched to a warning about false teachers. "Earnestly contend" means *wrestle intensively*. It comes from the Greek word *agonize*. "Once" means that it is a finished product. We are not to expect more and certainly not different information. Evil men try to change the revealed Word of God. That they are "ordained" (*written before*) probably refers to the fact that believers are warned that evil men would come and their punishment is certain; not that the specific individuals are predestined to this sinful behavior. Peter and Jude use similar illustrations of the fact that God's judgment cannot be avoided.

LIFE STEP What a privilege to catch the heartbeat of someone barely known and yet who had the opportunity to grow up with Jesus Christ.

Jude 8-11

What is the writer saying?

How can I apply this to my life?

Jude says that false teachers are antinomian (against the law) and anti-lordship (v. 4). They are immoral, anarchists and profane (v. 8). The "dignities" of verse 8 would be spirit beings (angels, demons and Satan). In contrast, even the highest angel in heaven – Michael the archangel – is respectful when he talks to Satan. The particular episode Jude alludes to occurs in Deuteronomy 34 but without these details. *The Assumption of Moses* is an ancient religious writing that Jude may have read. That he relates information from non-Biblical sources does not imply that they are inspired. It only means that God led the author to use information from that source. These false teachers are promoting an early form of Gnosticism, which teaches that physical matter is intrinsically evil and therefore, allows for immorality. It is not clear why they would speak evil of angels. Over in Colossians 2:18 a group is condemned for worshiping angels. At any rate, a very important principle is developed here. One of the marks of a false teacher is that he proudly brags about being able to boss Satan and demons around. Ironically, the Gnostics claim to have superior, hidden knowledge of the spirit world. Both Peter and Jude say that they don't have a clue (v. 10, see also 2 Peter 2:12). They are condemned along with: Cain, the first murderer who refused God's required method of worship (Genesis 4); Balaam, the prophet for hire (Numbers 22-24); and Korah ("Core"), the Levitical priest who challenged Moses's authority and wound up seeing some of his followers burnt by God, and others swallowed up by the earth (Numbers 16).

LIFE STEP Arrogance is a mark of sinful man. We should filter every comment and thought evaluating our arrogance level. If we find ourselves repeatedly erring in this area it is time for deeper spiritual introspection to find the source of this sinful attitude.

Jude 12-19

What is the writer saying?

How can I apply this to my life?

Jude uses six illustrations of the false teachers' uselessness. They are a stain at the church's communion table. They are pigs feeding themselves and not others. They promise spiritual drink, but can't satisfy anyone's thirst. They are fruit trees that not only have no fruit, but they are up-rooted. They are violent waves pouring forth pollution. They are shooting stars – all sound and fury, but vanish as soon as they appear. Their destiny is eternal blackout. Jude quotes godly Enoch (who walked with God and God took him, Genesis 5). The quote does not come from the Bible. It comes from the so-called Book of Enoch, one of many religious writings of the ancient Jewish world. It almost certainly is not written by Enoch, for it does not appear in human history until the first century B.C. God's inspiration overcomes any weakness in the source. In fact, God could have told Jude that this is what

Enoch said, without any other written source. The information communicated, however, is all known from other biblical passages such as Daniel 7:9-14. "Ungodly" occurs four times in verse 15. It refers to an aggressive antagonism to the person of God. Antinomian means *against the law* while "ungodly" means *against God Himself*. It is gratifying to think that not only sinful behavior, but also the arrogant words men speak against God will be publicly judged and, in the process, corrected. These false teachers manipulate others with flattery (v. 16). Other apostles have already warned that this is how sinful men behave apart from the Spirit of God.

LIFE STEP To be forewarned is to be forearmed. We should brace ourselves for the disdain of sinners and have a gentle response to continue to interest them in the claims of Christ.

Jude 20-25

What is the writer saying?

How can I apply this to my life?

Praise God for His faithfulness and protection in your life this year.

Jude is rushing to get this urgent communication to his beloved brothers in Christ. The amount of words might have been limited to the paper Jude had at hand. Since time and space is limited, the communication is terse and pointed. These are the items foremost on Jude's mind. The recipients are "beloved" (v. 20). The root of the word is *agape*, the word for *self-sacrificing love*. "Building up" (v. 20) comes from three Greek words: *to build + house + upon*. The key is the foundation which is specified as "your most holy faith." We are saved by faith, and we continue to grow by faith. Our faith is bolstered by our prayer life in which the Holy Spirit guides our thoughts and prayers, and interprets our weak words to God the Father. Notice that in verses 20 and 21 all three members of the Trinity are mentioned. The Greek word *tereo* refers to believers twice in Jude. In verse 1 we are "preserved" in Jesus Christ. In verse 21 we are to "keep" ourselves in the faith. This is the only sphere in which God's love and mercy can be given. This does not mean that we *lose* salvation if we *lose* our faith. It does mean that someone who is truly saved would never *lose* his or her faith. Perseverance to the end is a mark of a truly born-again individual. As we seek to influence others for Christ, in some cases we take a low-key approach (v. 22) while in others we must be firmer in our admonitions (v. 23). Verse 22 is probably referring to weak believers who are being swayed by the heretics. Verse 23 is referring to the unsaved heretics who are still savable if they repent, but the rescuers need to be very careful because their error is toxic.

LIFE STEP

After many warnings Jude closes with a magnificent benediction. God is great, God is good, and we should thank Him for everything that He is and everything that He does.

Jeremiah is one of the two principle writing prophets of the Old Testament, the other being Isaiah. Two *Major Prophets,* Daniel and Ezekiel, began to serve as prophets when Jeremiah was in the later years of his ministry. Thus they were the younger protégé prophets in relation to Jeremiah. Three *Minor Prophets* were also serving the Lord during Jeremiah's younger years, Nahum, Zephaniah and Habakkuk.

There's a great deal of prophecy in the Book of Jeremiah, but there is also much in the book about Jeremiah the Prophet himself; his character, his burden, and his commitment to the Lord and to the Scriptures. Jeremiah, born into a family of priests of Israel, was about twenty years old when was called by God to be a prophet. Close to him was the scribe Baruch, who took dictation from Jeremiah. One hundred forty years after the destruction of the northern half of Israel by the Assyrians Judah, the southern half of Israel, was being threatened by a new enemy, the Babylonians. Jeremiah, concerned about the situation, writes out of a burdened heart (he is called "the weeping prophet") regarding God's sure judgment of His people unless they repent. His call is a call to turn to Jehovah and cease their worship of other gods (chapters 7, 26). A reading of 2 Kings 22 to 25 and 2 Chronicles 34 to 36 will give you a good background and setting for this book.

Jeremiah preached for fifty years with a burdened heart. His ministry spans the reigns of the last five kings of Judah. The prophet lived a life of extreme conflict as he predicted God's coming judgment upon Judah by the empire of Babylon, which would be used as God's tool of judgment. Hated and threatened, he was jailed, humiliated by false prophets, and suffered rebuke for his Lord. Through it all he was faithful and true to his convictions. As we look at his life, it is easy enough to compare it with ours in that the majority of the people didn't want to hear of their responsibility and the judgment resulting from disobedience.

A study of the times of Jeremiah will reveal that idolatry prevailed including the worship of the "queen of heaven" (7:18; 44:19). Idol worship was practiced (chap. 2), "high places" were being built to Baal (32:35), and an awful system of the sacrificing of children to the god Moloch in the Valley of Hinnom (7:31-32; 19:2, 6). While Jeremiah predicted a *near* judgment on Judah because of their disobedience, he also gives assurance that God was not through with Judah and that in the *distant future* there would be a king and a kingdom. This certainly inspired hope among the few who were still faithful to the Lord and His Word. (23:3-8).

There are several prevailing themes that will be noticed in a study of this book. We see the longing heart of Jehovah, loving the people in spite of their condition. We see also the servant's heart in Jeremiah who was more concerned for others than himself. We have much to learn from his example. God's compassion is prominent in this book and the comfort that comes from the Lord in time of distress and trials.

As you read the Book of Jeremiah, note Jeremiah's concept of God:

- He is the Creator and is the sovereign Lord governing all things (23:23; 27:5).
- The Lord knows the hearts of all people (17:5-10).
- The Lord is the fountain of life to all who trust Him (2:13; 17:13).
- He has a tender and special love for His own people (2:2; 31:1-3).
- However, the Lord demands obedience and is offended by the pluralism of the day that accepted the worship of heathen deities encompassing Baal, Moloch, and the queen of heaven. (32:34).
- Note also the difference between reformation and regeneration. While there was a revival under King Josiah, the nation apostatized after Josiah's death.

In a day such as ours when immorality is prevalent, this book will be helpful in revealing the mind of God concerning such things. Moral corruption in Judah "followed the elimination of the fear of God and reverence for His law" (New Bible Dictionary). Yet the religious and political leaders, rather than dealing with Israel's immorality, encouraged it and practiced it themselves and contributed to its spread. Jeremiah also stressed that a morally-right lifestyle took precedence over the outward display of religious activity taking place at the Temple.

The Book of Jeremiah is a final collection of the events and sermons of Jeremiah that took place at different times during his lengthy ministry. Notice that the following outline of the book displays a final arrangement of the affairs and sermons from throughout Jeremiah's life:

Jer. 1	The Call of the Prophet, Jeremiah
Jer. 2-29	The Great Book of Doom, Jeremiah's Sermon of God's coming judgment upon Judah by the Babylonians.
Jer. 30-33	The Little Book of Consolation, God's future restoration of the Messianic Kingdom.
Jer. 34-45	The Book of the Personal History of Jeremiah.
Jer. 46-51	The Book of Prophecies against Foreign Nations.
Jer. 52	A Final Footnote: The Fall and Captivity of Judah.

Jeremiah 1:1-10

What is the writer saying?

How can I apply this to my life?

Jeremiah's home was Anathoth, a designated town of priests (Joshua 21:15-19). Jeremiah by birth was to be a priest; yet we see his ministry was changed when he was called of God to be a prophet (v. 5)!

While King Josiah's reign began in 640 B.C., Jeremiah began as a prophet in 627 B.C. (v. 2). Apparently, Jeremiah considered his official ministry to have ended in 586 B.C. (v. 3; after forty one years) with the destruction of Judah and its last king, Zedekiah, being taken captive to Babylon (39:6-7; 2 Kings 25:7). Yet, the last portion of his book (39:11–44:30) records events from Jeremiah's life after 586 B.C.

At first Jeremiah was reluctant. A prophet deals with the future, and in this case, a terrible time of judgment and destruction (v. 10). Jeremiah's defense was that he is too young [v. 6, "a child" referred to someone of about twenty years] and inexperienced to be a respected spokesman. He protests that he lacked abilities as a speaker (v. 6)!

Yet God's call of Jeremiah included a series of promises from God:

- God, in His foreknowledge (v. 5), had been arranging all that was needed for Jeremiah's call since before Jeremiah had been born!
- God thoroughly "knew" Jeremiah's strengths and weakness; He had not made a mistake in His choice of Jeremiah (v. 5)!
- God Himself would command where Jeremiah was to go and what he was to speak (v. 7).
- Jeremiah need not be afraid for the Lord would be with him and would deliver him from those who would seek to silence him (v. 8).
- The LORD then touched Jeremiah's mouth (v. 9) to show that He was supernaturally preparing and qualifying Jeremiah to speak.

We gain another important insight from these opening verses. The Lord was all-knowing. He even knew Jeremiah when he was in his mother's womb. This, of course, shows that the fetus is not an *it or* just a *collection of cells* but rather a *not-yet-born person*.

MONDAY 19

Jeremiah 1:11-19

What is the writer saying?

How can I apply this to my life?

Today's passage is intended to be a *confirmation* of Jeremiah's call as a prophet. The Lord visits him with two prophetic visions (vv. 11, 13). Notice the Lord asks Jeremiah what he *sees* which are described as *words from the LORD*. These visions served two purposes: (1) the visions graphically illustrated the Lord's message and (2) the visions authenticated the source of the messages. The first "word" would focus upon the speed of the delivery of the message. The second "word" points to the nature of the message that Jeremiah would be delivering. The visions are:

1. An almond tree (v. 11b). The Hebrew word for *almond* tree, *shaqed*, is related to the word *watching*, or *shoqed* (KJV uses "hasten," v. 12b). The intended play on words is that the Lord is like this *watching tree* that was *ever watching for the coming of spring*. It was the first tree to blossom in January and it quickly brings forth its almond fruit ten weeks later. Thus Jeremiah was given an intended metaphor: (1) the

Lord has not been asleep but has been *watching* Judah's sin and (2) the Lord was now *hastening* to bring the *fruit* of judgment upon Judah.

2. A seething pot (vv. 13-16). The second vision was a boiling pot sitting over a fire but on the verge of spilling over from the north to the south. Thus, Judah was in danger of being *flooded over* with an *evil* (i.e., a great disaster) coming from their north (v. 14). The invading armies would actually originate from Judah's east but these would follow the roads that first take them to the north of Judah (25:8, 9).

Next, Jeremiah is warned to "gird up thy loins" (v. 17, equivalent to our saying "roll up your sleeves so you are ready to go to work"). The LORD was warning Jeremiah to prepare him for Judah's hard-hearted response to Jeremiah's announcements of God's coming judgments; that is, Judah was not going to repent of her sin and idolatry (v. 16) to avert judgment. Rather, Judah was going to fight against the Lord's prophecies.

LIFE STEP

In a similar way we Christians have been given an assignment of *going into all the world to make disciples* (Matthew 28:18). How will the Lord help you to be a *defended city and a brazen wall* as he prepares and strengthens you for His service? How has the Lord been getting you ready to *roll up your sleeves* to serve Him?

TUESDAY 19

Jeremiah 2:1-13

What is the writer saying?

How can I apply this to my life?

PRAY Chile – For the perseverance of Chilean saints as only 38% attend church regularly.

We now begin the largest section of the book (chaps. 2-29), called The Great Book of Doom since it is a series of prophetic messages from God (2:1) concerning His coming judgment upon Judah.

Today's passage is the opening of Jeremiah's first message (2:1). It presents God's accusations against Israel as outlined below:

- 2:1-13 — God's faithfulness is contrasted with His young bride's unfaithfulness (v. 2, all Israel is in view yet only Judah remained).
- 2:14-30 — Israel has been wasted by her enemies (v. 18, Egypt and Assyria) because of her sin and backsliding.
- 2:31–3:5 — In spite of God's past punishments, Judah had not repented, they continue in rebellion (2:32), claiming to be "innocent" (2:35).

The message begins with a contrast of Judah's present, sinful separation from God (v. 5) and Judah's past devotion to God (v. 2):

- She had been full of unfailing devotion (v. 2a, KJV "kindness").
- She had loved God as a new husband (v. 2b). This love denotes affection, faithfulness, and loyalty to their marriage covenant.
- Her willingness to forsake all her comforts in Egypt and follow God (v. 2c) was proof of her love and confidence in God's ability.
- She had lived "holiness unto the LORD" (v. 3a), that is she lived *set apart* unto God, *dedicated* to a manner of life that pleased Him.
- She became a "firstfruits" offering to God (v. 3b; Leviticus 23:9-14)!
- She also came under His protection from other nations!

Yet she soon became an unfaithful wife who had gone far from God (v. 5). She began to *walk after vanity* (v. 5; *worthless things*; 1 Kings 16:13 relates this to the worship of idols) and became "vain" (worthless) herself. She completely forgot all of God's bountiful care (v. 7a) and, by her idolatry, defiled the land God had given her (v. 7b).

LIFE STEP As Christians, we are similarly referred to as the "bride of Christ." Are you living for Christ with *unfailing devotion*, *faithfulness*, and *loyalty*? Are you *willing to follow* where He leads and in a *dedicated* manner? How can these characterize your life today?

What is the writer saying?

How can I apply this to my life?

PRAY Nicaragua – Praise the Lord that the Church has doubled in the last 10 years!

This section is a series of pleas by the LORD for Judah to *turn* away from her sin and *return* to the LORD (vv. 1, 7, 10, 12, 14, 19, 22).

Jeremiah is developing the theme that God's people have *forsaken* (2:19) the Lord, to whom they were *married* (2:2; 3:14) and have repeatedly *played the harlot* (vv. 1, 6). Chapter 3 now amplifies this imagery with the idea of *divorce*; Judah's sister, Israel, had played the harlot and had not repented so the LORD "divorced" her (v. 8, i.e., the LORD had raised up the Assyrians to destroy the Kingdom of Israel). Two key words are used here. First, Israel is repeatedly referred to as *backsliding* (vv. 6, 8, 11-12, 14, 22) which means *a turning away*, and declares that Israel had *turned aside from correct path*. She had abandoned her reliance on God. Second, Judah is repeatedly referred to as Israel's *treacherous* sister (vv. 7-8, 10-11, 20) for Judah had also acted unfaithfully towards

God. Judah had not kept her covenant with God even though Judah had seen what happened to Israel for refusing to turn back to her covenant with the LORD (vv. 7-8). As a result, Judah's attitude was worse than Israel's; Judah had seen God's judgment but had "feared not, but went and played the harlot also" (v. 8b). And so, as a warning (v. 5), God had sent a drought upon Judah, (*the rains have been withheld*, v. 3). This had resulted in a *feigned* or pretended (v. 10b) cry to the Lord but, sadly, Judah had not been sincere. While there was an outward move of reformation under King Josiah (v. 6), there was no real turning of Judah's heart to God (v. 10).

We must not miss the Lord's attitude towards judging sin! God is merciful (v. 12) and His heart's desire, was to care for His people (v. 15)! All that the Lord asked of Judah was that she turn back to the LORD (v. 12), admit her sin (v. 13a), and begin again to obey His voice (v. 13c).

LIFE STEP The Lord would want us Christians to learn from the backsliding of Judah and to take heed (1 Corinthians 10:12) of our own lives. Have you also turned aside from God's path? Then, spend time in prayer as you turn back to God. Admit your sin and ask Him to guide you as you begin again to obey His voice.

Jeremiah 3:14-25

What is the writer saying?

How can I apply this to my life?

PRAY Australia – For churches to have strong, sound leadership that produces committed believers.

Today's passage is a continuation of Jeremiah's second sermon against Judah (3:6–6:30). We begin with an unexpected break (vv.14b-18) in the theme. Treacherous Judah is worse than backsliding Israel (v. 8), and Jeremiah presents a vision of the distant future. This parenthetical section is building on God's assurance to Israel that He will "not keep anger forever" (v. 12b). When they turn from their backslidden condition (i.e., having turned aside from the correct path) the Lord will show His hand of blessing on their behalf (note the three "I will's," vv. 14-15).

The parenthetical section (vv. 14b-18) is looking to the future millennial condition of Israel when the Lord will reign on the earth (v. 17a). The key characteristic of that future day will be the Lord's bringing back His people, one from here and another from there (v. 14b), as He restores a remnant of Israel back to Zion, the poetic name for the land promised to Israel. Surprisingly, the ark of the covenant, which had been the focal point of worship at the tabernacle and at the temple, will be *remembered no more* (v. 16b). In the future, the ark will be replaced by "the throne of the LORD" (v. 17; Ezekiel 43:7). Evidently Jesus Christ will become the focal point of worship as He rules from the future temple at Jerusalem. His rule will extend over all nations who will go to Jerusalem to worship Him (v. 17b; Zechariah 14:16-19). Also note that Judah and Israel will come together, being reunited as a single nation (v. 18). The two houses were separated in 931 B.C. and have never come together since. Yet God intends to bless both houses "in those [future] days" (v. 18) as a father blesses his sons.

Sadly, Judah did not turn from her treachery and backsliding but was continuing in her perverted ways (v. 21, i.e., twisted behavior). As a result, in Judah's near future, she would look in vain to the LORD for her salvation (v. 23) from the coming destruction by the Babylonians.

LIFE STEP Perhaps your life has been filled with *twisted behavior*! The Lord would also say to you, *My child, you have turned aside from the right path, return to me*! Would you say to Jesus, "Thou art my Lord?"

Jeremiah 5:1-3, 12-19

What is the writer saying?

How can I apply this to my life?

PRAY Bahamas – For Christians to guard themselves from materialism.

Our passage begins with the LORD sending Jeremiah on a search; "Run ye to and fro through the streets of Jerusalem" (v. 1). God's judgment was coming but the people of God were refusing (v, 3) to listen to His warnings so here He has Jeremiah begin a series of ten action sermons that dramatize God's message so that the dull-of-hearing people of Jerusalem will take notice.

The LORD tells Jeremiah that if he finds just one person who practices justice and seeks the truth, then the Lord will pardon Jerusalem for her sins. This illustrates the spiritual state of God's people. Their hearts were hardened and refused to return to the Lord. They were denying the LORD's coming judgments, that is, there will be no evil, no sword, and no famine (v. 12). They were also saying God's prophets were full of "wind" and did not speak for the Lord (v. 13). As a result of their attitude, God's judgment is pronounced (v. 14). Because of Judah's refusal to listen to Jeremiah, God would make his words like a fire that would devour them (v. 14b). Furthermore, the Lord announces that He would bring a mighty nation as the instrument of God's judgment upon Jerusalem (v. 15 – We learn later that this is Babylon). Their quivers of arrows would be as an open grave into which the Jews would fall (v. 16). These invaders would also eat up the harvest, the bread, and the flocks, leaving Judah impoverished (v. 17).

Yet, a promise is given, "I will not make a full end of you" (v. 18; 4:27), God, who is faithful and merciful, would keep alive a remnant of His people. And so, when this remnant would later ask why the calamity had come, Jeremiah was to answer, "Since Judah had forsaken God to serve foreign gods in their own land, God would have them serve foreigners in a foreign land" (v. 19).

LIFE STEP We, too, need to learn the lesson that a spiritual walk with God can never be compromised or abandoned with impunity. And so, we Christians are also warned not to make provision for the flesh (Romans 13:14). Don't be like ancient Jerusalem – you must listen to God's prompting to turn from your sin in repentance! (1 John 1:9)

What is the writer saying?

How can I apply this to my life?

PRAY Costa Rica – For godly young people to embrace their role in reaching their generation for Christ.

In this sermon (3:6–6:30) Jeremiah has reproved Judah for her sins and has threatened them with God's judgments. Now he is sent on a new mission to publish (v. 20, *to cause all to hear*) a question from God, "Why do you not fear Me?" (v. 22), thus asking, "Why do you not respect (to hold in high regard) Me and obey My commandments by righteous living?" Three aspects of their foolish lack of understanding (v. 21a) and spiritual blindness (v. 21b) are pointed out:

- They refused to heed the lesson of God's control over nature; here displayed by His "perpetual decree" (v. 22; Psalm 104:9) that holds the seas to the boundary of the sands of the seashores. In their foolish thoughtlessness they failed to understand that, as the LORD is present in and has control over nature, so the LORD is present with them and will have His way in their lives (v. 23)!
- They were displaying ingratitude for God's love and care for them (v. 24) by

their withholding (v. 25) similar acts of compassionate love for others. Rather, they were setting snares and traps to take advantage of downtrodden and needy people (v. 28).

- And so an appalling and horrible thing was happening (v. 30); the people of God were supporting each other in their injustice and greed (v. 28). Prophets, who should be speaking against sin, were speaking falsely (v. 31a). Priests, who were to instruct the people in God's ways, were acting so as to benefit their own corrupted authority (v. 31b). Sadly, people condoned and loved this twisted situation (v. 31c) that allowed them to continue in their sinful ways!

The prophet Jeremiah ends with the publishing of a final question, "What will you do when the end comes?" (v. 31) Sadly, there was no answer to this question. Their spiritual blindness had caused them to fail to see the overwhelming flood of God's judgment coming upon them.

LIFE STEP Have you been living like ancient Judah? Have you foolishly forgotten that the Lord expects a return on His investment in you? How can you this week do some deed of compassionate love for a needy person? How can you live for righteousness and justice?

SUNDAY 20

Jeremiah 6:10-20

What is the writer saying?

How can I apply this to my life?

PRAY   Finland – For immigrants to encounter Jesus in a real and attractive way.

In his second sermon (chaps. 3:6–6:30), Jeremiah has been confronting God's people about their sin and warning them of the approaching judgment from the Lord. Today's passage is the climax of this second sermon describing the several reasons for the coming invasion:

- The people's ears were closed to the Word of the Lord (v. 10) at this crucial time in Judah's history. Sadly, no one was listening.
- Therefore the Lord was angry at and weary of His people (v. 11).
- The Lord's judgment would be poured out upon all ages and classes, with every part of their lives being affected (vv. 11-12).
- Rather than being distraught over God's coming judgment, all Judah's people continued to be greedy for gain (v. 13a).
- False prophets and priests were proclaiming a false prophecy of a coming peace (vv. 13b-14).
- Yet these prophets and priests were without shame as they completely inverted the truth of the Lord's coming judgment (v. 15).

At this point the LORD gives them a stern warning in story form, "stand in the ways, and see, and ask for the old paths" (v. 16). To "stand in the ways" pictures a traveler on a road who has come upon a fork in the road. The man must consider which path to take. A wise traveler would *see* if there was anything or anyone at the fork to guide him on to the good way. So an old man was found, *the ancient ways*, who could direct the traveler to the good way (Job 8:8; Deuteronomy 32:7). The man, *Mr. Ancient Ways*, would advise the traveler to take the way of righteousness and avoid the way of shame.

The people of Judah were at this fork in the road, but they would not listen to *Mr. Ancient Ways*. "We will not walk" as you have warned us (v. 16c). A second advisor, a watchman, also warns them, yet they say, "We will not hearken" (v. 17; Job 22:15). Therefore, judgment would come upon Judah for they *would not listen to my words* (v. 19).

LIFE STEP   As Christians, we too must stop at *forks* in our lives to consider which path is the good way to take. We have the Word of God to act as our ancient advisor to the path of godliness (Proverbs 3:5-6). How can you today hearken to its good advice?

Jeremiah 7:1-11

What is the writer saying?

How can I apply this to my life?

PRAY Bolivia – For the Holy Spirit to bring about maturity in the lives of those studying for the ministry.

This begins Jeremiah's third sermon, The Temple Sermon (chaps. 7-10). It best fits the historical situation where King Josiah had repaired the temple and found a copy of the Law, (books of the Pentateuch, 2 Kings 22:8-20; 23:21-23). This had a profound effect upon the king as he realized how far the people had departed from the will of the LORD.

As a result of the repair of the temple, the finding of the Law, and the command of Josiah to all the people to keep the Passover (2 Kings 23:21), great numbers of people from all Judah (Jeremiah 26:2) were coming to worship at the temple! Remarkably, we see the LORD instructing Jeremiah to stand at the entrance to the temple (v. 2) and to preach against the people who were coming to worship; "Amend your ways and doings" (vv. 3, 5)! Jeremiah was to declare that God knew that these worshippers were still holding on to many of their faults and evil ways.

They came to worship, but not with pure hearts! By their triple acclaim (v. 4), they were saying, "Surely this great temple will protect us from Jeremiah's prophecies!" Being superstitious, they were using it as a talisman! They also assumed that their ceremonial observances would supersede any need for personal holiness in conduct.

Amend here is a command meaning, *to change one's conduct by removing faults, so as to please God.* Four changes were wanted:

- They were to be honest in their dealings. People with civil power were to administer honest judgments (v. 5b). In business, godly people were not to oppress (v. 6a, i.e. to cheat) helpless people.
- They were not to take life by violence or for unjust gain (v. 6b).
- They were not to follow or worship other gods like Baal (vv. 6c, 9b).
- They were to stop disobeying the Ten Commandments (five of the ten are mentioned here, v. 9) and live holy lives before God (v. 10).

LIFE STEP Do you see how this applies to us Christians? You cannot truly worship the Lord Jesus on Sunday and not "amend" your wrong conduct during the rest of your week! What changes need to be made in your weekday conduct so that your life will be pleasing to God?

TUESDAY 20

Jeremiah 7:18-28

What is the writer saying?

How can I apply this to my life?

PRAY — Nigeria — For Northern Nigeria youth, who are enticed by Muslims with promises of material goods and wealth, to know the truth about Jesus Christ.

After what had happened to Israel (ten northern tribes), Judah should have seen that God would judge them, too, for worshipping false gods. Instead, many in Judah had drifted far from the God of Israel (v. 21). Whole families were worshipping the queen of heaven (v. 18; also 44:17-19, 25). Apparently, their worship was done with the clear intent of provoking the Lord (v. 18c).

"Queen of Heaven" was the title the Babylonians had given to their chief goddess, *Ishtar*, a goddess of war and fertility associated with the moon. She was worshipped throughout the Near East under various names; Ashtar, Aphrodite, etc. All kinds of evil sexual practices are a part of her worship (such as sacred prostitutes). Commonly, at each new moon, *moon-cakes* (v. 18b) were made and offered to her.

The LORD then makes a point. When He first called the fathers of Israel out of slavery in Egypt, He had commanded them to "obey my voice" and to *walk in all my ways* (v. 23). The LORD's emphasis had been upon a holy walk while living apart from sin and other gods. Yet, the Jews thought they could satisfy God by keeping the Levitical religious services (v. 21) while still doing as they pleased at other times. As a result God said, *Mix all your sacrifices together in a pile and eat them at your leisure* (v. 21), which was abruptly saying, *Your continual sacrifices have no religious value to God*!

The point is not that the Lord hated sacrifices; after all, He commanded them with meticulous detail. Rather, the sacrifices were intended to be a reflection of an obedient life. Remember God's word to Saul, "To obey is better than sacrifice" (1 Samuel 15:22).

How sad and yet how prevalent in our world today that much is done in the name of religious ritual to appease God for our wrong doings. Obedience is still vital; not simply obedience in ritual and form, but obedience that comes from the heart (Deuteronomy 6:1-15).

LIFE STEP — Since the best way to honor God is to obey Him and walk in His ways, how can you choose to conduct yourself today so as to declare your love for God? What would be the most important *spiritual sacrifice* you could offer up to God today? Ask the Lord to help you.

Jeremiah 8:20–9:9

What is the writer saying?

How can I apply this to my life?

PRAY Guatemala – For the rapid and accurate completion of the 17 Bible translation projects in progress.

Jeremiah's reaction to the LORD's pronounced judgment (8:13) upon Judah was dismay (v. 21). In spite of the many opportunities for God's people to repent, ("harvest is past, the summer is ended" — v.20), they were not going to be saved from the coming judgment.

Because his people were going to be hurt (v. 21a, used literally, *broken into pieces*), Jeremiah says he was also hurt (v. 21b, used figuratively, a deep feeling of "*broken heartedness*"). He says that his grief had turned his heart black (v. 21b) because there was no light of hope left! As a result, Jeremiah was reduced to weeping (9:1). Note his balance; Jeremiah had a love and sympathy for the people, while he wanted to escape from the presence of their sin (9:2a). Next he says there was "no balm in Gilead" (8:22, a medicine made from sap of an evergreen tree) for this sin-sick people. Their "physicians" were false prophets who failed to advise repentance from sin

(8:6) and a returning (8:5) to the LORD. As a result, there was no healing for their sin-infection! Rather the infection had spread:

- Verse 9:2 – they all were adulterers and treacherous men.
- Verse 3 – they were bowmen who shot lies as arrows.
- Verse 4 – they were all neighbors who sought to betray each other.
- Verse 5 – they cheat with deceptive balances and without truth.
- Verse 6 – they have openly chosen to live in the midst of deceit!

Our passage ends with a declaration from the LORD of judgment upon Jerusalem and all the cities of Judah (9:7, 9, 11). The LORD proclaims that He will melt them and try them (v. 7). These are terms used of metal smiths who purify metal (6:29); the impure metal must be "melted" so that contaminating dross can be removed. Only then can the metal smith test (to examine) the metal for purity.

LIFE STEP Each of us Christians can praise the Lord Jesus as our physician for He has the healing "balm" which will cleanse us from our sin-infections (1 John 1:9)! How can you act today so as to be trusting in the God of truth to cleanse you from bad relationships, bad talk, bad conduct, bad business practices, and bad choices?

Jeremiah 9:12-24

What is the writer saying?

How can I apply this to my life?

PRAY Cuba – For God to save and call to service many of the 1,000,000 Cuban refugees living in the United States.

The passage before us begins with questions for the wise men of Judah. A wise man would surely understand what was taking place and would be able to explain why the land was ruined and laid waste.

The passage implies that no wise man was found to answer the questions so the Lord Himself steps forward and gives the answers that should have been provided by the wise men of the nation!:

- They had forsaken the law; not obeying or walking in it (v. 13).
- Also, they walked after their own imagination, after *Baalim* (the plural of Baal, that is, the *Baals*; thus picturing here a following of the various Canaanite gods and evil practices associated with each of them). Amazingly the people of Judah had learned these wicked behaviors from their fathers (v. 14)!

Next we have three declarations of judgment on Judah because of their sin (notice the repeating "Thus saith the LORD"; vv. 15, 17, 23).

War: First the LORD will send them the poisonous waters (v. 15, "gall") of war (v. 16, "a sword") that will scatter them far from Israel.

Weeping: Next, the LORD says conditions will be like the weeping of women at a funeral (vv. 17-20). They will lament for the Jewish men killed in battle who will look like cut grain left ungathered in the fields (v. 22).

Warning: The LORD now warns that the people of Judah should not "glory" (v. 23, literally — *flash forth light*, thus to *boast of oneself*) in wisdom, power, or wealth. Rather one's *glorying* should be, "that he understands and knows" God (v. 24a). The most important thing in life is to know the Lord, who is loving-kindness, just, and righteous (v. 24b). The Lord delights in those who invest their time seeking to gain an intimate knowledge of the true character of God (v. 24c).

LIFE STEP Most people in our world today seek after these same ways of *glorying* in themselves, through education, power, and wealth. Yet God, who has all knowledge, power, and wealth, is delighted when we Christians declare as our goal, "That I may know Him…" (Philippians 3:10). Write out a "Post-It" note, and then post it, declaring your goal to obtain a better understanding and knowledge of God.

Jeremiah 10:1-13

What is the writer saying?

How can I apply this to my life?

PRAY For safety, salvation decisions, and consecration commitments during Word of Life Snow Camp weekends.

Today's passage is a contrast between the living God (v. 10) and idols of wood (v. 5). It is an underlying subject to the main focus of Jeremiah's sermon, Judah's incomplete return to the LORD (chaps. 7-10).

The passage alternately presents a cutting sarcasm of idols followed by a doxology of praise to the LORD — idols (vv. 3-5); God (vv. 6-7); idols (vv. 8-9); God (v. 10); idols (v. 11); God (vv. 12-13); idols (vv. 14-15); God (v. 16).

Jeremiah's description of idols looks at the vain (vv. 3, 15) work of the makers of idols; all their efforts are futile and worthless. Both the idols and those that worship them are brutish (vv. 8, 14 – senseless). Yet God's people had become fearful (v. 2) of these idols that could not speak (v. 5) and were breathless, powerless falsehoods (v. 14).

What a contrast to the one true God, whose name is Jehovah!:

- He is great and His name is great in might (v. 6).
- All should fear this One, who is the King of nations (v. 7a).
- Among all the wise men "there is none like thee" (v. 7b – also v. 2, likely referring to the magicians' encounter in the book of Daniel).
- He is the true (genuine), living (idols are lifeless), and everlasting God (idols decay, v. 10a). He is in a class by Himself (v. 6)!
- All nations together will not be able to resist His judgment (v. 10b).
- God's creative hand is seen as "he made the earth by his power" and "established the world by his wisdom" (v. 12).
- The name "Portion of Jacob" (v. 16) points out God's continuing interest in His people, Israel (here given alternate name, 'Jacob').

Today, we Christians have substitute brands of manufactured idols. The Apostle John warned us of these, "Little children, keep yourselves from idols!" (1 John 5:21). Our contemporary idols include anything that captures our attention and demands our service, perhaps an expensive home or car, a business or career, an ambition or hobby.

LIFE STEP Upon what do you center your life's attention and affection? To what are you willing to sacrifice your money and time? If your answer is something other than Jesus Christ then it is your idol! How can you return your life's focus to the true and living God?

Jeremiah 10:14-23

What is the writer saying?

How can I apply this to my life?

Today's passage completes Jeremiah's third sermon (7:1–10:25), often called his Temple Sermon. He picks up again on his earlier subject (9:9-26), describing God's soon-coming judgment upon Judah and Jerusalem. Jeremiah is writing around 600 B.C. before the arrival of the Babylonians who will besiege the city of Jerusalem. While some Jews had already been taken away into exile (Daniel and others were taken to Babylon in 605 B.C.), those that remained were confident that they would remain in their land, continuing business as usual. The opening comment, "gather up your wares" (v. 17), is both an economic and personal warning, that is, bring to completion your business in the land and hastily pack a few personal items into a bundle and make ready to leave this land! Jeremiah is addressing the Jewish people as if they were already inhabitants of a besieged fortress (v. 17).

In verses 19-20, Jeremiah, as he prophetically sees the near-future of Jerusalem, becomes the personified voice of Jerusalem as she cries out while in the midst of her grief while being captured and destroyed. She also acknowledges the correctness of God's judgment upon her sin when she calls out, "Truly ... I must bear it" (v. 19b).

At verse 21, Jeremiah contemplates the reasons for the coming catastrophe. He declares that those chiefly to blame were the nation's leaders who should have been pastors, or "shepherds," guiding the people of Jerusalem. Yet they had become senseless (KJV uses old English, "brutish"), which is a figurative use of the literal idea, *unable to see because of the smoke of fires they have set ablaze*! They were blinded because they were not seeking what was pleasing to the LORD (v. 21b). As a result, God would see to it that their attempts to prosper (v. 21c, *observing and arranging things to bring about success*) would all fail. These blind pastors had failed to understand that the LORD controls the ways of a man and not the man himself (v. 23).

LIFE STEP   So then how can you avoid living a life that brings to nothing (v. 24) all that you desire to prosper (v. 21)? The answer is not to get *blinded in the smoke of the fires you yourself have set ablaze*! The answer is to stay focused on the ways of the Lord!

SUNDAY 21

Jeremiah 12:1-17

What is the writer saying?

How can I apply this to my life?

In chapter 11, two conspiracies by evil-hearted Jews had been revealed, one against King Josiah the other against Jeremiah. Today's passage is in response to these events. First, we have Jeremiah's *Song of Lament* (vv. 1-4) about the treacherous (v. 6) situations. Next is the LORD's response, a *Song of Rebuke* (vv. 5-17).

Jeremiah is wrestling in prayer with age-old questions: *Why do the wicked prosper?* (v. 1), *Why does God allow the fruit of the ungodly to grow* (v. 2) while all the land mourns (v. 4) under God's judgment? Since the LORD is righteous (v. 1a), this situation doesn't seem right! And so, he prays that the wicked might receive their just reward (v. 3).

The LORD ignores these questions and presses home that things were going to get worse! God says, *My dear Jeremiah, if you are worn out after running against footmen, how will you compete in your race when you have to contend with horses* (v. 5a)? Then the LORD says, *If you are stumbling while running on a peaceful terrain how will you manage when your path is in the thickets along the swollen Jordan River* (v. 5b)? Was Jeremiah's faith only able to hold in easy times?

Finally, in verses 7-13, the LORD declares that He, too, had been betrayed:

- The situation was as if the LORD's own dearly beloved family (i.e., Judah) had forced Him to forsake His house and His heritage (v. 7).
- They had turned on the Lord like a lion (v. 8).
- They, like birds of prey, were being attacked by other birds (v. 9)
- They are like wicked shepherds who have destroyed *my* vineyard, *my* loved ones, *my* portion and *my* land. And yet no one cared (v. 11)!

As a result, the sword of the Lord (v. 12, i.e., God's judgment) would destroy Judah from one end to the other. God was going to send spoilers (i.e., armies of Babylon) to destroy Judah and her evil neighbors. By this God would bring His people back to Himself (v. 16).

LIFE STEP   What is the character of your faith? Is it like Jeremiah's, only able to function on easy terrain and unprepared for difficult paths? How can you avoid being indifferent to things important to God as you lay to heart (v. 11) His mission for your life?

MONDAY 21

Jeremiah 13:1-11

What is the writer saying?

How can I apply this to my life?

PRAY United States – Pray that the Holy Spirit would bring a spiritual unity across churches that goes deeper than race and culture.

This is the first of five *visual aids* used in this chapter: a sash (vv. 1-11, KJV uses *girdle* 8x), wineskins, a flock, a woman in labor, and stubble. The situation was that God's people were refusing to hear God's words (vv. 10, 11), so God directed Jeremiah to use these dramatized attention-getters to illustrate God's point.

In the ancient world, a sash, as an article of clothing, served as a belt to carry a sword or money pouch, but looked like a short skirt. It was worn by soldiers, kings, and priests. It was often made of leather and cloth. It could be highly decorated with gold (Daniel 10:5) or embroidery (Exodus 28:39) to declare a person's position, association or allegiance.

God used the linen sash that Jeremiah was to purchase and wear as a picture of His relationship to Judah. God had always intended Judah (and all Israel) to be His fine linen sash decorated with gold and embroidery that declared that they were God's special possession. God desired to proudly display His people as a valued possession with the important function of carrying the cherished things of God. They were to carry God's Word to the world. They were to hold the sword of the Lord as they defended the holiness of God. But the Jews had become filled with great pride and evil and were walking after other gods (vv. 9, 10). They were now a marred and dirty rag that was profitable for nothing (v. 7).

Jeremiah's actions of taking the sash far away to the Euphrates River, hiding it there, and then recovering it after it had become "marred" and "good for nothing" showed the state of God's people who had forsaken the Lord. They went from being a garment on display to a marred and good for nothing rag (v. 10). They had flirted with the pagan world and would reap the results; they would become like a lost garment along the Euphrates in far-away Babylon.

LIFE STEP While this *sash visual aid* is an Old Testament picture of God's relationship with Israel, it still teaches us much of God's desired relationship with Christians. How can you keep your life clean and functional so that God can use you for His purposes? How will you live today so God can put you on display as one of his valued possessions?

Jeremiah 14:7-22

What is the writer saying?

How can I apply this to my life?

PRAY

Korea – For seminary graduates to humbly commit themselves to less prominent, rural pastorates.

The Palestinian Covenant in Deuteronomy 28 makes it clear that when God's people sinned there would be punishment. Specifically, there we read, "If thou wilt not hearken unto the voice of the LORD thy God, to observe to do all his commandments and his statutes…all these curses shall come upon thee, and overtake thee" (Deuteronomy 28:15). Again, "The LORD shall send upon thee cursing, vexation, and rebuke, in all that thou settest thine hand unto for to do" (Deuteronomy 28:20). We should not be surprised, then, to find God doing what He said He would do.

In today's passage, Jeremiah becomes a spokesman for his people, saying, "We have sinned against thee" (v.7). Their theology was right, referring to the Lord as being their hope and savior in time of trouble (v. 8a). The LORD alone was the mighty man who could *save* them (v. 9). Yet, the Lord saw beyond their words; He saw their love of wandering away from God and their unwillingness to refrain their feet from carrying them back into sin (v. 10, note "backslidings" of v. 7).

Their plea of "leave us not" (v. 9) was impressive, but hollow to the Lord. God responds with, "I will not hear their cry," and "I will not accept them" (v. 12). In fact, the people were surprised by the LORD's failure to act as Judah's Savior; they were saying God appeared to them as a foreigner who had been ambushed while travelling through their country and was thus unable to provide any assistance to the people of the land (v. 8b).

Apparently the people were also claiming that it wasn't their fault that the false prophets had lied to them (v. 13). The Lord responds, "I sent them not" (v. 14). Three specific judgments were upon them: sword, famine, and pestilence (vv. 12, 15, 16, 18). To each of these, the false prophets responded claiming it would not be so (v. 13).

LIFE STEP

The lesson here is that confession and prayer must be more than just a religious ritual; it must be real! Yes, we, too, can be like these people; they spoke the right words (v. 20) but did not have a right heart (v. 10). Ask the Lord to help you to be honest and truly sincere as you pray in repentance to God, turning from your sin. Then you can seek His help in your times of trouble! Remember: God looks on the heart.

WEDNESDAY 21

Jeremiah 15:1-2, 11-16

What is the writer saying?

How can I apply this to my life?

PRAY China – For the effective use of radio and the Internet in reaching and discipling the Chinese.

Warning, today's passage is God's announcement of His rejection of Jeremiah's third prayer for divine deliverance for Judah (14:19-22)! Sometimes it really is too late to pray for God to turn away from His announced and soon-coming judgment! God's people had persisted in their sin, now judgment was sure. Even if Moses and Samuel had been there to plead their cause, (both of whom interceded at critical times for the people – Exodus 32:9-14; 1 Samuel 7:5-11), it would not have changed the LORD's intended judgment upon Judah, summarized by death, the sword, famine, and captivity (vv. 2-4 *Captivity* means captured in wartime then taken back to the conquering country as plunder).

While the sins of Judah had been increasing for generations, it had culminated in the terrible idolatries committed by evil king Manasseh (v. 4, 686-642 B.C., 2 Chronicles 33:1-10, which was just prior to Jeremiah's

call as a prophet in 627 B.C.). As a result, God had announced that Judah would be removed into all the kingdoms of the earth (v. 4).

Verse 10 is a personal appeal by Jeremiah concerning his own grief as God's prophet delivering a message of judgment, that is, the whole land was against him. Verse 11 is the LORD's response to Jeremiah's personal appeal. God promises that Jeremiah would be vindicated when the time of judgment finally arrived. This was specifically fulfilled when King Zedekiah requested Jeremiah's help (chaps. 21, 37-38).

Verse 12 continues the LORD's response with a rhetorical question that emphasizes the inevitability of God's coming judgment. The *northern iron* in verse 12 refers to Babylon. Judah's treasures would be lost and they would be taken to this land they did not know (vv. 13-14).

LIFE STEP Sadly we Christians often have need of warnings to repent from sin before it is too late to seek God's forgiveness. Consider Paul's statement to the Christians at Corinth. "For this cause many are weak and sickly among you, and many sleep (have been taken home to Heaven)," 1 Corinthians 11:30. Are there sins in your life that you have been foolishly hanging onto? Unlike Judah, will you repent from sin while God is ready and waiting to forgive and cleanse your life from the sin?

THURSDAY 21

Jeremiah 17:1-13

What is the writer saying?

How can I apply this to my life?

Jeremiah begins with a stinging judgment upon Judah because sin was chiseled, or graven, upon their hearts (v. 1). An image of ancient tools is used; of iron chisels for cutting into stone and of diamond-tipped iron rods for inscribing letters into metals. He was saying that God intended to judge Judah with exile and servitude (v. 4) because God's Law should have been chiseled upon their hearts (Deuteronomy 6:6-7)!

The next stanza (vv. 5-8) looks at another of Judah's sins; her political leaders' hearts had turned away from the LORD (v. 5b) and were no longer relying upon the LORD. Instead, they were trusting in man (v. 5a), a reference to Judah's alliances with Egypt and others for protection from the coming Babylonians. As a result, Judah had become like a desert juniper tree (v. 6) which must struggle for existence in a stark climate. Judah was no longer the blessed plant in a rich land (v. 7).

In the third stanza (vv. 9-13), Jeremiah seems to step away from his sermon to reflect upon the principle of God's working in the world; He will inevitably punish evil just as He will surely reward and prosper good! Why, then, has Judah continued on such a foolish path of life? Jeremiah finds his answer as he reviews what he has known about the hearts of people (vv. 1, 5, 9-10). His first observation is that the heart is deceitful (v. 9a); it is insidiously deadly and more dangerous than expected. He also observes that the heart is desperately wicked, which is to say it is as one who is incurably wounded or sick.

We must also note that later in the Book of Jeremiah, the LORD declares that He will one day write his Law in their hearts (31:33). Then in the New Testament we learn that the Lord Jesus became the Mediator of this promised New Covenant from God (Hebrews 8:6-10; 10:16-20) and the Holy Spirit is the *cutting tool* that writes God's law upon the hearts of Christians (2 Corinthians 3:1-3)!

LIFE STEP Christian friend, it is important to set your affection on things above as we live in this polluted, deceitful world (Colossians 3:2) that seeks to chisel sin upon your heart, too! How has God been trying to chisel His law on your heart (Hebrew 10:16)?

FRIDAY 21

Jeremiah 18:1-12

What is the writer saying?

How can I apply this to my life?

PRAY Papua New Guinea - Pray for the schools that are engaged in outreaches and religious instruction throughout the school year.

Today we have another of Jeremiah's action sermons, this time using the illustration often called *The Potter Working at his Wheel.* Since Judah continued to refuse to repent of their sin as a result of Jeremiah's prophecies concerning God's coming judgment, God had Jeremiah switch strategies by using illustrated lessons.

Jeremiah is sent to a potter's house where God is going to illustrate the way in which He would deal with His people. We see the potter, with obvious skill, forming a vessel of clay until some defect is revealed that marred, or ruined, (v. 4) the vessel — perhaps part of the clay was too stiff or perhaps a small stone or other debris was found within the clay. The potter would then remove the defect, destroying the original vessel, and begin again to shape the purged clay as it pleased the potter.

As we read the paragraph we are impressed with the sovereignty of God. "Cannot I do with you as this potter" (v. 6)? We also see

a message of grace here, too. God says He can make Judah, purged of defects, into a pleasing vessel again (v. 4b). While God is sovereign and in full control, He assures the nation that if they would submit to Him and keep His commandments He would bless them (v. 8).

So we see that God is both sovereign and yet tender hearted, that is, *wanting to forgive as an act of His grace.* If they insisted on rebelling, God would surely bring to pass His judgment (v. 10).

Their response was not the one for which Jeremiah had hoped. They said, "We will walk after our own devices" (v. 12). Be careful that you do not find yourself doing the same thing, telling God, "It's no use; I will do my own thing and walk after my own plans." Rather, you should say:

"Have thine own way, Lord, have thine own way.
Thou art the potter, I am the clay.
Mold me and make me, after thy will,
While I am waiting, yielded and still."

LIFE STEP We are clay in the potter's hand. God would have us yield to His shaping our lives. Are you willing to let Him have His way with you? Are you willing to submit to His hand as the potter and accept what He does in the remaking? Tell Him that today. See what He will do!

SATURDAY 21

Jeremiah 20:7-18

What is the writer saying?

How can I apply this to my life?

PRAY Paraguay – For pastors to actively model the disciplines of prayer, Bible study, and witnessing.

Do you ever feel like quitting? Do you ever feel caught between rejection and isolation, wondering about yourself? Well, these are the feelings expressed by Jeremiah.

Jeremiah had preached to the common people (19:2), warning them of the LORD's threatened judgment. He then repeated this message at the temple (19:14). His message was rejected (19:15), and resulted in his being arrested by the chief officer of temple, a priest named Pashur (20:1). Jeremiah was then beaten by Pashur and placed in stocks.

As a result, Jeremiah, filled with anguish, complains to the LORD:

- His preaching had only resulted in his being ridiculed and laughed at (vv. 7-8). The people only jested at Jeremiah's warnings.
- More menacing was the fact that some were plotting against him, waiting for him to stumble so that they could destroy him (v. 10).

- And so he complains to God that he had been deceived (v. 7). He should have remembered that he was told it would not be easy (1:19). And so we must conclude that Jeremiah has deceived himself!
- He also was tempted to say, *I quit* (v. 9), because of the hardships he was facing and because of the people's lack of repentance to the LORD.

Jeremiah then sees his own self-deception and recognizes that God intends good for him (v. 11; Romans 8:28-30). He also recognizes again that those persecuting him would ultimately stumble and be disgraced. And so Jeremiah once again commits his cause (v. 12) to the LORD.

Sadly there follows a second look into the depths of despair (vv. 14-18)! This portion is best understood as a poetic contrast between the preceding spirit of thanksgiving (v. 13) and Jeremiah's earlier spirit of despair. In effect Jeremiah is here saying I had said in the time of my self-deception *cursed be the day I was born* (vv. 14-18).

LIFE STEP Christian, you too can find victory over despair and discouragement! Life will have its ups and downs, but we must never question God's intent to do good for us, nor His abiding presence that enables us to do His calling. Remember, in all circumstances *nothing is able to separate us from the love of God* (Romans 8:39)!

SUNDAY 22

Jeremiah 21:1-14

What is the writer saying?

How can I apply this to my life?

PRAY Pray that God will bless the ministry and outreach of your local Christian radio station.

In today's passage we have a delegation sent by Zedekiah, king of Judah, to Jeremiah to inquire (v. 2) of the LORD concerning the Babylonian army who had come to make war against Judah (they began a siege of Jerusalem in 588 B.C. and destroyed it in 586 B.C.). Likely, Zedekiah and his delegation had hoped the LORD would again deliver Judah (v. 2b) as He had years earlier (701 B.C.) delivered King Hezekiah and Judah from the invading Assyrians (2 Kings 18-24). They had hoped for God to work wonders for them, but what they got was a declaration that the LORD was going to fight against them (v. 5)!

The LORD instructs Jeremiah to answer the delegation in three parts:

- The LORD's Answer to Zedekiah (vv. 4-7): God was going to insure that the Babylonians would enter into the city (v. 4). Also, He warns that the inhabitants of Jerusalem would die by famine (v. 7) and a plague (v. 6) during the siege. Finally, He says that Zedekiah and his royal court would be captured by Nebuchadnezzar (see 52:8-11).

- The LORD's Answer to the People of Judah (vv. 8-10): Because of Jerusalem's continuing sin, God had set his face against this city (v. 10). As a result, they had to choose between two difficult options: the way of life (to surrender), or the way of death (to stay in the city and die by famine, plague, or fighting). God had chosen to allow Judah's enemy to do this as His method of judging the sin of His own beloved people.

- The LORD's Answer to the Royal Family of David (vv. 11-14): Apparently, the extended royal family acted as the nation's judges, having control of the country's judicial courts. It is also apparent that the LORD considered their doings to be evil; they were neglecting their duties (v. 12b) and failing to be a defense of the oppressed (v. 12c). Thus, God would come down against them (v. 13).

LIFE STEP Again we are reminded that God is not mocked. Judah thought they could continue to play the game of living in sin but turning to the Lord when they were in danger. Are you playing the same game — living in sin yet expecting God to protect you when facing a danger? Are you like Judah's judges, delaying in your dealing with evil in your own life?

Jeremiah 22:24–23:6

What is the writer saying?

How can I apply this to my life?

PRAY Spain – Praise – Successful use of music in evangelization. Pray for more musicians and opportunities.

Today's passage forms the last two parts of Jeremiah's ninth sermon (21:1–23:8) against Judah's kings, who were false shepherds.

First we consider King Jehoiachin, here called Coniah and elsewhere Jeconiah (see 2 Kings 24:12 and Jeremiah 24:1). He reigned three months and was exiled by the Babylonians in 597 B.C. He would spend the next thirty seven years as a captive, which means Jehoiachin would outlive his uncle, King Zedekiah, who would be killed by the Babylonians in 586 B.C. Since the Babylonians put Zedekiah on Judah's throne before Jehoiachin's death, Jehoiachin was considered Judah's last legitimate king who finishes the 350-year story of Israel's kings (2 Kings 25:27-30).

This paragraph is Jeremiah's answer to a series of questions about why God removed Jehoiachin from the throne (v. 28). Because of Judah's and Jehoiachin's continuing sin, God had declared that even if Jehoiachin was God's own precious signet ring (v. 24), God would cast him off in judgment. To the people of Judah Jehoiachin was not a broken and unwanted pottery vessel (v. 28) to be left cast out in a distant land. Yet God is here declaring He was in control of Judah, not her kings! As a result God had decreed the removal Jehoiachin from the land. The land is then called as a witness of God's judgment (v. 29).

In chapter 23 verses 1-8, Jeremiah finishes his sermon to false shepherds by declaring a "woe," a prophetic announcement of judgment upon these unfaithful pastors, or those who feed and care for a flock. While they should have been *feeding* God's flock, they were destroying, scattering, and not attending to its needs (v. 2).

Jeremiah concludes with a vision that the LORD will gather a remnant of His flock (v. 3) and set over them faithful shepherds. He climaxes with a promise that God would also raise up a "righteous Branch" (v. 5) who will bring salvation (v. 6). This will be fulfilled by Jesus Christ, who is the Branch from David's own family tree.

LIFE STEP Christ has become THE LORD OUR RIGHTEOUSNESS (v. 6b). His righteousness is ours by faith. When we trust Christ as the One who saves (v. 6a) us from sin, we also receive His righteousness (2 Corinthians 5:21). How can you be one of God's righteous shepherds?

TUESDAY 22

Jeremiah 23:25-40

What is the writer saying?

How can I apply this to my life?

PRAY Finland – For more Finns to respond to the call to full-time Christian service and missions.

Today we take a look at Jeremiah's tenth sermon against Judah's false prophets (23:9-40). It has the Bible's greatest concentration of the words, "prophet" and "prophesy" (twenty occurrences), and the greatest concentration of the word, "burden" (eight times), meaning the message from God that a prophet was to carry to God's people. Similarly, we have the Bible's third most common use of "dreams" (six times), which is used more often only in connection with Joseph's and Daniel's interpretations of Pharaoh's and Nebuchadnezzar's dreams.

Jeremiah's tenth sermon centers on the evil practices of his peers:

Verses 9-15 – The false prophets were godless (v. 11, KJV – "profane" that is, not concerned about the holy things of God), promoting wickedness and spiritual adultery as they turned to Baal to obtain false hope.

Verses 16-22 – Their visions (v. 16) of the future are from their own hearts and not from God! Yet they said, "The LORD has said ... no evil shall come" (v. 17). But God said, "I have not sent these" evil prophets (v. 21).

Verses 23-32 – The dreams and prophesies of these lying prophets were only proclaiming the deceits of their own hearts (v. 26). Their dreams were not spiritually nourishing; being as beneficial as eating straw (v. 28). Sadly, God's people had become like other pagans, they were more fascinated with the interpretation of their own dreams than they were in reflecting upon God's name (v. 27) or studying God's Word (vv. 28-29)!

Verses 33-40 – The key here is the word "burden." The false prophets were claiming to have a burden, or message, from God while at the same time ridiculing Jeremiah by making *light* of his message concerning God's soon judgment upon Judah. As a result, the people of God were confused, asking, "What *is* the burden of the LORD?" (v. 33)

LIFE STEP Beware of influences that come into your life that are contradictory to God's Word, things like popular customs, ways of life, or scientific theories! Beware of peer pressures that draw you into life styles that are in opposition to the character of your Holy Father! How have you been negatively influenced by such corrupting things, and how can you return to a focus upon the holy name and Word of God?

Jeremiah 24:1-10

What is the writer saying?

How can I apply this to my life?

Here is an Old Testament parable. Its setting is after the Babylonians had carried King Jehoiachin (Jeconiah or Coniah) away from Jerusalem along with his princes, craftsmen, and smiths (v. 1, 597 B.C.) to begin a seventy-year exile.

The lesson begins when the LORD showed Jeremiah two baskets of figs that were set before the temple of the LORD. One basket had very good figs (v. 2a), which would have been the best-tasting, early-ripening first-fruits of the fig trees. The other had very bad figs (v. 2b), which had deteriorated to a point where they could not be eaten.

The LORD explained that the figs represented two groups of people. The good figs represented those had been carried away into captivity. This must have come as a surprise to everyone! While it had been considered a bad thing to have been forced into exile away from Judah, God here declared it to be a good thing, for He would personally acknowledge (v. 5) those that had gone into exile. God was saying it was a good thing, since the hardships of

their exile would cause them to turn from their sin. It would bring them to true faith in and reliance upon the LORD. God would acknowledge (v. 5) their repentance, that is, God would *notice and favorably care for* the repentant ones in exile. He would again set his eyes upon them for good (v. 6). God also gives these a great promise, saying the scattered people would one day return unto Him (v. 7). More than a physical return to Jerusalem is in view here. They would have a wholehearted return to a walk with God (v. 7b)!

The bad figs (v. 8) represented the Jews who stayed in the land. By staying behind they thought they had been blessed since they had avoided this apparent catastrophe. Yet they were the "bad figs" because they continued to be rebellious and live in sin. Because these would not return unto God (v. 7), God was going to bring upon them a great judgment characterized by misery, hurt, and reproach (v. 9). They would receive the sword, famine and pestilence (v. 10).

LIFE STEP Is your conduct in life such that the Lord will acknowledge you and your need for His notice and favorable care? Like the exiles of ancient Judah, are there things in your life from which you need to turn away? How can you today wholeheartedly return unto God?

What is the writer saying?

How can I apply this to my life?

For twenty three years Jeremiah had prophesied against the sins of Judah. Yet four times in this passage we read, "You have not listened" (vv. 3-4, 7-8).

It was now 605 B.C., the year the Babylonians would defeat a coalition of Egypt and her Near-Eastern allies, gaining control of the entire region. Before the year was out the Babylonian army would come to Jerusalem and deport many of Judah's chief citizens (Daniel 1:1).

Jeremiah summarizes the message being delivered all these years, *turn from your evil ways and practices (v. 5); especially, turn away from other gods (v. 6).* Only then would the people of Judah be allowed to continue in the land God had given to them. Otherwise they would provoke (vv. 6, 7) the LORD to anger and judgment. The land would be totally ruined, a desolation. Its people will be utterly destroyed, with its survivors exiled to serve the king of Babylon for seventy years.

This declaration adds three important new details. First, Jeremiah now identifies the enemy God would use to bring judgment. The enemy from the north (1:13; 4:6) was to be Nebuchadnezzar, the Babylonian king (v. 9). In addition, the Jews were going to serve Babylon for seventy years. Thirdly, Jeremiah declared that after the seventy years of Judah's exile, Babylon in turn would be judged because of her own wickedness (v. 12).

Note that God calls Nebuchadnezzar "my servant" (again at 27:6; 43:10), in that he would be used to carry out the will of God. Remember, God is sovereign and He uses any tool He desires. Just as God had used many prophets to urge Judah to repent from her sin and seek God's mercy, so now God would use an evil, idol-worshipping king to punish His own evil, idol-worshipping people, who would not repent!

Concerning the seventy-year exile of the Jews (v. 11), we note that they apparently had not obeyed God's command that the farmlands were to be allowed to rest every seventh year (Leviticus 25:3-5; 2 Chronicles 36:20-21). The LORD was now going to enforce his command.

LIFE STEP   The lesson is clear. We need to submit to God's will concerning our living the right kind of lives. Not to do so will result in His chastening hand upon us, too! Are there specific aspects of your own life where you are refusing to listen to God's holy Word?

Jeremiah 26:1-16

What is the writer saying?

How can I apply this to my life?

PRAY Italy – For more believers to attend Bible schools and seminaries before entering the ministry.

With today's passage we leave the largest division of the Book of Jeremiah, a collection of twelve sermons by Jeremiah that announce God's declarations of judgment upon Judah for her many sins.

Today we begin a small section of the book, sometimes called "The Conflicts of Jeremiah" (chaps. 26-29). This section of the book records a collection of responses to Jeremiah's sermons. These two collections, sermons and then conflicts, are arranged in parallel chronologies. Thus chapter 26, a conflict, is going back in time to tell of the people's response to Jeremiah's Temple Sermon (chapters 7-10). Note that at the beginning of both the Temple Sermon (7:1) and today's conflict (26:10) it is reported that Jeremiah was at the gate of the LORD's house, that is, the gate to the outer court of the temple at Jerusalem.

Chapter 26 verses 1-7 give a summary of the Temple Sermon and repeats the warning that, if they did not turn from their sinful ways in repentance, God would judge. Rather than repenting, the response of the people, priests, and prophets was one of anger, "Thou shalt surely die" (v. 8)!,

They became enraged at the idea that God would make the temple like Shiloh. Remember, at Shiloh the ark of the covenant fell into the hands of the Philistines (1 Samuel 4). Their response was that Jeremiah was a false prophet because God would never allow such a thing to take place. Jeremiah was arrested and taken to the gate of the Lord's house (v.10).

Verse 10 tells us that the princes of Judah convened a court. First, the religious leaders bring their accusations against Jeremiah (v. 11) and then Jeremiah defends himself by insisting that God had sent him (v. 12). Jeremiah also insists that God's punishment was conditional; it wasn't too late for them to turn back to the Lord (v. 13). Finally, if he were slain they would have been guilty of taking innocent blood (v. 15).

LIFE STEP The courage of the Prophet Jeremiah is clearly portrayed here. Obviously, Jeremiah had counted the cost of doing as God had directed him. He had decided to do what was right and not just what was safe! How about you? When you have the opportunity to speak for God, do you only speak when it is safe? What threatening situation will you be facing? How can you now ask for God's strengthening?

What is the writer saying?

How can I apply this to my life?

Apparently envoys from several nations were meeting in Jerusalem. We can surmise that they were planning a revolt against Babylon. While God had made it clear that His plan was for them to go into captivity as a part of His judgment upon their refusal to turn from their sin (vv. 6-7), they apparently had other plans. In this chapter, God tells the prophet to tell the envoys to report to their kings and submit to Nebuchadnezzar.

Again we have an *action* sermon entitled "The Yokes" (vv. 2-3), as God instructs Jeremiah to put a yoke on his shoulders. First, Jeremiah's "Yokes" message was delivered unto the various kings (v. 3), and then to King Zedekiah himself (v. 12). They certainly would ask what it meant and he would deliver God's message of submission to Babylon's rule. Going forward with their planned rebellion would only make matters worse; that is, they would be exiled from their homelands (v. 11).

If one idea stands out in this chapter it is *God's sovereignty* (v. 5). God is all-powerful and He gives power unto whomever He chooses to accomplish His will (v. 5b). Thus we see that God called the king of Babylon as his servant (v. 6). He was going to use him to bring Judah to repentance. All their conniving and planning would not prevail over the plan of God. In God's own time He would also deal with the sinfulness of the king of Babylon, but it would be in God's time and in His way.

Four times Jeremiah warns the Jews not to listen to the false prophets (vv. 9, 14, 16, 17) among them. These prophets had not been sent by the LORD (v. 15), and as a result their prophecies were only lies (vv. 10, 14, 15, 16). Yet the people were tempted to listen to their prophecies of hope even though these prophecies were not true.

LIFE STEP

The same truth is evident today; God is sovereign and has the right, as our all-powerful Creator, to direct our lives as He chooses. He will put you into His service as He chooses, even if that service is hard upon you. Since God also limits what He chooses to that which is just, good and merciful for us, we can place our trust in His choices. So then, what has God said that should be a directive for your life? How can you be about the business of doing as He has directed?

SUNDAY 23

Jeremiah 28:1-17

What is the writer saying?

How can I apply this to my life?

PRAY — Panama – Removal of obstacles for those translating the Scriptures and Christian literature.

The collection of *Jeremiah's Conflicts* continues. First, we read of Jeremiah's conflicts with the people (chap. 26). Then we read of conflicts with false prophets (chap. 27). Today we read of a conflict with a particular false prophet, Hananiah (eleven times, only found in the Book of Jeremiah).

Hananiah comes before Jeremiah and all the people telling them that God had told him that the yoke of Babylon was broken (v. 2) and within two years there would be peace. Also, King Jehoiachin (Jechoniah or Coniah) (v. 4) and the holy vessels (v. 3) would be returned from Babylon. Hananiah was challenging Jeremiah's sermon, "The Yokes," of the previous chapter. Jeremiah responds by saying, "Amen" which was saying, *While I wish this were so, it is not* (v. 6). Jeremiah reiterated the fact that his own prophecies of judgment would surely come true. Hananiah then breaks the wooden yoke off the neck of Jeremiah (v. 10) to dramatize his claim that the power of Babylon was broken.

God was displeased and told Jeremiah that he was to make yokes of iron to replace the broken yokes of wood (v. 13). God was making a vivid point that his intentions were unalterable; that is, Judah and her rebellious neighbors would serve Babylon, as oxen serve the farmer.

Jeremiah also said to Hananiah that the LORD had not sent him and he had made "this people to trust in a lie" (v. 15). Of course, people would rather believe a lie when they are given unpleasant news. We are reminded that in the future Tribulation that people will again trust a lie. The *lie* will be personified in the Antichrist (2 Thessalonians 2:11).

To emphatically declare His own support of Jeremiah, the LORD announces that within the year the false prophet Hananiah would die. Jeremiah was careful in verse one to tell us the date — the fifth month of the fourth year (August/September 593 B.C.). We read in verse 17 that the false prophet died in the seventh month, less than two months later!

LIFE STEP — These events give us a warning against taking a stand against the clear teaching of the Word of God. We need to listen to the Word and be sensitive to it, even when it tells us things that we would rather not hear. How can you trust in the truth of God's Word?

MONDAY 23

Jeremiah 29:1-14

What is the writer saying?

How can I apply this to my life?

PRAY Ecuador – Pray for church growth to continue to increase and for a renewed emphasis on evangelism.

This chapter presents us with an interesting development. Since many Jews had already been exiled to Babylon several hundred miles away, this chapter tells the story of the conflict between Jeremiah and Shemaiah as they send letters between Jerusalem and Babylon:

(1) from Jerusalem, Jeremiah's letter to the exiles at Babylon (vv. 1-23).

(2) from Babylon, Shemaiah's letters to many at Jerusalem (vv. 25).

(3) from Jerusalem, Jeremiah's second letter to exiles at Babylon (vv. 30-32).

Jeremiah's first letter was sent to the elders who were carried away captives (v. 7). The letter addresses these exiled Jews who seemed to have no hope. They were restless and uncertain about the times. God told them to settle down and live normal lives (vv. 5-7), as they would be there for seventy years (v. 10). They were to carry on their social lives, their family lives, and seek peace. They were even to pray for those who held them captive (v. 7). They should remember that God was in control. The letter then tells the exiles not to be upset by the false prophets who tried to deceive them into thinking that their situation would only be temporary (v. 8). They were to be good Jews in a non-Jewish land. This speaks to us as we Christians are in the world, but not of the world.

Jeremiah's letter then gave them assurance that the Lord had a plan for them, "to give you a future and a hope" (v. 11). He was calling on His people to look beyond their present circumstances to God's perfect plan for their lives. They were to call on Him and seek Him (vv. 12-13). Yes, He would hear them even though they were far from Jerusalem and the temple. Also, God would turn away their captivity (v. 14, i.e., let them return home). Verses 12-14 are a reminder to the exiled Jews that God had a purpose in their exile; to force the Jews to come back to God with all their hearts (v. 13; see Deuteronomy 30:1-10).

LIFE STEP Christian friend, God continues to think thoughts toward you (v. 11). He knows your needs. He has a special plan for your life. So how can you handle depressing situations in your world? By looking beyond those difficult circumstances and trusting Him with your future. How can you trust in God during your current difficult circumstances?

Jeremiah 30:1-11

What is the writer saying?

How can I apply this to my life?

PRAY North Korea — Protection and perseverance of nearly 100,000 believers confined in North Korean camps.

With this passage the tone of the book changes from declarations of coming judgment to messages of hope. We are beginning a four-chapter scroll of God's plan for the future restoration of Judah and Israel (v. 3). While frightening judgments would still fall upon Judah, yet here God promises to bring again His people back from captivity (v. 3). These chapters have been entitled the "Little Book of Hope and Comfort," which give balance to the longer section of Jeremiah's prophecy we have now completed, often called the "Great Book of Doom" (chaps. 2-29).

Note that Jeremiah was to *write*, not speak, these new words from the LORD, likely because many Jews had already been exiled in the earlier deportations by the Babylonians (605 and 598 B.C.) and written copies could be carried to them. Also, the most devastating attack was upon Judah in 586 B.C. Thus, God's message of hope would be needed by the survivors of the soon-coming destruction of Jerusalem.

There are several key themes included in this text:

- The LORD would bring again Israel and Judah from captivity, causing them to return (vv. 3, 10).
- They would learn that God's purpose was to save Israel (vv. 7, 10, 11) even though they would be scattered far away (v. 10; Zechariah 8:7).
- Because the multitude of Judah's sins had increased (v. 14c), the LORD was going to wound Judah (v. 14b) with terrible wounds beyond healing (v. 14). Yet the LORD also promises that He would heal their wounds and restore their health (v. 17).
- A future time would come when all Israel would no longer serve foreigners (v. 8) but would serve the LORD their God (v. 9).
- Similarly, a future time would come when the LORD would raise an heir of David's family who would reign as Israel's king again (v. 9b). Of course, that heir to David's throne is Jesus Christ!

LIFE STEP Similarly, we do not fear (v. 10) the Lord's purposes for us! The Lord desires to save us from sins and troubles and so we, too, can rest in Him. Notice that a privilege of being saved is that we, too, may serve Him. How can you be about the business of serving the Lord?

WEDNESDAY 23

Jeremiah 31:15-30

What is the writer saying?

How can I apply this to my life?

PRAY China – Special need for study Bibles and children's Bibles and safety for those transporting them.

Today's passage dates from a time between the early deportations of Jews from Judah and Judah's final destruction by the Babylonians. It continues the announcement of a coming new covenant between God and both the house of Israel and the house of Judah (v. 31).

It is a poetic look at Rachel, the mother of two of the twelve sons of Israel (Genesis 42:13), Joseph, father of two of the ten tribes of the Northern Kingdom of Israel, Ephraim (v. 18) and Manasseh, and Benjamin, who becomes a part of the Southern Kingdom of Judah. Rachel's weeping (v. 15) and tears (v. 16) for her children, Israel and Judah, will be rewarded:

- Rachel is granted a renewed hope (v. 17); her children will come again to their own borders (v. 17), that is, to live in their own country.

- The LORD declares that this will be accomplished by creating a new thing in the earth (v. 22). Thus, by special application of His own power, the LORD is going to do something unprecedented in the world, something like His creation of Adam and Eve! Further study of Scriptures reveals that this promise was fulfilled by means of the virgin-birth of Jesus (Isaiah 7:14).

- The result will be a new beginning (v. 27) for Israel and Judah. Just as the LORD had recently overseen their destruction, so in the future He will personally oversee their rebuilding (v. 28).

- There will also be a new covenant between the LORD and Israel, since the former covenant made through Moses (Exodus 19:5) had been broken (v. 32).

LIFE STEP An important detail for us Christians concerning this great prophesy is that included in the "new thing" that God was going to do in the world was the fact that He intended to graft in among the Jews a wild olive branch (that is us Gentiles who have become God's chosen people as Christians! Romans 11:17-24). By this means, God intended for us Christians to also have a *new beginning* in life through the work of the Lord Jesus. How is God's new beginning evident in your life?

THURSDAY 23

Jeremiah 31:31-40

What is the writer saying?

How can I apply this to my life?

PRAY Venezuela – Perseverance and patience for those discipling believers from dysfunctional backgrounds.

These several verses give us the principle articles of the LORD's promised new covenant. First, we note it is a *new covenant* in contrast to the old *Mosaic covenant* between God and the nation of Israel. The principle articles of the new covenant include:

- The new covenant will not be written on tablets of stone but will be a living thing, written upon the hearts of God's people (v. 33). Thus the new covenant is inward in its emphasis. It is personal rather than national, that is, an emphasis upon each individual person coming to faith in the Lord and thus receiving a new heart.

- Israel and Judah, who had been God's people in name only, will be presented by God as "my people" because their hearts and deeds will be truly dedicated to holiness before God (v. 33c).

- All of God's people will know Him. This knowledge will come from the Holy Spirit's new work of teaching believers from within their own hearts (v. 34a; Ezekiel 36:24-32; Joel 2:28; John 14:26).

- The LORD is going to forgive Israel of all her sin (v. 34b). This will be accomplished by means of the substitutionary sacrifice of Christ. He will suffer death and judgment to pay for the sins of all who place their faith in Him (Isaiah 53:4-6; Matthew 26:27-28).

- The LORD Himself will be the One who guarantees this new covenant (vv. 35-40)! God guarantees that He will preserve Israel as a nation (vv. 35-37) and rebuild of the city of Jerusalem (vv. 38-40).

It is very important to understand that this covenant relationship is yet future and pertains primarily to Israel. A failure to differentiate between the *Jew*, the *Gentile*, and the *church* causes much confusion. Read 1 Corinthians 10:32 for a clear indication that these are three distinct groups. While the ultimate fulfillment of the promises of the new covenant will occur during the millennial reign of Christ over Israel, the church participates in some of the benefits of this new covenant.

LIFE STEP God has always been true to His Word. What He promises He will do. He has promised to forgive your sin, to teach you by His Spirit, to write His Word upon your heart. How will He work in your life?

FRIDAY 23

Jeremiah 32:1-15

What is the writer saying?

How can I apply this to my life?

Today we read another of Jeremiah's action sermons, "The Purchased Field" (the seventh of ten). The passage begins with a clear dating of the time which places Jeremiah's sermon in 587 B.C. Thus this takes place during the Babylonian siege of Jerusalem, 588-586 B.C.

Because Jeremiah spoke the truth when he had prophesied that the Babylonians would end their siege by capturing Jerusalem and King Zedekiah, Jeremiah had been shut up in prison by Zedekiah (v. 2).

Now an odd thing takes place. While in prison, Jeremiah is told by God that his cousin would come to him and would ask him to buy the cousin's family farmland saying, "for the right of redemption is thine" (v. 7). When the cousin did come, Jeremiah knew what he must do (v. 8). The cousin was following a provision that God had long before included in the Law of Moses (Leviticus 25:25-28); that is, if a relative is forced to sell the family farm due to poverty, then a relative with the money was to buy it so that the land would stay in the family and as a result the land could be redeemed by the cousin in the future.

The question must be asked, why would you buy a field, paying good money, when you knew that the very parcel bought was soon to be taken and destroyed by the enemy? On the surface this seems to be a foolish purchase making no sense at all. What we must understand is that Jeremiah was not buying land because it was financially profitable, but because he trusted in God's future promises concerning the land!

What Jeremiah was doing was demonstrating simple faith in the Lord. He believed that God would someday give the land back to His people. God intended this action sermon to be a public testimony of Jeremiah's own faith in what he had been prophesying, namely that God was not finished with Israel. While in the near future judgment and exile were coming, God would ultimately restore them to their land.

LIFE STEP When your future seems difficult, you too need to trust the Lord, knowing that He has a plan for your future. Are there things God has asked you to do which will allow God to strengthen your faith?

SATURDAY 23

Jeremiah 32:16-27

What is the writer saying?

How can I apply this to my life?

There was a lot that Jeremiah didn't understand about his situation or God's purposes. His opening words "Ah Lord God" indicate *Lord, things are out of order!* After all, Jeremiah, while unjustly imprisoned in a city under siege for over a year, had been directed by God to buy a cousin's farm a few miles out from Jerusalem in the very area occupied by the invading Babylonians. While Jeremiah's situation was confusing, he continued to be confident in God. Note that he did not allow his own confusion to paralyze his obedience; he bought the land. Yet Jeremiah's response in today's paragraph is an excellent example of a believer's prayerful reply to his own seemingly impossible situations.

- While Jeremiah had troubling issues to bring before God, he begins his prayer, not with his troubles, but with praise. Jeremiah will get a handle on his troubles by reminding himself that God is the great omnipotent Creator for whom "there is nothing too hard" (v. 17).

- Then Jeremiah speaks of the loving-kindness, justice, and wisdom of God (v. 18a). Because God is also omniscient, that is, *all-knowing,* ("Thine eyes are open upon all," v. 19), He is able to recompense or repay justly the sins of men (v. 18). Jeremiah was looking beyond the greatness of the Babylonian army to the greatness of God.

- Next Jeremiah rehearses Israel's history to review the truth that God had always been patient and just with Israel (vv. 20-23). The past actions and deeds of God confirmed Jeremiah's present faith in God!

- Finally, Jeremiah presents his quandary (vv. 24-25), that is, he had purchased the field but the Babylonians are here to destroy all!

Note that God answers Jeremiah (v. 27) with a truth that Jeremiah already knew but needed to again apply, "I am the LORD,.... is there anything too hard for me?" (Compare v. 17 with v. 27).

LIFE STEP Are you facing circumstances that are difficult or even insurmountable? Then it is important for you to get your troubles into a right perspective! Will you begin your prayer time with adoring worship and then with a reminiscing of God's past care for you? Reflecting upon who He is will help you remember that nothing is too hard for Him!

SUNDAY 24

Jeremiah 32:28-44

What is the writer saying?

How can I apply this to my life?

PRAY France – For missionaries to integrate well into French culture and to persevere amidst slow results.

In the verses before us we have the Lord's answer to Jeremiah's prayer (vv. 16-25). The answer is in two parts; first will come the judgment of God (vv. 28-35) against Israel, then the second part gives us the restoration of God (vv. 36-44).

Three times we read of Israel provoking God to anger (vv. 29, 31-32) by means of their sin. They were worshipping other gods, especially Baal (v. 29). Israel's people had increasingly allowed the works of their hands to become evil (vv. 30-31). The people, the political leaders and the religious leaders had turned their backs to God, not receiving His instruction (vv. 32-33). Pagan worship had been set up in the temple (v. 34). Most hideous was their sacrificing their own children in the Valley of Hinnom. They were passing them through the fire unto the god, Molech (v. 35). It is no wonder that the Lord was angry and would bring destruction upon Judah (vv. 28-29).

Jeremiah also got a glimpse of hope as the Lord looks to the future and speaks of the final restoration of a repentant people. Note the "I wills" in the second part of God's answer (twelve occurrences, vv. 37-44; you might want to mark them). Yes, the day would come when the Lord would gather them out of all countries (v. 37) and restore them. This is based on God's *everlasting* covenant (v. 40). This is the same as the *new covenant* we read about in the last chapter (31:31).

Circle the words *as* and *so* in verse 42 and then connect them to show that the same Lord who punishes will bless and restore. Note verse 40 shows that it will be the work of God in their hearts that causes them to one day steadfastly follow God (see also 31:33). This promise will be fulfilled in the kingdom age of one thousand years, after the coming of Christ in power and glory.

LIFE STEP Has your life been in constant turmoil because of God's judgment upon sin in your life? Perhaps you need to be saved from your sin. Perhaps you are already a Christian but you need to now repent of sin that has increasingly produced evil in your life! Just *as* God brings judgment into your life *so* will He bring blessing and restoration.

MONDAY 24

Jeremiah 33:1-13

What is the writer saying?

How can I apply this to my life?

PRAY Bermuda – Pray for unity among believers so that God's agenda can remain the focus of their hearts.

Today's passage presents a second word from the LORD to Jeremiah while he was confined to the palace guardhouse of King Zedekiah, during the siege of Jerusalem by Nebuchadnezzar (32:2) that lasted from 588 to 586 B.C. Jeremiah had been arrested because he had prophesied that the army of the king of Babylon would take the city.

The LORD begins His message by reminding Jeremiah (and all Israel) of both the power and character of the One who speaks: (v. 2)

- The *Maker* of all (i.e., all earth and heaven): A reminder that the LORD has the power to accomplish what He says!
- The *Former* of all: A reminder that the LORD shapes things in accordance with His will. Like a molder of clay (Isaiah 45:9), God formed Adam (Genesis 2:7), the dry land (Psalm 95:5), Israel (Isaiah 43:1), and even Jeremiah (Jeremiah 1:5).
- The *Establisher* of all: A reminder that the LORD not only brought into being all things but also made preparations for and continued to provide for all these things.

From this foundation the LORD reveals to Jeremiah *mighty things* (v. 3), that is, future things that only God could *unlock* about Israel's future. The following secret things are then unlocked for Jeremiah:

- In the near future (in one year!), Jerusalem will be filled with dead bodies of the houses (families) of Judah (vv. 4-5). This will be the result of God's anger upon the wickedness of Jerusalem (v. 5).
- Yet, in the distant future, God says He will turn everything around:
  - "I will bring it health" and "cure them" (of their wickedness) (v. 6).
  - "I will cause the captives of Judah and… Israel to return" (v. 7).
  - "I will cleanse them from all their iniquity" (v. 8).

3. The LORD also promises that people will again sing, "Praise the LORD… for the LORD is good; for His mercy endures forever" (v. 11).

LIFE STEP God is still concerned about cleansing (v. 8) us Christians from our sins today! What sin have you allowed to take up residence in your heart? How can you confess your sin to the Lord (1 John 1:9) so that He might cleanse and cure (vv. 6, 8) you from sin's effect in your life?

TUESDAY 24

Jeremiah 33:14-26

What is the writer saying?

How can I apply this to my life?

PRAY Papua New Guinea – For the unity found in Christ to transcend ethnic differences among believers.

The words "Behold, the days come" are found sixteen times in Jeremiah. It is the word from the Lord about the future. While often they refer to the judgment of the people, the last nine times they look beyond to the millennium when Christ will restore the land to His people. Verse 14 says it simply that He would perform what He promised. This is true with all the promises of God. What He promises He will do! Count on it. Next, He speaks of the Branch of righteousness, the Lord Jesus Christ, as the one who will reign. Both the royal (v. 15) and the religious (v. 16) aspects of His kingdom are seen. Be sure and compare verse 16 with Jeremiah 23:6 where "THE LORD OUR RIGHTEOUSNESS" refers to Christ. Here, (Jeremiah 33:16) it refers to Jerusalem. What it is saying is that the city will take the name of the person reigning in the city. *Jehovah Tsidkenu* identifies both the Son and the city. What a great time of blessing the millennium will be! The Prince of Peace will occupy the city of peace. The place and the person will have the same name for the place is the place of the person. Christ will be preeminent. But how sure of this can we be? The answer, of course, is as sure as the promises of God. What He promised He will perform. But the impact of the promise is seen in the words *if* (v. 20) and *then* (v. 21). That is, the promise is as sure as the covenant (the existence) of the day and the night. We have this reiterated in verses 25 and 26.

LIFE STEP For each believer today, Christ is *JehovahTsidkenu* – The Lord our Righteousness. We have His righteousness (2 Corinthians 5:21). As Edward Mote (1797-1874) said in the hymn "The Solid Rock": "Clothed in His righteousness alone, Faultless to stand before the throne."

WEDNESDAY 24

Jeremiah 35:1-6, 12-19

What is the writer saying?

How can I apply this to my life?

PRAY

Greece - Pray that God would use Greece as a springboard to reach over 20 nations that need to be evangelized.

Events of this chapter took place some fifteen years earlier than chapter 34 (perhaps 601 B.C. and 586 B.C.). It is apparent that Jeremiah placed it here as a contrast between the tenacity of the Rechabites for obedience and Judah's refusal to receive instruction from God's Word (thus, disobedience, v. 13). This chapter is also Jeremiah's eighth action sermon, sometimes called *The Wine Party where no one drank.*

The Rechabites were distant relatives of Jethro, the father-in-law of Moses. Through Jethro, this small group of nomadic foreigners became associated with Israel. Later the Rechabites assisted King Jehu in eliminating Baal worship (2 Kings 10:15-27, 820 B.C.) in Israel. Recently, this nomadic clan had been forced to move within the wall of Jerusalem due to the approach of the Babylonians (v. 11). Their ancestral father had instituted a rule of life for his people that included a command not to drink wine (35:6-10). Thus Jeremiah expects readers to see the faithfulness of the Rechabites to their ancestral father's command when they refused to drink the wine he set before them (v. 5).

In contrast to the Rechabites (vv. 12-19), we find the men of Judah and the inhabitants of Jerusalem rejecting the right way and violating the Word of the Lord. They refused to listen to the Lord (v. 15) or His servants, the prophets. Verses 15 and 16 together clearly point out the contrast, "Ye have not inclined your ear…the sons of Rechab have performed the commandment of their father."

The contrast is clear and pointed. Israel had been put to shame by the honorable obedience and faithfulness of this clan of Gentiles to both their ancestral father and to their adopted God, the LORD God of Israel! How often do we find this so in our day? We find people with little light, even those who are unsaved, that are found more loyal to a right and moral life style than the average believer is to his Heavenly Father.

LIFE STEP

Obedience is so vital to the Christian life. Jesus put it this way, "Seek ye first the kingdom of God and His righteousness" … all other "things" are secondary (Matthew 6:33)! To be honorably obedient to our Lord Jesus, to what will you have to say "no" today?

Jeremiah 38:1-13

What is the writer saying?

How can I apply this to my life?

PRAY El Salvador – For more Bible schools and funds to meet the needs of the staff and students.

Today we skip ahead to the middle of a series of events near the end of the siege of Jerusalem by the Babylonian army (586 B.C.). In the previous chapter, Jeremiah had been cast into an underground dungeon by Jewish leaders only to be rescued by King Zedekiah, who returns Jeremiah to the palace guardhouse.

Apparently Jeremiah used the relative freedom of his palace detention to proclaim his message, *all that remain in this city shall die* … (w. 2-3; cf. 32:1-2); that is, their only hope was to desert to the Babylonians. Apparently enough people were heeding his warning and abandoning the city (v. 4b) that soon four powerful officials (v. 1) went to Zedekiah demanding that Jeremiah be handed over to them to be put to death (v. 4). Sadly, Jeremiah was given to his enemies. They have him lowered into a deep-but-nearly-dry water-storage cistern where he sunk into the mud (v. 6). Here he was left to die without food or water!

But there was a righteous man, who was also a government official, named Ebed-melech (v. 7). This Ethiopian appealed to the king concerning Jeremiah, saying the four officials had done evil (v. 9). As a result, the King allows Ebed-melech to rescue Jeremiah (w. 11-13). Jeremiah was again placed under palace detention and protection.

Let's consider this obscure man of righteous character:

- Ebed-melech set aside personal safety so that he might act with compassion and sympathy towards Jeremiah (Galatians 6:10)!
- Ebed-melech needed great courage to act upon what was right (Joshua 1:7). He would have known that he was risking retaliation.
- Since he was able to greatly influence the king, Ebed-melech must have been of consistent integrity, good reputation, and righteous conduct in previous palace business matters (Ephesians 4:25-29).
- Ebed-melech was a man who trusted in the LORD. As a result he would be commended and defended by the LORD (39:15-18).

LIFE STEP How can you be like Ebed-melech in your world today? How can you determine to do what is right and good in an unpopular situation? How can you choose to be compassionate to someone in need? How can you trust the Lord for His enabling today?

FRIDAY 24

Jeremiah 39:1-2, 11-18

What is the writer saying?

How can I apply this to my life?

As Jeremiah had long warned, judgment day now comes as the Babylonian army captured the north-central part of the city of Jerusalem. The siege had lasted from January, 588 to July, 586 B.C.

By this time, Nebuchadnezzar had put his son-in-law, Nergal-sharezer, in charge. A royal military court inside the city walls demonstrated Nergal-sharezer's authority (v. 3). Nergal-sharezer (directing the captain of the guard, Nebuzar-adan) will finish putting down the Jewish rebellion, preside over the city's destruction, and direct the exile of the captive Jews (vv. 8-10).

Zedekiah still led the remaining Jewish forces in the southern parts of the city (v. 4). Yet knowing all the city would soon to be occupied, Zedekiah flees (v. 4). He is pursued and captured near Jericho (v. 5). Zedekiah is taken to Nebuchadnezzar in Lebanon (v. 5). His sons and all of Judah's nobles are brought before him and killed (v. 6). Zedekiah's eyes are then put out

and he is carried off to Babylon in chains (v. 7) as a war trophy. Sadly, Zedekiah had not listened to Jeremiah's last words of advice (38:17-23) to give the city to the Babylonians, which would have allowed the city to escape destruction!

Be sure to note that this climactic passage begins *the times of the Gentiles*! Daniel will talk to Nebuchadnezzar about this prophecy, referring to Nebuchadnezzar of Babylon as the *head of gold* since he would be the first Gentile king to rule over Jerusalem (Daniel 2:38). Christ referred to it saying, "Jerusalem shall be trodden down of the Gentiles, until the *times of the Gentiles* be fulfilled" (Luke 21:24).

Also in this chapter we have Nebuchadnezzar instructing the Babylonian officials to *look well* after Jeremiah (v. 12). In addition, we have the LORD's announcement that He would care for Ebed-melech since Ebed-melech had endangered himself to rescue Jeremiah (vv. 15-18).

LIFE STEP Be a Jeremiah! He had remained true to the Lord through many years of service. He had always spoken the truth. He had been an example. Yet after the city was destroyed, he chose to continue with the poorest of God's people to whom he could help the most. To whom can you speak the truth? To whom can you be of service?

SATURDAY 24

Jeremiah 50:1-7, 17-20

What is the writer saying?

How can I apply this to my life?

PRAY   Nigeria – For the staggering growth of the church to continue and for the body to become mature.

Our last lesson in Jeremiah tells of God's coming judgment of Babylon. This is the final in a series of prophetic judgments delivered by Jeremiah (chaps. 46-51) against Egypt, Philistia, Moab, Ammon, Syria, Elam, and Babylon. Altogether these prophecies answer the question, "If God would judge His own people (first Israel and now Judah) for their sin, what will God do concerning the conspicuous sins of the heathen nations around Judah?" (*Bible Knowledge Commentary*, v, 1, p 1192)

This begins Jeremiah's longest prophecy (50:1 to 51:64)! A copy was made for Seraiah, the 'quartermaster' (51: 59b) at Jerusalem who would be deported with others to Babylon. Seraiah was to read aloud the scroll (51:61) at Babylon then he was to bind it to a stone and cast it into the Euphrates River while declaring, "Thus shall Babylon sink, and shall not rise from the evil that I (the LORD) will bring upon her" (51:63-64).

Jeremiah was speaking of the Medo-Persian invasion of Babylon (539 B.C.) when they *sank* the city of Babylon by diverting the Euphrates River, which ran under the city walls, creating an entrance into the great city. Yet, this prophecy was only partially fulfilled when Babylon was occupied. Thus the prophecy also looks to the future, to the final fall of religious Babylon (Revelation 17-18, the power center of the Antichrist).

This opinion is corroborated in verses 4 and 5 and 17-20, which speak of that wonderful future restoration of God's people, Israel. There we read, "The iniquity of Israel … and the sins of Judah … shall not be found: for I will pardon them" (v. 20)! God will forgive the sins of His people and will again bring blessing upon them.

As we conclude this study we should remember that Jeremiah has taught us that God cannot tolerate sin. Jeremiah also teaches us that while Judah continued to sin, they were still loved by God. God even promised to ultimately restore them. Today they are set aside, while the Lord Jesus is gathering another people for His name, the church.

LIFE STEP   Remember, God has not changed! Christian, if there is sin in your life, God wants to forgive and restore you, too! Confess your sins to the Lord and He will cleanse you of your sins (1 John 1:9)!

The Book of Acts is a book of transitions. The author, Dr. Luke, is clearly affected by Paul's mission and terminology. Two themes dominated Paul's early writings. In the book of Galatians he confirms that the Gospel he is preaching is not a new gospel but the same gospel that has always been preached. In his second and third epistles (1 and 2 Thessalonians), Paul deals with the fact that the church was an unexpected interruption to the "times of the Gentiles" as sketched out by the Old Testament prophets. This interruption he would later describe as a "mystery" (*musterion*) in the book of Ephesians. For Paul a "mystery" was a previously unrevealed selection of truth and therefore not discussed in the Old Testament. What Paul describes in theological terms, Luke fleshes out in more concrete terms. Luke paints the picture that illustrates Paul's theological presentation.

Luke has already written the gospel that bears his name. That gospel depicts Christ in light of Paul's primary gospel emphases. He now begins a new volume with a new purpose. This is not an extension of Luke. The two should not be considered as two volumes devoted to one subject, that is, recounting the history of the period. In each book Luke is careful to *order* his portrait to communicate two very distinct messages. The message in Acts deals with the subject of God's kingdom, which was promised to Israel in the Old Testament. He answers two specific questions. Why did the kingdom fade into the shadow of the church? And, how did the church assume her role as God's present worship system?

There are a number of secondary transitions in the book but the most important is the transition from the kingdom to the church. The church, which begins in Acts 2 at Pentecost, is not revealed immediately. In fact, it is not until the arrival of the apostle Paul that the *mysteries* of this new age are revealed to us. In Acts chapters 1-6, Peter is the prominent apostle and the preaching is very much geared to the Jewish people and the kingdom they expected. In Acts 3:19-21 Peter preaches as if that kingdom is about to come at any moment.

In Acts chapters 7-12 the narrative begins to move between Peter and Paul. The Gospel begins to expand to the Samaritans who were partly Jewish by descent (Acts 8:14), and to a proselyte who was a Jew only by conversion (Acts 8:36), and to a God-fearer, who was in essence a Gentile (Acts 10:44-45). Acts chapters 13-28 are dominated by the apostle Paul and Gentile missions. This one man in these few years was said to have turned the world upside down (Acts 17:6). Clearly the doctrines of the Church Age are unfolding before our eyes and the kingdom promised to Israel fades into the background.

The book is generally outlined with reference to Acts 1:8, "But ye shall receive power, after that the Holy Ghost is come upon you: and ye shall be witnesses unto me both in Jerusalem, and in all Judea, and in Samaria, and unto the uttermost part of the earth."

I. The Witness to Jerusalem Acts 1-7

II. The Witness to Judea and Samaria Acts 8-9

III. The Witness to the Uttermost Part Acts 10-28

This is a very fair representation of the contents of the book. What we need to understand is that the movement is not just geographical. As the Gospel moves out from Jerusalem and begins to turn the world upside down, the worship and fellowship system that has been in place since the time of Moses is gradually discarded and replaced with a new way *to love God (worship) and love your neighbor (fellowship).* This new *way* is what we presently call the church. It is not a new way of salvation. That can never change. It is a new way to worship God and to love your neighbor. Just as the whole Mosaic system was built upon these two commandments, so the church now fulfills that role.

The changes in the interaction among believers that we see developing in the Book of Acts are a result of the change in ministry focus that occurs. In chapters 1-7 Peter is the central figure. In chapters 8-13 both Peter and Paul are visible. After chapter 13 Peter is almost entirely absent from the accounts. And yet Luke is still focused on the kingdom-promised-to-Israel issue. He opens the book with a reference to this kingdom, "When they therefore were come together, they asked of him, saying, Lord, wilt thou at this time restore again the kingdom to Israel" (Acts 1:6), and closes with a similar reference, "And Paul dwelt two whole years in his own hired house, and received all that came in unto him, Preaching the kingdom of God, and teaching those things which concern the Lord Jesus Christ, with all confidence, no man forbidding him" (Acts 28:30-31).

Luke organized his material so that the reader would not mistake his intent. He wanted the reader to understand that Paul never lost his belief in or his enthusiasm for the kingdom that was promised to Israel. He never broke faith with the Old Testament prophets. He was the apostle to the Gentiles and the revealer of the Church Age, but he never let go of the truth that the Lord might return and set up the kingdom promised to Israel in his own lifetime. Therefore Luke's history of the development of the early church supports Paul's theological teaching that the church does not replace Israel. God has a future plan for both Israel and the church with both categories of believers enjoying the blessings of God forever.

Acts 1:1-11

What is the writer saying?

How can I apply this to my life?

The "former treatise" referred to in verse 1 is the Gospel of Luke (see Luke 1:1-4). As the author of both this book and of the gospel that bears his name, Luke sought to arrange his material in as orderly a fashion as possible (Luke 1:3). Theophilus, literally "friend" (philos) "of God" (theos), was more than likely a wealthy Gentile who could have financed all of Luke's research, writing, and distribution costs.

This first section introduces the major themes that will be developed throughout the book. Luke's selection of this particular question asked by the disciples is not a random choice. It is a carefully designed literary devise used to alert the careful reader to the primary purpose of the writing. The book of Acts is designed to answer this simple question, *Since the Messiah has come, how can the kingdom still remain imminent*? The Church Age and its imminent conclusion at the Rapture allow the kingdom to be an about-to-happen event even though an unexpected worship system has come into play.

Jesus tells the disciples that there will be some momentous changes coming. The pouring out of the Holy Spirit was the first event of this new thing, the Church, but in Joel it was also associated with the start-up of the kingdom. In effect, Jesus was telling them that they did not need to know what was about to happen, but either the kingdom would start or an equally momentous event that required similar manifestations. The Holy Spirit would come as prophesied, but the direction of human history would be determined by something else. Jesus leaves the impression that the kingdom is still a viable option for the disciples.

LIFE STEP We live in a world of *instants* and waiting has become a lost art. If we are ever going to experience everything God has for us, we need to learn to wait on the Lord.

MONDAY 25

Acts 1:12-26

What is the writer saying?

How can I apply this to my life?

PRAY   Ecuador – Pray for God to call more laborers to reach the impoverished of Quito and Guayaquil.

The events recounted in Acts 1:12-26 are a clear indication of the disciples' mindset about the future. They are not planning for the start of a new worship system; they are busy making preparations for the kingdom as promised to Israel. It is clear that the number 12 was not an arbitrary choice for the number of disciples. Jesus had told them that they would sit on twelve thrones and rule the twelve tribes of Israel. But when Peter looks around the room he saw only eleven men who were officially recognized as apostles. The first "act" of these apostles was to replace Judas who had revealed himself to be unworthy of that calling.

The methods that Peter uses to make this decision may seem a little unusual to Church Age believers. We do not cast lots to choose pastors or deacons. Luke includes this as a reminder to the readers that the Church Age has not yet begun. These men are using the methods taught to Old Testament Israel to resolve such a matter. Peter, who was appointed second in command by Jesus in Matthew 16, takes his responsibility seriously and in Jesus' absence uses one of the options available to Old Testament rulers for similar situations. In situations when the king needed an answer from God he could use the Urim and Thummin (part of the High Priest's garments) or he could cast lots. The former were no longer available in Israel; therefore, Peter uses the lots. God's answer is as sure. Matthias is Judas's replacement

This is very important to the theme that Luke is trying to develop. There does not appear to be any doubt in the minds of these men that Jesus is about to return and the kingdom is about to be set up and they have done their duty to ensure that twelve qualified men are ready to rule with Him.

LIFE STEP

Any confusion over how the events in the Book of Acts apply to the church today is a result of not understanding Luke's purpose in writing. The initial "acts" of the apostles were intended to launch the kingdom offered to Israel. This included miraculous acts as *sign-miracles* that God did not intend to be repeated in every generation of the church.

Acts 2:1-13

What is the writer saying?

How can I apply this to my life?

As one travels along any highway in America, there are places where two or more routes join for what is sometimes a significant number of miles. However, the time eventually arrives when the paths part and the driver has to choose which route he wants to take. As we drive that road, there is no way to know which cars will go which way. We are entering just such a period in the Book of Acts. We know which road we are going to take but the rest of the drivers around us have different agendas. We know that the church starts in Acts 2, but for the persons involved in this adventure this has not yet been revealed. The apostles are about to make the same offer to Israel that Jesus made when He was on this earth. They believe that if Israel will repent the kingdom will be set up.

In order for this offer to be legitimate, all of the criteria set down by the Old Testament must be met. One of the signs that the prophets foretold concerning the coming of the kingdom was a general *pouring out* of the Spirit. See Isaiah 32:15; 44:3; Ezekiel 39:29; Joel 2:28; and Zechariah 12:10. The Spirit had been given before to certain individuals but never in such an indiscriminate way. In this case there is a visible and widespread pouring out of God's Spirit upon all who were in that place. This was always intended by God to be a sign of the approaching kingdom, but in this case it is the merging of two roads, of two possible futures. One of those futures, the kingdom, had already been revealed; the other, the church, was only a potential future at this point that had not yet been revealed. It was still a mystery.

LIFE STEP God never intended men to seek miracles for the sake of benefitting from the miracle. The miracle was always a sign of a spiritual reality. We are to pursue spiritual strength and live with a sense of expectancy that He could come for us today.

What is the writer saying?

How can I apply this to my life?

Peter could have chosen any of a number of passages from the Old Testament to explain this event. The crowd standing before him knew their Old Testament and therefore knew that the pouring out of the Spirit was a sign of the coming kingdom. They may not have been willing to accept it, but they were familiar with the concept. Peter chooses to quote from the book of Joel because it is one of the earliest prophetic writings and introduces the coming of the Spirit as a key indicator that must occur just prior to the time of Israel's salvation. The Old Testament did not say that this would be the only time that the Spirit would be poured out but that this event was a necessary first step at that specific time. In this moment two futures coexist in the same way that two routes may exist as a part of the same highway.

The uncertainty is real. Israel faces a very important choice. Will she repent and accept Jesus as her Messiah, or will she continue on the path of rebellion and reject Jesus? Just as the historical nation of Israel stood on the border of the promised land and listened to the report of the twelve spies, the people now stood at the edge of the messianic kingdom and listened to the twelve men who had followed Jesus for the previous 3 ½ years. This was a choice that the nation had to make. Would they step up and claim what God had promised, or would they fall back into the hardship of Gentile oppression? Israel felt that they were indispensible to God because of their necessary part in the kingdom; God is about to demonstrate that we should never try to use prophecy to manipulate God.

LIFE STEP The generation that left Egypt with Moses did not enter the place of promise. They looked at things through the eyes of facts and figures and physical reality. History is repeating itself and God is about to implement another waiting period for His beloved people.

Acts 2:22-36

What is the writer saying?

How can I apply this to my life?

PRAY Cayman Islands – For Christians to spread the Gospel to the millions of tourists that pass through each year.

Having explained the significance of the immediate miracle (tongues), Peter now begins to tie this to the recent events that have taken place in and around Jerusalem. Those recent events would be the trial and crucifixion of Jesus Christ. Peter starts his apologetic with Scripture. The first pillar in his argument is that God had always intended that the Messiah would be put to death and resurrected from the grave. This was the truth that the disciples themselves had difficulty grasping. See Luke 24:46. Throughout Christ's ministry they had resisted this event. They thought that it would disqualify Jesus as their Messiah. But now Peter understands the Old Testament Scriptures and begins to minister to the crowd in the same way that Jesus had ministered to them. He opens the Scriptures and shows them that the crucifixion was not a detour or misstep in the messianic mission. David had clearly revealed such to be the case in Psalm 16. If the Messiah is to provide a new kind of life, the old life must pass. To live with Christ one must die with Christ.

David himself understood this when he penned the Psalm that Peter quotes. He knew that he could not defeat the grave, but he also knew that another would come and that that One would shatter the bonds of death and set the captives free. Jesus led the way into death and back again. David was not speaking of a resurrection; he was speaking of a rescue. Jesus entered the grave to rescue those who had no hope in their own strength.

LIFE STEP Some commentators resist the idea that Psalm 16 is speaking about Christ. They imply that Peter is misusing this passage. This is not the case. To defeat death, the Messiah had to die in order to look death in the eye and walk away the victor.

FRIDAY 25

Acts 2:37-47

What is the writer saying?

How can I apply this to my life?

PRAY Japan – For more men to choose active church ministry over an obsession with career advancement.

The reaction to Peter's sermon is marvelous. In the same way that this message had opened the disciples' hearts, it now pierced the hearts of the assembled crowd. They call out to Peter and ask what they should do. Peter tells them to repent and be baptized. This verse has caused a lot of controversy among believers. On the surface, at least to modern readers, it seems to imply that one must be baptized in order to be saved. But the modern reader is not the intended reader. If a modern believer were to hear in a sermon that one must *die daily* or be *crucified with Christ*, he or she would immediately put that into a proper context. We understand such metaphors.

A Jewish person living in the first century would understand baptism terminology in the context of John the Baptizer. Baptism was simply an outward confession of an inward reality. It was part and parcel of the message that Peter had just preached. Unless we identify ourselves with the death, burial and resurrection of Jesus Christ there is no hope to defeat death. Baptism says that. It is a confession that the person being baptized is renouncing self-righteousness and choosing to be resurrected in newness of life. Baptism is an act of faith and as such is no different than a word of faith. Paul tells us in Romans 10 that we must believe in our hearts and confess with our lips. Confessing with the lips simply means to *officially* agree with God's terms for salvation. Baptism was simply a way of demonstrating that one was in agreement with the death, burial and resurrection provision of Christ.

LIFE STEP God has always designed outward acts of faith to be informative. Baptism is a very memorable way of recognizing that we are buried with Christ in order to be raised in newness of life.

221

Acts 3:1-11

What is the writer saying?

How can I apply this to my life?

The narrative immediately jumps to an incident that takes place shortly after the Pentecost sermon. Peter and John are heading to the temple when they encounter a man who was lame from birth. This is the first miracle recounted since the Spirit came upon the apostles at Pentecost. That Luke spends as much time as he does on the event makes it significant to the central theme of the book. The fact that it created such a stir among the patrons of the temple would clearly indicate that this type of thing has not been happening regularly in Jerusalem even though the Spirit had been poured out. The apostles, led by Peter, were about to embark on a journey filled with wondrous signs and irrational responses. These signs did not randomly occur within that believing community. They are always linked to the apostles.

How and why they are linked to the apostles is what Luke is about to reveal in the coming chapters.

It is also of note that this occurs at the very doorstep of the political body (the Sanhedrin) which had illegally tried Jesus and condemned Him to death. It is open proclamation that the Apostles were finished hiding and that the Good News would continue to be preached publicly and in the power of the Spirit at the very seat of resistance. This Great Light that came out of Galilee was about to turn the ancient world upside down. And at the middle of this storm were twelve rather ordinary guys.

LIFE STEP

We sometimes get so enamored with the miraculous that we forget that such power is always secondary in importance. It is the message that saves. Power like this in the wrong hands is as great a danger as it is good in the right hands. We need to take care in what we ask because power corrupts and total power totally corrupts.

SUNDAY 26

Acts 3:12-26

What is the writer saying?

How can I apply this to my life?

PRAY Australia – Pray for churches to understand the 'post-modern' society in Australia and reach out to generations who increasingly see God as irrelevant.

As a crowd begins to materialize trying to figure out what has happened, Peter seizes the moment and begins to give an explanation for what has just occurred. Peter does not talk about himself and his part in what has just taken place; he talks about Jesus. He talks about His death, burial and resurrection. He keeps it simple. And yet, there is a kind of oddness to this sermon. Consider verses 19-20. Peter is telling this crowd that if they repent and turn to Jesus that Jesus will return from heaven and that He will set up the "times of refreshing" predicted by the Old Testament prophets.

This is why we believe that the Book of Acts is about transitions. Here at the beginning of the book the apostles are still preaching the gospel of the kingdom. They are still convinced that the seventieth week of Daniel 9:24-27 is about to begin. The nation of Israel is being given one more opportunity before

God formally institutes a new worship system, that is, the church. There is no question that the church began at Pentecost; there is uncertainty about when believers realized that the church began at Pentecost. God's knowledge of events is outside of time and allows Him to set events in motion before outcomes are revealed in time and space. The disciples are operating by kingdom principles because they still hope that Israel will accept their Messiah. Until the church is unveiled, there is still a real decision to be made within time. What God knows never invalidates what God offers.

LIFE STEP We are sometimes tempted to belittle the importance of decisions simply because God knows the outcome. Human responsibility is not diminished by divine sovereignty. We know this only because God says so, not because it is reasonable.

Acts 4:1-12

What is the writer saying?

How can I apply this to my life?

PRAY Netherlands Antilles – For doctrinally sound literature to be printed in the Papiamento language.

One cannot help but be impressed with the transformation that has taken place in Peter's life. It was not too long ago that Peter was hiding in the shadows and denying that he even knew Jesus. This was equally true for all of the apostles. The transformation that had begun at the end of Luke's gospel (24:36-49) has so transformed these men that they now stand fearless before the very authorities from whom they previously hid.

Luke makes it a point to list the dignitaries that were present on this occasion. This was not a minor gathering. These were the most important and powerful religious leaders in Israel. These were the same men that had conspired to have Jesus crucified. Luke wants it to be as clear as possible that the religious establishment in Jerusalem were given every opportunity imaginable to repent and accept Jesus as their Messiah. The Gospel did not formally go to the Gentiles until God had exhausted every possibility with respect to Israel. Peter makes this point very clear. Notice his statement in verse 11. Jesus has become the stone which caused Israel to stumble.

Verse 12 indicates exactly why these men could not accept their Messiah. They wanted a salvation that was under their control. They did not want Jesus to be the sole mediator between God and man. They wanted their names to be *up in lights* along with Jesus' name. Salvation is a God thing. It can never be subjected to any human authority. Israel lost it all because she kept holding out for a better deal. With Jesus there are no better deals. He alone can save.

LIFE STEP One of the most difficult things for men to do is to give up all control of their destiny. We always want to have a *security blanket*. Unfortunately, the only thing that can come between us and Jesus is us.

Acts 4:13-22

What is the writer saying?

How can I apply this to my life?

The confrontation begun in yesterday's passage continues to play out in today's. The spiritual leaders of Israel realize that they are at somewhat of a disadvantage. The fact that a forty-year-old man who had been lame for many years is now standing before them a whole man is somewhat intimidating. They are not tempted to believe in the message that was being preached; rather they feared the response of the crowd if they acted too hastily.

Compare this mentality with that of the apostles. While it is true that Peter resisted their instructions to stop preaching the name of Jesus, he did not do so in a disrespectful way. Even though Peter could have felt justified in giving these men an earful, he did not. He honored these authorities in the same way that he would have had they not crucified Jesus. When Peter proclaims that men ought to obey God rather than men, he is not suggesting that believers have no obligation to worldly powers. In fact, he is saying the opposite. The only time that it is appropriate for believers to resist earthly powers is on those rare occasions when the earthly power commands a believer to do something that is the exact opposite of what God has commanded.

On those rare occasions the believer ought to follow Peter's example. He was never disrespectful or confrontational. He showed deference to these men and only objected when they directly forbade the preaching of the gospel. At that point Peter explained his predicament. He did not say one thing and then go out and do another. All his dealings with these authorities were totally transparent.

LIFE STEP Whether at home, at school, or at work, we all have authorities in our lives. Even in difficult times we must honor them.

WEDNESDAY 26

Acts 4:23-37

What is the writer saying?

How can I apply this to my life?

PRAY Bolivia – Revival for churches who are growing in number but lack commitment in their lifestyle.

James captured the spirit of today's passage when he wrote, "…count it all joy when ye fall into divers temptations (various testings)" (James 1:2). The apostles were not unaffected by the threats that they had just received. They returned to the larger group of believers and recounted all that had been said. Notice all the positive blessings that flow out of what many might be tempted to consider a major setback. The immediate response is prayer. This prayer straight away puts the trial into a scriptural perspective. They do not call upon the Lord to remove the threat; rather they ask that they might have the courage to carry on with this important work.

The second thing that happens is that the whole body of believers becomes united. They are together with one heart and one soul. This kind of unity is an awesome demonstration of the Spirit's work. Too often we look for the power of the Spirit to make us special. That does not take any power. It is natural for humans to want to stand out, or be cool, or to do their own thing. What takes a miracle is when a diverse group of believers become one.

Finally, we see the love of the Spirit shed abroad in the hearts of these people. They truly love one another in deeds and not just words. They willingly sell their possessions in order to support the community. If the Council would have known the unifying reaction, they never would have threatened this company of believers.

LIFE STEP Too often when we pray we ask God to change others. We should never ask God to do such a thing unless we have asked God to change us first. By the way, it often happens that when we change, the other person does not need to.

What is the writer saying?

How can I apply this to my life?

The narrative concerning Ananias and Sapphira can be a very chilling one. There does not appear to be any similarity between this event and what one commonly experiences in churches today.

We need to realize that we are still in the transition between the Jewish economy and the church age. The apostles are still preaching the kingdom of God and they are still planning on Jesus returning and setting up His kingdom at any moment. There are a number of comparable incidents that take place in the Old Testament. Achan is destroyed because he stole some merchandise from Jericho. Uzzah is killed because he touched the Ark of the Covenant. Elisha's servant contracted leprosy because he took payment from Naaman. Uzziah was afflicted with leprosy when he entered the temple and offered a sacrifice. During that dispensation, there were different rules than those that govern the Church Age. The events that we read today are a stern warning that Peter and the rest of the apostles were high ranking officials in the coming kingdom. There are some very significant differences between the mediatorial kingdom as it existed in the Old Testament and the Church Age. If we do not keep this in mind, we can be misled by some of the occurrences in the Book of Acts. Many of the uncomfortable occurrences in Acts would be very normal occurrences under the Mosaic system. We need to be careful that we do not use the early part of Acts as a pattern for church administration.

Acts 5:12-23

What is the writer saying?

How can I apply this to my life?

For just a moment it appears that the message of salvation is beginning to win the day in Jerusalem. The sick are being laid out in the streets so that Peter's shadow might fall on them. And yet Israel is about to snatch defeat out of the jaws of victory. Behind the scenes, the same religious leaders who orchestrated the crucifixion of their Messiah were now busy plotting as to how they would respond to this revival. The evil in this world never naps. No good deed goes unnoticed.

While it is specifically the leadership of Israel that is in the crosshairs, it should not be overlooked that the population in general went along with those leaders. This is a hard pill to swallow. No matter how much healing the apostles did, when the time came to choose sides, the people went along with their leaders. Sin damages the heart. People will generally choose that which is in their own self-interest. However, when it is a matter that involves God, people will often choose to die rather than accept a helping hand.

It seems logical that if God opened the doors of the prison to set the apostles free, that this would be evidence that God was working through these men. When people do not want to believe, no amount of evidence is going to change their minds. In Luke 16:31 Jesus told them that even if someone came back from the grave, they would not believe him. All of the events that have transpired in Jerusalem have had little effect except to enrage the officers of the Council.

LIFE STEP Jealousy is a cruel master. One would think that everyone would be encouraged when needs were met and lives were rescued. But it was not so. The leaders of Israel cared more about who got the credit than they did about the suffering of the people.

SATURDAY 26

Acts 5:24-32

What is the writer saying?

How can I apply this to my life?

PRAY

For young people in your church to see the need and commit to full-time Christian service.

It is not hard to sense the court's desperation. They thought this matter would be done with once they had taken Jesus out of the mix. Apparently, they did not think that the disciples had what it would take to carry on the mission. They seem shocked that these twelve uneducated Galileans were somehow turning Jerusalem upside down with their teaching.

As on the previous occasion (4:19), Peter is very respectful in dealing with these rulers. He does not rail against the Council but simply states that whenever he was forced to make a choice between obeying God and obeying man, he would always choose God. This was not a slap in the Council's face because they all would at least technically agree with this statement. In effect Peter was tying their hands.

Peter goes one step further this time. He makes reference to the *signs* that have been taking place all over the city. These things were not rumors coming from another country. These events were taking place right under the Sanhedrin's noses. They could not be ignored. As it was with Pharaoh, these "signs" only serve to harden the hearts of these men. The more love God shows, the more men seem to reject Him. The reason that God did not set up the kingdom in the first century is because His people did not want Him. They wanted a kingdom that was run by their rules and not by God's.

LIFE STEP

Willfulness can have tragic results. We often fight for our own way to our own detriment. It is so easy to get so focused on how we want things to be that we miss all the good things that are happening all around us. Take time to appreciate God's goodness in your life.

Acts 5:33-42

What is the writer saying?

How can I apply this to my life?

PRAY Honduras – For righteous men to be appointed as judges to halt corruption and institutional violence.

This episode may seem even a little humorous to our modern minds (if there can be any humor in a flogging.) The disciples are found innocent but they are beaten mercilessly before being released with a stern warning. This only emphasizes the irrational behavior of the Council. They were so frustrated because every step they took to crush this new *religion* only seemed to breathe additional life into the cause.

Gamaliel is mentioned only a couple of times in Scripture: here and in Acts 22:3 where we are told that he was Paul's teacher. The Talmud (Jewish scriptures) teaches that he is the grandson of Hillel. If such were the case, then he would seem to be a very respected member of the Sanhedrin. That he is not mentioned in the trials of Jesus is a bit of a mystery but he very well could have been out of town. The fact that he seems to be less emotionally caught up in the situation may indicate that he did not participate in the events surrounding Jesus' death. He makes a very good point and the rest of the Council is persuaded to follow his advice. There is an ancient church tradition that Gamaliel converted to Christianity and that he was baptized by Peter and John together with his son and Nicodemus. Whatever the case, he was clearly a respected member of the Jewish council.

As with the first encounter, these events serve only to encourage the disciples and they continue to preach the gospel with even more enthusiasm. In particular they are preaching that Jesus is the Christ, that is, the Messiah who can set up God's kingdom on Earth.

LIFE STEP These early believers constantly turned negatives into positives. They never saw the glass as half empty. They knew that opportunity was always knocking.

Acts 6:1-15

What is the writer saying?

How can I apply this to my life?

PRAY Dominican Republic – For church leaders and their congregation to be good witnesses in tense and inequitable situations.

A growing church is a recruiting church. Leadership is essential for many reasons. In chapter six we are introduced to the second wave of church leadership. While the word "deacon" ("serve" in verse 2) is used in the passage it is unlikely that this is referring to the office of deacon as we understand it today. These men were not initially called to a teaching/preaching ministry but some of them quickly developed into gifted preachers. The immediate need had to do with the serving of the food. In the confusion of numbers, some of the needy were being overlooked at the community meals. The apostles immediately arranged for seven men to be responsible for this area of ministry. Two of these men, Stephen and Phillip, quickly became a part of the preaching team and had an immediate impact.

The text first focuses on Stephen. It is not clear why the Sanhedrin chose to single him out, but it seems likely that they were trying to avoid the public outcry that might have resulted if they grabbed one of the twelve. The text is clear that Stephen was performing many signs and wonders and that people were beginning to recognize his leadership abilities. The council made its first move against Stephen in order to see how such an act would be perceived by the general population. As with Jesus, they put forward false witnesses who claimed that Stephen was speaking out against the Temple and the Law.

 LIFE STEP Serving the Lord in *small* matters is the training ground for future leaders. Never despise those who "serve tables." This is where God looks when the big shoes need to be filled. Start small but always think big.

Acts 7:1-16

What is the writer saying?

How can I apply this to my life?

Stephen's appearance in the text seems so short and yet it is so meaningful. He went from serving tables to standing before the Sanhedrin in just a matter of weeks. This is the longest recorded sermon in the Book of Acts and one of the longest in the Bible. In it Stephen demonstrates an incredible understanding of the Old Testament. He weaves together the old truth with the new truth that was revealed in Jesus Christ in such a way that the crowd is incensed.

The message starts with a quiet tone to it. It has a soothing quality that draws the hearers in. Stephen makes those who have gathered feel comfortable. He speaks of Abraham and Isaac and Jacob. He traces the working of God from Abraham's call in Mesopotamia to his sojourn in Egypt. Stephen rehearses the promises of a son (seed) and the land, which he pointed out to his hearers, where they were now dwelling (v. 4). He then reviews the deliverance and sojourn in Egypt through Joseph.

The main point of Stephen's message is found in verse 51, "as your fathers did, so do ye." Earlier, Jesus made the same criticism of this generation (Matthew 23:31-32). Stephen's message illustrates this history of hard-heartedness and rebellion against God's guidance. One cannot but be amazed at how God uses this *new* convert.

LIFE STEP There is a gap between the objective and the personal. Many of us have a clear and clinical understanding of the gospel and of the Savior, but it has never become personal. What Stephen does in this sermon is make the Gospel a personal matter.

What is the writer saying?

How can I apply this to my life?

PRAY Colombia – For boldness and perseverance among missionaries who live with the threat of violence.

One of the charges against Stephen was that he rejected the Law of Moses. We notice in today's passage that Moses was not immediately accepted by the children of Israel. In fact, while Moses was on the mountain the crowd below forged an idol from silver and gold and danced before that idol as they had done in Egypt. In this message Stephen is making the point that Israel has never changed. He implies that the Council, by failing to accept Jesus, was siding with the crowd that rejected Moses in the first place.

The crowd that faced Stephen knew all of these narratives. Many of them were experts on the Law. They always pictured themselves as the true heirs of Moses and the guardians of his Law. Stephen is suggesting that they are actually the spiritual children of those ancient ancestors who rejected Moses and caused him to flee into the wilderness where he would live for the next forty years.

Human nature is very adept at this very thing. We have no problem seeing the subtle but devastating effects of sin in the lives of others but when the finger of Scripture begins to point our way, we often become blind to the very same danger. The crowd is still calm but the storm is approaching.

LIFE STEP Our towns and cities are filled with churches that no longer preach or teach the gospel as it is revealed by Scriptures. We look around with complacent expressions never thinking that this could happen to us. Peter warned that we must take heed because, when we think we stand, we are often just about to fall.

THURSDAY 27

Acts 7:30-43

What is the writer saying?

How can I apply this to my life?

PRAY Bermuda – For unity among believers so that their testimony will be clear and unhindered.

Today's passage continues with the account of Moses' life. Moses is the one that God calls to from the burning bush (v. 30), and sends to deliver the people from bondage – and for a second time they refuse him (v. 35). Through Moses, God shows His power unto Pharaoh by great signs and wonders. God parts the Red Sea for Israel and causes the same water to drown the Egyptian army. While he is on Mount Sinai receiving the Law, the people's hearts are turning back to the evil ways they learned in Egypt.

Stephen makes one especially important point in these verses. He reminds them that God promised Moses that He would raise up another prophet like Moses from among the people. This introduces the main point of the sermon. If historical Israel would not accept Moses with all the "wonders and signs" that they saw, why would this present generation think that they would receive another like Moses with open arms? Does it not seem likely that Israel would reject the new Moses in the same way and for the same reasons that they rejected the old Moses?

Jesus is that new "Moses." He brought a new revelation from God. He came to His own people with many signs and wonders, but his own people received Him not. They claimed to be followers of Moses but they were followers of the people who had rejected Moses. Stephen is telling them that this is not an exception; this is the way that it always was with Israel. They wanted the Law to serve them; they did not want to serve the Law.

LIFE STEP This is a great truth that each one of us must understand clearly. If we do not take great care, we will always use the Law to promote our own worthiness. Law, as a means to righteousness, was meant to humble us, to break us; it was never meant to empower us.

Acts 7:44-60

What is the writer saying?

How can I apply this to my life?

As we come to the end of Stephen's sermon, we need to ask why Luke spent so much time on this particular sermon. This is especially true since Stephen, apart from this sermon, does not play a very large role in the Book of Acts. There are two important elements within Luke's central message that pivot on the events surrounding Stephen's death.

First, Stephen's sermon explains why Jesus did not return from heaven and set up the physical kingdom right there and then. Why did Israel spend an extra forty years in Egypt? Because they rejected Moses' leadership. Why did Israel spend an extra forty years in the wilderness? Because they rejected Moses' leadership. Was God willing to set up the kingdom that he promised to David right there and then? Yes, He was. The reason that it did not happen was the same reason that Israel had missed out in the past. They rejected Moses, that is, the *other* Moses. Just as He did in the past God gave Israel more than one chance. They had rejected God the first time when they allowed Herod to murder the forerunner, John the Baptist. They had rejected God the second time when they manipulated the Romans into murdering Jesus. Now they reject for the third and final time by picking up stones and with their own hand murdering Stephen, a man filled with the Spirit. In a sense they rejected each member of the trinity.

Second, Luke is about to introduce a new stream of narrative into the story line. That storyline has to do with the redirecting of the gospel to the Gentiles. We will talk about that tomorrow.

LIFE STEP God's grace is a marvelous and powerful thing. There is one thing however that it will never do; it will never force anyone to accept a Savior that they do not want. God's love must be accepted; it will never be forced on anyone.

Acts 8:1-13

What is the writer saying?

How can I apply this to my life?

PRAY South Africa – For the church to cultivate multi–racial relationships and to model unity in Christ.

As mentioned yesterday, the stoning of Stephen is a pivotal moment in the book of Acts. We all recognize these kinds of moments when they occur in modern literature. A new face is introduced into the story line in such a way that everyone knows that it is significant to the development of the plot. So it is here. At the very moment that Stephen lies still on the ground having breathed his last breath, Luke introduces Saul. Saul is not throwing stones but he is sitting off to the side watching over the outer garments of those who were carrying out this deed (See Acts 22:20.).

From this point on the storyline in Acts changes. For the next five chapters the plot alternates between the Twelve and Saul/Paul. Emphasis on the kingdom wanes while talk of the church increases. The kingdom has been offered to that generation for the final time. God's temporary replacement is now beginning to more clearly emerge from the shadows. The man that God uses to define this new age is Paul.

There is a sense in which Paul's life corresponds perfectly with what was happening in the churches. Those who had once been considered enemies and afar off (the Gentiles) were now welcomed into the new worship system without any formal restriction such as circumcision. Paul, who we first meet as an avowed enemy of the Gospel and the last person anyone would expect to be saved, now becomes the primary spokesperson for this new era.

LIFE STEP God's ways are not our ways. We are left to marvel at many of God's choices. If you ever feel that you have nothing to offer, just remember Saul. Who could have guessed?

Acts 8:14-25

What is the writer saying?

How can I apply this to my life?

Philip's trip to Samaria follows quickly on the heels of the introduction of Saul/Paul. It brings the focus back to the Twelve and their ministry while at the same time shifting the focus from a Jewish audience to a half-Jewish audience. Having these two events so close together only serves to reinforce the transitional elements.

Luke also begins to clarify the exact purpose of these *signs and wonders* that have been taking place all over Jerusalem. Remember, God never acts without purpose. In Samaria Philip leads many people to the Lord but Luke focuses on the conversion of a very prominent magician named Simon. This individual had mastered the fine art of the illusion. He immediately understood that Phillip was doing something that he had never seen before.

Simon is even more impressed when Peter and John come from Jerusalem and distribute these *powers* to everyone in the audience. Do not miss this point! Sign gifts were exactly what God said they were, signs! But what were they a sign of? Luke makes it clear that these were the signs of an apostle. Only an apostle could give sign gifts to another person. Other people like Philip could exercise a sign power but they could never distribute such a power to another person.

Nowhere in the Book of Acts or in the remainder of the New Testament does a person exercise sign gifts without having direct contact with an apostle.

LIFE STEP We know from the Book of 1 Corinthians that sign gifts such as tongues did not come without some complications. They could be used inappropriately. That God was willing to allow these "complications" only serves to emphasize how important the apostles were.

Acts 8:26-40

What is the writer saying?

How can I apply this to my life?

PRAY   Aruba – Pray for an end to rivalry among churches, as it hinders the effectiveness of their witness.

The storyline immediately shifts from Samaria to an Ethiopian eunuch. Keep in mind that Samaritans were genetically connected to Abraham. They were in a sense half-Jewish. This gentleman is clearly non-Jewish by genetic standards. However, it becomes clear as one reads the text that he is a proselyte. A proselyte was a Gentile who followed all the requirements of the Law (such as circumcision) so that he was a Jew religiously. Step by step Luke is showing how the gospel expanded from being exclusively Jewish to include an ever-expanding cross section of mankind. Luke is tracing the expansion of the gospel from Jerusalem to Samaria and it is about to explode unto the uttermost parts of the earth. This gentleman from Ethiopia marks another step in this process. His baptism is important because it demonstrates that he is fully accepted into this new worship system and will not have to endure *partial* membership anymore.

For a modern believer all of this seems rather ho-hum, but it was not only revolutionary in that world, it was considered to be heresy. God was introducing a new way to worship and fellowship on Planet Earth. It was an assembly without walls. It was new and shocking to those who had been raised under the Mosaic Law but it was clearly a work of God and not of man.

LIFE STEP   We sometimes miss so much because we ask the text to meet us where we are. We try to uncover some morsel that we can relate to our present experience. Try seeing the text the way the original readers experienced it. That is where the real excitement is.

TUESDAY 28

Acts 9:1-9

What is the writer saying?

How can I apply this to my life?

PRAY New Zealand – For Bible schools and churches to convey a mission emphasis among their people.

Chapter 9 refocuses our attention on Saul who has been commission by the Council in Jerusalem to search out and arrest members of Jesus' group in Damascus. The text describes Saul as "breathing out threatenings and slaughter." This does not sound like someone that would listen to a gospel presentation.

Keep in mind that Saul was being called for a specific purpose. Each of the twelve disciples were directly called by Jesus Christ and they were all directly taught by Jesus. God did not need to use this dramatic event in order for Saul to be converted. He used this very visible sign so that all Christians would clearly understand that Saul was not one bit inferior to the Twelve. In Galatians 1-2, Paul is very adamant that his Gospel, even though it was the same Gospel, originated directly from Jesus in the same way as the rest of the Apostles received their Gospel.

It should be noted that although Saul was persecuting Christians, he was doing so for theological reasons and not from jealousy. He genuinely believed that Jesus was a false Messiah and that he was serving the one true God of the Old Testament Scriptures. This is not to excuse what Paul was doing. Being sincerely wrong is still being wrong. There are many who have done great evil in the name of God. Such evil should not be excused. In the Day of Judgment many will say, "Lord, Lord," but Jesus will disown them by saying, "I never knew you."

LIFE STEP One of Satan's most effective lies is to say that we all serve the same God but He has a lot of different names. There is only one true God and knowing Him is the only way to have eternal life.

Acts 9:10-22

What is the writer saying?

How can I apply this to my life?

PRAY South Africa – Fruitful ministry of the nearly 2,000 South African missionaries serving abroad.

Luke's writings are clearly influenced by Paul's teaching. Yesterday Galatians 1-2 was significant to Luke's story. That was Paul's first letter and the first issue he deals with in his first letter was his own independent status as an apostle. We remember from Acts 1:21-22 that the primary apostles were only chosen from among those who were with Jesus from the very beginning of His ministry and who received their Gospel directly from Him. Paul claims to be an equal with these pillars of the church. He claims that he is different from Stephen and Philip because he was taught directly by Jesus in the same way as the original Twelve.

What Paul says in Galatians is confirmed here in Acts. We might expect that if Paul were such an important addition to the early church that God would have sent Peter to give him back his sight. God does not. Instead He sends Ananias,

a disciple living in Damascus. God is intentionally taking Paul down a path that will demonstrate to all who believe that this man who had once persecuted believers was now to be accepted as a co-apostle with the Twelve.

There is something else that is special about this healing. Only the apostles could give the Holy Spirit to others, but in this case, because Paul was an apostle, no apostle was present when he received this gift. His salvation and call are in every way possible kept distinct from the existing apostles so that he might be an Apostle to and for the Gentiles.

LIFE STEP People often complain that *the devil is in the details*, a colorful way of saying that keeping track of all the details is a difficult task. Luke is a master of the details. God orchestrated every aspect of what was happening in the early church so that His purposes would be absolutely clear. We must always pay attention to the details in Scripture.

THURSDAY 28

Acts 9:23-31

What is the writer saying?

How can I apply this to my life?

PRAY Canada – That increasing political polarization will not threaten the unity and witness of believers.

Saul has an immediate impact in the synagogues because he still had an open opportunity to speak freely. It is a little difficult to see the timeline here in Acts 9, but according to Galatians 1:16-17 Saul spent 3½ years in seclusion in the Arabian Desert being taught by the Lord. As best we can understand, this would seem to have taken place between verses 22 and 23 of Acts 9. What might appear to be happening rather quickly to us ("and after that many days were fulfilled") is really happening over several years. The first twelve chapters of Acts cover over fifteen years. By the time Paul visits the Apostles in Jerusalem over five years have passed since the day of Pentecost. The conversion of Cornelius told in Acts 10 occurs about five years after that.

So, it is not as if Paul gets saved one day and they are trying to kill him a week later. It is also worth noting that Paul's time in the desert allowed the *rumors* of his conversion to become dimmed and when he did go to Jerusalem there was a lot of fear that he might still be on a mission to destroy the church. The fact that the apostles themselves are mentioned as being very careful in this matter reinforces the point that they have not yet met with Paul face to face. It is interesting to note that the persecution of the church eased up for a few years. It is also interesting to realize that it has been ten years since Jesus died and the gospel has not yet formally gone to the Gentiles.

 LIFE STEP When we read a book like Acts we should never read it as *just* history. We can gain insight into the author's message by noting what he left out of the story as well as what he left in.

Acts 9:32-43

What is the writer saying?

How can I apply this to my life?

PRAY   Mexico – For Bible schools to be characterized by doctrinal accuracy, depth, and personal integrity.

Jumping ahead five years, the storyline once again reverts to Peter. The churches in and around Judea and Galilee have been enjoying a time of peace and expansion. It appears that everyone is comfortable with this arrangement. However, Jesus had told the disciples that the witness was to go to the uttermost parts of the earth. It is now time for the next move.

Peter had been travelling throughout the region. Lydda was a town not too far from Joppa, currently known as Jaffe or Yafo (The letter "J" is pronounced as a "Y" in Hebrew). It was a little more than halfway on the road from Jerusalem to Joppa. Luke recounts a healing that happens at Lydda and then Peter is called to Joppa where he raises another saint, Dorcas, from the dead. The fact that the saints called Peter when Dorcas died would seem to imply that Peter may have done this sort of thing before in other locations. There were incredible miracles happening throughout the region but it was still basically a Jewish church. Samaritans and proselytes were welcomed into the church but the big barrier had not yet been breached. We are ten years into the book of Acts and as yet not one Gentile has been welcomed into the church. We may assume that many of the believers were still offering sacrifices and attending services at the temple. But all of this is about to change. Today's passage is designed to set the stage for what is about to happen in chapter 10.

LIFE STEP   So many things that we take for granted in our relationship with Jesus Christ were astonishing developments to those who first experienced them. What is happening here in the book of Acts shook the early church to its very foundation.

Acts 10:1-8

What is the writer saying?

How can I apply this to my life?

PRAY Germany – Salvation of former East Germans who bear the affects of Marxist indoctrination and lies.

To this point all conversions in the Book of Acts have been either Jews, half-Jews (Samaritans), or Jewish proselytes (the Ethiopian eunuch). Cornelius is the first recorded occasion of a Gentile being converted directly to Christianity. The amount of space given it by Luke in the Book of Acts stresses its importance. Today's passage introduces us to Cornelius and the events that led up to Peter's visit. He is called "one who feared God." This designation was used by Jews to refer to a Gentile who was unwilling to fully convert to Judaism, but who was committed to both monotheism and to the Jewish ethic. For the most part Cornelius would follow Jewish practices but would be uncircumcised. Tomorrow in verses 9-22 we will examine Peter's vision. In that vision Peter sees a "vessel." The word itself is so flexible that it could be translated "thing." Contained in the "vessel" were a large variety of domesticated and wild mammals (four-footed beasts and wild things), reptiles (creeping things) and birds (fowls). The common tie between all these was the fact that they all were unclean, that is, forbidden by the Mosaic dietary laws (see Leviticus 11).

God is preparing Peter for the delegation that was about to arrive from Cornelius. God also wanted Peter to realize that He had the right to change certain aspects of His program. The Gospel was about to make an incredible leap; so much so, that in a few short years the church would become almost exclusively Gentile.

LIFE STEP Cornelius may at times have wondered if his commitment to the God of the Jews would ever result in anything good. His piety did not go unnoticed. God does not miss the smallest offering made in His name.

Acts 10:9-22

What is the writer saying?

How can I apply this to my life?

PRAY   Pray for those who teach in your church to be faithful to the Word.

Peter is not immediately sure what the vision means. While he is trying to figure it out, the delegation from Cornelius arrives and the Spirit clearly instructs Peter that their arrival is in conjunction with the vision. Based on the discussion in verse 22, it would appear that at least one of this group was Jewish. Most likely both of the servants were.

The phrase "doubting nothing" in verse 20 is very instructive. Clearly under normal circumstances Peter would have doubted that taking the gospel to Cornelius was the right thing to do. Peter was still in the *go-only-to-the-lost-sheep-of-the-house-of-Israel* mode. Had he not had the vision come to him, he would have most likely dismissed Cornelius's vision as some cruel hoax. But now, through the eyes of faith, Peter was beginning to get a glimpse of just how the Gospel was to go "unto the uttermost parts of the earth."

How does a man who sat and listened to Jesus say, "Go into all the world," become so limited in his thinking? Constantly throughout the Gospels and in the book of Acts the Apostles underestimated the power and the breadth of God's program. Up to this point, Peter probably thought this command was referring to the Jews who were scattered through the Roman Empire. He may never once have considered that God was about to turn the whole world upside-down.

LIFE STEP   In a similar fashion to Peter, we sometimes underestimate the extent to which God wants to work in our lives. We are happy with the portion we have. Let us pray that God will enlarge our vision in order that we might endeavor to do the great work to which God has called us.

Acts 10:23-33

What is the writer saying?

How can I apply this to my life?

PRAY Korea – For the message of the gospel to penetrate North Korea's isolation from the modern world.

It should be noted that Peter did not enter into this meeting without trepidation. He clearly has many misgivings about a Gentile becoming a part of the family of God without first going through some initiation into the nation of Israel. Peter was still under the impression that salvation was primarily a Jewish thing. One can almost feel the awkwardness as Peter and Cornelius meet for the first time. Peter is struggling with a lifetime of teaching that told him everything about this situation was wrong, and Cornelius was overwhelmed with the possibility that he could be accepted into the family of God as a full partner and no longer have to worship as a second class citizen.

The contrast between the two could not be greater. One was a soldier and, while he may have had a special place in his heart for the Jewish people and their God, as a general rule, soldiers were despised by the religious Jews. The other was a Galilean fisherman, a man that most soldiers would not consider much above a slave or a piece of property. And yet here on this day God had brought them together to participate in one of the greatest peace accords ever recorded in human history. A wall that had existed for untold generations was about to come down. The event that occurs on this day will shape the history of the world for the next two thousand plus years. The gospel is about to go international. The church is about to engage the whole world.

LIFE STEP As we read the Book of Acts we sometimes are amazed by the miracles that Peter and the other apostles performed. Don't miss the gift inside because of the awesome wrapping on the outside. God is doing something really big here in Acts 10.

Acts 10:34-48

What is the writer saying?

How can I apply this to my life?

PRAY Indonesia – For missionaries to reach every inhabited island to share the Gospel.

Peter's message is short and to the point. He opens with a very important statement, one that will be debated throughout most of the rest of the Book of Acts. That issue has to do with the Gospel and the Gentiles. Peter, in verses 34-35, sets forth a new and powerful truth very clearly. The Gospel is in no way limited to the Jews. It is available to all men, no matter what their nationality, without any connection to the nation of Israel. A man did not have to become a Jew in order to be saved.

Notice the elements contained in this message. These are the same components that would become the essentials of Paul's gospel. First Peter establishes the deity of Jesus. In verse 36 He is called Jesus Christ and "Lord of all." Next Peter emphasizes Jesus' humanity. He is Jesus of Nazareth and empowered by the Holy Spirit. His death and resurrection are described in verses 39-41. Because of these things salvation from sin is available to all men by faith (v. 43). Notice the opening phrase of verse 43; all of these things were according to the Scriptures. This simple gospel message marks the first time that all reference to the nation of Israel is removed. Peter, who was first given the keys to the kingdom, has opened the door for a truly international gospel.

In all times of great change God has validated these changes through the use of signs and wonders. So it was that when Cornelius responded in faith to Peter's message there was an outpouring of the Holy Spirit similar to the Day of Pentecost. Peter correctly accepts this outpouring as the divine seal of approval on the preceding events.

LIFE STEP The gospel has never changed. Salvation has always been by faith. However, how God makes His gospel known sometimes does change.

WEDNESDAY 29

Acts 11:1-15

What is the writer saying?

How can I apply this to my life?

PRAY Bulgaria – For freedom from the media and local government's constant attempts to obstruct any form of evangelical outreach or growth.

It is in our nature as men to resist change. But our God is not a dead or stationary piece of gold or silver such as many men worship. He is a God who has instituted many dramatic changes in His workings with the human race. When Peter returns to Jerusalem with his account of the Gentile conversions, there is a great stir among the Jewish believers. They immediately react negatively to the very idea that a Gentile could be saved without first converting to the Jewish faith. Peter, however, is very forceful in his retelling of the events that led him to share the Gospel with Cornelius. He is absolutely clear that it was God who had initiated this change and not he.

We should note however that this change was instituted only on the basis of clear and authenticated revelation from God. It was not just a response to changing culture and moral values.

Truth is eternal. Programs can change. These changes are always done in such a way that there can be no question as to Who has instituted it. Peter not only had the vision. His decision was verified by an outpouring of the Holy Spirit at Cornelius's conversion. This outpouring of the Spirit resulted in the distribution of *sign gifts*. These gifts have value only when there is an event or messenger that needs to be authenticated. Signs without the thing that is to be signed are a contradiction.

LIFE STEP Imagine you are travelling along an interstate highway. Your tank is on empty and you see a sign for a gas station. You pull off at the exit and find that the sign is there but no gas station to accompany it. You feel deceived. So it is with signs and wonders; where there is no new revelation, there are no signs.

247

Acts 11:16-30

What is the writer saying?

How can I apply this to my life?

Even though a Gentile *God-fearer* named Cornelius had already become a believer, there was still no concerted effort to reach out to the Gentiles as a whole. Verse 19 makes this very clear. But a Gentile outreach was beginning to occur in Antioch. Barnabas (his name means *comforter*) was sent by the church in Jerusalem to make sure that the new churches being formed in Gentile regions were being formed in a godly manner. But God had a different mission for Barnabas. He did not remain in Antioch, but was sent from there to Tarsus to seek a new believer named Saul. For one year Saul and Barnabas ministered in the church in Antioch. The church needed to be sure that these two men met the qualifications essential for missionary service. They did not want to commission them too quickly.

The gift of prophecy (a sign gift) was very important to the early church. It not only served to authenticate the apostolic ministry, but it also provided much needed direction to a church that had none of the books we now know as the New Testament. Both of these needs, however, disappeared with the completion of the New Testament and the passing of the apostles. One such prophet is Agabus. The prophecy here concerns a famine that will affect the whole Roman Empire. That famine did indeed take place during the reign of Claudius (41-54 A.D.). This prophecy had a profound effect on the church. They were immediately concerned not for themselves but for the church in Judea.

LIFE STEP Many years have passed since the Lord confronted Paul on the Damascus road. Paul has spent many years in preparation for his role as an apostle. Always seek to do the Lord's will in the Lord's time.

FRIDAY 29

Acts 12:1-11

What is the writer saying?

How can I apply this to my life?

The "Herod" mentioned in this chapter is Herod Agrippa II, a grandson of Herod the Great. Under this persecution, James, the brother of John, became the first apostle to be martyred. Verse 3 gives a good picture of the general response of the Jewish community to Christianity.

The reason Peter was not immediately executed was because of the Feast of Unleavened Bread. This took place during the seven days immediately following the day of Passover (today the two holidays are combined into the *Week of Passover*). Because these were holy days the Jews would not look favorably on any execution during this time. The word translated "Easter" in verse 4 is actually the word for *Passover*.

The story of Peter's miraculous rescue from prison is very popular. It does, however, raise a question. Why did God engineer such a miraculous escape for Peter but let James die? It appears that God's plans for each person are individually designed for that person.

Peter's release from prison is one of the most dramatic events in the whole of the Book of Acts. He is not only in a prison cell but he is chained between two soldiers. Perhaps the Romans remember how Jesus mysteriously disappeared from a sealed tomb. His life is in immediate jeopardy, but Peter sleeps soundly. An angel awakens him. Peter's response to this escape is very revealing. He is apparently in some sort of trance during the rescue (vv. 8-10) and finds himself alone and free on a Jerusalem street. He was so amazed by what the Lord had done that it was not until he was standing alone on the street that he was able to accept that this had actually happened.

 LIFE STEP Rejoice that God's plan for your life is uniquely tailored for you and cannot be compared with His plan for anyone else. We each must bear our own cross and not seek to be trading crosses with our neighbor.

SATURDAY 29

Acts 12:12-25

What is the writer saying?

How can I apply this to my life?

PRAY Bolivia – For boldness and integrity as national leaders attempt to shut down the cocaine industry.

In today's passage Luke describes the response of the believers who have been praying for Peter's release. A prayer meeting is taking place at a house owned by Mary, John Mark's mother. A young girl, Rhoda, responds to Peter's knock at the door. She is so excited to tell those who are praying about what has happened that she forgets to open the door. Peter stands outside while she tries to convince those who are praying for Peter's release that Peter has actually been released. What a shock they received when the door is opened and there stands Peter.

Another response to Peter's release is recorded by Luke — Herod's. Unable to accept the supernatural, he assumes that it is an inside job and has the jailers executed. His failure to execute Peter so shamed him that he left Jerusalem and went to Caesarea. This effectively ended that particular series of persecutions.

Herod's story does not end there, however. Josephus, a contemporary Jewish historian, records that Herod stood proudly in his robe of silver so that the people called out and declared him to be a god. "At the same time he was seized by a severe pain in his belly, which began with a most violent attack. He was carried quickly into the palace, and when he had suffered continually for five days from the pain in his belly, he died, in the fifty-fourth year of his age and the seventh of his reign." Herod's power to hurt the church had been taken from him, but the word of God, which he attempted to stifle, flourished.

LIFE STEP Herod's audacity only served to embolden and empower the spread of the Gospel. Expect resistance but do not be discouraged by it. God is still in control.

SUNDAY 30

Acts 13:1-13

What is the writer saying?

How can I apply this to my life?

PRAY Jamaica – Leadership within the government and churches to be untainted by corruption or compromise.

The church at Antioch must have been quite a place. Verse one gives a list of some of the prominent men who ministered there. Paul and Barnabas are well known characters in the New Testament. Simeon and Lucius are not so. Some have suggested that Simeon is Simon of Cyrene who carried the cross of Christ. In Mark 15:21 we are told that he had two sons, Alexander and Rufus. The fact that Mark mentions them is a clear indication that they were known to the Roman churches. (Mark's gospel was written for Roman Gentiles.) Paul in Romans 16:13 makes reference to a Rufus and to his mother, "Salute Rufus, chosen in the Lord, and his mother and mine." It is possible that Paul considered the mother of Rufus as a mother because he stayed with them while he was in Antioch.

It would appear that the church was seeking direction for its next move. The decision to select Paul and Barnabas seems to have come unanimously. The four prophets who ministered in that church were in agreement. It is important to note that the church fasted and prayed about direction and did the same once they had received it. They did this even though they had "prophets" in their midst. Thus Paul, Barnabas and John Mark set out on the first of three great missionary journeys recounted in the Book of Acts. The first thing they encounter is opposition. Herod may have been removed, but Satan has many ways to resist.

LIFE STEP Prayer can easily be put on the back burner. When we are seeking for direction in a particular area, prayer comes naturally. But once we receive that direction we often charge into the fray without sufficient prayer to ensure success.

Acts 13:14-25

What is the writer saying?

How can I apply this to my life?

PRAY Slovakia – For financially secure believers who will sponsor the Bible training of young Slovakians.

A group of three set out from Antioch on this first missionary journey. Paul and Barnabas are well known but in today's passage we focus on the third member, John Mark. It was at his mother's house that the church had prayed for Peter. Their journey brought them first to the island of Cyprus. They traveled the island from east to west, starting out in the capital of eastern Cyprus, Salamis. They then traveled to what is now known as Asia Minor (modern Turkey). John Mark abruptly leaves the party. Little is said of this but Paul and Barnabas will later part company over Mark's worthiness for service.

As Paul enters into the city of Antioch in Pisidia we begin to see a pattern that he would follow in all his missionary journeys. He first announces the Gospel in the synagogue. Why Paul chose to do that probably has more to do with practical matters than theological.

Members of the synagogue would know much of the background material necessary to give the Gospel a context. Furthermore, the God-fearing Gentiles associated with the synagogue would give Paul an open door into the non-Jewish community. The phrase and "ye that fear God" would be a direct reference to those God-fearing Gentiles present in the synagogue. This in a sense mimics the greater commission given to the Twelve for Jerusalem (Jews), Samaria (half-Jews and proselytes), and the uttermost parts (God-fearing Gentiles).

LIFE STEP Paul always followed the path of least resistance when he approached the evangelism of a city. He never compromised the Gospel but he always sought the best place to gain a beachhead. He used the opportunities at hand to the best of his ability. He didn't try to reinvent the wheel. A key to ministry is to make the most of the opportunities God provides.

TUESDAY 30

Acts 13:26-41

What is the writer saying?

How can I apply this to my life?

PRAY Chile – Reconciliation among believers who have been deeply divided by past political problems.

This passage, combined with tomorrow's, contains the heart of the Good News that the apostle preached. The city is Antioch in Pisidia, a province in Asia Minor. Paul is in the synagogue on the Sabbath and is invited to address the audience. His sermon began in 13:17. It is clearly geared toward the predominantly Jewish crowd that is before him. We pick up the sermon at verse 26.

In 1 Corinthians 15:3 Paul later writes, "For I delivered unto you first of all that which I also received, how that Christ died for our sins according to the Scriptures." Three times (verses 27, 29, 33) in this opening portion Paul emphasizes that the things that happened to Jesus Christ were not a failure in God's plan. Rather these things all happened according to the preannounced plan of God. This was an important point to Paul and ought to be an important point with us. God always intended that Jesus should die as He did. It was all a part of God fulfilling His promise. There is clearly continuity between the Old Testament and the New Testament. The barrier is found in the fact that the nation of Israel has misunderstood the Old Testament.

In like manner, all the opposition we encounter is a part of God's plan. Paul never even considered that the things he suffered were not a part of God's plan. Read 2 Corinthians 12 to get an overview of the kinds of opposition that Paul faced. Acts only shares a small part of the story.

LIFE STEP

The gospel did not appear in a vacuum and it cannot exist in a vacuum. The Old Testament is a necessary background to the gospel message. Without it we have no way to understand the significance of many of the things that happen in the New Testament. The New Testament adds to the Old and completes the Old; it does not replace it.

WEDNESDAY 30

Acts 13:42-52

What is the writer saying?

How can I apply this to my life?

PRAY Fiji – For the success of church planting ministries, as Mormons and Jehovah's Witnesses grow in numbers.

Spiritual blindness is a cruel master. It not only blinds a person's heart and mind but it seeks to impose this blindness on others as well. So it was with the Jews in Antioch of Pisidia. They not only rejected the Gospel themselves but they did not want anyone else to accept it. In this pattern the world has not changed. In a society that accepts all manner of immoral behavior and protects it as a minority, there is only one group that will not be tolerated – those who stand for truth. Those who defend God are called bigots and enemies of freedom.

These Jews, as they did with Jesus, used the courts and civil authorities to do their dirty work. Their concerns were not a misguided zeal for the souls of men but for their own pocket books and their own reputations within the community. This radical idea that salvation was absolutely free shook them to the core. But it was when they saw people leaving their assembly and converting to Christianity that they became envious. The act of shaking the dust off their feet was instituted by Jesus in Luke 9:5 and Matthew 10:14. The act was specifically directed toward the Jewish community rather than the city as a whole and was a symbol of excommunication and tantamount to calling a man a heathen. The believers who remained behind were not discouraged by this turn of events but filled with joy and the Holy Spirit.

LIFE STEP The Gospel is as much a tool of division as it is of unity. To those who believe, it is the tie that binds our hearts together in Christian love; to those who reject it is a stumbling stone and matter of much resentment.

THURSDAY 30

Acts 14:1-13

What is the writer saying?

How can I apply this to my life?

PRAY North Korea – For the unblocking of Christian radio broadcasts that reach into North Korea with the Gospel.

Paul and his band of missionaries proceed to Iconium, where once again he begins his ministry in the Jewish synagogue. As in Antioch of Pisidia, there is an immediate and sizable response to the gospel among both the Jews and the Gentiles. The opposition once again originates with the Jews. They begin a propaganda campaign that poisons the minds of the civil authorities and once again Paul is forced to leave the city for fear of his life. Perhaps we could conclude that Satan won another victory, but that is not the case. In reality this may be better viewed as God's way of keeping His missionaries on the move. It is always interesting to realize that many of the persecutions that the church experienced were almost like throwing oil on a fire.

The missionaries now move on to the Derbe/Lystra area. In Lystra Paul is preaching and sees a man who has been crippled from birth. Perceiving that he has the faith to be healed, Paul commands him to stand up. When he does, the crowd jumps to a very wrong conclusion. They assume that Paul has done this in his own power and that he must be a god. Thus begins a sequence of events that will have severe consequences later in this chapter. This illustrates another danger that is always present when sign gifts are used. There is always the temptation to magnify the sign above the message. People do want the miracles but often that is all that they want.

LIFE STEP Life isn't fair and trials cause us to grow strong. Today's passage certainly reinforces that idea. Paul only wanted to help people and for his efforts they plotted to kill him. These events had two specific purposes. They were exactly what Paul needed and they furthered the plan of God.

Acts 14:14-28

What is the writer saying?

How can I apply this to my life?

PRAY Japan – For the Holy Spirit to help believers overcome ancestral influences by the study of God's Word.

We pick up the story from yesterday. The crowd mistakenly considers Paul to be one of the gods and starts to worship him. When he refuses their worship the crowd turns on him. Urged on by enemies who have followed the missionaries from Antioch and Iconium, the crowd stones Paul and leaves him for dead.

Luke repeatedly indicates the plotting of the Jews to discredit the Gospel and to hinder its progress. This is clearly a part of the argument of the book. The Gospel has been sent to the Gentiles because the Jews have rejected it. In verse 19 it is at the urging of Jews from Iconium that the people in Lystra stone the Apostle. Being left for dead, he is revived shortly after the crowd leaves and after briefly returning to the city, he heads for Derbe. Some have associated Paul's description in 2 Corinthians 12:2-4 with this event. From Derbe Paul backtracks through the cities that he has already visited.

In each one he "ordained" elders. Right from the start local churches were given autonomy. Paul established local leadership in each assembly that had been born during his initial contact with these cities. The fact that Paul authorized these leaders does not mean that they were not recommended by the assemblies themselves. Additionally, if Paul had made these decisions by himself, it was designed to initiate the process in churches that knew little of church organization.

LIFE STEP Local churches were planted by the apostle Paul but they were not controlled by him. Each church was ruled by men chosen from their own midst. This is one of our most important responsibilities as believers: to appoint leadership within our churches that will honor God and allow the church to flourish.

Acts 15:1-12

What is the writer saying?

How can I apply this to my life?

As the Gospel spread to the Gentiles an inevitable controversy began to arise. Do Gentile believers need to be circumcised? When the Gospel was almost exclusively Jewish this was not a problem, but as more and more Gentiles entered the church, there arose a faction within the community of believers that insisted that Gentile believers must be circumcised. These discussions became rather intense — so intense that it was decided to send a delegation led by Paul and Barnabas to Jerusalem to meet with the elders of that church and the other apostles to resolve this matter.

The converts within the Jerusalem church who were advocating Gentile circumcision were converted Pharisees who had a hard time letting go of their ceremonial past. Peter, as the leader of the Apostles, is the first to speak. It was Peter who had opened the door to Gentile conversion in Acts 10 when he preached to Cornelius, an uncircumcised Roman soldier. He asks, if the Holy Spirit accepted Gentiles apart from the Law and circumcision, why should we as men try to require it? Peter's characterization of the Law as a "yoke" is very appropriate. It seems that the more legalistic believers were arguing that it should be used as a means for sanctification (spiritual growth) at a minimum and maybe some were even requiring it for justification (salvation). In the book of Galatians (which was written about this time) Paul seems to indicate that the biggest issue was with respect to sanctification.

LIFE STEP Rules and regulations, whether in the Old Testament or the New, were always meant to be a diagnostic tool. God never suggested that they could make anyone righteous. Laws can tell us we are sinners but they cannot do anything about the problem. For that we need faith in God and His provisions for spiritual growth.

SUNDAY 31

Acts 15:13-29

What is the writer saying?

How can I apply this to my life?

PRAY Costa Rica – For the youth to turn to the Gospel and not to drug addiction for comfort.

After unrecorded speeches by Paul and Barnabas, James addresses the assembly. This James is not the brother of John but is the *half-brother* of Jesus and the author of the book of James. He appears to be the chief elder in the Jerusalem church. The fact that he makes the final decision is very appropriate. According to Galatians 2:12, many of those claiming that circumcision was required were using James's name in support of these claims. Also, James would be held in high esteem by the believing Pharisees, since he was one of them. Finally, since he was the senior pastor in Jerusalem, it was only appropriate that as a matter of respect he be given the last word.

James's conclusion amounts to an all-out victory for Paul and Barnabas and the *apart from the law* gospel they have been preaching. The three restrictions that James places on this decision are included to address some practical problems that could result from this ruling. If Jews and Gentiles are to live harmoniously in the church, it is imperative that the Gentiles be sensitive to the Jewish believers. Since meals were an important part of the lifestyle in the early church, James suggests two ways that Gentiles could help their Jewish brothers feel more comfortable. Food offered to idols and animal blood (by itself or in the meat) would be particularly offensive. The Jewish community was used to a high standard of morality, but Gentile believers were not. James feels that for fellowship to continue, Gentiles must adopt a more biblical form of sexual purity.

LIFE STEP To flaunt our Christian liberties in the face of those who have sensitivities different from ours is as wrong as requiring circumcision to be saved. Enjoy your liberties but use them wisely.

Acts 15:30-41

What is the writer saying?

How can I apply this to my life?

Even spiritual leaders can have legitimate disagreement. Paul and Barnabas were both filled with wisdom but disagreed about whether or not Mark should go with them on their second missionary journey. Paul objected to Mark going because Mark had quit the team in Pamphylia on the first missionary journey. His desertion had probably caused a number of hardships.

Barnabas, however, was Mark's relative and he saw qualities in the young man that Paul did not. Both men stuck to their positions and the result was a division between the two. Instead of one missionary team, there were now two. Whether there was a right or wrong in this dispute is immaterial. Paul, to his credit, later commends Mark in his epistles (Colossians 4:10; Philemon 24; 2 Timothy 4:11). It would appear that God used this circumstance to double the missions program of the church at Antioch. Was Mark ready to go with Paul at that time? Probably not. Did he need the discipleship that Barnabas could give? Probably. In the final analysis, this legitimate disagreement was resolved in such a way that everyone involved benefited.

Silas is chosen as Paul's new partner. Silas had been sent to Antioch by the Jerusalem church after the council in chapter 15. This benefited Paul when the false teachers claimed that they were officials of the Jerusalem church. He also, like Paul, was a Roman citizen, a fact that provided much legal protection and could open many doors.

LIFE STEP   As believers it should be our policy to avoid conflict as much as possible. There are times, however, when we must take a stand. If we do so in the right spirit, as Paul and Barnabas did, such confrontations will result in positive consequences.

Acts 16:1-13

What is the writer saying?

How can I apply this to my life?

PRAY Romania – Funding and godly staff for the expansion and establishment of Bible schools and seminaries.

Paul and Silas recruited Timothy, a young man who was probably saved during Paul's first visit to the city of Lystra. They were planning to continue their work in Asia Minor. The churches were young and the needs were great. The fields were truly "white unto harvest" (John 4:35). Twice they attempted to enter regions that they had not formerly visited and twice they were forbidden by God. The exact manner by which God communicated His desires to Paul is not stated. It may have been by prophecy or direct communication to the apostle. The effect, however, was clear. The missionary team was being pushed to the west and the north.

On the northwest corner of Asia Minor was the port city of Troas. It was there that Paul received what is known as the *Macedonian Call*. God used a vision to communicate this call to Paul and immediately the apostle made plans to cross over to Macedonia. Notice Luke's use of the word "we" in verse 10. It can be assumed that Luke joined the party in Troas. This is the first of several "we" sections as Luke intermittently joins the missionary team. These "we" sections are further proof that Luke was indeed the author of this book.

Paul heads to the major city in that part of Macedonia, Philippi. It was a colony started by the Romans for military purposes. It would therefore be very familiar with Roman law. This fact would come into play when Paul revealed his Roman citizenship to the magistrate.

LIFE STEP Clearly Macedonia was not Paul's first or second choice for missionary service, but we need to be a light where God has placed us; not discouraged because we wish we were somewhere else.

What is the writer saying?

How can I apply this to my life?

PRAY Angola – For the Holy Spirit to ignite a passion for youth evangelism among believers.

Luke chooses to record three conversions that occur in Philippi. The first was Lydia, a God-fearer (16:14). It would appear that there was no formal place of worship such as a synagogue in this city. The Jewish community was either too small or nonexistent. Traditionally, in such cases Jewish people worshipped near a body of flowing water. Therefore, Paul went to the riverside on the Sabbath where Jews, proselytes and God-fearers might worship. It was one of these God-fearers that responded to the gospel and offered her home as a center for Christian worship.

The second convert is entirely different from the first. A young slave girl who was possessed by a "spirit of divination" took it upon herself to advertise for the apostle. Her ability to tell the future was a very marketable commodity in that city. The word translated "spirit" is "pythoness." Clearly this future-telling ability was given to her by demonic powers. In an obvious case illustrating that the ends do not justify the means, Paul rejects this woman's endorsement and casts out the demon that had been afflicting her.

The matter with the fortune-teller creates enough of a stir that Paul and Silas were brought before the magistrate who orders them to be beaten and cast into prison. It seems clear that the Gospel has the ability to offend people no matter where it is preached. From a human perspective things do not look very promising. But God's ways are not our ways. All of these things had a purpose and tomorrow we will appreciate the beauty of God's plan.

LIFE STEP Many who labor in the field of Christian service become discouraged when the opposition seems to be winning. We sometimes even mutter, "Good guys always finish last." The facts are exactly the opposite. Only the good guys finish. Cheer up, God knows and God has a plan.

THURSDAY 31

Acts 16:25-40

What is the writer saying?

How can I apply this to my life?

PRAY Panama – For this nation of diversity and potential to be used to bless the world.

Paul and Silas could not have been very comfortable as they sat in the dark and gloomy dungeon at Philippi. Their backs were raw from the beating they had just endured and the stocks made getting into a comfortable position impossible. The fact that they could not sleep did not discourage them. At midnight they are still singing praises to God. In James 1:2 and Romans 5:3 the Scriptures command us to rejoice no matter how evil the times may be. We often dismiss this as some kind of *deep* joy that dwells at the core of our hearts as outwardly we agonize about a particular situation. Paul and Silas were singing. This was not manufactured emotion. It was two guys who trusted God and knew that whatever happened to them was in God's plan and therefore the best thing possible.

At that point, an earthquake rattles the prison and every door is opened and all the restraining devices come off the prisoners. The jailer is the third convert we are told about in Philippi. He, assuming that the prisoners have fled, is about to kill himself when Paul calls out from the cell. Not only were Paul and Silas still there, but all the other prisoners, as well. The jailer reacted in a totally different way to his trial than did the missionaries. He didn't know the God who ruled the universe so that rather than rejoice in difficulties, he panicked and was about to commit suicide. The difference between the two was the hope that believers have in their Lord.

 LIFE STEP We sometimes cry out to God for an explanation when we find ourselves in trying times. We need to be reminded that God is the God of the prison cell just as much as He is the God of the winner's circle. Wherever He leads, He will supply.

Acts 17:1-9

What is the writer saying?

How can I apply this to my life?

PRAY Colombia – For God to break the spiritual strongholds in the cities of Medellin and Cali.

The next major city that Paul visits is Thessalonica. It was the capital city of Macedonia. As usual, Paul begins his ministry in the synagogue. He ministers there for three Sabbaths, showing from the Old Testament Scriptures that Jesus must be the Christ. Paul's sermons convinced only a few of the Jews but many of the Gentile proselytes and God-fearers turned to Christ.

This brought an immediate reaction from the synagogue officials. They were incensed that prominent Gentiles were being attracted to Paul's preaching of the Gospel and leaving the synagogue. They enlisted the help of some unsavory characters from the area and started a riot that eventually arrived at the house of a Gentile named Jason. We can assume that the missionaries were using this as a place to live or for worship services or both. Since Paul and Silas were not present, Jason was dragged before the courts and a security was taken from him. Exactly what Jason would forfeit if any more trouble occurred is not clear. His money, his home, or his life are all possibilities. Because Paul did not want to jeopardize his friends, this effectively ended his ministry in Thessalonica.

Because the text tells us that Paul ministered in the synagogue for three Sabbaths does not necessarily mean that that was how long he was in Thessalonica. He was probably forced to move his services after that time but he continued to minister in Thessalonica for several months.

LIFE STEP While the Gospel brought peace and joy to the lives of individuals who believed, it brought turmoil to the community. The Thessalonians accused Paul of "turning the world upside down." The Gospel is a two-edged sword.

SATURDAY 31

Acts 17:10-21

What is the writer saying?

How can I apply this to my life?

PRAY Kenya – For church leaders to live exemplary lives and to speak out against sins prevalent in society.

The Bereans receive what is perhaps the greatest compliment given to any of the cities that Paul visited. They were more noble than the Thessalonians because they searched the Scriptures to see whether Paul's gospel was accurate. The written Word of God was clearly their sole authority.

Even with this positive reception trouble also emerges in Berea. The members of the synagogue in Thessalonica, upon hearing that Paul is preaching in Berea, send representatives to agitate the community against Paul and Silas. One may wonder how a few people from another city can exert such a powerful influence. In the Roman Empire, all religions had to be approved by the government. If anyone belonged to an illegal religion they were considered to be criminals. As such they could be arrested and all of their property confiscated. Some corrupt government appointees were looking for any excuse, not primarily to arrest people, but to confiscate their property. It was considered to be a great financial opportunity when Rome would appoint someone as governor and opportunities such as this were the reason. If the Jews from Thessalonica were able to convince the authorities that a new and illegal religion was being promoted by the members of the synagogue, there could have been some very severe sanctions. From Berea Paul heads to Athens were he finds a very different opportunity to address the citizenry.

LIFE STEP

In a world that is more concerned about experiencing God and doing the work of the ministry, do not miss that it was the Bereans who were more noble because they searched the Scriptures.

SUNDAY 32

Acts 17:22-34

What is the writer saying?

How can I apply this to my life?

PRAY Bulgaria – Pray for reconciliation among believers concerning past conflicts and compromises.

Paul's sermon before this group of philosophers in Athens is much different than the one he preached in the synagogues. The central content remains the same but it is packaged in such a way that it retains the interest of the crowd. His opening remarks are a classic example of how one should go about presenting the Gospel. He starts where his listeners are. The statue with the inscription "To An Unknown God" is a vivid and concrete illustration that opens the door for Paul to speak about Jesus. They cannot summarily reject Paul's God for they themselves, by erecting this statue, admit that there are gods that they do not know, and if such gods exist it would be unethical not to listen to see if perhaps this stranger does know just such a god.

Throughout the sermon Paul uses this same technique. He does not quote the Old Testament but rather quotes from their own philosophers (v. 28). By using thoughts and concepts that are known to them, Paul is able to unlock and illustrate new truths that are unknown to them. The Gospel itself will never change, but the style and manner in which we present it must. If the Gospel is to be effective, it must be heard and understood. If Paul would have spoken to these men as he did to those who attended the synagogue, they would not have clearly understood the message. Paul does not waver or leave out any of the truth. He is as transparent as he always was, but he uses different illustrations to keep the message simple.

LIFE STEP Truth is fragile. Christians are often easily convinced that we can use man's so-called wisdom to win a man to Christ – that we can use his own weapons against him. The fact is that God has given us all the content we need; it is called the Gospel.

Acts 18:1-17

What is the writer saying?

How can I apply this to my life?

PRAY Uganda – For God to call witnesses to the Karamojong, Pokot, and Jie, nomadic people.

From Athens Paul moves southward to Corinth. This city was famous for its depraved life style. Located on a narrow neck of land between southern and northern Greece, it was both a seaport and a land route. This meant that thousands of travelers passed through this city each year. With this volume of visitors it is easy to see why prostitution and other such activities abounded. But just as it was an ideal location for Satan to market his poison, it was also an ideal location for Paul to maximize the impact of the Gospel. The crowds were coming to him and moving on to other locations. Two men are mentioned in this passage. Titus Justus is a Gentile who lived next door to the synagogue. Verse 8 mentions Crispus, who was the ruler of the synagogue. These two names are forever engraved in Holy Scripture because they were willing to help the Apostle Paul as he ministered in Corinth. Too often little acts of kindness or support go unnoticed in our communities. God does not miss these little things.

Paul's stay in Corinth was not entirely without incident. God had promised him that no harm would come but He did not promise there would be no attacks. Almost humorously, Luke recounts that the ruler of the synagogue tried to enlist the aid of civil authorities to stop the spread of the Gospel. Paul was brought before Gallio, a man whose reputation for fairness and wit are well attested in secular histories. Not only does Gallio dismiss the charges as frivolous, but he seems to approve of the beating of Sosthenes the ruler of the synagogue.

LIFE STEP Believers ought to appreciate the little things that others do. We ought to show gratitude and we ought to do the little things that make others grateful.

Acts 18:18-28

What is the writer saying?

How can I apply this to my life?

Very few people apart from the apostles are singled out for individual attention in the Book of Acts. One such person is introduced in this passage, Apollos. It seems clear that this man became very influential in the early church. Paul makes multiple references to him in the book of 1 Corinthians and those in very elite company; Jesus, Peter and Paul (see 1 Corinthians 1:12).

Aquila and Pricilla were Paul's first converts in Corinth (Acts 18:2) and were tent-makers by trade as was the Apostle. They then accompanied Paul when he left Corinth and traveled with him to Ephesus. The events told in these verses happened in Ephesus while Paul was out in the provinces round about.

The events surrounding Apollos' conversion are important more for what does not happen than what does. This will become much clearer in tomorrow's passage. One of Luke's secondary themes in the Book of Acts has to do with the sign gifts of Spirit empowerments. There are two reasons for this. First, Luke wants the reader to know that Paul was exactly like Peter and the rest of the Twelve. He could give new converts spiritual gifts. Second, Luke wants us to know that these empowerments were strictly limited to the apostles. This was how a community could know if someone was an apostle. He could give someone else the ability to perform signs. This would distinguish a true apostle from false teachers.

LIFE STEP Many today long for visible signs of the Spirit's work such as occurred in the Book of Acts. What they miss is the purpose for such gifts. Sign gifts were specifically designed to authenticate the apostles. It was like a signature; forgeries were exposed and rejected.

What is the writer saying?

How can I apply this to my life?

The chapter break at this point is rather unfortunate. Luke is trying to set two stories side-by-side just as he did with Peter and Phillip in chapter 8. In that case Philip had a great ministry in Samaria but no one received the empowerments of the Sprit until Peter and John came and laid hands on them. The end of chapter 18 has a faith update but there is no mention of the Spirit. In today's passage Paul meets twelve disciples of John the Baptizer. They had left Israel before Jesus' ministry. He asks them if they would like some spiritual gifts and is surprised to hear that they have not even heard of such a thing. Paul then asks them how they got saved and they mention John. Remember, Apollos was also saved under John's ministry.

At this point Paul gives them an update on all that has happened since they had been saved under John's ministry. They welcome this good news and are baptized. Paul then lays his hands on them and they receive the Holy Spirit and begin to speak in tongues and prophesy. The concept of receiving the Holy Spirit in the Bible generally refers to an empowerment of the Spirit not the indwelling of the Spirit. Confusing the two can create a lot of misunderstanding. People are indwelt by the Spirit when they are saved. People are empowered by the Spirit under very specific and rare situations. It this case the empowerment was to identify Paul as an apostle. Remember, in order for a sign to be effective it must be unique. If everyone can do it then it is not a sign. Only apostles could distribute sign gifts.

LIFE STEP Gifts such as tongues and prophecy may seem to be a blessing that we miss out on because there are no apostles today. But remember, the Bereans were more noble because of their time invested in studying Scripture. The completed Word of God is our power source!

THURSDAY 32

Acts 19:11-22

What is the writer saying?

How can I apply this to my life?

PRAY Nigeria – For the 168 people groups who are inadequately reached due to lack of workers, churches, and Bible translation.

Following as it does on the heels of Paul's encounter with the twelve disciples of John, this passage is a great example of someone usurping authority that does not belong to him. It is dangerous (and forbidden) to dabble in the spirit world. Demons exist and are powerful. The power of exorcism is one of the sign gifts. It is always listed with healing the sick and raising the dead. Unless we have been authorized by Jesus Christ to cast out demons we should not claim to have the power to cast out demons. Praying for those we suspect to be controlled by demons is the appropriate course of action today. Likewise we are authorized to *pray for healing* but not *to heal* the sick. Sharing Scripture with any unsaved person will eventually enable them to say "no" to Satan and "yes" to God if they will to do so.

Satan is a very real and present danger, but only in clearly defined ways.

Christians can be externally influenced by Satan and his forces, but demons cannot control the believer from the inside. James is clear about this when he says that sin occurs when we are drawn away by our "own lusts" (James 1:14). 2 Corinthians 6:14-18 shows clearly that light and darkness cannot coexist in one place.

These Jewish exorcists had apparently been *successful* in casting out demons previously. When they tried to do it with the legitimate authority of Jesus Christ, they were attacked and beaten by the demon possessed man. It would therefore seem that their initial successes were only apparent and not genuine. Demons clearly play games with those who are supposedly casting them out. This event however, so impressed those who engaged in these types of things that a huge revival breaks out in the *exorcist* profession.

LIFE STEP There is no magical formula for casting out demons. That particular sign gift has passed, but prayer has always been a more powerful weapon and it is still available.

269

Acts 19:23-41

What is the writer saying?

How can I apply this to my life?

PRAY Pray for the peace of Jerusalem (Psalm 122:6).

Opposition to the gospel is eventually going to come. Paul had a profitable stay in Ephesus, but soon his preaching began to adversely affect a certain very influential portion of the community, the silversmiths. The practice of biblical Christianity will always generate opposition from the world. Benign Christianity is a lifeless Christianity. This, however, does not justify going out of our way to cause a conflict. Paul himself commanded that we should live at peace, if possible, with all men (Romans 12:18).

This opposition was spearheaded by Demetrius. There is no doubt that his major concern was monetary, but he wrapped his greed in the guise of religious commitment. It is sad how committed people can become to false gods and develop false systems. Their commitment often far exceeds the commitment of followers of the true God.

In this passage we see a good example of what Paul meant when he wrote in Romans, "For rulers are not a terror to good works, but to evil" (Rom 13:3). If we behave in a peaceable and responsible way, the government will very often become our friend. That is exactly what happened in Ephesus. This is what it means to be in the world but not of the world. Once Demetrius the silversmith got the ruckus going, it soon spun out of control. No one could speak. For two hours the crowd filled the theater and continuously shouted, "Great is Diana of the Ephesians." This event marked the end of Paul's sojourn in Ephesus.

LIFE STEP We sometimes assume that the powers that be are going to resist us without reason. As much as possible we need to take advantage of the opportunities that our government provides for us and avoid unnecessarily antagonizing them.

Acts 20:1-12

What is the writer saying?

How can I apply this to my life?

PRAY New Zealand – For missionaries to capitalize on this nation's love of sports as a means of evangelistic outreach.

Returning from Greece Paul stopped at a port on the northeast corner of the Aegean Sea. He stayed there in Troas for seven days. While there another amazing incident occurs. It is not that someone fell asleep while Paul was preaching that is so amazing, for Paul admitted to being a poor public speaker (2 Corinthians 10:10). It is what happens afterward.

This young man, Eutychus, was seated in a window. Windows in those days did not come with glass so out he tumbled and crashed to his death in the street below. Paul graciously raises Eutychus from the dead. Paul then goes back to the message.

This is a far cry from the so-called *faith healers* of today. Today's healers never deal with the kind of traumatic injuries that must have occurred in this story. They do not go to hospitals or morgues. They always do their so-called healings in an environment that is totally under their control, much like a professional magician. They do not go to the sick; they ask the sick to come to them. This is not a small matter. If we are going to claim that these things are happening today just as they did in Acts, then they ought to happen *just as they did in Acts* and not in some sterile and managed environment. Paul held no healing service, but when a need arose he met it. It is awesome to realize that to Paul it was no big thing to resurrect someone from the dead.

LIFE STEP There are some today who would claim the office of apostle. These are incredibly big shoes to fill. Anyone who makes such a claim will have a hard time living up to it. One of the criteria is established right here in this passage.

Acts 20:13-24

What is the writer saying?

How can I apply this to my life?

From Troas Paul proceeds to Miletus, a seaport to the south of Ephesus. Paul did not go into the actual city of Ephesus, but rather the elders of the church came to Miletus to meet with Paul. Paul had spent almost two and a half years with these men. They were old and dear friends with whom Paul had shared both good times and bad. This is his farewell speech to them and it is charged with emotion.

Paul first of all asks them to remember his ministry among them. It was a ministry fraught with danger and hard work and yet the apostle labored with patience and love. Paul says that he "kept back nothing" if it would be of benefit to the Ephesian believers. His was a ministry of total commitment.

We get a little glimpse into Paul's mindset in verses 22-24. When he says that he is "bound in the spirit" he means that he is driven by an inward force. He is committed to go to Jerusalem. He is uncertain of the future, but he does know that "bonds and afflictions" wait for him there. Paul's situation was a good news/bad news dilemma. The good news was that Jerusalem held a new opportunity for him to serve the Lord. The bad news was the increased opposition he would experience. Some have wondered if the Holy Spirit was telling Paul that he should not go to Jerusalem. It is best to give the apostle the benefit of the doubt in this matter. Look at the end of verse 24. He is not going to let anything stop him from finishing the job that Jesus Christ had given to him.

LIFE STEP Do we have this kind of determination in serving the Lord? What would it take to stop us from witnessing to a neighbor? What would it take to get us to witness to a neighbor? Resolve that is crushed by opposition is no resolve at all.

Acts 20:25-38

What is the writer saying?

How can I apply this to my life?

PRAY Korea – Protection and perseverance of nearly 100,000 believers confined in North Korean camps.

Paul, in dramatic fashion, declares that he has met his entire duty to the people of Ephesus. He knows that there will be no more missionary journeys. He is going to Jerusalem for an uncertain future. There is one thing that he does know for sure: he has done his best and he has done his duty.

But Paul knows that the wolves are ever vigilant. No weakness escapes their notice. They are experts at corrupting and misrepresenting God's truth. Every church and every ministry must be on guard. They will come and they are effective. The apostle now turns over the responsibility for the church in Ephesus to the elders. No effective work for the Lord Jesus Christ will go unchallenged by Satan and his ministers. The wolves Paul speaks of here are false teachers. By the way, the wolves do not always wear nametags. The wolves have no concern for the flock of God, they are only out for personal advantage.

What a bittersweet time this must have been for the apostle. Bitter because he had to tear himself away from a group of believers that he loved dearly. Sweet because he was embarking on God's will for the rest of his life. Before he left, however, he shared with them a few things that they needed to know. Look at verse 33. Don't these things fit the false teachers to a tee: silver, gold and fine clothes. Paul didn't take the Ephesians' money; he worked to support himself. Paul always taught that a church ought to support its pastors, but he also taught that the Gospel ought to be preached free of charge.

LIFE STEP When we take the Gospel to another people group, we should always be sure that the Gospel is preached free of charge. It is not only the church's responsibility to care for its own ministers, but also to provide for the taking of the Gospel to the "uttermost parts."

TUESDAY 33

Acts 21:1-14

What is the writer saying?

How can I apply this to my life?

PRAY

Ghana — For evangelistic outreach in the northern region, which has had less exposure to the Gospel.

When Paul arrives in the port city of Caesarea he stays at the house of Philip, the same one who led the Ethiopian eunuch to the Lord. He is now married with four unmarried daughters. Philip's daughters have the gift of prophecy but, since it would be improper for them to prophesy in the presence of men, Agabus, who came down from Judea was called upon to prophesy. Notice that prophecy is not a spontaneous event. It appears that the prophet had some control over when he would prophesy. This would be very important for maintaining order in the worship services where more than one prophet was present.

His prophecy seems to greatly concern everyone but Paul because Paul has heard similar prophecies before and has already settled in his own mind what he must do. God's will is not altered by the circumstances of life. It remains constant in a constantly changing environment.

Paul's comment in verse 13 is classic. It was not the danger of the future that most concerned Paul; it was the tears of his friends. Those tears were breaking his heart. Those who suffer most in a time of testing are not always the ones who are directly involved. Sometimes those who look on but are unable to help suffer greater frustration. Even those who were arguing that Paul should not go to Jerusalem eventually acknowledged that God's will should be done.

LIFE STEP

Why did God send these prophecies if He wanted Paul to go to Jerusalem? We cannot say. But just because danger may lie ahead, we should not allow that to stop us from doing what we know God wants us to do.

WEDNESDAY 33

Acts 21:15-26

What is the writer saying?

How can I apply this to my life?

Today's passage is one that many interpreters have anguished over. Why did Paul give in to the pressure of James and the other leaders of the Jerusalem church and take this vow. The answer lies in 1 Corinthians 9:20-22. "And unto the Jews I became as a Jew, that I might gain the Jews; to them that are under the law, as under the law, that I might gain them that are under the law. To them that are without law as without law, (being not without law to God, but under the law to Christ,) that I might gain them that are without law. To the weak became I as weak, that I might gain the weak: I am made all things to all men that I might by all means save some." To Paul the outward act was less important than maintaining every possible opportunity to present the Gospel. Just as with meat offered to idols, Paul did not see any intrinsic evil in taking a vow.

At this point it would appear that in the church at Jerusalem the Jewish believers were still involved in some of the ceremonies of the Mosaic law. They did not do this as a means for salvation or sanctification, but out of respect for the civil laws within the Mosaic code. We must always remember that the Law of Moses was both a *political* and a religious document. While Christ ended much of the ceremonial law, there were still civil laws that could and should have been followed. It is also important to realize that the book of Hebrews had not yet been written. Temple worship seems to be forbidden from that point on. As far as Luke is concerned, even at this point there are still transitional elements in play.

LIFE STEP

Transition was the key word for this book. Paul was right to participate in practices that had not yet been terminated by God's revelation. That does not give us the right to do the same since we live after the later revelation was given.

Acts 21:27-40

What is the writer saying?

How can I apply this to my life?

In spite of Paul's attempts to meet all of the standards necessary to enter the Temple, the people, when they recognized him, were outraged, not because of anything that he had done, but because they thought he had broken the law and brought Gentiles into the temple. In a fashion similar to what happened in Ephesus, a mob quickly formed and it was their intent to kill Paul. Once again the authorities came to his rescue. The Captain of the Guard was shocked when Paul could speak Greek and even more startled to know that he was a Roman citizen. It was the military's responsibility to protect all citizens of the realm. The allies of the ministry often come from unexpected sources.

Paul's response to all this turmoil is somewhat amazing. With everything that was going on around him, he was continually looking for an opportunity to get to preach to this large assembly of people. Paul never saw a crowd that he did not want to preach to. Some may have been discouraged that so many people wanted to kill them. But Paul saw the silver lining in every cloud. Where else would these people ever get the chance to hear the gospel? This approach to life is one that characterizes Paul. He saw every tribulation as a cause for rejoicing for the opportunities it provided. Anxiety accomplishes nothing. Opportunities often come in strange packages.

Paul gets his wish and for a brief moment the angry mob is hushed and Paul speaks to them in their own language. He wanted every barrier to the Gospel to be removed.

LIFE STEP What is our perspective on life and ministry? Do we see the potential dangers, or the opportunities. Paul saw life from a different angle than most people do. He always looked for an opportunity in every situation and invariably he found one.

Acts 22:1-16

What is the writer saying?

How can I apply this to my life?

Having been given the opportunity by the Captain of the Guard, Paul begins to share with the crowd before him. He speaks to them in Hebrew. This immediately caught the attention of the Jews and increased their interest in what he was saying. He also mentioned that he knew the High Priest and the elders of Israel. He mentioned Gamaliel under whom he had studied and shared that he was at one time a persecutor of the Christians and was trying to wipe them out. All of this would have grabbed the interest of the people who were listening. Paul was building bridges to these people. He understood that it was necessary to use everything at his disposal to get an opportunity to share with these people.

Having gained their attention, Paul immediately shares the Gospel. He tells them about his encounter with Jesus Christ on the Damascus road. One of the neat things about this sermon is that people could check out the facts. Many of the people who had known the old Paul were still around in Jerusalem. The lives that we have lived were always intended to be a preparation for the present. In God's overall plan each of us is being prepared for the opportunities that come our way.

Paul's technique here is great. He keeps them interested by unfolding events from his old life little by little. The stoning of Stephen must have been a well-known event in Jerusalem. Paul just kind of mentions that he was a part of that. He actually held the coats. But he is also weaving in the Gospel. Look at verse 16.

LIFE STEP Paul was given the opportunity to defend himself. The opportunity he took was to preach Christ. If we are looking for opportunities to witness, the opportunities will come. But, they may not come in the way that we are expecting.

Acts 22:17-30

What is the writer saying?

How can I apply this to my life?

PRAY Mexico – For outreach to teens as churches tend to gear all programming to adults.

It is very probable that some of the people present would remember the things of which Paul spoke. A stoning could not have been a very common occurrence in Jerusalem, especially since the Sanhedrin did not possess that authority. Most who stood there that day would know about those events and some may have been involved.

Paul had gotten his opportunity to preach, but he was probably disappointed with the response. The crowd was enraged and demanded that he be put to death. The soldiers, not ready to kill Paul, decided to scourge him. It is at this point that Paul makes use of his Roman citizenship. In those days citizenship was a privilege not an entitlement, and very few people were actually citizens of Rome. The chief captain had to pay a huge sum of money to get his certificate of Roman citizenship. Once the soldiers realized that Paul was a Roman citizen they decided not to scourge him but to give him a hearing in the "council." This council was the Sanhedrin, the highest Jewish court allowed by Roman law. This was the same council that tried Jesus and the same group that stoned Stephen. It was not necessarily the same men but the same council. It is probable, however, that some of the same eyes that Jesus looked into were now staring at Paul.

To Paul this was just another opportunity to share the story of his Savior. When Stephen stood before this group twenty years prior to this, he had no protection. Paul had his Roman citizenship to make sure that he could return to preach another day. It certainly was no act of cowardice to use this privilege, but a wise use of a divine provision.

LIFE STEP Paul did not always make his citizenship known to the authorities. Perhaps it was because none of his companions were citizens and he did not want them to suffer alone.

Acts 23:1-10

What is the writer saying?

How can I apply this to my life?

As Paul stands before the Sanhedrin his greatest desire is to have an opportunity to clearly present the gospel. He wants to ensure that the men present would be listening attentively. The trial does not start well. Paul enters a plea of not guilty, and is immediately slapped in the face by command of the high priest. This was in clear violation of the law. Deuteronomy 25:2 says that a man may be struck only when found guilty and then he is to lie on the floor to be beaten. The council has not convened to determine whether or not Paul is guilty; they have already decided that in their own minds and have illegally skipped to the sentencing phase.

But Paul, as an ex-associate of the inner circles, soon sees an opportunity to get a more meaningful hearing. The Sanhedrin was composed of Pharisees and Sadducees. One of the bitterest disagreements between these two groups was over the physical resurrection of humans. The Pharisees taught that there was a future resurrection and the Sadducees denied it. When Paul said that he was being called into question about the resurrection, it would be impossible for the Pharisees to let him leave without hearing his argument. To them it would be like admitting that the Sadducees were right. Paul's hopes, though, were not realized. The argument between the two groups became so bitter that the captain had to escort Paul out of the building, a rather unexpected ending to such a prestigious meeting.

LIFE STEP Yesterday Paul used his citizenship to help him escape one beating. Today he uses his knowledge of the theological controversies between the Pharisees and Sadducees to help him deal with another difficult situation. Opportunity wears many faces.

Acts 23:11-22

What is the writer saying?

How can I apply this to my life?

It seems reasonable to think that things were not going exactly the way Paul had imagined they would. He surely had hoped that the Gospel would have touched a few of the many who had heard him speak. As far as we know, no one responded to the message. In verse 11 the Lord encourages Paul. He makes it clear that Jerusalem was not Paul's final goal. Rome has always been the destination that God had in mind. The Gospel has always had two purposes. For some it is a fountain of life, but for others it only serves to confirm their disobedience. Luke wants it to be clearly understood that God did not abandon Israel; Israel abandoned God. Paul may have been the Apostle to the Gentiles but even he was given an opportunity to preach to the nation that he loved.

It is amazing that the very people who were trying to accuse Paul of breaking the Law were breaking the Law in an attempt to murder him. It makes no sense, but that is the way it is with sin. The Jews were destroying the very thing they were claiming to protect because of an almost insane hatred for Jesus and his messenger, Paul. The Sanhedrin itself was conspiring with criminals in an attempt to have Paul murdered. At every turn it seems that the Jewish authorities are resisting God, just as Stephen had prophesied. Their hearts were blind, cold, and treacherous. But there is good news. Paul was spending a lot of time with Gentile soldiers.

LIFE STEP Opportunity ignored is opportunity squandered, whether it is an opportunity to accept Christ or an opportunity to preach Christ. For Israel this was opportunity lost but for the Gentiles it was an open door. Never say no to an opportunity because there is no guarantee that opportunity will come again.

TUESDAY 34

Acts 23:23-35

What is the writer saying?

How can I apply this to my life?

PRAY Finland – For the hopelessness that pervades society to be replaced by the joy of salvation.

Paul is beginning to be a problem for Claudius Lysias, the chief captain in Jerusalem. A plot to kill Paul has been uncovered. Therefore the captain decides to send Paul away from Jerusalem to Caesarea where the governor lives. This was designed to reduce the amount of time and personnel invested in protecting the prisoner. Along with the apostle, the captain sends a letter describing the events surrounding the arrest and so-called trial.

When Paul arrives at the palace, he is immediately granted an audience with the governor. After reading the letter and a few moments of questioning, Paul is dismissed and sent to the official residence of the governor, Herod's judgment hall. Once again Paul, on account of his arrest, is given an opportunity to reach people who would otherwise be inaccessible to him. The actions of those who are trying to kill Paul have produced an increased availability of the Gospel. Paul is constantly brought in contact with individuals who have probably never heard the Gospel.

Paul could very easily have complained about the unfairness of his situation. He could have grumbled about the lies that were being spread about him. But Paul saw the big picture. God was providing an escort and free transportation to Rome.

LIFE STEP

We wonder sometimes why Luke chose to include all the details that he did in his book. Each one of these little trivialities is a part of God's plan to bring Paul to the city of Rome. But more importantly, along the way Paul is able to preach the Gospel to many people who would otherwise never have had the opportunity to hear. God's ways are not our ways!

WEDNESDAY 34

Acts 24:1-16

What is the writer saying?

How can I apply this to my life?

Notice how the lawyer for the Sanhedrin tries to flatter the governor and at the same time twist the facts to his own advantage. He even accuses the chief captain of misbehavior. He raises the specter of *police violence* in an attempt to coerce Paul out of the governor's hands and into his own. No attempt was made to bring in any *neutral* observers. Those who accused Paul were willing to stoop to any means to discredit and destroy him. They are not interested in what was fair or right. Their only concern was whether or not they won.

Paul in his turn points out the inconsistencies in the prosecution's account of the events and introduces what really started the trouble among the Sanhedrin, the controversy about the resurrection of the dead. His purpose in doing this was to help Felix, the governor, to realize that their problem with him was not political but religious.

He knew that Felix would not try him for a religious squabble. Even in that ancient world, the authorities were wise enough not to involve themselves with internal religious disputes.

But by bringing up the resurrection Paul does more than just shift the focus toward religion, he opens the door to discuss the very heart of the Gospel message. The Sanhedrin may have no interest in Paul's gospel but undoubtedly there were those within the court whose ears would perk up on hearing about such a matter.

LIFE STEP We often follow Paul's example and begin gospel presentations by introducing the resurrection. One of the most common and helpful ways to begin a gospel presentation is to ask, "If you were to die tonight, do you know where you would spend eternity?"

Acts 24:17-27

What is the writer saying?

How can I apply this to my life?

PRAY No interference from civil authorities in the cities where street evangelism takes place.

Today's passage is a continuation of Paul's defense before Felix. It is worth noting that Paul did not say anything about offering a sacrifice. While he was willing to give in to the temple ritual in some respects, he did not yield in any area that would in any way hinder the Gospel. When he says that he was "purified" in the temple, he is referring to the vow he took and the shaving of his head.

At the conclusion of the hearing, Felix decides that he needs to hear more evidence before making a final decision and, therefore, places Paul under house arrest. Clearly Felix was at least familiar with Christianity, here referred to as the "way." Accordingly he gives Paul great liberty so that he was able to carry on a productive ministry from his *prison*. As difficult and unfair as the situation seemed it was still a part of God's plan for the apostle. All God's decisions that must be called *God's will* are not necessarily pleasant. Sometimes the greatest opportunities come from the most difficult of situations.

Sometime later Felix has Paul present the gospel to him and his wife, and although Felix was under so much conviction that he literally shook, there is no indication that he was ever saved. In fact, he kept Paul in prison hoping to receive a bribe from some of his friends. Thus Paul spent the rest of Felix's term as governor under house arrest. Felix could have let Paul go at any point during this time but was more concerned about keeping the Jews happy than he was about treating Paul fairly.

LIFE STEP Every person who heard the Apostle Paul did not get saved. Felix came close but still rejected. We will not win everyone to whom we witness. This should not discourage us. Each opportunity that comes along is provided by the Lord.

Acts 25:1-12

What is the writer saying?

How can I apply this to my life?

The Jews in Jerusalem had not forgotten about Paul. As soon as the new governor was installed, they immediately began plotting Paul's murder once again. They presented their charges against Paul to Festus and asked that Paul be brought to Jerusalem. They do not seem to be very creative, since once again their plan is to ambush and kill him along the road. Festus, however, invites them to come to Caesarea again and present their charges against the apostle. And once again Paul will be given an opportunity to present his case (and the Gospel) to a new audience. It seems that the more the Sanhedrin tried to keep Paul from preaching, the more opportunities they created!

As with the first go 'round their charges are again unsubstantiated, but Festus is clearly leaning towards turning Paul over to the Jews because he wants to appease them. Paul at that point uses the last defense he had: he appeals to Caesar. It was the right of any Roman citizen to be tried in Rome by the court of Caesar. Remember, very few inhabitants of the Roman Empire were citizens. This *appeal option* was originally designed to protect the inhabitants of Rome from being mistreated by the courts of a foreign country. But all citizens, even those who were not actually born in that city, were given this right. Thus Paul finally started on the journey he had long wanted to make. He was headed for Rome, a city in dire need of evangelizing.

LIFE STEP Paul was always willing to wait upon the Lord's timing. He did not appeal to Caesar the moment he was arrested. He waited until his hand was forced. There is no need to rush God. Paul was under house arrest for over two years but he knew that God would work out His plan in His time.

Acts 25:13-27

What is the writer saying?

How can I apply this to my life?

While Paul was imprisoned at Caesarea awaiting transportation to Rome, Herod Agrippa II (grandson of Herod the Great and son of Herod Agrippa I who had James killed in Acts 12) came for a visit, perhaps to welcome the new governor. While he was there, Festus thought it would be great entertainment to have the King hear what Paul had to say. King Agrippa has no authority over Festus, but is an expert in Jewish affairs and has wanted to hear Paul for some time (v. 22). It is possible that he was looking for some advice, but most likely he was just looking for a good way to pass a few hours. Whichever the case, Paul was once again given a great opportunity to present the Gospel to people who may never have had the opportunity otherwise.

Bernice is not Agrippa's wife, but his sister (their other sister is Drusilla). Agrippa and Bernice have an incestuous relationship. Bernice, for a time, becomes the mistress of Emperor Vespasian, and then of his son, Titus. However, she always returns to her brother.

Festus shares with his guests the events that led up to this present occasion. Also, he includes how Paul refused to go up to Jerusalem to be judged, choosing rather to appeal to Caesar. This may have created a problem for Festus because he did not have any formal charges that would make sense to Rome.

LIFE STEP Murphy's Law suggests that everything that can go wrong will. While there is a lot of truth to this, we must realize that every situation in which we find ourselves can be seen as an opportunity to do something for God.

Acts 26:1-18

What is the writer saying?

How can I apply this to my life?

PRAY Colombia – Pray for the safety and accuracy of those participating in Bible translation projects.

Paul is permitted to speak in his defense. The gesture "stretched forth the hand" is a common way of beginning a speech. Agrippa would no doubt be very familiar with Jewish customs, having grown up in the area. As Paul starts to talk about the resurrection of Jesus, the intensity in the room must have taken a tremendous leap. This topic must have been a source of much conversation and embarrassment to the local authorities. It has only been about twenty-two years since the crucifixion took place. Against this politically and perhaps personally charged backdrop Paul once again begins to rehearse his testimony.

Paul continually appeals to Agrippa's knowledge and expertise of Jewish customs. It must be remembered that Paul is not on trial here, but is being given an unbelievable opportunity to give his testimony. In fact, Paul's purpose here is to see Agrippa and others converted (vv. 28-29). Paul tells of his pre-conversion life, his upbringing and the fact that he lived as a Pharisee. He speaks of the hope of the promised Messiah and that of the resurrection. Paul then tells of his zeal in persecuting Christian believers.

As Paul wraps up today's portion he quotes the commission that Jesus gave to him on the Damascus road. He understands clearly that the center of God's work is moving from the Jews to the Gentiles. He also knows that the center of Gentile power is Rome. He is not looking to be released; he is looking to continue his mission in Rome.

LIFE STEP It is easy to miss the forest for the trees. We sometimes get so caught up in the immediate trial that we are in that we fail to even consider the big picture. The immediate must always be subordinate to greater purposes in life.

Acts 26:19-32

What is the writer saying?

How can I apply this to my life?

Paul continues his defense before Herod Agrippa. In verse 24, Festus, who was obviously from a different region of the empire, interrupts. He thinks that Paul is crazy. Paul, however, turns to Agrippa. As a young man, he had probably heard of the slaughter of the infants in Bethlehem. He had probably been alive when James had been killed and when Peter had escaped so easily from the prison. The crucifixion and the resurrection were events that were well known throughout the land. Paul says, "...this thing was not done in a corner." Maybe it was Agrippa's curiosity about these things that had happened in his younger days that kept him listening; maybe it was a sincere search for the truth; maybe it was just for the amusement value; but listen he did. By the time Paul was finished Agrippa was ready to acquit him of all charges. We might be tempted to think, "If only Paul had not appealed to Caesar." But remember, if Paul had not appealed to Caesar, he would not have been around to speak to Agrippa.

Four of the saddest words in the history of the world occur in today's passage: "almost thou persuadest me." Agrippa was so close and yet so far. Salvation was within his grasp, but he let it slip away. No one ever knows how long the Lord will continue to speak to his or her heart. Now is always the time to respond to God. Tomorrow is never the time of opportunity. Make the most of what God brings into your life today. Redeem the time because the days are evil.

LIFE STEP The present is a gift. This is a very special time in an eternity of moments. Eternity stretches like an infinite road ahead of us. But the present is most precious because it is the only time when we can make a decision that will determine what our forever will be like.

Acts 27:1-13

What is the writer saying?

How can I apply this to my life?

Notice that the text once again uses the pronoun "we" indicating that Luke has joined the delegation once again. That may account for the numerous details that are included in these verses. And yet, the inclusion of these details is not just a random occurrence. These are people that would be in Rome when Luke's manuscript was published. These are people that a reader could ask if what Luke was writing was true.

There were other prisoners on the ship but as to their identity we can only speculate. Luke probably does not name them because they would not be considered reliable witnesses in the court of public opinion. Paul would be treated much better than the usual prisoner because of his Roman citizenship. When they stop at Sidon, Paul is permitted to visit his friends.

Much of today's passage is taken up by a detailed description of the route that the ship travelled. Such details may have been of special interest to Luke or they may have been more significant to the ancient readers. Paul does warn the centurion that danger lies ahead but given the circumstances it is not surprising that he is totally ignored. The journey goes on and trouble lies ahead.

LIFE STEP For most of the people on this ship the trip began like any other trip. They had no clue that their world was about to be turned upside down. We need to remember that every day is kind of like that. Each day is another journey and we never know when the rocks may appear.

Acts 27:14-29

What is the writer saying?

How can I apply this to my life?

PRAY Bolivia – For caring youth ministry in a land where 80% of children are living in extreme poverty.

Today we find Paul in a ship on his way to Rome. Bad weather has trapped them as the sailors valiantly attempt to make the dangerous voyage around the southern tip of Italy. The vessels of that day were much smaller than the ships we have today. The situation became so critical that the crew had thrown all the cargo overboard. Even the essential ropes and tools for sailing the ship were thrown away. But still the vessel was in distress.

After three days without seeing the sun or the stars, which means they had no idea of where they were, Paul stands up to give them some good news and some bad news. The good news is that no one will die. The bad news is that the ship will be lost. Since Paul was a prisoner, it is not clear how this revelation was received, but when things get really bad, people seem to be much more open to listening to a *man of God*. Paul could

have been frustrated because of yet another delay in his journey to Rome, but instead, he became a source of strength and comfort.

When all seems to be lost Paul has a vision from God. In this vision an angel reaffirms the promise he has received from Jesus that Paul would get to Rome (see 23:11). Paul encourages the crew that not only would he appear before the emperor, but also they would all survive for his sake.

LIFE STEP God's ways are not our ways. If it were left up to us, we would give Paul an uneventful journey to Rome, but God has other plans. There are 276 people on this boat and they are about to get an up close and personal look at the Gospel.

Acts 27:30-44

What is the writer saying?

How can I apply this to my life?

PRAY Spain – For the Holy Spirit to remove religious cynicism, the lasting stain of the Spanish Inquisition.

In Paul's vision the angel had promised that every person on board would be saved if they stayed on board. The sailors have been measuring the depth of the water and realize that they are getting close to land. They prepare the lifeboat and are about to desert under the pretense of lowering the anchors. This time the centurion listens to Paul and he cuts the ropes that are holding the lifeboat so that all on board will have to stay on board.

Paul encourages all the men to eat. With the storm and inherent difficulty in food preparation, little or nothing has been eaten in the previous two weeks. There seems to be a renewed strength among the crew and in the morning land is spotted and an attempt is made to get to the beach. The ship, however, runs aground on a reef and begins to break apart from the pounding of the surf. Before jumping overboard, the soldiers plan to kill all the prisoners. Knowing Roman law, they fear for their lives. If a soldier loses his prisoner, he would lose his own life or face the same punishment as intended for his prisoner. Fortunately, Julius opposes the plan and takes command. He orders those who can swim to go first, and the others to follow on planks or other items that would float. After all was said and done, all 276 persons that had set sail were alive and standing on solid ground.

LIFE STEP As with everything about Paul's life even a tragedy turns into an opportunity. Not one of those men would ever forget Paul and if they remembered Paul they would also remember the Good News that he was always preaching.

Acts 28:1-16

What is the writer saying?

How can I apply this to my life?

Exactly as Paul had prophesied the ship is wrecked, but Paul and all the rest of the people on the ship are spared and find themselves on an island called Melita. This is the island we know today as Malta. The people who live there are called "barbarians" in the text but that simply means that they did not speak a commonly known language such as Greek or Latin. They are very friendly and fix a fire for the castaways. As the people gather about the fire, God's purpose for the events of the last few days begin to unfold.

Two things happen that single Paul out for special attention. A poisonous snake bites him but he is not harmed, and he heals a prominent individual's father. Thus that campfire becomes a center for evangelism as the apostle shares the good news of salvation with as many as will listen.

And so, after a long and adventurous journey, Paul finally arrives at the city where God had told him he was headed. As he draws close to Rome the word is spread and an excitement begins to build among the believers of that city. He had written them a letter over two years prior to this arrival and they had looked forward with great anticipation to his visit ever since. The tears Paul wept as he left the believers in Ephesus were not forgotten as once again he is welcomed back with open arms into the Gentile world. He would always be a Hebrew of the tribe of Benjamin but he would be forever tied to the people for whom he had been called to be an apostle, the Gentiles.

LIFE STEP   The progress of our lives often seems to drift along by means of an intricate chain of chance events and encounters. This little island was not a scheduled stop on the journey and even if it were, Paul, a common prisoner, would never have been allowed shared the Gospel. But he did!

Acts 28:17-31

What is the writer saying?

How can I apply this to my life?

PRAY Ecuador – Pray for the protection of evangelical churches from prejudice, threats, and violence.

The year is about A.D. 60 and even though the Book of Acts ends at this point, the life and ministry of the apostle goes on for many more productive years. During this his first stay in Rome, Paul is under house arrest. He writes the books of Ephesians, Philippians, Colossians, and Philemon. He also has an incredible ministry to the saints in and around Rome.

Paul is released after two years and for the next five years visits a number of different locations, Ephesus, Macedonia, Crete, Nicopolis, and Troas. We learn much of this from his letters. In A.D. 67 he is once again arrested and taken to Rome. This imprisonment is much different. Instead of house arrest he is placed in a traditional dungeon. He has none of the comforts that he knew during that first stay. It is from there that he writes his final epistle to his son in the faith, Timothy (2 Timothy). The following year, A.D. 68, Paul is beheaded in Rome. The same human authorities that God had used to protect and transport Paul for so much of his trip to Rome are now used by God to usher him into glory.

The book closes with a seemingly odd reference to the kingdom. But this only serves to tie the reader back into the even bigger picture. Yes, Paul was the apostle to the Gentiles, but he never relinquished the belief that God would one day reestablish His relationship with Israel and deliver the kingdom that He had promised to Abraham, and Moses and David.

LIFE STEP If you met Paul in A.D. 35, you would never have dreamed that this man could turn the world upside down for God. But he would. It is not the man that makes the difference; it is the God behind the man. Put your life in God's hand and he can do great things in and through your life.

HABAKKUK

The name Habakkuk means *embrace* or *embracer*, perhaps because of the prophet's love for God. Beyond that we know nothing about him from a personal standpoint. We do know, however, that the time of his prophecy was just prior to Nebuchadnezzar's invasion of Judah (605 B.C.). At that time Daniel and others would be taken captive to Babylon.

Behind the writing of the book is a problem that Habakkuk faced. He begins with an exclamation, "O Lord, how long shall I cry and thou wilt not hear!" (1:2) The problem? He could not understand why God was not judging the nation of Judah for her obvious sins. And so this book becomes a *theodicy*, or a defense of God's justice. God answers this problem by telling Habakkuk that He will judge Judah and will use Babylon to do it (1:5-11). This only causes the prophet to have a greater problem, for this would mean that God would be using an even more sinful nation to punish His own people, and God is too righteous to resort to such measures (1:12–2:1). God's answer to this problem is twofold. His primary answer is the key to the book. Man is to live by faith in God, that is, man is to trust God to do that which is right. The second part of the answer is to show Habakkuk, and us, that sin, in this case that of the ungodly Babylonians, does not and will not go unpunished (2:2-20).

Habakkuk learned his lessons well. The third and final chapter of the book is a psalm of prayerful praise that centers on God. The final verses of that chapter show that the prophet is no longer focused on circumstances, but on God. No matter what happens all around him, he can rest in the Lord. The key verse of the book is Habakkuk 2:4, a verse that is quoted three times in the New Testament, "The just shall live by his faith." It is, in fact, one of the most important verses in the entire Bible. It is included in the text of three New Testament books: Romans, Galatians, and Hebrews. In Romans 1:17 the emphasis is on *the just*, in Galatians 3:11 the emphasis is on *shall live*, and in Hebrews 10:38 the emphasis is on *by faith*.

Some final thoughts from Warren Weirsbe: Habakkuk shows us how to deal with life's problems. Admit them honestly. Talk to God about them. Wait quietly before Him in prayer and meditation on the Word. When He speaks, listen, and obey. Never run away from the difficulties of life because God wants to use those difficulties to strengthen your faith. Never doubt in the dark what God has told you in the light. The just shall live *by faith*!

OUTLINE

1. The Dialogue (1:1-2:20)
   a. Habakkuk's First Complaint (1:1-4)
   b. God's First Response (1:5-11)
   c. Habakkuk's Second Complaint (1:12–2:1)
   d. God's Second Response (2:2-20)
2. Habakkuk's Psalm of Praise (3:1-19)
   a. Praise for God's Person (3:1-3)
   b. Praise for God's Power (3:4-7)
   c. Praise for God's Purpose (3:8-16)
   d. Praise because of Faith in God (3:17-19)

The theme of Zephaniah is "The Day of the Lord." It is a book of *bad* news. But, thankfully, it doesn't end that way…there is some *good* news for those who "trust in the name of the Lord" (3:12).

God must judge sin. In this message He promises to do exactly that. Judgment falls first on God's people, Judah, and then on the Gentile nations. The pronouncement of judgment begins with these words: "I will utterly consume all things from off the land" (1:2). That's the bad news. But following judgment, salvation is also available in the "day of the Lord" (1:7, 14). This phrase occurs many times in Old Testament prophecy and can be understood in two ways. First, it can refer to a present judgment, such as the impending invasion of the land by the Babylonians that took many Jews captive (see the book of Daniel). Second, it can refer to a future time when God will judge sinners (the Tribulation Period) and bless His people (the Millennial Kingdom). The text of Zephaniah makes it clear that its major emphasis is for the distant future. It also explains why that period of judgment is unique (Daniel 12:1; Matthew 24:21).

Zephaniah was a contemporary of Jeremiah, who prophesied during the reign of godly King Josiah during the latter years of the southern kingdom (Judah). Zephaniah was a grandson descendant of King Hezekiah (1:1) and therefore had access to the palace. His name means *the Lord hides or protects*, or *hidden in the Lord*. Since the messages of the Old Testament prophets came from God Himself, their personal names often had significance to their message. With judgment coming, certainly the safest place to be was "hidden in the Lord."

King Josiah received Zephaniah's warnings and, under his direction, the Israelites began to correct their ways—at least on the surface. They pulled down idols, judged false priests and prophets, rebuilt the temple, and started celebrating the neglected Passover. But, Zephaniah questions the sincerity of their repentance. The idols in their *homes* had been removed, but not in their *hearts*. Greed, disobedience, and wickedness still characterized the people of Judah.

Despite dire warnings of judgment, Zephaniah promises restoration for those who sincerely respond to God. His announcement of the coming day of the Lord – a coming day of doom, using terms that could be no darker – also promised a day of blessing that was just as bright as the doom was bleak.

OUTLINE

I. Blastings (Bad News) in the Day of the Lord (1:1–3:7)
   a. Judah in that Day (1:1–2:3)
   b. Nations in that Day (2:4-15)
   c. God and that Day (3:1-7)

II. Blessings (Good News) in the Day of the Lord (3:8-20)
   a. The Remnant Cleansed (3:8-13)
   b. The Remnant Restored (3:14-19)
   c. The Remnant Blessed (3:20)

SUNDAY 36

Habakkuk 1:1-11

What is the writer saying?

How can I apply this to my life?

"The burden which Habakkuk the prophet did see." That's how the book begins. We need to understand what the word *burden* implies. The book records a question and answer session between Habakkuk and God. The burden is not a reference to the prophet's questions but to the Lord's answers to those questions. We could rephrase verse 1 as, *The ominous announcement which Habakkuk, the prophet, did see.*

Habakkuk was perplexed over God's tolerance with the sinful behavior of Judah. He asked God, *How long, Lord, are you going to put up with their wickedness? If You don't do something about it You have made the law powerless. Justice has been perverted and the wicked have restrained the righteous. How long will such behavior prevail?* (vv. 2-4).

Such questioning of God may seem out of line, but God does not rebuke Habakkuk. Instead, He answers him, *I am doing something about it. This will be hard for you to believe. Behold (look around), I am going to use your barbaric neighbors, the Chaldeans (Babylonians), to judge My people. They are a nasty nation, but I am going to raise them up to do My work of judgment* (v. 6). This answer deepens Habakkuk's distress. God, of course, can control the nations for His own purposes (Daniel 2:21). That is what He tells Habakkuk He is going to do. This nation that He describes as terrible and dreadful (v. 7), fierce (v. 8), violent (v. 9), and scoffers of kings (v. 10) will carry out the judgment that Habakkuk knew was well-deserved. The Chaldeans will assume that their victories were due to their own greatness. They won't know that God ordained the judgment they carried out.

LIFE STEP Sin always has consequences, but because God is longsuffering it does not always come immediately. Judah thought judgment delayed was judgment forgotten. Don't ever let that happen to you. "Always," in the words of Donald Barnhouse, "stay confessed up." (cf. 1 John 1:9)

Habakkuk 1:12-2:1

What is the writer saying?

How can I apply this to my life?

God's answer (vv. 5-11) to Habakkuk's question (vv. 2-4) only increased Habakkuk's anguish. Habakkuk is astonished that God would use the barbaric Chaldeans to punish His people. He asks a second question, bolder than the first. His question challenges the very character of God. In effect he says, *How can you do this? Are You not my Holy One?* (v. 12). Habakkuk reasons that God's holiness should have prohibited Him from using something as dirty as these barbarians to accomplish His will. In effect he says, *Are you not of purer eyes than to behold evil, and canst not look on iniquity. So how can You look on them that deal treacherously?* (v. 13). Habukkuk is puzzled as to how God could look on these perverters of justice, and use them to carry out His justice. How can He stand there silently when the wicked destroy those more righteous than they?

Habakkuk goes on to characterize the savagery of the Chaldeans. They sit like fishermen by the sea, a sea generously stocked with human fish (he's charging God with reducing mankind to the level of fish), pulling in fish after fish, sacrificing to their nets (those nets brought them their profit), eating until they are full, ("their portion is fat, and their meat plenteous" v. 16), and dumping their leftovers on the water's edge to die. How long, God, are you going to let this go on unchecked? (vv. 14-17).

Habakkuk then pauses (2:1) to await God's response to the charges he has leveled against Him (1:12-17). In his mind he stationed himself as a watchman upon a look-out tower. He wanted to be in position to get an early answer from God to pass on to others. He also appears to be bracing himself for a rebuke. He contemplates what he should answer when he is reproved (2:1).

LIFE STEP   Habakkuk didn't understand what was happening all around him, and why God didn't bring it to a halt. But he never stopped doing what God had called him to do. He was a prophet, so he took up his watch. Let us, even in days of confusion and darkness, continue to shine as lights in an ever-darkening world.

TUESDAY 36

Habakkuk 2:2-14

What is the writer saying?

How can I apply this to my life?

Dr. Ron Blue says, "God does not mumble. He speaks with clarity and forthrightness." This passage is proof of that. Habakkuk has leveled some serious charges at God, and has asked some very pointed questions. Now, as he stands watch upon the tower, God answers, "Write the vision, and make it plain upon tablets, that he may run that readeth it." God wanted it permanently recorded, with clarity, so that when it was delivered to others (this was not for Habakkuk alone) it would be clearly understood.

When dealing with prophecy, patience is necessary. But when the prophecy comes from God, you can be sure that it is true and will take place at God's appointed time (v. 3). God's answer to Habakkuk in effect is, *Yes, My eyes are too pure to approve evil; the wicked shall be punished.* In the meantime He reminds Habakkuk that "the just shall live by his faith" (v. 4). He follows up His

exhortation for patience by detailing five woes that will fall upon sinners. (Three of these woes are in these verses; two are in the following section.) A woe is an exclamation of distress pronounced in the face of the disaster of coming judgment (cf. Isaiah 3:11; 5:11; 10:1).

Woe #1, because of intimidation, greed, aggression, wanting that which is not his (vv. 5-8). *Woe #2*, because of covetousness, exploitation, and extortion which are clearly prohibited in Old Testament Law (vv. 9-11). *Woe #3*, for violence, cruel suffering, building cities with the blood and sweat of others less fortunate (vv. 12-13).

In contrast, God's future kingdom on earth will feature a reign of righteousness (v. 14). This thrilling prophecy, to be fulfilled in the millennial kingdom, is not only given here, but in four other Old Testament passages (Numbers 14:21; Psalm 72:19; Isaiah 6:3 and 11:9).

LIFE STEP *Patience* is a good word when life's circumstances and the world around us seem unfair. But to gain God's perspective you must ask Him for answers. Habakkuk did, and we should as well. They are to be found in His Word if we will just be patient. *The just live by faith.*

WEDNESDAY 36

Habakkuk 2:15-20

What is the writer saying?

How can I apply this to my life?

The quick glimpse at Israel's wonderful future in the millennial kingdom has interrupted the five woes pronounced upon the Babylonians for their cruel, sinful behavior. The text now returns to the last two *woes*.

In *woe #4*, once again the focus is on the Babylonians' barbaric behavior. In this instance it is upon the inhumane indignities they sometimes forced upon their victims. For example, giving wine to his neighbor in order to get him drunk, thereby inducing some sort of disgraceful behavior in order to bring him to shame (v. 15). But one day the Lord will turn the tables, and what they thought was glory will be turned to shame, for they will drink, get drunk, and be exposed before God as sinful people (v. 16). And the cup they drink from will come from the Lord's right hand, clearly a picture of divine punishment. (vv. 15-17).

Woe #5, the final woe, condemns Babylon's idolatry. God asks this penetrating question, "What profiteth the graven image?" The answer, of course, is no profit. Idols are lifeless creations of their own worshipers that can neither teach nor even speak (v. 18). With withering satire God pronounces His *woe* on the sin of idolatry. How ridiculous to call out to a dumb idol, "Awake!" (Remember Mt. Carmel and the prophets of Baal? 1 Kings 18:26-29.) The idol has no breath to respond (v. 19). *But*, here comes the great contrast, "The Lord is in His holy temple: let all the earth keep silence before him." How wonderful to serve and worship a living, self-existent, eternal, and holy God who rules the universe from on high (cf. Psalms 11:4; 18:6, 9; Micah 1:2-3). The lesson for Habakkuk is simply this: Stop complaining. Stop doubting. God is in control. Sin will be judged. Righteousness will prevail. Stand in silent and patient awe as you await His intervention. (vv. 18-20).

LIFE STEP Heed the instructions to Habakkuk and do the same. And remember, *the just live by faith*. So live!

Habakkuk 3:1-19

What is the writer saying?

How can I apply this to my life?

PRAY Taiwan – For renewed minds, committed discipleship, and humble service to characterize the church.

The book of Habakkuk begins with a confused prophet. He sees his people's sins and says to God, *How long are You going to tolerate such behavior?* God answers by saying that judgment is coming at the hands of the Babylonians. His perplexity increases. *How can You do this? They are even worse! They, too, need to be judged.* God says, *They will be*, and in chapter 2 He describes just how. With that answer, Habakkuk becomes a changed man. No more is he complaining or questioning. Here in chapter 3 he is simply offering up to God, who once again has demonstrated that He's got everything under control, a wonderful prayer of praise and worship.

He begins by asking God to carry out (revive, preserve) the work He has just described. It is a work of judgment both on His people and on Babylon. While not fully comprehending God's ways, he is satisfied that they are best (v. 2). He then goes on to review Israel's history (vv. 3-16). He compares the appearance of God at Sinai (v. 3) to a thunderstorm, with its darkness and flashing lights (cf. Psalm 18:9-14), and then relates some of God's judgments in days gone by. He compares pestilence (v. 5) with Exodus chapters 7-12; judgment on the *rivers* with Exodus 7:20-25 and the *sea* (v. 8) with Exodus 14:13-31; the *sun and the moon stood still* (v. 11) with Joshua 10:12-13. Habakkuk uses these events of the past to form the background for God's future judgment on His enemies (v. 12) and for the deliverance of His people (v. 13).

The final three verses (17-19) provide for the reader one of the finest confessions of faith ever recorded. Paraphrased, it says, *Though everything around me falls apart – vineyards, fields, flocks, herds – yet will I rejoice in the God of my salvation, for He provides for me the strength needed to face the trials ahead.*

LIFE STEP Habakkuk has many lessons to teach us. At the top of the list would be that just as God has a plan for Israel, so He does for us. Habakkuk sought God's direction as to that plan. We should do the same as we endeavor to serve Him in our day. Remember, *the just live by faith* in Him.

Zephaniah 1:1–3:7

What is the writer saying?

How can I apply this to my life?

The theme of Zephaniah is *The Day of the Lord*. It contains *bad* news. However, thankfully, it does not end that way. There is some *good* news for those who "trust in the name of the Lord" (3:12).

The first and larger portion of the book deals with the *bad news*. The early verses (vv. 1-3) predict a worldwide judgment occurring on the day of the Lord, broadly stated in verse 2: "I will utterly consume all." On that day, every trace of idol worship and all other false gods will be obliterated, and those who turned back from the Lord will be judged (v. 6). Not even God's holy city, Jerusalem, will escape (v. 12). God's judgment will be so severe that men will wander around like blind men, stumbling in the dark (1:17-18). In the near future, the Babylonians under Nebuchadnezzar would defeat Judah and destroy Jerusalem, thus partially fulfilling this prophecy. Ultimately this predicted judgment will be finalized in the Tribulation Period.

With such severe judgment in view, the doomed were called together to seek repentance (2:1-3). If they repented, "it may be that you will be hidden [the meaning of Zephaniah's name] in the day of the Lord's anger" (v. 3). In verses 4 to 15, the Gentile nations around Israel will be judged: Philistia (west); Moab and Ammon (east); Ethiopia (south); and Assyria (north). Judah and Jerusalem will also be judged (3:1-7). Jerusalem is particularly criticized because she ignored the special blessings from God and had become filthy and polluted (3:1). Four charges are leveled against Judah in verse 2: She did not obey, receive correction, trust the Lord, or draw near to God. Because God is absolutely righteous, He could no longer tolerate such evil. The nations were cut off which should have caused Judah to take note and shape up. She didn't repent, however, so she is rebuked and punished.

LIFE STEP God must discipline wrong behavior, especially in His own children (Hebrews 12:6). But true repentance and confession of sin will bring forgiveness and cleansing (1 John 1:9). Be sure to heed the lesson Judah failed to learn.

What is the writer saying?

How can I apply this to my life?

PRAY
El Salvador – For those taking Bible correspondence courses to gain a passion for studying the Word.

The second and smaller portion of the book deals with *good*. In these verses the tone of the book changes. In the first seven verses of chapter 3, Zephaniah scolds Jerusalem's leaders for the deplorable, sinful condition into which Judah had fallen. They were ignoring the Lord's presence and pursuing corrupt activities despite His offer of deliverance (vv. 6-7).

Finally, there is a glimmer of hope. In verse 8 we read, "Therefore, wait ye upon me, saith the Lord." The very hopelessness of the sin of the people makes divine action necessary, and in that action comes hope. From verse 9 through the rest of the chapter and book (v. 20), Zephaniah describes the millennial age and some of its blessings. He says the Lord will restore to the people a pure worship ("language"), an obvious contrast to the blasphemy of idolatrous worship that God was planning to judge.

In verses 10 through 13 a remnant of the Jewish nation is regathered, a remnant without iniquity or deceit (v. 13). They will sing and shout for joy (v. 14), for Christ Himself will be reigning in their midst (v. 15), a guarantee of safety (v. 16). The regathered are commanded to abstain from fear ("Let not thine hands be slack," i.e., the posture of one who is discouraged) and to be encouraged because of His presence (vv. 16-17). And to those who are sorrowful (v. 18), God is going to make all things right. His enemies will be defeated, the disenfranchised regathered and praised by God (v. 20, the fulfillment of Israel's destiny, Deuteronomy 26:19). Will this happen? Absolutely, "says the Lord" (v. 20). This is a promise confirmed by His name.

LIFE STEP
Good news, bad news. It all depends on one's relationship to Jesus Christ. For Israel that good news is yet future. But for you it can be today. Christ died for your sins. If you have already trusted in the good news, thank Him. And if you have not trusted in Him, why not do it today? That will be good news (see Acts 16:31).

DEUTERONOMY

Pentateuch means *five books*. Deuteronomy is the fifth of the Five Books of Moses. It is a review of the whole Law of Moses for the generation that was born during the forty years of wilderness wanderings. Deuteronomy means *Second Law*. It contains Moses' last instructions before he was killed by the Lord on Mount Pisgah (Nebo) on the east side of the Jordan River. Moses was allowed to see the Promised Land, but because of his disobedience in the second *water from the rock* incident, he was not allowed to enter the Promised Land (Numbers 20:8-12). The book was written about 1400 B.C. The book is considered to be the constitution of the new nation of Israel. It presents the government of national Israel as a theocracy (*God rule*). While God was the highest ruler, He is pictured ruling through human mediators such as Moses, Joshua, the Judges, and eventually the Davidic kings climaxing with Messiah Himself in the full manifestation of God's kingdom on earth. Outline of the book:

Past Journeys	1-4
Present Obligations	5-26
Future Possibilities	27-30
Moses' Last Days	31-34

In the ancient Middle East, when a superior power made a covenant with an inferior group, there was a set pattern to the terminology of the contract (known as a *suzerainty treaty*). It would include the following items, as does the book of Deuteronomy:

- King's Greatness Described
- Review of the King's Past Gracious Dealings
- Conditions of the Covenant
- Violent Warnings for Disobedience

Copies of the treaty would be placed in the temples of the two sides and read regularly for review and reminder. Since God's and Israel's temples were the same, some suggest that the *tablets* (plural) in the Ark of the Covenant were actually two copies of the law given to Moses on Mount Sinai.

Notable sections of Deuteronomy would include the Ten Commandments (5:6-21), the *Sh'ma*, a theological statement of Jewish monotheism (6:4), the background for the use of the phylacteries and mezuzah (6:5-9), the primacy of the land promises to Israel (8:7-9; 29:1–30:20), capital punishment for false teachers (13:1-5) and spiritists (18:9-15), God's year-long *honeymoon* for newlyweds (24:5), the prediction of the *wandering Jew* (28:64), and God's tender love and eternal concern for His chosen people (32:10; 33:26). The importance of the book of Deuteronomy is seen in the way in which the New Testament authors use the book. Seventeen of the twenty-seven books of the New Testament quote the book. Perhaps the most impressive statistic is that in Christ's wilderness temptations, He rebuffed Satan all three times with scriptural quotations from the book of Deuteronomy.

Deuteronomy 1:1-18

What is the writer saying?

How can I apply this to my life?

Moses will soon die at 120 years of age. He spent his first forty years in Egypt in the Pharaoh's court. He was a shepherd in the land of Midian (to the east of Egypt and south of Israel) for another forty years. At eighty years of age God sent him back to Egypt. Now forty more years have passed in the wilderness wanderings, and Moses is led to prepare the new generation for his departure and their entrance into the Promised Land. The place names give us a good idea of their movements and the extent of the territory promised them. Horeb (v. 2) is another name for Mount Sinai. It would be the southern-most place mentioned. The Euphrates River is the northern-most place mentioned. The distance is about 550 miles. The eleventh month (v. 3) in the Jewish calendar would be February. Spring was coming and soon the children of Israel would observe their first Passover in the Promised Land (in the month of March, Joshua 5:10). With the naked eye we can only see about five thousand distinct stars. Today scientists tell us that there are billions of stars in the universe. To liken something to the stars in the sky speaks of a large number that is almost impossible for humans to count (v. 10). We know that the number of Israelites was about 2.5 million at this time (based on Numbers 26). Moses reviews the bureaucratic arrangement designed to help administer the affairs of such a large number of people. He graciously does not mention all the conflict he experienced with the people. He didn't feel a need to because by this time every one twenty years and older had died off. The Amorites (v. 7) are singled out for destruction. The word means *high lands* and was a synonym for the Canaanites. They practiced infant sacrifice and gross immorality.

LIFE STEP Transitions: When planned, they can powerfully influence the next generation for good. When poorly handled, it can take years to recover.

Deuteronomy 1:19-31

What is the writer saying?

How can I apply this to my life?

Verse 2 informed us that it took the Israelites eleven days to travel from Horeb to Kadesh-barnea. The distance is about 140 miles, which would average twelve miles per day. Kadesh means *consecrated*, a reference to the presence of the tabernacle there. It became the pivot point of the wilderness wanderings. There the time of wandering judgment started. Earlier, in Genesis 14:7, it was called Enmishpat (*well of judgment*). In Numbers 20 it is given a third name, Meribah (*strife*). It was here that Miriam was buried and Moses sinned by striking the rock the second time. In verses 19-31 Moses reviews the failures of the Israelites. He uses a literary device known as *corporate solidarity*. Even though the Israelites who disobeyed were dead, Moses speaks as though the current generation was at fault. This is not to imply that the sins of the fathers are passed onto the children, but rather that the children have the same potential for disobedience. At this crucial juncture in their history they need to steel their minds against a similar rebellion and a similar fate. Most of Israel is mountainous (v. 24). Eschol means *cluster* as in cluster of grapes. It was a fertile valley near Hebron, about fifty miles north of Kadesh-barnea and twenty miles south of Jerusalem. Remember, Amorite means *high place* and they were *going up* to fight the Amorites (v. 28). Anakim refers to *giants*. Moses reminds the new generation that God was willing and able to protect their fathers. Their fathers lost heart and failed. They should not repeat the performance. When their faith falters, they should remember the great deliverance from Egypt (v. 30).

LIFE STEP Failure is so depressing. Gossips revel in failure, perhaps excusing their own poor performance. Wise people learn from failure and take steps not to repeat it.

TUESDAY 37

Deuteronomy 1:32-46

What is the writer saying?

How can I apply this to my life?

PRAY Philippines – For missionaries to the 13,000,000 plus living in Manila to affect every level of society.

Verse 33 refers to the shekinah glory of God that led them through the wilderness wanderings. It was a pillar of fire at night and a cloud of smoke by day. It represented God's presence with His people. The word *shekinah* does not mean glory. It means *dwelling*. God dwelled with His beloved chosen people. It is also the root word for *tabernacle* and *tent*. God was *tabernacle-ing* or *tenting* with His people. Jesus took on the *tabernacle* of human flesh that He might represent the Godhead to mankind (John 1:18). God in His Spirit existence may seem *wholly other*, but the ultimate *Great Communicator* desires to reveal Himself to His creatures and to do so, took on a form that we can identify with—human flesh. Of all that rebellious generation, only two adults, Caleb and Joshua, were allowed to survive the Wilderness Wanderings and then enter the Promised Land (vv. 36-38). Caleb means *dog*. That sounds harsh until you remember that even in Biblical times, the faithfulness of a dog to its master was known (ancient dog cemeteries have been uncovered in Israel). If anything can be said about Caleb, he was faithful to his God. His father's name, Jephunneh, means *he is ready*. Joshua means *Jehovah is Salvation*. It is the Hebrew form of *Jesus* and comes from the same root word as Isaiah and Hosea. What a dynamic duo those two men must have been. At 85 years-of-age, Caleb says, "give me this mountain" (Joshua 14:12). Joshua's father's name is repeated twenty nine times in the Bible, always to identify Joshua, but we know nothing about him. Perhaps we can conclude that such a great son must have had a fine father! (His name, Nun, means *fish* referring to fruitfulness).

LIFE STEP If God were to open His Word once again and add some more books to His Bible, would you or I be worthy of inclusion in the great story?

What is the writer saying?

How can I apply this to my life?

PRAY Bulgaria – That Christians would be protected from the violent attacks of neo-Nazi groups.

The forty years of Wilderness Wanderings (2:7) is broken into sub-sections. They took thirteen months and twenty days getting to and being at Mount Sinai (Numbers 10:11). The trip and events at Kadesh-barnea added another ten months. Following the failure, they then spent another thirty eight years until they entered the land. Verse 14 brings the story to the fortieth year (2+38). Chapter 2 mentions a number of the local peoples. Some we know a lot about, others very little. These details are interesting and support the historicity of the account. If the story were invented, then the storyteller would have explained the significance of every actor in the story. Since he doesn't, it affirms the reality of the story. The three enemy nations that we do know are all related to Israel. Edom came from Jacob's twin brother Esau. Moab and Ammon were the sons of Lot, Abraham's nephew. The river Zered (v. 14) was the natural boundary between Edom and Moab. It flowed into the southeastern corner of the Dead Sea. Chapters 2 and 3 describe the battles with the two Amorite kings, Sihon and Og, that gave the entire eastern side of the Jordan to Israel, except the territories of Edom, Moab, and Ammon. Two tribes (Reuben and Gad) and half of Manasseh decided to settle in this area. The victory over Sihon and Og was a memorable one (v. 21). *Og* is the root of the English word *ogre* (!). He was one of the last giants of the ancient world (3:11). Moses is enthused with these victories and the promise of more as they get ready to cross the Jordan. He begs God to allow him to go, but God tells him to stop asking (v. 26). For a second time Moses acknowledges that he too had failed to have faith in God like their fathers (1:37 and 3:26 "for your sakes" implies *in fairness to you*). On Mt. Pisgah (*Cleft*) Moses looked into the Promised Land and died.

LIFE STEP Even the great Moses had to pay a steep price for his disobedience. What blessings do we miss out on because of our poor attitude or behavior?

What is the writer saying?

How can I apply this to my life?

PRAY Ukraine – For outreach to eastern Ukraine, which is much less exposed to the Gospel than western Ukraine.

Moses knows that he will soon die. What must it be like to know that you are going to die very soon? Is every breath precious? Does every meeting and event trigger thoughts of "I will never pass this way again?" It is hard to say in Moses' case because he had already tasted the supernatural. Perhaps death was no more intimidating to him than getting up in the morning. Most intriguing: did he know that God was not done with him and would return him to the earth on the Mount of Transfiguration (Matthew 17) and perhaps as one of the two witnesses (Revelation 11)? "That ye may live" (v. 1) is not talking about *meriting salvation*. Salvation has always been by faith. Law observance was designed to aid in the believer's growth (sanctification). *Living* also refers to the physical blessings associated with obedience as opposed to *dying* which is the ultimate physical punishment for disobedience (like Nadab and Abihu and Ananias and Sapphira who were not necessarily unsaved people). The challenge of verse 2 is repeated in Deuteronomy 12:32 and Revelation 22:18-19. It does not apply to the whole Bible at once (otherwise we'd have no additional books after Deuteronomy!) but to each individual inspired book. Don't change the teaching of the book as originally given.

Deuteronomy 3:29 says that the children of Israel were currently at "Beth-peor" (*House of the god named Peor*). Verse 3 in today's section reminds them of the tragedy of Baal-peor (*Lord Peor*, probably also called Chemosh). This is a reference to Numbers 25 and the sin of the Israelites in worshipping the god of the Moabites and Midianites. 24,000 died in judgment. This had just happened and would be a fresh memory.

LIFE STEP Human history is a warning to the new generation. We study the past to learn the mistakes of the past and should determine not to repeat them.

Deuteronomy 4:21-31

What is the writer saying?

How can I apply this to my life?

PRAY **PRAY** Ghana – For godly leaders who will help bring guidance and stability to this newly democratic society.

Having reminded the Israelites of their recent failure, Moses reflects again on his own personal failure. Despite his general godliness and effectiveness for the Lord, God was not going to allow him to enter the land. The love of God cannot be used as a justification for slighting His holiness. "For your sakes" (v. 21) implies that his chastisement would be a good example and warning for them. Moses then warns them that their greatest temptation will be to worship the gods and goddesses of the Gentiles around them. Amazingly, this was their first downfall upon leaving Egypt some forty years earlier. God had no sooner delivered them from Pharaoh's army by parting the Red Sea than they were dancing around the golden calf at the base of Mount Sinai. The psychology is almost unbelievable, but the implication is that we would have fallen into the same trap. How often does God show His sovereign hand in our life only to have us shrivel into a ball of faithless flesh the next time a challenge comes our way!? Moses' greatest fears were realized in the subsequent history. The golden calf would come back, resurrected by the rebel Jeroboam to keep his subjects from traveling to Jerusalem to worship Jehovah (1 Kings 12:28). Baal worship would return (1 Kings 18). Isaiah and Jeremiah would thunder against the idols. Finally, it was the Babylonian Captivity that cured the Israelites of polytheism. Ironically, when Jesus came to them about five hundred years later, they were so convinced of monotheism that they rejected Jesus as a deity thinking that the Father could be the only personality in the universe possessing deity. In the terminal generation, demonic idol worship will once again compete for man's allegiance to the Creator God (Revelation 9:20).

LIFE STEP The messenger must deliver the message, even if few listen. Ask God to give you a chance to speak up for Him today.

Deuteronomy 4:32-40

What is the writer saying?

How can I apply this to my life?

PRAY Dominican Republic – For God to send workers to the 4,000 villages that have no Gospel witness.

Moses tried to get out of his leadership job forty years earlier by arguing that he was not a good public speaker. Well, these verses are eloquent, powerful, and moving. I wonder how any Israelite ever fell away from the Lord after these convicting and convincing arguments. His scope is all encompassing. He goes back to the beginning of time. He flatters their intellect by asking if any of them had ever heard anything remotely close to God's dealings with them. It may seem to be an exaggeration to think that these poor slaves would have had access to much information, but remember, Egypt was the greatest empire on the earth at that time. When Moses left Egypt, the great pyramids had already been standing for over eight hundred years. Even slaves and servants catch wind of what their masters know. The knowledge of the world flowed to Egypt and nothing could compare to the stories of Jehovah's care for His people. Apparently no one in the world at that time could convincingly claim that God had spoken to them out of a fire like He did with the Israelites (v. 33). "Temptations" (v. 34) refers to the *testings* that God poured out upon the Egyptians in the ten plagues. Each plague attacked one of the supposed gods of the Egyptians, proving "before your eyes" (v. 34) that Jehovah is superior. In fact, He is not only superior; He alone is God. The other *gods* had a severe problem—they didn't even exist (v. 35)! Obedience to this great solo God is the only way to true happiness and success. "Earth" in verse 40 refers to the Promised Land. God is giving it to them "for ever."

LIFE STEP It would be easy to condemn the Israelites if it weren't for the nagging thought that in many ways our failures are not much different—and we've had more light than they! We cannot presume upon God's grace. We are saved by grace, but we are blessed as we obey Him.

Deuteronomy 5:1-21

What is the writer saying?

How can I apply this to my life?

After a lengthy review of Israel's history, Moses now formally reminds the nation of the specific laws God delivered to them at Sinai (Horeb). This chapter is the third occurrence of the Ten Commandments in Scripture. Most people know about Exodus 20. They also appear in Leviticus 19, which, interestingly enough, many commentators feel is the Old Testament passage that the entire book of James is based on. Horeb means *dryness* and may refer to the entire mountain range while Sinai was the particular peak God descended upon. Sinai could refer to an ancient pagan moon god named *Sin*. If that is the case, then the only true God is pictured taking back what was falsely dedicated to an imposter. Sinai could also come from the Hebrew word for *thorny* which would refer to the treacherous ravines that make travel difficult there. Moses underscores the fact that even though his listeners are the new generation, the law from Horeb was for them. They can't avoid obeying it based on the argument that the contract was made with their fathers, not them. "Made a covenant" (v. 2) is literally, *cut a covenant*. It refers to both the process of engraving the covenant on stone and also the cutting of a sacrificial animal to ratify the covenant (with the implication that if either party breaks the covenant, they will be chopped up like the animal. Genesis 15:1-21). Moses says that God spoke "face to face" to them (which was the original intent and practical outcome) but then he qualifies his statement with the detail that actually he was the mediator because of their fear of God speaking directly to all of them. One feature of the development of God's program in Scripture is that He has elected to always administer His program through human mediators. Christ is the final and ultimate mediator.

LIFE STEP How many times does God have to say something for it to be true? Once is the logical answer, but when He repeats information, then we really need to listen!

Deuteronomy 5:22-33

What is the writer saying?

How can I apply this to my life?

PRAY Australia – For the 630,000 university students who need a gospel witness.

God wrote the Ten Commandments on two tablets. Traditionally, we envision this as five commandments on one tablet and five on the other. This very well may have been how it was done. A second possibility (or additional detail) is that in ancient treaties, two copies were made, one to be placed in the temple of the one party and the other to go into the temple of the second party. The god would watch to see that they were obeying the treaty. In the case of Israel, God and His people shared one temple so both copies went into the Ark of the Covenant in the Holy of Holies. In verses 22-33, the main idea is the awesomeness of our God. His appearance, although veiled, is overwhelming to everyone except Moses. All the people request that God stop talking to them. They want Moses alone to run the risk of being consumed by the holiness of God. They agree to trust Moses to repeat accurately what

God says, and that in fact, they will obey what Moses says God has told them to do. This appears to be pleasing to God and Moses does not object. However, later Korah will lead an unsuccessful rebellion against Moses out of jealousy. In hindsight, it might have been wise for Moses to ask for a few eyewitnesses to his encounter with God. God mentions twice in this section (vv. 29, 33) that He desires to physically bless Israel. Their only requirement was to obey Him. Over a period of forty days, God gave Moses a total of 613 regulations. There are 365 prohibitions (for the days in the year?) and 248 affirmations (by Jewish tradition, one for every bone in our body but that is not the modern "bone count"). The New Testament says that apart from the indwelling Spirit of God, it is impossible for sinful men to obey such laws. The Israelites were doomed before they even got started!

LIFE STEP When faced with temptation we must flee to God for strength and refuge. We cannot face the world, the flesh, or the devil in our own strength.

Deuteronomy 6:1-11

What is the writer saying?

How can I apply this to my life?

PRAY Serbia - Due to political changes, there are many open doors for the Gospel. Pray that the church would seize this time in history to evangelize youth.

Can you imagine what it would be like to know that you will be entering a land, killing the inhabitants, and taking their houses, farms, orchards, wells, and vineyards? After only knowing slavery and then being vagabonds, a nice cozy farm would be the stuff of dreams. Moses said that it was a land that "floweth with milk and honey" (v. 3). In comparison to the wilderness they were wandering in, it would be a paradise. "Milk" refers to goat's milk that was drunk fresh or turned into sour cream, yogurt, butter, or cheese. "Honey" was both bees' honey and the sweet paste made from grapes and dates. Can you imagine the interpersonal struggles as the farmland was divided among the various families? Fortunately, the law was a fence to protect them from foreign contamination and to guide them in their interpersonal relationships if only they would follow it. Chapter 6 is the ultimate expression within Judaism of the importance of learning, studying, teaching, and following the Law throughout the generations. Verse 4 is the *John 3:16* of Judaism, both in the sense that it is the most popular of Old Testament verses and also because it succinctly defines Jewish theology. It is called *the Sh'ma* based on the first word of the verse, "Hear." It is used within Judaism to announce strict monotheism. Amazingly, the name for God appears three times and the word *one* is not the Hebrew term for *singularity* but rather the word for *unity in diversity*. From verse 8 comes the practice of wrapping the leather straps on the left hand, arm, and forehead (called phylacteries) when praying. These have scriptures in the headpiece and arm piece. Verse 9 led Jewish people to place the little metal mezuzahs in their doorways with scripture verses inside, which they kiss when entering and leaving the home.

LIFE STEP According to this passage at what time of day or night can we relax and not think about God? How often do you think of your "significant other"? Should we treat God any less?

WEDNESDAY 38

Deuteronomy 6:12-25

What is the writer saying?

How can I apply this to my life?

What generation Christian are you? Have you noticed a distressing trend in our churches? A man and his wife get gloriously saved out of a life of rebellion and self-centeredness. They eagerly teach their children all about their newfound faith. The children grow up impressed with the salvation story of their parents and happy to claim Christ as well. They grow up in the church, marry church people, and then set about to establish the third generation. Here's where some Christian dynasties fall apart. The children of the third generation know nothing of the horror of sin. They become bored with *churchianity* and find the world to be an appealing taboo. A distressing number of third and fourth generations drift back towards the world. The dangers of the world and the great deliverance offered by God have not been successfully transmitted and the glamour of the world is too strong. I suspect we do not try hard enough. The power of the world, the flesh, and the devil is regularly underestimated. If we had a full understanding of the enemy's strategies, I wonder if we would continue to enjoy the TV programs, videos, and music that currently *entertain* us? Massah means *testing* and refers to events surrounding the first striking of the rock for water (Exodus 17:1-7). The Passover meal was specifically designed to be an annual reminder of what God did for Israel. Here in Deuteronomy 6:12-25 every day is a potential *Passover discussion* with the children. Unfortunately, the Old Testament contains over one thousand years' worth of failure (Moses to Malachi). When the New Testament story opens four hundred years later, the situation has not improved and the people reject and crucify their Messiah.

LIFE STEP Repeated failure is not an excuse to quit. Every generation has to be won afresh. Every member of every generation has to be won specifically. Where do you stand in this *Conflict of the Ages*?

THURSDAY 38

Deuteronomy 8:1-10

What is the writer saying?

How can I apply this to my life?

PRAY   El Salvador – Praise the Lord for the establishment of a democracy and for religious freedom.

Chapter 7 commands the Israelites to completely destroy the Canaanites lest their moral and religious corruption contaminate Israel. They are not to intermarry lest they be tempted to worship their gods (as eventually even Solomon did). They are not to fear them since God has already promised victory. They are to destroy all the idols and places of false worship. Chapters 8-10 give reasons why Israel should be faithful to God and God alone. God brought them out of Egypt. He is the one who took care of them for forty years in the wilderness. He gave them the manna from heaven. No one else ever received manna (manna means *what is it?*). Despite it being nutritious, the Israelites eventually resented it. God says in verse 3 that He purposely limited their diet to teach them to look beyond the physical to the spiritual. What is our diet like? Do we have a greater variety and a vaster amount of physical or spiritual food? God protected their clothing and shoe leather for forty years. How much of our wardrobe is older than five years? Jesus quoted verse 3 when tempted by the devil in the wilderness (Matthew 4:4). In fact, all three of the verses He used to deflect Satan's temptations come from the Book of Deuteronomy. We forget or try to ignore the fact that *disciple* comes from the same root as *discipline*. Humans naturally avoid *discipline*. That is why so many of us are overweight, out of shape, and struggle with high blood pressure and high cholesterol. Amazingly, we admire athletes and military personnel who highly discipline their bodies. Certainly God expects more of His children than what many currently offer.

LIFE STEP   Reward is available for believers when they enter the Promised Land. Is that Heaven for us? Or perhaps some discipline in this life would provide reward in this life as well—healthier living, longer life, richer life, more satisfying life?

FRIDAY 38

Deuteronomy 8:11-20

What is the writer saying?

How can I apply this to my life?

PRAY   Cuba – Protection for those making undeclared mission trips into this country.

Verses 11-20 warn against falling in love with the gifts of their God and not God Himself. God warns about becoming complacent. How often in human history have soldiers been lulled into dullness by rich parties? Humans with their lack of discipline take the path of least resistance. Once the crisis passes and we are stable, there is a tendency to forget the urgency of maintaining a close walk with the Lord. In fact, God even warns against pride in verses 14 and 17. We have a tendency to take credit for our own success. Certainly many men and women deserve their success in the sense that they diligently work for it. However, even the most talented and diligent individual owes his very breath to God and should not be taking credit for his lot in life. If they stop giving God the credit, it is hard to understand why they would begin to give other gods thanks (v. 19). We can blame it on the deception of Satan or just the perverseness of the human heart. In the confusion that sin brings, the human heart longs to worship something, but that something is patterned after ourselves. The *worship* that we create for this god made in our own image also flatters our egos and tempts our senses. Hence the beautiful art, music, and architecture associated with most of the religions of the world. Or the fleshly expressions of the fertility cults were justified as an innocent picture of agricultural fertility. What an unfair competition between Judaism and Baal worship on the human level. Baal worship cries, "Come, visit my temple prostitute!" Judaism offers, "Come, submit to circumcision." The pleasure of sin exists, but only for a brief period. To put starch in their souls, God warns that if they indulge in the banquet of this life, they will actually become a banquet for the vultures of the field.

LIFE STEP   Eat from the good hand of God, or be eaten! The follower of God must take the long view. Do we want to be happy for a moment or for eternity?

Deuteronomy 9:1-12

What is the writer saying?

How can I apply this to my life?

PRAY   Mexico – Protection of believers in Chiapas and Oaxaca who are persecuted for their faith.

By this time they have witnessed the great victory over the Egyptians, the miracles in the wilderness, and the defeat of Sihon and Og. You would think that there would be no question about God's ability to protect them. Moses anticipates that the living enemy ahead is more frightening than the memory of the dead enemy behind. The Canaanite cities were well fortified and some of the giants (v. 2) were still defending those cities. Moses also anticipates the human tendency to interpret everything with self in the center. God was going to protect them for His purposes (to destroy the sinful Canaanites, v. 4) and His great namesake (v. 5); not because of their worthiness. Paul explains in 2 Timothy 2:13, "If we believe not, yet he abideth faithful: he cannot deny himself." God doesn't pull any punches. How unpleasant it would be to be labeled a "stiffnecked people" (v. 6). He says that they have been this way for the entire forty years (v. 7). Amazingly, all of these people except Joshua and Caleb would have been younger than twenty at the time they departed from Egypt or not yet born. Still, God acts as though they were rebellious because they possessed the same human nature that their parents did. The tying together of persons and events is called *corporate solidarity*. They might not have been there, nor done these things, but by connection with their parents, it is as though they were there and did those things. Subsequent events prove that they were of the same nature since almost immediately there are problems in the Promised Land (see the book of Judges). Corporate solidarity also explains why Jesus started His ministry with forty days of fasting in the wilderness. It was to identify Himself with these people and with Moses.

LIFE STEP   But for the grace of God, there go I. It is so tempting to point the finger at the Israelites until we contemplate the rebellion of our own hearts. What "Israelite-like" attitude or activity do I need to forsake today?

Deuteronomy 9:13-29

What is the writer saying?

How can I apply this to my life?

Moses relays the conversation between God and himself, as God wants to destroy the Israelites. God makes an attractive offer to Moses; let me destroy the people and I will start over with you. Some question why a sovereign God, who already knows what He is going to do, would make such an offer to a mere man. We need to remember that God, as an infinite Spirit Being, is difficult for humans to comprehend. Therefore, He frequently speaks of Himself as though He were a man with a face and arms and hands, and so forth. These are *anthropomorphisms*, speaking of God in human terms that we can understand. It would seem that His conversation with Moses is also for our benefit; to show the depth of His annoyance with the sin of Israel and also to give Moses a chance to reveal his love and concern for Israel. In the sovereign plan of God, He decreed that Moses' intercession for forty days would move His hand to protect and not destroy Israel. Can you imagine no food, no drink, and all prayer for forty days and nights? What a godly and self-sacrificing man Moses was! Taberah is another place where Israel provoked the Lord (v. 22). It means *burning* because fire from the Lord consumed the complainers (see Numbers 11:3). Massah means *testing* and is the place of the first striking of the rock for water (see Exodus 17:7). Kibroth-hattaavah means *The Graves of Lust*. Here God gave them quail to eat but many died because of their incessant complaints (see Numbers 11:34). Moses continues to catalog their rebellion (at least of their fathers) and concludes that he asked God not to destroy Israel for two reasons, both of which center on God's glory: 1) His promises to Abraham, Isaac, and Jacob, and 2) His reputation among the Gentiles.

LIFE STEP Prayer secret: Pray for things that will bring glory to God. He delights to honor Himself and His plan. We need to discover His will and then pray that it be done.

Deuteronomy 10:1-10

What is the writer saying?

How can I apply this to my life?

PRAY New Zealand – For the emergence of a new generation of godly Maori leaders to evangelize their culturally alienated people.

God invited Moses up Mt. Sinai a second time and with His own finger He wrote the Ten Commandments on the tablets of stone. The new set is placed in a wooden ark. Shittim or Acacia wood grows in the desert and is valued for cabinetry. Israel had this ark from 1440 B.C. until we lose sight of it in 586 B.C. with the destruction of the first temple by Nebuchadnezzar. Tradition says that the prophet Jeremiah hid it. Perhaps it still exists somewhere in the world. Beeroth (v. 6) means *wells*. Israel stopped there twice in the forty years, but we know little about it or the descendents of Jaakan (*twisted one*) who lived there. Mosera means *bond*. Aaron died near Mt. Hor, so Mosera must have been nearby (Numbers 33:37-38). We don't know what Aaron means. His third oldest son, Eleazar, became high priest in his place (sons Nadab and Abihu were killed earlier for offering strange fire on the altar). His name means *God Helps*.

Later in Israel's history, the office of high priest inexplicably jumps to the fourth son's line (Ithamar). The judge and high priest Eli was apparently the first of Ithamar's line to be high priest. Because of Eli's failures, God announced that the office would revert to Eleazar's line which it did about one hundred years later in the time of David in the person of Zadok (see 1 Kings 2:26-35). Gudgodah (v. 7) means *cleft* and was the fortieth place Israel encamped (Numbers 33:32, here called Hor-hagidgad). Jotbath means *pleasantness* probably due to the abundant water there. Levi was the tribe of the high priest. Now it is named the tribe of all priests. They would not be given territory. Instead they lived in cities scattered among the other tribes as their local *pastors*.

LIFE STEP God is a God of decency and order. He expects our lives to be orderly in our spiritual disciplines and in our contribution to society.

Deuteronomy 10:11-22

What is the writer saying?

How can I apply this to my life?

Moses is repeating material, but repetition is good for remembrance. There are 613 laws to follow but Moses condenses them to their logical base: reverence and love the Lord with every fiber of our being. The history of humanity is one long struggle of man's will against other wills. Man's sin blinds his eyes to the foolishness of resisting the will of One infinitely more intelligent. His commandments are designed, not to make man miserable, but rather to give him the happiest possible life. Israel was to rest in the fact that God meant them well. They are challenged to remove indifference, insensitivity, and sin from their inner man (v. 16). Verse 17 uses His highest title, His covenant name, LORD (Jehovah or Yahweh). He is compassionate, especially to the vulnerable (v. 18). They were currently vulnerable and should have taken heart from that promise. They would also one day become secure and when they became secure, they were to practice compassion with those less fortunate than themselves. "Fear" (v. 20) can refer to trembling fear but here the primary idea is *respect to whom respect is obviously due*. The Hebrew word for *cleave* (v. 20) is the same word used in Genesis 2:24 where God says that the man should cleave unto his wife in marriage. It refers to a strong bond, like a powerful adhesive, that will destroy one or both parties if the bond is broken. The Hebrew word for praise in verse 21 is *hallel* as in *hallelujah* (Praise Jehovah). Another Hebrew word for praise is the root of Judah from which the word *Jewish* comes. To be *Jewish* is to be a praiser of Jehovah.

LIFE STEP   We can't match wits with Jehovah. We can't give Him advice. So what does He want from us that we can give?

Deuteronomy 11:1-15

What is the writer saying?

How can I apply this to my life?

Seventy people went down to Egypt and 2.5 million came out four hundred years later. They owe Him their great numerical growth and stupendous redemption from Egyptian slavery. Notice how often in Deuteronomy Moses refers to the content of the Law as *statutes, judgments*, and *commandments*. In verse 1 a fourth term is added to this list, *charge*. These terms are somewhat parallel. *Charge* refers to a serious obligation, such as guard duty in the military. The Hebrew word is similar to the "Hear" of Deuteronomy 6:4 ("Hear, O Israel: The LORD our God is one LORD."). We are to *hear* and to *heed* His words. "Statutes" means *cut in stone*. This certainly is true of the Ten Commandments but applies metaphorically to anything important enough to be engraved. "Judgments" comes from the Hebrew word that is part of Jehoshaphat's name, *Jehovah Judges*. If you don't keep the charge

and statutes there is a consequence. "Commandments" comes from the Hebrew word that is part of *Bar Mitzvah*. We recognize the Bar Mitzvah ceremony as the right of passage into adulthood for a 13-year-old boy (or *Bat Mitzvah* at age 12 for a Jewish girl entering womanhood). The terms literally mean *Son (or Daughter) of the Commandment*. In this ceremony the Jewish person agrees to take on the obligations of the Jewish Law. Verse 2 shows God's delight in reaching out to help the Israelites. He exerts divine effort on our behalf. Dathan and Abiram (v. 6) were part of Korah's rebellion in Numbers 16. God reminds the Israelites that they have a motivation for obeying. In Egypt, the Nile was always there to provide water. Not so in Israel. They will depend upon God to send rain.

LIFE STEP What has God brought into your life to *encourage* you to trust Him and not your own capabilities? What can you do to improve your trust in Him?

Deuteronomy 11:16-32

What is the writer saying?

How can I apply this to my life?

In an agricultural society, one that accounted for 95% of the population at that time in human history, every waking moment centered on the fruitfulness of your land, animals, and wife. This is the reason why most competing religions involved fertility gods and goddesses (like Baal and Asherah) and fertility rites including temple prostitution. Verses 18-20 repeat Deuteronomy 6:6-10. Pious Jewish people pray formally three times per day; in the morning, afternoon, and again in the evening. They will wrap their left arm (closest to the heart) with leather straps, called phylacteries. The strap will be wrapped on the hand in such a way as to spell the Hebrew letter *Shin* on the back of the hand (it looks like a capital *W*). It is the first letter of the name for God, Shaddai (*Almighty*). The root of Shaddai means *mountain* and *breast* and as such speaks of both His protection and His provision. The leather strap has a headpiece with a leather box containing some portions of Scripture. The box hangs on the forehead, literally fulfilling verse 18. Jewish men cover their head with a kippa or yarmulka (out of reverence to God) and also cover their head and shoulders with a white and blue prayer shawl (the same colors as the modern Israeli flag). Their prayers are read from a prayer book and the body bounces to the rhythm of the words so that the entire person is caught up in prayer. Conservative Jewish families will place a mezuzah on the left doorframe of their house. The word means *door post* in Hebrew (v. 20). It has a little scroll of scripture inside. It also has the letter *shin* on the front for Shaddai. It is customary to kiss your fingers and touch the mezuzah reverently when passing. Today, Mount Gerizim (the Mountain of Blessing) has trees but Mount Ebal (the Mountain of Cursing & the altar) is bald (v. 29)!

LIFE STEP Fathers: The only time you don't have to teach is when the family sleeps! Every waking moment is a teaching/learning opportunity. How can we make the most of them all?

FRIDAY 39

Deuteronomy 15:12-23

What is the writer saying?

How can I apply this to my life?

PRAY Guatemala – For the growth and maturity of the churches in the nation.

Chapter 12 warns against worshipping other gods. Chapter 13 warns against false prophets. Chapter 14 covers tithing and clean and unclean animals. Basically, only herbivores could be eaten. Chapter 15 discusses poverty and social justice. All debts were cancelled every seventh year (the sabbatical year) to give the poor another chance. Likewise, if a poor Jewish person had to sell himself as a slave to pay his debts, the contract would last only six years. In the seventh year, he would be free (v. 12). In fact, he was to be sent away with adequate provisions to get back on his feet financially in the open society. This was a way for the wealthy Israelite to show his appreciation to God for brining him out of slavery in Egypt and blessing him financially. The slave also was available to work 24/7 for those six years and more than repaid the initial debt (v. 18). At the end of the six years, if the slave decides he would rather keep working for the master, he could make his position in society permanent. The ceremony involved the public piercing of the ear (vv. 16-17 see Exodus 21:5-6). This cultural practice is the background to the statements by Paul and Peter that they were *bondservants* of Jesus Christ. The Israelites were to show their gratitude to God by offering the firstborn males of their herds and flocks. This was not a total financial loss to the farmer because he and his family got to enjoying eating some of the sacrificial meat. The sacrifices could only take place at the Tabernacle and later the Temple. This is why Jewish people today do not sacrifice—they have no temple. Non-sacrificial meat could be eaten at home (vv. 21-22) but in no case could blood ever be eaten (v. 23).

LIFE STEP It all seems so easy, so well organized, so clearly explained, so filled with promises. The Israelites failed. Would we have done any better? Where are we making similar mistakes in our obedience to the New Testament admonitions?

Deuteronomy 16:1-17

What is the writer saying?

How can I apply this to my life?

The Jewish calendar is a lunar calendar with thirty days per month. Every several years they add a *leap month* to bring the lunar calendar back into sync with the solar calendar. The ancients also started the calendar in the spring close to the equinox (resurrection, newness of life). Abib (v. 1) is the *first month* and corresponds to March. The Passover was the first *holy day* (holiday) in the religious cycle. Passover speaks of the action of the death angel *passing over* the homes protected by the covering blood of the lamb. As the fathers put that blood on the lintels and doorposts of their homes, they would be making the sign of the cross in the doorway and 1 Corinthians 5:7 says that Christ was our Passover lamb. As such, He was spotless, put on public display for three and a half years to prove His perfection (Passover lambs were inspected for 3½ days), and not a bone was broken (Exodus 12:46). Abel sacrificed a lamb for a man. At Passover a lamb died for a family. At the Day of Atonement an animal died for the nation, but with Jesus, the lamb died for the sins of the whole world. Originally, Passover was one day and the feast of unleavened bread the next seven days. Today, the two are merged into the week of Passover. Yeast and leaven are illustrations of sin. Getting the leaven out reminded the Israelites of their hasty departure from Egypt and the need to get the sin out of their lives. Moses skips some of the holidays listed in Leviticus 23 to 25. He hits the *pilgrim holidays*; the ones that required a trip to the Tabernacle. The three pilgrim holidays are Passover in March, Pentecost fifty days later in May or June, and Tabernacles in September or October. Pentecost (v. 9) celebrates the wheat harvest and the Law as the spiritual staff of life. Tabernacles (v. 13) is the harvest home festival (see Zechariah 14).

LIFE STEP Do we show sufficient gratitude for all that God does for us? How can I give Him the sacrifice of praise today?

SUNDAY 40

Deuteronomy 18:9-22

What is the writer saying?

How can I apply this to my life?

PRAY

Bermuda – Pray that Christians in Bermuda would get more involved financially and spiritually to support missions.

Deuteronomy 16:18–17:20 discusses God's plans for the political and legal administration of the new nation of Israel and 18:1-8 discusses the financial provisions for the priests. The rest of the chapter discusses the proper way to contact the unseen world. The Canaanites practiced gross immorality including homosexuality. They offered their children as human sacrifices. They also attempted to contact the spirit world, discern the future, and influence the future through various spiritist practices. It might be interesting to know the details of each of the practices mentioned in these verses, but one principle of spiritual warfare is that we don't want to unthinkingly elevate or flatter Satan by studying too deeply his wicked ways. Suffice it to say that Satan is alive and well on planet earth and that deception and self-destruction are still his chief goals (see John 8:44). All we need to know from these verses is that the only acceptable way to contact the unseen world is by praying to God (not even to His angels!) and then allowing Him to speak to us through His messengers (the prophets and apostles) which now is recorded in our Bibles. Lest the children of Israel despair of adequate information from the unseen world, Moses promises that there will be another prophet *like* him (v. 15). In John 1:19-22, it appears that the Jewish leaders of Jesus' day viewed this prophet as distinct from the Messiah. The New Testament concludes, however, that they are one and the same (Acts 3:22). In what way was Jesus *like* Moses? Answer: He was human and spoke for God to the people. In fact, Jesus embodied the three major branches of Israelite society: Prophet, Priest, and King.

LIFE STEP

Jesus is everything to me because He is God in the flesh. As God, He can supply my every need. As human, I can understand Him.

Deuteronomy 29:1-13

What is the writer saying?

How can I apply this to my life?

Deuteronomy 19 discusses the cities of refuge designed to protect those who accidentally kill another (manslaughter) plus civil law. Chapter 20 discusses the ethics of holy war. Chapter 21 discusses atonement for unsolved murders and various other criminal and civil laws. Chapter 21 discusses the treatment of women and rebellious children. Chapter 22 covers miscellaneous laws including prohibition of cross-dressing, wearing distinctive clothing, and marriage issues. Chapter 23 discusses situations that limit a person's access to the sanctuary, rules for the military camp, treatment of slaves, and dealing with prostitution. Chapter 24 considers the needs of the weak, defenseless, and poor. Chapter 25 talks about punishment, fair treatment, levirate marriage, and the destruction of the detestable Amalekites. Chapter 26 describes thanksgiving ceremonies. Chapter 27 relays details of a memorial to be built upon entry into the Promised Land. Chapter 28 is a long section of blessings for obedience and cursings for disobedience. Chapter 29:1-8 reviews Israel's history. It is the introduction to the formal offer of the covenant to the new generation (vv. 9-13). They are gathered and expected to carefully consider the details and then to accept or reject the covenant before they enter the land. From our New Testament vantage point, it would have been best for them to cry out to the Lord expressing doubt that they had the moral fiber to live up to such a lofty code of conduct. Practically, Moses did not provide that option and the pride of man would naturally keep him from such a humble self-evaluation.

LIFE STEP   Discretion is the better part of valor. These things were done for our example (1 Corinthians 10:1-11). Let us learn from Israel's mistakes and not repeat them in our generation.

TUESDAY 40

Deuteronomy 29:14-29

What is the writer saying?

How can I apply this to my life?

PRAY Paraguay – For salvation decisions resulting from radio broadcasts to the 90,000 Germans living there.

Moses makes sure that everyone in the camp of Israel realizes that they will be included in this oath. No matter how important (v. 10) or insignificant (v. 11), they, as members of the society, will affect the rest of the society by their behavior. Verse 18 is quoted in Hebrews 12:15, "Looking diligently lest any man fail of the grace of God; lest any root of bitterness springing up trouble you, and thereby many be defiled." The English poet and minister, John Donne, wrote in the seventeenth century, "No man is an island." His idea was that every person affects someone else by his behavior. In fact, not just by their behavior but also by their attitudes towards the covenant. Outward conformity with inward scorn will negatively affect everyone (v. 19). "Be sure your sins will find you out" is a close parallel, but here it is even deeper:

"Be sure that the secrets of your heart will be publicly revealed." Sodom and Gomorrah we know. Admah means *red earth*. Zeboim means *gazelles*. These cities were also destroyed along with Sodom and Gomorrah (Genesis 19:28 and Hosea 11:8). The Assyrians fulfilled verse 28 when they deported the ten northern tribes in 722 B.C. From that day until today, there have always been more Jewish people living outside of Israel than within. Babylon deported the two southern tribes in 586 B.C. and destroyed Solomon's Temple. Fifty thousand struggled back seventy years later, but Israel has never fully recovered, not even with the proud modern state of Israel.

LIFE STEP

In the fable of the scorpion and the frog, against his better judgment, the frog permits the scorpion to ride on his back across a rushing stream. Despite his promise not to sting and knowing that in stinging he guaranteed his own drowning death, the scorpion stung the frog. He answered the dying frog's angry question, "But why?" with "It is my nature." Better be sure your nature is purified because in the end, that is all that will be left to a watching world.

Moses looks beyond the judgment and captivity of the Jewish people to their repentance and restoration. "Shalt return" (v. 2) is the root idea of *repentance*. It involves a change of mind, heart, and activity. It has an emotional element, but merely being sorry is not enough. That remorse must lead to a change of mind and a change of behavior. 2 Corinthians 7:10 says, "For godly sorrow worketh repentance to salvation not to be repented of." While repentance is part of the true salvation experience, there are those who repent but it apparently wasn't a true repentance for they eventually turn away from the true God (John 6:66). God is looking for obedience and that of a whole-hearted nature (v. 2). A test of the genuineness of your own repentance is whether your children follow suit. Since humans possess free wills, parents can't be completely responsible for the behavior and attitudes of their children, but on the average, a godly home should produce godly children or at least children who know the issues and are not *pretend Christians*. God gives strong warnings about judgment, but equally strong promises of ultimate restoration (v. 4). Verse 6 refers to the New Covenant of Jeremiah 31. The Law was a rigid set of exterior rules. What humans need is power from within. It comes in the person of the Holy Spirit who performs a heart operation and empowers us to understand and obey God.

LIFE STEP "No man is an island, entire of itself; every man is a piece of the continent, a part of the main. If a clod be washed away by the sea, Europe is the less....Any man's death diminishes me, because I am involved in mankind; and therefore never send to know for whom the bell tolls; it tolls for thee." – John Donne (1572-1631). Our attitudes and behavior affect everyone around us, and potentially the history of the entire world!

THURSDAY 40

Deuteronomy 31:1-13

What is the writer saying?

How can I apply this to my life?

PRAY Poland – For surrendered believers willing to take the Gospel to thousands of unreached villages.

Moses is up in years. He spent forty years in Egypt, forty years in Midian as a shepherd, and forty years leading the children of Israel to this point. God told him he could not enter the land, so he is turning over the leadership of the people to Joshua (v. 3) and the priests (v. 9). Joshua has been a good second-in-command. He was the first commander of the Israelite army (Exodus 17:9). He went up Mt. Sinai with Moses while Aaron and the seventy elders stayed behind (Exodus 24:13). He was honored along with Caleb for faithfulness at Kadesh-barnea (Numbers 26:65). Toward the end of the wilderness wanderings he was further honored and affirmed by God as the next leader (Numbers 27:18). "Go out and come in" refers to the legal act of leading the people (Numbers 27:17). Moses was demoted from that legal position because of his sin in the second smitten rock incident (Numbers 20:12). Moses encourages them in verse 6. Notice that God uses the same terminology with Joshua in Joshua 1:6-9 "Be strong and of a good courage: for unto this people shalt thou divide for an inheritance the land, which I sware unto their fathers to give them. Only be thou strong and very courageous, that thou mayest observe to do according to all the law, which Moses my servant commanded thee: turn not from it to the right hand or to the left, that thou mayest prosper whithersoever thou goest. This book of the law shall not depart out of thy mouth; but thou shalt meditate therein day and night, that thou mayest observe to do according to all that is written therein: for then thou shalt make thy way prosperous, and then thou shalt have good success. Have not I commanded thee? Be strong and of a good courage; be not afraid, neither be thou dismayed: for the LORD thy God is with thee whithersoever thou goest."

LIFE STEP Would we patiently listen to the reading of Deuteronomy in one session? Do we spend enough time in Bible reading and prayer to really know God?

Deuteronomy 32:1-14

What is the writer saying?

How can I apply this to my life?

PRAY God's guidance for staff and candidates participating in the Word of Life Missionary in Training program.

If God allowed you to know the time and manner of your death, would you want to know? Moses was told that his death was imminent (Deuteronomy 31:14). Did that affect what he had for breakfast that morning? Should it have affected his daily choices? Moses is told to write a song as a reminder of what God had done for the children of Israel. Deuteronomy 31:24-26 says that the book was deposited alongside of the Ark of the Covenant as a reminder of all that God had commanded them. Who wrote these verses describing what Moses did? Probably Joshua wrote it because in 31:19 Moses *and* Joshua were told to write this song (the verb *write* in Hebrew is plural). It seems strange that a *song* would be *spoken* (31:30) but in Hebrew singing is more of a poetic chant than a musical song. Content is the primary issue. In verse 1, the heavens and the earth are called to witness the contract between God and the Israelites. Moses goes back to the dawn of human history. From the beginning God had planned to use the Jewish people to minister to the Gentiles. The number of Jewish people foreordained was in proportion to the Gentiles needing mediation with Jehovah. Israel was positioned in the *navel* of the earth—centrally located with the Gentiles arrayed around them for easy access (v. 8, see Ezekiel 5:5). The "apple" of the eye is the pupil (v. 10). The eye is the tenderest part of the human body. When enemies touch Israel, they are poking God in the eye! Olive trees prefer rocky soil and bees often build hives in the crags of rocks (v. 13).

LIFE STEP The mother eagle is very protective with the eggs and hatchlings. She plucks her own down to feather the nest, but as they mature she removes the down making the nest uncomfortable. Eventually she pushes them out but swoops down to catch them on her back if they can't fly! So will God!

What is the writer saying?

How can I apply this to my life?

Moses' final address to the nation contains prophetic blessings for the twelve tribes. Jacob did the same before he died in Genesis 49. All the prophecies are important but several are truly astounding. In Genesis 49 Jacob is brutally honest in his criticism of his first three sons, but then extremely positive to the fourth, Judah, and announces that the Messiah would come from Judah (49:8-12). In Deuteronomy 33:12, it is announced that God would dwell in the territory of Benjamin. Jerusalem actually was in Benjamin and David chose it for his capital partly to blunt King Saul's influence (Saul was from Benjamin). Asher would "dip his foot in oil" (33:24). Some modern enthusiasts have mistakenly taken this to be a prophecy of petroleum wealth. Actually, Asher controls the area of Carmel famous to this day for the lovely olive orchards (olive oil!). Jeshurun (33:26) means *Upright One* and is a term of endearment for Israel. Deuteronomy 33:26 and 27 form a powerful and precious summary to the entire book: "There is none like unto the God of Jeshurun, who rideth upon the heaven in thy help, and in his excellency on the sky. The eternal God is thy refuge, and underneath are the everlasting arms." Amazingly Genesis 49, Deuteronomy 33, and Deuteronomy 34:1 all place the tribe of Dan in the far north. This is where she eventually ended up, but initially she was given territory in the extreme south (Joshua 19:40-48; see Judges 18). Moses died and God buried him. The mystery surrounding his death and burial led to interesting speculation (see Jude 9). Physical contact symbolizes the passing of blessing, power, and authority (v. 9). Remember Elisha and Elijah's mantle.

LIFE STEP "Face to face with Christ, my Savior, Face to face—what will it be, when with rapture I behold Him, Jesus Christ Who died for me?" – Carrie Breck

There are times when all those theological explanations just don't cut it; times when the gap between what we know and what we feel is like a vast empty void; times when our soul wants to express itself to God but the words just don't seem to come. It is just for those times that the Wisdom books (Job, Psalms, Proverbs, Ecclesiastes, and Song of Solomon) were written.

These books deal with down-to-earth feelings and down-to-earth questions. They are concerned more with our physical and emotional welfare than they are with religious theories or systems. These are lessons for living, guidelines to godliness, schooling for success. Each of these five books deals with a different aspect of surviving on Planet Earth.

These books are relevant to all human experiences. The problem of suffering, the conscience twisted by sin, the fragility of human life, and the passionate love of woman and man, to mention only a few of the matters dealt with in these books, cut across national and ethnic lines to include all of the human race. "The spokesmen in these books formulate questions that have lain in man's subconscious mind, often without his having the courage to bring them to the surface." [C Hassel Bullock, *An Introduction to the Old Testament Poetic Books* (Chicago: Moody, 1979), 17]. Job is the first of these books and deals with the problem of evil and suffering.

The lifestyle and historic references in the book indicate that Job lived before the time of Abraham. It is the longest story in the Bible from the earliest period of biblical history. The book does not identify the author. It could have been Job himself or the relatively wise and godly young friend in the story, Elihu (*He is my God*). Certainly Moses is a candidate, since God moved Moses to write other large portions of the biblical record. Since Solomon was known for his intense interest in wise sayings and theological and philosophical discussions, the Holy Spirit might have used him to record this story. Perhaps it was well-known among the people, handed down from one generation to the next.

The book opens in Heaven with a discussion between God and Satan. There is no question that God instigates the ensuing discussion and draws Satan into a conversation about personal behavior and its relationship to adversity. This is the most fundamental dichotomy that exists in the created universe. There does not appear to be any immediate correspondence between righteousness and adversity. There is, however, a correlation between godliness and sorrow.

The mistake that Job and his friends made was in trying to find a correlation between the *righteousness and adversity* and ignoring man's responsibility in the area of *godliness*. Men long to live in a world where fairness reigns. They want to be able to think that the *good* live long and prosper. But, in reality, it rains on the just and the unjust. The difference is not a matter of *happenings* but rather our attitude towards those circumstances. The just man interprets the "rain" differently than the proud one. He looks at all of the events of life through the eyes of faith.

Job's journey is one of clarification. It is a journey into the depths of living by faith. It is a journey constructed by an omniscient God to bring His choice servant into a better understanding of a salvation that is by grace alone through faith alone, a salvation that means more than justification, a salvation that sustains a man in the greatest adversity that one could ever imagine.

The following outline is a helpful memory aid:

Job in the hands of Satan, 1:1–2:10
Job in the hands of men, 2:11–37:24
Job in the hands of God, 38:1–42:17

Job 1:1-12

What is the writer saying?

How can I apply this to my life?

The book opens with a description of Job. He was a wealthy land owner, but more than that, he was, in God's words, "a blameless and upright man, one who fears God and shuns evil." One would be tempted to think that such a man would be exactly the kind of person that God wanted him to be, a man that could put his feet up and enjoy the good life that God had given him. But that would be wrong. The journey we take in this life is one of reliance, not autonomy. The lessons to be learned are the lessons that only weakness can teach. Jesus put it succinctly, "The first shall be last and the last shall be first." This is not to say that Job was in any way deficient by human standards, it is only to say that spiritual growth is a privilege that never fades. It is a glimmer of light that shines brightest in a dark place.

God looked at Job and saw one awesome servant. He saw that Job had one awesome life, but God knew something else. He knew that Job's life could be better. God knows life; He knows real life. So He turned to Satan and said, "Have you considered my servant Job?" Thus begins one of the most troublesome journeys to be found anywhere. This is not a punishment for Job. It does not happen because God wants Job to be *more upright*. It happens because God loves Job and He wants Job to have then best life possible. When it comes to His children, God is always in the grace business. Man's problem is that he does not always believe that such is the case. We allow the trials of this life to become temptations and doubt God's love.

LIFE STEP Whenever Satan attacks believers, he has to go through the Lord first. We can trust that the Lord only allows Satan to test us as a part of His gracious plan for our best possible life.

Job 1:13-22

What is the writer saying?

How can i apply this to my life?

PRAY Jamaica – Outreach to the "barrel children" who are the destitute underclass, whose parents have emigrated elsewhere and occasionally send them support.

The series of *evils* that befalls Job is hard to comprehend from a human perspective. It is even harder to believe that God has allowed Satan to do this. A life that had been so pleasant the day before turns into a torture chamber for Job. Everything that he had was taken from him in a series of manmade and natural disasters. Even his family was not spared. The thought that begins to grow in each of our minds is, "How could God allow that to happen?" God allowed Satan to kill Job's children. How can that be? Doesn't Job's righteousness count for anything? Here is the key point. Job had no personal righteousness. All that he had was given to him by God, especially his righteousness. It is the unfairness of the events that draws us into the story, but it is this supposed unfairness that God wants us to reconsider. If this were a fair world, would we not all be spending an eternity in the fires of Hell?

Does God *owe* us anything? Did God *owe* Job anything?

The writer of this ancient book wants us to grasp this concept. He wants us to ask a different question: "Why would God take such interest in a single person and begin to unpack a sequence of events that would overwhelm Job with His grace." We might be tempted to ask how this qualifies as grace. But if it is not grace then what is it? Is God condemning Job? Is He unable to protect Job? Has His love for Job grown cold? Can God be anything but loving toward his children? The God who willingly gave Himself for Job would never allow anything to happen to Job that was not designed to bless Job. The true grace of God sometimes comes in strange packages.

LIFE STEP Life in God's family only gets better as the days go by. That can only be known by faith and that is why we are called "believers." It's what we do.

Job 2:1-13

What is the writer saying?

How can I apply this to my life?

PRAY Australia – Pray that the people would turn to Christ and not to the secularism that pervades society.

Any one of us would be tempted to think that after such a devastating day the Lord would give Job time to recover and perhaps even comfort him in his distress. Instead, at the next opportunity, the Lord once again engages Satan in a conversation about Job. And again Satan claims that Job only worships the Lord because of all the protection and blessing He provides. In the initial go round, Satan was forbidden to touch Job's person, but now God gives Satan permission to harm Job physically, short of taking his life. Job is covered with painful sores from head to foot.

It is worth noting that Satan did not ask for permission to attack Job internally. This option was not available to Satan. In recent days there has been much talk about demon possession and demon bondage. Since the focus of this book is about a case of extreme testing, one would think that if such were a possibility that Satan would have brought it up. Satan can only attack the believer from the outside. He may be able to afflict the body but he cannot touch the soul.

The arrival of Job's friends accomplishes two purposes. First, it serves to reinforce the intensity of Job's suffering. His friends were overwhelmed by Job's condition. Second, it moves the conversation from heaven to earth. Job's friends were not privy to the conversations that had just taken place. They are looking at these matters from an earthly and human perspective. Their goal is simple: to make some sense out of all that has happened. The journey begins here, a journey that all of us will take at some point or points in our lives. A journey for answers to life's most perplexing problem: Why do righteous people suffer?

LIFE STEP As we read this account, we need to ask ourselves where we should look to find such answers. Can they be found in us or must they be found with God?

Job 7:1-16

What is the writer saying?

How can I apply this to my life?

The thirty five interior chapters are a series of speeches by Job's three friends. Each is followed by a response from Job. There are three cycles of speeches. Elihu is only involved in the last cycle and Job does not respond to Elihu. Cycle one covers chapters 3-14 (Eliphaz, Bildad, Zophar); cycle two chapters 15-21 (Eliphaz, Bildad, Zophar); and cycle three chapters 22-37 (Eliphaz, Bildad, Elihu). Elihu gives four speeches.

In this first series of speeches Job's friends argue that God blesses the godly and punishes the ungodly. Satan has already given his assessment of the matter. He suggested that man's faith in God is directly related to services provided and man's prosperity. Eliphaz is the first to speak and suggests that man brings trouble upon himself because God is always fair (Job 4-5). Our passage today picks up in the middle of Job's response to Eliphaz. Job's central thesis is a common one. He believes that he is justified in his complaint against God because he did nothing knowingly to deserve the severe trial that he is enduring. He refuses to criticize God but will not accept his situation without an explanation. Job is willing to suffer but only on condition that he knows why. And he wants to know why so that he can correct his ways.

In today's passage Job points out the frailty of human life. He acknowledges the weakness of the flesh. He does this in order to strengthen his contention that all he wants is an answer. See 6:24, "Teach me and I will hold my tongue; Cause me to understand wherein I have erred."

LIFE STEP

It is not always sinful to ask the Lord why something has happened in your life (Jesus asked "Why?" from the cross). The mistake is to demand such an answer before we trust God and are contented. Sometimes God just wants us to live by faith. Trust Him. He does know what He is doing.

Job 9:1-20

What is the writer saying?

How can I apply this to my life?

In chapter 8 Bildad presents his analysis. He bases his argument on God's character. Because God cannot twist or ignore justice, he reasons, Job must have done something to *earn* this trial. These kinds of arguments are made today. Well-trained scholars will sometimes pick an attribute of God and use that attribute to deny a rather clear teaching of Scripture. For example, some pick the love of God as the primary characteristic of God and then argue that a loving God could never send anyone to hell, especially not people who have never heard the gospel. No man can fully understand the person of God or how his known attributes interact one with the other. We can all agree that God is just, but does that force us to conclude that every trial is a punishment? Maybe trials are good things.

In today's passage Job answers Bildad. He correctly concludes that God's activities are all in keeping with God's character. He cannot violate His own integrity, but Job still maintains that he himself is guiltless. He knows that this tribulation is not condemnation for known sin, but he still cries out in frustration. Verse 19 sums up this frustration. Like Bildad he uses God's attributes to justify his anxiety. God is omnipotent so there is no one to stop His purposes and He is also the supreme judge so that there is no one who can force Him to give an accounting for that behavior. It seems that we just have to trust Him. Job has still not come to the point where he is willing to ask the right question. He still thinks that his suffering is a *bad* thing.

LIFE STEP Life often deals us some unexpected and painful blows. It sometimes seems that our whole world is coming apart at the seams. Is it possible that God had a discussion with Satan prior to our trial? More importantly, would that matter?

Job 9:21-35

What is the writer saying?

How can I apply this to my life?

It is important for us to keep in mind the larger context from which this passage is taken. The issues we are dealing with are not going to be solved this early in the narrative. The thing to note is that all of the discussion to this point has originated from Job's deep depression and disillusionment. Job would have come to similar conclusions if this had happened to one of his friends. It is not that he does not believe the same things that his friends are saying. He is not denying the basic arguments; he is simply claiming that they do not apply in his case because he is guiltless. All of the discussion to this point is based upon the unbelievable emotional and physical pain that Job is enduring.

This is also the common worldview today. Pleasure is good; pain is bad. We determine the quality of our experience by how it feels. This is the anomaly that Job faces. He knows God is a good God but he is unable to reconcile that with his day-to-day experience. He says that he is without guilt and that he hates his life. At the very core of this complaint is the greatest challenge that we as believers face. Will we believe what God tells us about the circumstances of life or will we believe what our hearts tell us about these trials?

Job is struggling to answer the most difficult question that exists in our universe, the question of evil. But to this point all of his attention is directed toward the trial. In effect, he is trying to protect God from what he considers to be an injustice.

LIFE STEP It is very easy for man to worship God in the comfort of prosperity but do we respond the same way when the music dies and the world becomes cold and empty? Is God sufficient for the valley of the shadow of death? Whatever controls how we feel is our god.

SATURDAY 41

Job 10:1-2, 8-22

What is the writer saying?

How can I apply this to my life?

PRAY   Czech Republic – Pray for the establishment and growth of Christian institutes and seminaries.

In the Gospels Jesus is very clear about loving our enemies. His whole point is that it takes no faith to love our friends. There is no challenge. But loving one's enemies is a different matter altogether. What if they turn on us and kill us. Is it not a fool's errand to think that we can love those who hate us? From the world's perspective this is true. We live in a world where we do not give gifts, we exchange gifts. We live with an idea that all things need balance. Our sense of justice is based on this core belief. But what if that belief is wrong? What if real blessing comes from giving and giving and giving some more? What if receiving is the spoiler in our lives. What if it is really more blessed to give than to receive?

Job hated his life because he thought that his life had been diminished by recent events. He knew how precious life was. He knew the great care that God had taken in creating man in His own image. But he did not understand how such a gracious God could allow him to suffer without at least an explanation. Job sees only darkness on the road ahead. He does not know how he can carry on. He knows that God has intentionally allowed this trial to come into his life, but from the core of his being he believes it to be some form of judgment. His heart tells him that this should not be happening to him. And yet his faith tells him that the Lord is not a mean-spirited or careless God. He is the God of all that is wonderful, the God of life itself. Job is confused.

LIFE STEP   In one sense the book of Job can seem like a broken record. Job's friends keep coming up with more and more reasons that this trial is of Job's own making. But do we not do the same when we determine the quality of our lives based on physical prosperity?

SUNDAY 42

Job 12:1-4, 13-25

What is the writer saying?

How can I apply this to my life?

PRAY Peru – For the continued work of the Holy Spirit among the Quechua and Aymara people.

Zophar's argument, found in chapter 11, is similar to the others. He proposes that God cannot be tricked and that He knows sin when He sees it. Job and his friends are trying to answer *grace questions* in a *works world*. They cannot seem to break free from the moment and understand the true grace of God. The reason that Job is so frustrated in this discussion is that he still buys into their basic philosophy. He is convinced that the quality of his life has been affected adversely by recent events. Given that assumption, he is looking for an answer that does not exist.

Job gets the theology part of the problem. He knows that God is a God of wisdom and might (v. 13); he knows that God is a God of counsel and understanding. And yet he still has this huge knot in his stomach. He still wants answers.

But consider what Job has already confirmed. He knows about God. He knows the kind of power that He has. He knows about His loving-kindness. He knows about His wisdom. Given all of these facts, there is a rather simple conclusion: these things happened because God wanted them to happen, and, given what he knows about God, that ought to resolve all of his issues. Could he trust the God of the universe to take care of His children and to lavish His grace upon them? It is somewhat like the question, "Can God create a rock so big that he cannot lift it?" This is a question designed so that it cannot be answered (and therefore is an invalid question). Job wants to know why God punished him but God only and always intended it for good. That is what it means in Romans 8:1. There is no condemnation.

 LIFE STEP What question should Job have been asking? If humans are to count it all joy when they fall into various trials, would it not be better for Job to ask how the quality of his life was improved by the recent events?

Job 13:1-18

What is the writer saying?

How can I apply this to my life?

Job continues his response to Zophar in our text today. He points out to Zophar that he already knows that God judges sin (vv.1-2). Job goes on to say that the only one who can give him satisfaction is God and God alone. He exclaims, "I would speak to the Almighty and I desire to reason with God." This may seem a little arrogant to us, but it is a very appropriate request. It is God's answers that matter. Truth cannot originate with the one created because the creation is not eternal. Only the Absolute can offer absolutes. Only God can answer the questions that man has about life because God is the Creator of that life. God knows life. God knows meaning. God knows best.

Job is respectful in his request. He is asking the right Person but he is not asking the right question. He cries out, "Though he slay me, yet will I trust Him, but I will maintain (argue) mine own ways before him" (v. 15). This same scenario will happen again later in the Old Testament. In a similar way Habakkuk stands before the God of the universe and cries out for an explanation. "I will stand upon my watch, and set me upon the tower, and will watch to see what he will say unto me, and what I shall answer when I am reproved" (Habakkuk 2:1). Neither Job nor Habbakkuk is given the explanation they request. God's answer to both Job and Habbakuk is as true today as it was the day it was given. It is the heart of Paul's gospel: "the just shall live by faith." Faith is not a means for man to achieve a goal. It is the goal. The faith life is the only real life. Faith transforms living. It is a lifestyle. Real life is from faith to faith. Job wanted an answer to believe in; God wanted Job to believe in the promise that had already been given.

LIFE STEP   Do you trust in the Lord when things go wrong? Tell the Lord today that you trust in Him and will continue to no matter what happens to you.

Job 14:1-15

What is the writer saying?

How can I apply this to my life?

In this passage we see Job giving a view of life from that of a sufferer. He compares his life with the rest of the creation in an attempt to move God in his behalf. Job points out, for example, that when a tree is cut off it has the hope of being able to sprout again from the roots. But it is not so with a man. "Man lieth down and riseth not, till the heavens be no more" (v. 12). At first glance one might think that Job has no concept of an eternal life and an eternal home in the future. Some even suggest that in the Old Testament there was no understanding of life after death. Such thinking takes a very narrow view of this passage. It is true that Job did not have a detailed understanding of future events like we do, but that is because there was no need for this information at this point in the development of God's plan. Job did understand that the present heavens and earth were not designed for eternal living and that when these were renewed so would he be renewed. He makes this hope clear throughout the book. He knew that sometime in the future there would be a new universe in which he and others like him would live forever.

He also understood that a man only gets one chance in this present world. He understood that once this life ends there will be no second chances. Before the new heavens and new earth come into existence there will be a judgment. Once a man, woman or child passes from this world, destiny cannot be changed.

LIFE STEP The present is all we have. It is a gift. It is an opportunity. It is also a very fragile thing. There are no second chances after death. Paul suggests that we redeem the time because the days are evil. Using the time wisely and knowing its value is how wise people conduct their lives.

What is the writer saying?

How can I apply this to my life?

In chapter 15 Eliphaz begins the second round of speeches. He does not introduce a new argument but brings new evidence to support his contention that man brings trouble upon himself because God is always fair. He tells Job that he was being foolish and dodging the issues. In today's passage Job begins his second response to Eliphaz.

Job's argument appears to be that in his case the punishment does not fit the crime. He agrees that God is fair but He cannot understand how God is acting fairly in his case. The fact that Job's enemies have been given power over him is unimaginable. He feels that he has been turned over to the wicked. Interestingly this is again very similar to Habakkuk's complaint regarding Israel's enemies, the Babylonians. Both men are willing to admit that they do not deserve God's blessing, but they still argue that a man ought to be treated fairly according to his comparative righteousness. If Job is to endure this trial, then those who are more wicked ought to be treated even more severely.

This may be the most common complaint in the world today. In fact, it may be the most common complaint ever. Job would have been less troubled if his enemies would have experienced equal or worse treatment from God. This sense of fairness is the enemy of joy and contentment. It destroys a man's understanding of the world around him. Grace and fairness cannot coexist in the same worldview because grace by definition is unfair. It is unmerited favor. Until a man is willing to reject *fair*, he will never appreciate the awesome grace of God.

LIFE STEP   It is too easy to look around us when we are suffering and see someone who is less deserving than we are getting rewarded despite their bad behavior. It is at that point that faith must kick in. Can we trust the God of this universe to do right??

What is the writer saying?

How can I apply this to my life?

PRAY

United Kingdom – For many teens to be saved through Christian camping and outreach events.

In today's passage Job's second response to Eliphaz continues. Read verses 11-16 very carefully. These verses give us a clear picture of Job's despair. He has lost all sense of comfort and joy. He feels utterly abandoned. His pain has darkened his soul and Job sees no possible way that he will ever smile or laugh again in this life. For him life is over and he sees death as his only friend. Physical and emotional pain can do this to a man, even a great man like Job. Remember, he was the most upright man on the planet. The fact that these three friends were here to *comfort* him only added to the problem. Job knew that they were not as upright as he was. He feared as much as anything else that men would think him a hypocrite (v. 8). Not only did he lose all that he held dear, but "upright" men would all assume that he must have gotten what he deserved. Why? Because that was how Job thought before all of this had happened to him. Now he was totally confused. It was all so unfair and pointless. His life was gone and so was his reputation.

It is interesting to note that the further Job walks down the *fairness* road the more depressed he becomes, and Job's friends keep bringing him back to that road. When Job centers his thoughts on God, he seems a little more objective, but when he considers his situation as compared to everyone else's, despair dominates his thinking. Job was not getting godly counsel and it was compounding the problem. Job seems to be getting more and more depressed as the conversations move along. This was not necessarily a matter of personnel, but one of message. This fairness message is always counterproductive.

LIFE STEP

We are told that there is wisdom in a multitude of counselors. But counsel can be a two-edged sword. Not all counsel is equal. Seek out godly counselors or your view of the problem may get worse.

Job 19:19-29

What is the writer saying?

How can I apply this to my life?

In chapter 18, Bildad tries once again to get his point across to Job. Remember, he believes that because God cannot twist or avoid justice, Job must have done something to *earn* this trial. He tells Job that he is being chastised, and that it will not stop until he repents and gets his life right with the Lord. Until he does this, he will continue to walk in darkness.

We need to understand that chastisement (*discipline*) is not a bad thing. We are told in Hebrews 12 that the Lord chastens those He loves. It is a part of God's fatherly responsibility to discipline his children. However, Bildad is using the concept to put Job down. Not all chastening is because of sin. We sometimes use chastening in a preventive way. We do not wait until a child plays in traffic to train them to stay in the yard. A fence takes away a child's freedom but it does so in order to protect that child. He or she may resent and despise the fence but it is still an act of love and protection.

We see in this passage a clear claim by Job that he does not view the grave as the end of human existence or as the end of a flesh and blood reality. He knows that there will be new heavens and a new earth and that he will stand before God in that time and that place. He has hope about the future but takes no pleasure in the present. In fact, he warns his friends that, given their reasoning, the same or a worse thing may happen to them.

LIFE STEP   Job still sees no light at the end of the tunnel. He knows that his real problem is with God but he continues to argue with his friends. Until a man is right with God, he cannot expect to be at peace with his friends. Every joy in life is based upon a right relationship with God. The real question is, "What does a right relationship with God look like?"

Job 23:1-12

What is the writer saying?

How can I apply this to my life?

Today we will look at a part of Job's third response to Eliphaz. In chapter 20, Zophar gives his second speech. His basic argument continues to be that God cannot be tricked and that He knows sin when He sees it. Job responds to Zophar in chapter 21. In Chapter 22 Eliphaz tells Job that a person can get away with evil for a little while, but it will eventually catch up with him. He tells Job that if he will only repent, then God will build him up and that God will put evil away from his home (22:23).

In his answer Job continues to stress that the trial he has suffered does not prove that he has sinned more grievously than those who accuse him. He wants only to have the opportunity to present his case before the Almighty. Job seems to be convinced that by doing this he will somehow be justified in the eyes of both men and God. Job does not want his stuff back, he wants his reputation back.

Note what he says in verse 10, "But he knoweth the way that I take; when he hath tried me, I shall come forth as gold." Job does not despise the trial; he longs for the trial to conclude so that his (and God's) reputation will be restored. He is still convinced that this ordeal has an attached good that will somehow outweigh the bad. He cannot bring himself to believe that this tragedy was in and of itself a true grace of God. Somehow it must be a blessing in disguise. Why does he believe this? Because he has convinced himself that he has the ability to determine what is good and what is evil.

LIFE STEP We tend to view faith as a means to an end. The *end* that we want is sight (*proof*) which is <u>by definition</u> the opposite of faith. This is a contradiction. Hope that is seen is <u>not hope</u>. The same is true of faith. We cannot demand to see God before we will live the Christian life because believers can only live by faith.

SUNDAY 43

Job 26:1-14

What is the writer saying?

How can I apply this to my life?

PRAY   Austria – Legal and social barriers to the gospel to be destroyed as newer laws have restricted rights.

In chapter 25 Bildad gives his third speech on the subject. He agrees with Job that no one can be sufficiently righteous because all men are like worms before the Lord (25:6). In today's passage Job responds to Bildad. He appears to agree with Bildad on this point. There is no one like God. To compare our righteousness to His is foolish. God is altogether holy. He is in a class all by Himself. Job uses a series of illustrations to emphasize how magnificent the Lord is.

It is clear from this passage that Job knows that he has no righteousness of his own. His *righteousness* is a gift from God. This is a key point throughout Scripture. If men are going to survive the Day of Judgment, they need a higher kind of righteousness than what they can perform. "All have sinned and come short of the glory of God" (Romans 3:23). Men need a "glory-of-God" righteousness. The only way that anyone can have such a righteousness is if God transfers His righteousness to their account.

Job is concerned with the kind of righteousness that James speaks of in James 2:21, "Was not Abraham our father justified by works when he offered Isaac his son upon the altar?" This refers to the visible fruit-of-the-Spirit righteousness that God provides in the believer's life so that men will see that person's good works and glorify his Father who is in heaven. Bildad was confusing external righteousness with personal righteousness. Only God has personal righteousness. The believer's righteousness is a gift from God.

LIFE STEP   This distinction between the two kinds of righteousness is very important for the believer to understand. We can misunderstand the external evidence of God's love for us, but we can never do anything to affect the personal righteousness once it has been transferred to our account.

Job 28:12-28

What is the writer saying?

How can I apply this to my life?

PRAY Portugal – For a mighty work of the Holy Spirit in the predominantly Catholic provinces of the north.

Job's friends, as we saw yesterday, were confusing the two kinds of righteousness that the Bible talks about. They failed to understand that what was happening to Job could not be about condemnation because that was all dealt with by Job's possession of God's righteousness. Job's problem had to do with the second kind of righteousness that is supposed to grow in a believer's life. In the New Testament this is called the fruit of the Spirit. In the Old Testament it is often referred to as wisdom, namely, *skillful living*. Job believed that he was living more skillfully that many of his contemporaries and, therefore, he should not be treated more severely than they.

Job now points out that wisdom is as much a gift from God as is righteousness. Man is no more capable of living righteously than he is of being righteous. Job's complaint is becoming much more difficult to answer. If God has provided all of the daily righteousness one exhibits, how can He now be chastening Job because Job does not have a sufficient supply? Job concludes, "The fear of the Lord, that is wisdom."

The concept of fear in this passage is much different than the modern English word would imply. It speaks of a much deeper relationship than just being afraid. Just as fear often paralyzes a person emotionally and thereby controls their actions, the Old Testament expects mankind to have an action-controlling relationship with God. If a person has claustrophobia (fear of enclosed spaces), they sometimes lose control of their behavior when forced into a small room. Our relationship with God ought to so control our lives. Not because we are afraid but because we believe Him.

LIFE STEP Faith without good living is no faith at all. Skillful living occurs when a person's life is shaped by what he or she believes with the result that it conforms to the ideal life described by God's commandments.

Job 32:1-16

What is the writer saying?

How can I apply this to my life?

PRAY Taiwan – Greater sense of responsibility among believers who tend to let leadership do everything.

To this point the three friends who have been counseling Job have been very close to Job's age. Remember, in the time that Job lived men lived much longer than they do today. But a younger friend was also present. Because of his comparative youth, he has been ignored in the conversation and in the storyline to this point. It is very possible that this incident was written as a drama to be presented live before an audience. Note that all the things that happen to Job are reported verbally by a servant. Consider that the conversation has continued at length with one participant sitting there silently hour after hour. There must be a kind of suspense building as to who he is and why he is there. All of that is answered in today's passage.

At this point Elihu crashes into the conversation. He is so angered by what is taking place that he dares to speak. His anger is directed toward Job's three friends and not toward Job himself. He is frustrated that they have no answer for the problem. Elihu gives four speeches, none of which elicit a response from Job. He acknowledges that his interruption is inappropriate but claims that God often gives understanding to those that one might least expect (v. 8). Because Job does not answer any of Elihu's speeches, we are left on our own to assess what he has to say. Today's passage does not give us any of the actual argument that Elihu will make but it gives a justification for why we should listen to such a young man.

LIFE STEP There are two practical lessons that we can take from today's passage. First, we can see that Elihu waited until the older men had their say. Second, we can see that the older men did not put Elihu down when he entered the conversation after waiting an appropriate amount of time.

Job 32:17-33:6

What is the writer saying?

How can I apply this to my life?

Elihu continues his insights after having listened to Job and his three friends for hours. You can tell that he has wanted to say something for quite a while (vv. 17-19). At this point Elihu begins to lay the groundwork for the answer that he is about to give Job. Do not forget what the confusion is. These men are trying to justify the acts of God in time and space. They are dealing with the age old problem of evil and why it seems to flourish on Planet Earth. They want a reasonable God who does reasonable things.

Elihu claims that his solutions have been forged within a person created by God and one who has lived his life in accordance with the desires of his Creator. He is not claiming that his message was given to him by God, but that by extension, because he was created by God and that he desires to serve God, his answers should be honored. He does not have the life experience that the others have but he is still a product of God's creative activity. He does not suggest that his answers are right but that they ought to be taken seriously. This is a very respectful and appropriate way for a young man in that culture to introduce his suggestions.

This is a very long introduction. It illustrates for us the high priority that the ancient world placed on maturity. It is a lesson that our present culture has in many ways rejected. Youth is idolized. It is considered a distressing thing to look old. We do all that we can to hang onto youth. This is probably because we prize strength and appearance above wisdom.

LIFE STEP Wisdom does not happen overnight. It grows slowly and matures only in the valleys. It should be our most prized and sought after resource.

What is the writer saying?

How can I apply this to my life?

In chapters 33-37 Elihu give four separate speeches. Job does not respond to any of the four. The central idea in these speeches is that God is refining the righteous. Of all the solutions this is the only one that does not discredit Job and, therefore, Job does not respond to it. Also, there is a sense in which Elihu does make a significant move in the right direction, but he does not take his solution to the place that God wants it to be. Yes, God is refining the righteous but the end cannot justify the means. With God the process is as meaningful as the outcome. God does not want us to trust in just future blessing, He wants us to believe that we are blessed today.

God calls to Job out of the whirlwind. He questions Job's basis for assigning meaning to the events that have just taken place. Over the course of these eighteen verses God asks Job a stream of questions for which the answers are always, "No." The point that God is making has to do with foundation. Job and all of his friends have made a judgment about the series of tests that have just taken place in Job's life. Without exception they have considered these to be a misfortune. But on what basis are they suggesting that such is the case? A starving person would think that a peanut butter and jelly sandwich was a treasure. A wealthy ruler might be insulted if he were offered the same. God is asking Job how he as a mere human thinks that he can determine what is good and what is bad. All events of life only have the meaning that was intended by God. If God intended it for good, then who are we as mere men to argue with the Almighty?

LIFE STEP   A sketch book of drawings by Picasso is valued at over 10 million dollars. Is it because of their excellence or because they are Picasso's? The events of life must be valued based on the Artist, not the appearance.

Job 40:1-14

What is the writer saying?

How can I apply this to my life?

PRAY Romania – For the lifting of government restrictions, which are hindering effective ministry growth.

After an extended series of questions (two chapters), the Lord finally draws the matter to a conclusion. Like the rest of the speech it is framed as a question. He basically asks Job, "The one who contends with God is the one who thinks that he can correct God. Are you seeking to correct me, Job?"

Job gets it. He now responds to God from a place of humility (vv. 3-5). Job realizes that he has gone much too far in his complaint. He crossed a line when he assumed that he was capable of judging an act of God. Job's problem ran much deeper than the words he spoke. It was an issue of the heart. Job thought that he knew what was best for him. God is not to be defined by the conditions that one experiences. The events are to be defined by the God that we serve. Life does not help us understand God; God helps us understand life.

God then instructs Job in the way he should walk. Can anyone of us by our own effort earn a moment of peace or joy? Is not every moment that we are not suffering in the fires of Hell a moment of pure grace? Are not the trials that we face in this life indescribable joy compared with the consequences that we would face without the grace of God? We live in days of incredible opportunity. What we complain about as insufferable agony would be considered a moment of greatest joy by those who face the torment of eternal death. These are not things that we can know by sight. They are things that we must accept by faith. It always boils down to what or who we are going to believe. Will we believe the pain we feel or the God we serve?

LIFE STEP We can only serve one God. Whoever or whatever controls how we feel is ultimately our god. If the Lord cannot tell us how to feel, then He cannot rule our lives.

Job 42:1-17

What is the writer saying?

How can I apply this to my life?

As we come to the end of the book of Job, we are left with more questions than answers. In fact, we are not given any answers. Job's response to God is simple, he changes his mind (repents) and despises (abhors) all of his questions. They no longer seem meaningful. Once he understands (sees) God, there are no questions left. He is content to live his life in whatever arrangement God deems appropriate. The point is that if God told Job the reason He allowed all that had happened, Job would be trusting in the explanation. With God it is never the *why* that matters; it is the *Who*.

The last part of today's passage wraps up a few loose ends. Job's three friends are rebuked by God because they did not speak correctly to Job. They totally misunderstood God's relationship to the circumstances of life. Elihu is not rebuked but neither is he commended. If his solution was the correct one then God would have commended his words to Job, but He did not. We may suggest here that Elihu proposed a possible solution that honored both God and Job even though it was not the right solution. God does refine the righteous but that is only a small part of what God is doing when He brings trials into the life of a believer. This is still a *why answer* not a *Who solution*.

Finally, we see all that had been taken from Job restored twofold. We may conclude from this that God's intentions for each of His children is for good, both in the process and the outcome. The process in this life must remain a mystery but the end results will always be understandable.

LIFE STEP Let us take care that we do not separate the outcome from the process. We sometimes view the trial (process) as a necessary evil that will be outweighed by the final blessing, but the process is also a blessing because it is God who controls it.

Any time believers take up sides and battle other believers, it hurts. It hurts even more when the adversaries are long-time friends. John is writing to churches where this is happening. A new philosophy has infiltrated the church body and believers are confused. They want to know which side is right. They want to know if both sides are believers. They want to be sure that they are believers.

This situation is not that unusual. It is early in church history. The believers are striving to serve the Lord. Some so-called believers from another area come and begin to teach new ideas. They have a new view of sin, a new view of revelation, a new view of Christ. A number of church leaders soon embrace this teaching and ... Presto! ... a church split is in progress.

The genuine believers are caught in the *love-versus-doctrine* snare. They want to love these men because they claim to be Christians, but their presence in the assembly is causing young believers to be led astray due to false doctrine. Some are even unsure about who is right and who is wrong. They want direction. They want assurance. And that is exactly why John writes this epistle.

Things are not all that different today. It would be nice if we lived in a unified church where everybody believed exactly the same way. It would be nice if we could just let everyone believe whatever they wanted and not have to worry about it. Unfortunately, we don't and we can't.

The struggle is not for us to decide who is saved and who is not saved; the struggle is with fellowship. When John wrote this epistle, his purpose was exactly this: to guide us in the area of fellowship. He wants us to be in fellowship with God and with all other believers who are in fellowship with God. He wants us to know that we are saved.

This is not a book about what salvation is or the doctrine of eternal security. It is a book about assurance—a book about feeling saved. How do we know that our religion is the right one? How do we know that Heaven is our home? It is one thing to know the doctrine of eternal security; it is quite another to know for sure that we are saved. John has written this book for exactly that reason: so that we can know that we have eternal life.

John sees four relationships that affect how we feel about our salvation: Our relationship to the Word of God (1:1–2:6), our relationship to the people of God (2:7–3:24), our relationship to the Spirit of God (4:1–21) and our relationship to faith in God (5:1-13). The last few verses of the book review the confidences that we have as believers.

SUNDAY 44

1 John 1:1-4

What is the writer saying?

How can I apply this to my life?

PRAY Indonesia – For the Muslims to be exposed to the Gospel by the few missionaries remaining.

One writer comments, "John wrote his Gospel to prove the deity of our Lord, assuming His humanity, and his first epistle to prove His humanity, assuming His deity." John announces, "…we have heard [Him], which we have seen [Him] with our eyes, which we have looked upon, and our hands have handled, of the Word of life" (v. 1). Using three different means of evidence – hearing, seeing, and touching – John establishes his proof of our Lord's humanity.

John has to do so, for heretics, called *Gnostics*, are challenging that truth. There are Docetic Gnostics (*dokeo* – "to seem"), who argued that the Lord *only seemed* to have a body, that is, He was a *phantom*, so to speak; and Cerinthian Gnostics (after Cerinthus), who distinguished between the physical-man, Jesus, and the divine-spirit, Christ. They claim that the Christ came upon Jesus at His baptism and left Him at the cross.

John identifies Jesus as "the Word of life" (v. 1). He then details his fellowship with Him and expresses his desire that his readers might experience the same. The Greek word for "fellowship" is *koinonia*, and carries with it the idea of one person having a joint partnership with another in *something possessed in common* by both. He wants to share with his non-eyewitness readers his first-hand knowledge of the life of the Lord gained through the senses of sight, hearing, and touch.

LIFE STEP You can *possess in common* with John a fellowship with God the Father and His Son, Jesus Christ! As the Spirit of God guides you in your study of the Word, you can see/hear/touch the Lord Jesus through John's eyes/ears/hands witness to you! Take a minute and write out a favorite aspect of your "fellowship" with Jesus. What part of your walk with Jesus brings an overflowing joy (v. 4) to your life?

1 John 1:5-10

What is the writer saying?

How can I apply this to my life?

John now begins his first subject (1:5–2:11), the truth that God is light. John tells us that those who want to have fellowship with God must *live in that light*. Christ taught this same truth (John 1:4; 3:19; 8:12; 9:5; 12:46). Light is contrasted with darkness (v. 6) as a picture of the absolute nature of God. God is *all light* – thus completely holy – "in Him is no darkness at all" (v. 5).

Having identified God's character, John develops a series of "if" statements that alternate between right and wrong responses to God:

1. First, some are saying they "have fellowship with him [God]," while they continue to *walk in darkness*. This is ridiculous and untrue. Just as you cannot carry a light into a room and claim that it is still completely dark, so you cannot be carrying the *light from God*, while still walking in darkness (v. 6). Light and darkness cannot *share* the same space!

2. A second "if" statement begins at verse 8. Some are claiming to have a character *free from a sin nature*. Not only are those folks liars, but they are self-deluded. Their claim demonstrates that the truth is not in them. On the other hand, the believer who recognizes he is a sinner and confesses his sins will experience God's forgiveness (v. 9).

3. A third group is claiming to have *never sinned* (v. 10). This is a claim that makes God out to be a liar, since the entire Gospel message rests on the fact that every man is sinful and needs a Savior.

LIFE STEP

So then, we cannot walk in darkness — it destroys fellowship. But then, neither can we walk perfectly in the light (that is why God offers His forgiveness if we confess our sins to Him!). Thus, we learn that a part of our fellowship with God is to (1) seek to walk in the light, and (2) to confess our sins when we fail to walk as children of God's light. Well then, how can you have a better walk with God in the light? And what do you need to confess to God so He can forgive you?

1 John 2:1-6

What is the writer saying?

How can I apply this to my life?

PRAY Finland – For creative, committed believers willing to invest their lives in this country's youth.

Chapter two brings a change of tone. John moves away from the confrontational instruction of the first chapter where he deals with the "if" situations involving doctrinal error. Now, using an affectionate tone, he is addressing his believing family members, referring to them as my "little children," a title he uses often (2:12, 28; 3:7, 18; 4:4; 5:21).

He begins by offering a warning (v. 1) and a promise (v. 2). The warning: *Don't sin. That's why I'm writing.* The promise: *But if you do, God has provided a way for you to respond, so don't lose heart.* It is found in "Jesus Christ the righteous" who serves as the believer's "advocate" (v. 1), coming alongside as his defender and to plead his case in God's courtroom. There, He acknowledges the believer's guilt and presents His work on the cross as grounds for acquittal.

John makes it clear that what Christ did at Calvary was for all mankind, not just believers (v. 2). There He became man's "propitiation." "Propitiation" refers to God's anger against sinners being satisfied by Christ's death in their place. The death of Jesus made it possible for a holy and righteous God to be merciful to believing sinners. Jesus took the punishment we deserved. Wow, think of it! A divine sacrifice provided by the Divine One, Jesus Christ the Son of God! Please understand — if there are those who do not experience the benefit of Christ's payment, the fault lies not in the sacrifice, but in the sinner who fails to accept it.

John then answers the question, *How can I be assured that Christ is my propitiation and my advocate?* in verses 3-6. It is found in a lifestyle of obedience to His commandments, and in walking as He walked.

LIFE STEP Does your daily life reflect the truth that Jesus is your propitiation and your advocate? How is your obedience and daily walk? His great sacrifice should bring about a lifestyle pleasing to Christ. So then, what has changed in your lifestyle since you asked Jesus to save you?

WEDNESDAY 44

1 John 2:7-11

What is the writer saying?

How can I apply this to my life?

PRAY Austria – Over 75% of Austriains call themselves Christians but at the same time 80% have been involved with the occult. Pray that the truth of the Scripture would boldly go forth.

John emphasizes "fellowship." A component of fellowship is love. A believer in fellowship with God, who is consciously walking in fellowship (1:7), is walking in love toward his *brothers in Christ* (v. 10). Conversely, the believer out of fellowship with God will find that he cannot get along with God's people. John's point is that members of God's family are to love one another. To that end John writes an "old" (v. 7) and yet "new" (v. 8) commandment about Christian love.

God's command to love goes back to earlier books of the Bible (Leviticus 19:18, Deuteronomy 6:5), where man is commanded to love God and his neighbor. Jesus combined those in Matthew 22:34-40, stating that they summarized all the Law and the Prophets (thus, all the rest of the Old Testament). But now the "old" commandment is also "new," for Christ gave new meaning to and example of the word "love."

Notice also that love becomes "new" to believers as they exercise it in their own lives (v. 8). As Christ loved sacrificially, so should we. The darkness that surrounded us prior to salvation is "past" (v. 8), and "the true light [of Christ] now shineth" in our lives (v. 8).

John is giving us another way to evaluate the genuineness of our fellowship with God! The person who claims to exist in God's light yet hates his brother is in the dark (v. 9). However, the one who loves his brother (in real actions, not just in words) is in the light. Conversely, the brother-hater exists in darkness, and is in danger of stumbling over unseen obstacles, for he cannot see where he is going (v.11).

LIFE STEP Take time to check out your *love-quotient*. How have you demonstrated a Christ-like, others-minded love to your brothers and sisters in Christ in recent days? This *love from God* seeks to serve others without demanding anything in return! Ask God to show you someone in need of some help. How can you be of service to them?

What is the writer saying?

How can I apply this to my life?

Brotherly love between members of God's family must be obvious. John now addresses these members, and does so by grouping them according to their spiritual status. He lists his instructions to them according to where they are in their Christian walk:

1. "Little children" (2:12-13b). The COMMENCEMENT of the Christian Life. These are the newborns in the family of God. Their sins have been forgiven.

2. "Young Men" (2:13-14). The CONFLICT of the Christian Life. Moving on to manhood does not come without a struggle. Learning how to handle the Word of God gives victory over the wicked one.

3. "Fathers" (13a). The CONSUMMATION of the Christian Life. These have now progressed to the level of spiritual fathers. They are people of spiritual maturity, having grown in their knowledge of Him.

Having identified their spiritual-growth status, he gives to all three groups this caution: "Love not the world, neither the things that are in the world" (v. 15). This is not the "world" for which Christ died, but the *world system* that is hostile to Christ. While this evil *world system* will *pass away* (v. 17), it continues to be deceptive and dangerous, using as its tools both "lust" and "pride" (v. 16).

John cautions believers to *abide* in their walk with God. Abiding means to continually be *camping out* with God. The believer needs this to win the victory over this world system. The believer's defense is to continue doing the "will of God" (v. 17).

LIFE STEP What is the *level* of your Christian walk? Since the *world system* is a danger at every level, are you planning for spiritual victory? Are you abiding in the will of God and obeying the Word of God? What do you need to *do* today to *abide in God's will*?

FRIDAY 44

1 John 2:18-22

What is the writer saying?

How can I apply this to my life?

PRAY Nigeria – Protection for those working among the Fulani people and other Muslim groups.

In these verses John contrasts true and false teachings about Jesus. Those who claim fellowship with God are to pursue truth, not false teaching. One cannot believe lies and have fellowship with God.

John reminds his readers that the one called "antichrist" is coming (see Revelation 13:1-10; Matthew 24:5, 24). While that Antichrist has not yet appeared, John wants his readers to understand that they are in the beginnings of the last time period (v.18) which ends when he appears. John says that since there are those with the *spirit of antichrist* already on the scene, that the "last time" has begun (this is the time period between the First Coming and the Second Coming of Christ).

John warns that many with *against-Christ* attitudes and doctrines are already on the scene. These "antichrists" are dangerous for they have infiltrated the visible church. They have characteristics like Christians ("they went out, that they might be made manifest that they were not all of us," v. 19) and were *church members* but not true believers!

They also deny the deity of Jesus. They say that the man, Jesus, is not the Messiah of the Old Testament (v. 22, "Christ"). Their false teaching makes them liars (v. 22).

If Jesus is not God and the promised Messiah of the Old Testament, then His death could not pay the infinite price for our sin. In the same way, if Christ had not become a flesh-and-blood man, then He could not become our substitute when He died upon the Cross. Jesus had to be both God and man in one person to become our Savior!

LIFE STEP Thank Jesus Christ, God the Son, for His great love for you, for it was His love that led Him to become a man so that He might also be your Savior!

SATURDAY 44

1 John 2:23-27

What is the writer saying?

How can I apply this to my life?

PRAY Fiji – To increase their role in sending missionaries to other small countries of the Pacific.

John continues his emphasis on the foundational doctrine of Christ. Error here indicates that a person is not a part of God's family. The point: the Son and the Father are inseparable, and must be accepted together (v. 23).

John's advice is, when confronting the false claims of these antichrists, simply abide in the truths already learned, such as Christ's incarnation, holy life, death, and resurrection. These great truths are vital for ongoing fellowship and communion (v. 24).

John then says that belief in these great truths give the promise of eternal life (v. 25). Eternal life is far more than ongoing existence. It is a quality of life (not simply quantity) that can be experienced now. It is a promise Christ made repeatedly (John 3:15-16; 6:40; 17:3). Later John writes: "He that hath the Son hath life" (1 John 5:12).

John reminds them of these truths so they can avoid the seductive nature of these false teachers. Their lies lead to spiritual adultery (v. 26).

Their protection is found in the "anointing" which they have "received" (v. 27). The "anointing" comes from the Holy Spirit who uses the Word of God to teach them the truth. His indwelling presence provides the necessary spiritual discernment so that no child of God ever needs to be led away by error. The key, however, is found in the word "abide." Only this relationship successfully counters false teaching.

LIFE STEP Abide means *to permanently 'stay-at-home' in your beliefs* about Christ. Consider John's instructions. Be sure you have your doctrine of Christ straight. Write out a summary statement of your beliefs in Jesus Christ and then spend some time praising Him for who He is!

What is the writer saying?

How can I apply this to my life?

John closes chapter two with a challenge, one based upon the certain return of the Savior. The believer is to live a life that will give him confidence in Christ's presence! The key: *to be constantly abiding in Him*, a word picture meaning *to stay-at-home with Jesus*, that is, *living in close fellowship with Him*.

John points out that true sonship ("born of him," v. 29) is expressed in Christ-like characteristics such as righteousness, love, and truth.

"Behold" (3:1) is a command to *Pay Attention! Look at this truth until you have learned its implications!* God's love for us is "exotic, foreign-to-the-human-heart love" (Wuest). It is *agape* love. It is the type of love that gives without measure and does not ask for anything in return. It results in a new status as the children of God.

In verse 2, John compares the present and future of God's people. Our present reality is the privilege of being His children. While the future is still somewhat dim, one great fact stands out – we will be like Christ, a transformation that will take place at His return. To *be like Him* includes both physical changes – we get a new *resurrection body* – and spiritual changes of purity (v. 3), no sin (v. 5), and righteousness (v. 7).

This future "hope" (v. 3) encourages us to cleanse ("purifieth") our lives as Jesus was "pure" in His life. As "partakers of the divine nature" (2 Peter 1:4), we possess the ability to show the attributes of Christ in our daily lives as we are enabled by the Holy Spirit who dwells in us (3:24).

LIFE STEP Check yourself out. Since you are a child of God, does your life demonstrate a *pure life* to a watching world? What area of your life does the Holy Spirit want to *purify* further?

1 John 3:4-10

What is the writer saying?

How can I apply this to my life?

John turns his attention from Christ's future appearing (v. 2), to His past appearing (v. 5). His first coming had two objectives: (1) to take away sins (vv. 4-6), and (2) to destroy the works of the devil (vv. 7-8). The sinning child of God is demonstrating a failure to understand or appreciate what Christ did for him on the cross.

Furthermore, a person born of God (v. 9) lives a habitually righteous life. Thus, a person living in sin is demonstrating that he has not been born into the family of God (v. 6). Both *sin* and *lawlessness* are used here. Sin means *to miss the mark*. Lawlessness implies the more serious offense of *purposely disregarding God's law*.

It is likely that the false teachers are playing down the seriousness of *minor* sins. Thus, John insists that any sin is rebellion against God. John's point: one who abides in Christ does not continually practice sin.

Similarly, one who habitually sins has not come to know God in a permanent relationship (v. 6). In fact, one who practices sin is of the devil (v. 8), the source of sin. Ever since his fall (Isaiah 14:9-17; Ezekiel 28:12-15), Satan has been in revolt against God. We are not surprised that John declares that it was the "purpose" of God (v.8) to destroy the works of the devil by Christ becoming a man.

John concludes that true believers cannot practice sin because God's seed of a new divine nature dwells within them (2 Peter 1:4). From that divine seed comes divine characteristics, which we are responsible to develop to spiritual maturity (vv. 8-9). It is this holy lifestyle that distinguishes God's children from Satan's children (v. 10).

LIFE STEP   So then, to which spiritual family do you belong? If you say you have been born into God's family, do you see the fruit of that new life? Are there divine characteristics of a pure life growing in you? How about talking to God about an area of your life that needs some growth?

1 John 3:11-16

What is the writer saying?

How can I apply this to my life?

PRAY Poland – For the exposure of all false doctrines. Jehovah's Witnesses outnumber followers of Christ.

Verse 10 introduces an additional trait of a genuine Christian: love for the brethren. This command is not new. Christ Himself presented it in John 13:34-35. Believers are to have an extra measure of love for other believers. This was particularly important in John's day, since Christians could be put to death for not worshipping the Roman emperors as gods. Christian love for one another is vital for survival. John develops his point by citing a negative example: Cain's lack of human brotherly love for his brother, Abel (v. 12, Genesis 4). Cain, whose evil works were influenced by Satan, killed Abel because Abel's works were righteous. *Don't be surprised*, John says, *if you experience such hatred*, for the world will always hate Christianity. The world hates Christians because the Christian message is offensive to it (v. 13).

John now contrasts a Christian's love for other Christians with the hate that the world directs toward them. He notes that one of the ways we know that we have passed from death unto life is "because we love the brethren" (v. 14). When this love is not evident in a believer, he needs to consider if he has genuinely been born into God's family! Hatred is incompatible with Christianity. John is echoing Christ's words in Matthew 5:21-22, where He equates hatred with murder. Verse 16 gives the positive contrast, that is, a willingness, if need be, to lay down one's life for the brethren. Such is the extent of sacrifice that may be demanded of a Christian.

LIFE STEP Loving sacrifice for one another ought to be the norm among believers. Think back. Has there been a fellow Christian who has carried out some deed of sacrificial love on your behalf? Now *think about those around you*, is there some Christian that needs you to exercise sacrificial Christian love towards them? How can you begin acting as his Christian brother?

1 John 3:17-24

What is the writer saying?

How can I apply this to my life?

PRAY United States – 35% of all foreign missionaries are American. Pray that these missionaries would be able to work in partnership with local churches.

In verse 16 Jesus is presented as our model for true love – a love which is sacrificial. He is contrasted with the individual who claims to possess God's love, but who is unwilling to help a needy brother. He has the means, sees the need, but he *shuts* his heart, choosing not to help ("bowels," "compassion," heart, etc. – all references to the seat of one's emotions). It is a picture of one who has failed the test of love (v. 17).

Such behavior is to be avoided. Love is to be active, not simply verbal. True love is not hypothetical; rather it is demonstrated by "deed" (v. 18). Genuine, self-sacrificial love for fellow believers is proof of the genuineness of one's own position in God's family (v. 19a).

The remaining portion of verse 19 and verse 20 go together, and can be translated: "If our hearts condemn us, God is greater than our hearts, and knows all things. He will bring balance to our thoughts speaking comforting words to our hearts." Because the possibility exists that a conscientious believer may be plagued by unjustified guilt feelings, he can rest in John's word of comfort, that God, Who is all-knowing, is also all-loving.

Being freed from an accusing conscience allows us to approach God with great boldness (v. 21). Such confidence brings an assurance that God has heard our prayer and will give us a clear answer (which could be "no" or "later"!). There are some attached conditions: (1) we must be keeping His commandments; (2) we must be doing that which pleases Him; (3) we must believe in His Name, that is, in all He is; and (4) we must love one another (vv. 22-23).

The chapter closes with a return to the abiding principle that makes keeping Christ's commandments possible (v. 24).

 LIFE STEP Check out your love life. Have you by-passed an opportunity to show special concern to a fellow believer? Ask God (v. 22) to help you to see and then do that which is pleasing in His sight as you lovingly serve others today!

THURSDAY 45

1 John 4:1-6

What is the writer saying?

How can I apply this to my life?

PRAY Saudi Arabia – For Saudi believers to have the ability to meet together in safety and have access to God's Word.

John argues that a person's heavenly sonship can be demonstrated by doctrinal truth, especially concerning the Person of Christ. With "many false prophets" in the world (v. 1), John warns that all speakers must be checked against the teachings of the Word of God. In John's day, the New Testament has not yet been completed. Therefore, John states that true teachers will confess that Jesus is the Christ, the Messiah. False teachers will not (vv. 2-3). In John's day, it is the Gnostic heresy that fails this test. Today, this doctrinal error marks many branches of liberal Christianity and the cults. Heresy in this area affects other areas of Theology. Example: if Jesus is not the Christ, then the Bible is not inspired. If Jesus was not the God-Man, then He was not an acceptable sacrifice for our sins, thereby invalidating our salvation.

John assures his "little children" that they have overcome the spirit of antichrist (v. 4). They have withstood the lure of false doctrine because the One in them (a reference back to the Holy Spirit; see 3:24; 4:2) is greater than the one indwelling the world.

In verse 4, John addresses his readers. In verse 5 he focuses on the heretics. They are clearly creatures of the satanic world system, thoroughly in tune with the direction Satan is taking it. They speak the world's language and find ready acceptance by the world.

In verse 6, John turns his attention to teachers of the truth. His claim: "We are of God," and those in tune with God would listen to men like John and the apostles whose message comes from God. Those deluded by the world and its thought patterns would not care to hear the truth.

LIFE STEP John would want to warn you about false teachers and the lure of false doctrine. How can you rely on the *One in you* to aid you in *overcoming* the error that comes your way? The Bible is God's Word, the true message from God. Jesus Christ is God's Son and our Messiah.

1 John 4:7-12

What is the writer saying?

How can I apply this to my life?

This passage begins another cycle of John's teaching, focusing on a genuine believer's display of love (see also 2:7-11; 3:10-24). The word "love" (*agape*) is used here, in various forms, thirteen times, plus twelve more times in tomorrow's selection.

John declares that love reveals God's essence: He is love (v. 8); it is His supreme quality. It summarizes all He says and does. Agape marks God's love for the world (John 3:16) and for sinners (Romans 5:8). It characterizes Christ's love for His church (Ephesians 5:25) and for individuals (Galatians 2:20). It is also the manner in which mankind is to love God.

He begins (v. 7) by calling his readers "beloved," for they have experienced God's love. That being the case, they should exhibit the same kind of love. Doing so demonstrates the genuineness of one's relationship with God. Notice that the opposite is also true. If this agape-type love does not exist in a person's life, such a person is giving evidence that a genuine relationship with God does not exist (v. 8).

In verse 9, we see an echo of John 3:16. God sent "His only begotten Son into the world," putting action to His words. His purpose: to provide eternal life for lost mankind. He was sent to be the "propitiation for our sins" (v. 10, that is Christ's death was the satisfaction of God's wrath upon our sin, Romans 3:25, 1 John 2:2). That love of God provides an example for His children. Just as God demonstrated His love toward us through Christ's incarnation and work on the cross, so should His children demonstrate love toward the rest of the family (v. 11).

LIFE STEP The Father has shown us great love. His love is a pattern we should follow. Ask God to bring someone to your attention today for you to love the way God loves.

1 John 4:13-21

What is the writer saying?

How can I apply this to my life?

Today John gives an additional test of a believer's relationship with the Father: the presence of the Holy Spirit (1 Corinthians 6:19). The Spirit is given to all believers at their salvation. He lives within the believer producing "fruit" (Galatians 5:22-23). He also "gifts" all believers (see 1 Corinthians 12). It is the outworking of these gifts that proves the Spirit's presence.

In verse 14 John testifies that he personally observed that the Father sent the Son into the world to provide God's offer of salvation to everyone. He was an eye witness of the Life of Christ. Verse 15 follows with a statement that *throws the doors open* to anyone who will walk through on God's terms: the acknowledgement and belief that Jesus Christ is His Son. Both John and his first readers have done exactly that: "We have known and believed" (v. 16).

Because a believer's relationship with the Father is confirmed by the presence of the Holy Spirit, he can stand before God with great confidence that "casteth out fear" (v. 18). What John is saying is that fear and love cannot co-exist. If fear is present, it is a rebuke to its possessor and an indicator that God's love has not truly captured his heart.

The inner working of the Holy Spirit declares that a true believer's heart has been captured by Christ. The result of the Spirit capturing a person's heart is that love will be put into practice (v. 21). Note that claiming to be a family member and saying, *I love God*, but failing to practice love, brands the person as a "liar" (v. 20).

LIFE STEP Do you still have lingering fears about your own salvation, your own death, or the final judgment of God upon your sin? A key application here is that the Spirit will witness to your spirit that you are genuinely God's child. As such you now possess eternal life (not a final death!) and you have obtained a Savior from the coming judgment of sin! If these fears persist, ask God to allow His great love to cast out such fears!

1 John 5:1-8

What is the writer saying?

How can I apply this to my life?

PRAY Serbia – For genuine forgiveness between ethnic groups that have been at war for so long. Pray that people would be able to rebuild trust and cooperation.

John continues to point out that a genuine love for God should result in our love for our brother in Christ. Our brothers would be those who have also come into God's family by responding to "whosoever believeth that Jesus is the Christ" (v.1) (the Anointed One sent by God to be our Savior, 4:14). This same doctrinal test has been used earlier (2:22; 4:2, 3, 15) to distinguish true believers from false Gnostic teachers (see 1:1-4). All believers, therefore, have a common link to the Father through Jesus and, therefore, love for one another.

That link is developed in verses 2-3. It looks back to three concepts featured in previous verses: love for God, love for His children, and love for His commands. John declares that one leads to another: loving God leads to loving God's people and obeying God's commands. We must recognize that keeping God's commands is a demonstration of our love for God and our faith in Christ as the Son of God (v. 5).

In verse 6, John begins discussing the person of Christ. He refutes Gnostic error by offering three infallible witnesses. First, the Holy Spirit: He descended on Jesus at His baptism in the form of a dove. Also, Christ Himself said that the Spirit's work was to witness of Him (John 15:26). Second, water: At the beginning of His ministry (His baptism) the Father identified Him as His Son (Matthew 3:13-17). Third, blood: A reference to the conclusion of His ministry (His crucifixion). Jesus did not receive "the Christ" (the anointing) at His baptism and lose it at the cross. Both at Jesus' baptism and crucifixion, the Father spoke as a witness to His Son's Deity.

LIFE STEP The evidence has spoken. Jesus is the Christ, the anointed One. He has given us commands to obey: love one another and keep God's commands. Think of how you could practice (1) a love for God, (2) a love for the people of God, and (3) a love for His commandments!

1 John 5:9-15

What is the writer saying?

How can I apply this to my life?

PRAY Uganda – Pray for the continued and steady growth of the ministries in Uganda. For God to supply workers and open doors of opportunity.

John asks his readers to think through their sources of authority. While they have accepted testimony from human witnesses (v. 9a), John declares that the witness of God Himself (v. 9b) is much greater.

John now moves from the objective (a witness has been offered, v. 9b) to the subjective (it is necessary for us to place our faith in Jesus who has been presented, v. 10a). What God has done is of no value until accepted (v. 10b). Once accepted, there is a confirming inner "witness" of the Holy Spirit to support the evidence offered (v. 10a).

On the other hand, the one who rejects the gift God has offered is, in effect, calling God "a liar" (v.10b), thereby questioning God's character (v. 10).

John next cites the record (v. 11): God has given "us" (those that believe Jesus is the Christ, v. 1) eternal life. We now possess a life that will never end. It is found in a personal relationship with His Son (v. 11); if you have the Son (2:23, 2 John 9) you also have life. Conversely, without believing in Jesus there is no hope of eternal life (vv. 11-12).

Just as the Gospel of John concluded with John stating his purpose (John 20:31), John does the same here (v. 13). The Gospel brings people to faith, this letter helps believers, challenged by heresy, to know with confidence that they have followed the truth about Jesus Christ (v. 13).

Knowing we are in God's family makes it natural for us to pray to God (v. 14). When we pray according to His will, we can be confident that He will hear and answer according to His will (see also 1 John 3:22, John 14:14; 15:7).

LIFE STEP Pause in gratefulness to God, not only for salvation offered and accepted, but also for the wonderful resource of prayer! All because of His Son, the Anointed One, our Savior Jesus Christ!

1 John 5:16-21

What is the writer saying?

How can I apply this to my life?

PRAY Colombia – Outreach to the 700,000 women and children displaced by drug wars and violence.

Two scenarios are presented (vv. 16-17); a "sin not unto death" and a "sin unto death." Since John emphasizes the first, let us begin there.

A brother, seeing another brother in sin, should pray for him, knowing that such is God's will. Since the term "brother" refers to a Christian, a "sin not unto death" refers to a genuine believer who has chosen to sin. Note that while God, for a time, will endure his sin, God will not allow him to sin indefinitely! The concerned brother should pray for the one sinning, requesting that God restore him to proper fellowship without having to end his "life" on earth by taking him to his eternal home to heaven. John does not request that we pray for the one committing a "sin unto death." This is God's business alone. While commentators are divided on this, it quite likely refers only to believers and therefore only to physical death (and not a spiritual, eternal death which could only

be the case for unbelievers). We note that because of sin, Old Testament believers like Moses and Aaron experienced death (Numbers 20:12, Deuteronomy 3:26-27), as did Ananias and Sapphira in the New Testament (Acts 5:1-11). While a child of God cannot commit sin that would nullify his salvation, he can commit sin so grievous to God that God would choose to end his life and call him home prematurely!

John closes with a summary: (1) born again ones do not habitually practice sin (v. 18, see 3:9); (2) we may know with certainty that we belong to God and not Satan's world system (v. 19); and (3) God has given us "eternal life," by means of the coming of Jesus Christ into the world (v. 20).

His final instruction is to "keep yourselves from idols" (v. 21), that is, anything that would remove God from His proper place in our hearts.

LIFE STEP Has God made you aware of and then burdened your heart for a genuine Christian brother or sister who is openly sinning against God? Then, would you begin to earnestly pray for this brother requesting that God bring about his restoration to a proper walk with Him?

What is the writer saying?

How can I apply this to my life?

PRAY Slovakia – Sensitivity among those ministering to Gypsies, as they are suspicious of outsiders.

In the introductory verses (vv. 1-3) of this little epistle, John, the author, calls himself "the elder." The emphasis is on age, not office, though in John's case both apply – he is the lone remaining apostle. We also meet the recipient, "the elect lady," which is a title of the church as a whole and "her children" a reference to its membership. Thus, this letter is intended to be circulated to all local churches. That is true of some of Paul's letters. Hence, this letter also applies to our present-day local churches.

John's greeting is similar to other New Testament writers, and includes the triplet of grace, mercy, and peace (v. 3). But it is also different, for it is expressed as a prediction (future tense) and not as a wish, as in many other cases. The church and its members receive these blessings from both Father and Son (v. 3), administered with both truth and love.

John then moves to a word of commendation (v. 4), for he was rejoicing that as he came in contact with her children, he found them "walking (continuously) in truth," just as God has commanded. Next he turns (v. 5) to the immediate reason behind his writing. He reiterates his constant *theme song*, "that we love one another." This command has been in place from the beginning and, in fact, was stated by the Lord Himself (John 13:34-35; 1 John 3:11). It must, however, be exercised within the guidelines of obedience. It must be put into action – action that is designed for the good of one another. Thus, John's charge is that they "walk after" this command (v. 6).

LIFE STEP How has your conduct with your Christian friends resulted in onlookers rejoicing in your love for one another? What might you plan to do with your friends so that John's "love one another" commandment to you is obvious to an onlooker?

THURSDAY 46

2 John 7-13

What is the writer saying?

How can I apply this to my life?

PRAY Philippines – That Christians currently working within the government will use their influence wisely.

Behind John's reason for his exhortation to his readers to "love one another" (vv. 5-6) is the presence of false teachers who are spreading heresy in the church. While believers are to love one another, they are not to extend such hospitality (v. 10) to those who would not acknowledge that Jesus came in the flesh (v. 7). John selects this key doctrine of the incarnation as the key test of a false teacher (v. 7). To reject this doctrine, marks a person as a deceiver and an antichrist.

John offers a warning and a command (v. 8): *Watch out! Be on guard.* Why? There are false teachers who have the potential of nullifying all the work that has gone into building the Church.

John's explanation for this stern warning is that some are not standing firm on the basic teaching that Jesus is the Christ, the Messiah. They are instead *going beyond* ("transgresseth") that teaching, as are the Gnostics in their *enlightenment*. John declares that these do not have God (v.9). On the other hand, the one who stays within the bounds of that which was originally taught has both Father and Son (v. 9).

Therefore, says John, *if someone comes to you with a false teaching, they are not to be helped in any way* (v. 10). If you fail to follow such directions and offer some form of hospitality, you become a partaker of his evil deeds. While love is to be expressed among believers, such love must be withheld from the heretic. The believer should not give even passive or unintended cooperation to the false teacher.

LIFE STEP Do you know someone who teaches a false doctrine? First of all, you should be praying that they would come to know the truth. Secondly, while you must continue to have a love for that individual, you must act in a manner that does not assist them in spreading their false teachings.

3 John 1-8

What is the writer saying?

How can I apply this to my life?

John again refers to himself simply as the "elder" (see 2 John 1). The recipient is Gaius, apparently a prosperous believer who is a leader in a local church. The subject is hospitality and traveling preachers. John expresses his love for Gaius (v. 1), his concern for his health (v. 2), and the joy he experienced in hearing that Gaius, probably one of his converts, is walking "in the truth" (v. 3). There is no greater joy (v. 4).

Verses 5-8 are a review of how we should care for traveling teachers and Gaius is commended for his example. If the traveler is one who shares similar convictions, hospitality is to be generously extended. Such a practice is a demonstration of faithfulness to God (v. 5) and makes the doer a *partner in the enterprise* of Christianity ("fellowhelpers," v. 8).

The text makes it clear (v. 6) that many traveling preachers have come Gaius's way. Later, these testified of his love towards them (v. 6). John encourages Gaius to send them on their way with a generous offering – giving as if you are giving directly to God. By his love, they are motivated to minister for "his name's sake," (v. 7). Their faithfulness is to be supported in every way possible by like-minded Christians, for the pagan world to which they are going has no obligation to do so.

The support of missionaries is not optional. As believers, we are responsible to provide for those who take salvation's message to the lost. Our assistance makes us co-workers with them in "the truth" (v. 8).

LIFE STEP

How are you doing in this matter? Does your conduct make it evident that you are *faithfully doing whatsoever* (v. 5) you can to *send them forth in a worthy manner* (v. 6)? Gaius's record is clear, and he is commended. What can you do this month (and every month after!) as a "fellowhelper," so that this commendation can be extended to you?

3 John 9-14

What is the writer saying?

How can I apply this to my life?

PRAY Don Lough Jr., Executive Director of Word of Life Fellowship, for wisdom as he leads.

In contrast to Gaius (v. 1), whose behavior is commendable, we meet Diotrephes, a man whose behavior is shameful. His love for the "preeminence" (*desiring to be first*, v. 9, meaning he is jealous of the influence of others like John) is causing great difficulty in the church.

John has written earlier to Gaius's church (perhaps a reference to 2 John, likely carried to the churches and then taught through by traveling teachers). This letter has been rejected by Diotrephes (v. 9). Diotrephes's opposition to apostolic authority results in John making it clear that he intends to come and expose his actions as rebellion (v. 10).

John's condemnation of Diotrephes is two-fold. First, his words: he spoke maliciously against John and his company. Second, his actions: he refused to accept the traveling Bible teachers that John had sent to the church. He also had acted to prevent anyone else in the church, like Gaius, from helping them, even to the point of excommunication (v. 10).

Diotrephes's actions were so forceful that John feels it necessary to exhort Gaius to continue his practice of genuine hospitality; Gaius is not to give in to Diotrephes's pressure. Rather, Gaius is to "follow [imitate] ... that which is good" (v. 11). In so doing, he would demonstrate his genuine relationship with God (see also 1 John 2:29; 3:9; 4:7; 5:1, 18).

A fourth character is now introduced, Demetrius. He apparently is the carrier of the letter to Gaius and is likely one of John's Bible teachers. John himself gives evidence that Demetrius is worthy of Gaius's hospitality (v. 12).

LIFE STEP Gaius, Diotrephes and Demetrius. One is a wealthy, yet generous church leader. One is a self-promoting church problem. One is a worthy teacher of Bible truth. If John were here today, how would he characterize your life? To what evidence would John point to make his case?

Thessalonica is located one hundred miles from Philippi and is a key city in northern Greece (ancient Macedonia). The Egnatian Way (a major East/West road) goes though her walls. She also has a splendid harbor, making her the chief port of Macedonia. She is the largest city in Macedonia with 200,000 inhabitants. There are some Jews, but it is basically a pagan city.

History:

315 B.C.	City is named after Alexander the Great's sister.
168 B.C.	Romans divide Macedonia into four districts and make it capital of its district.
146 B.C.	Named capital of all Macedonia.
42 B.C.	Declared a *Free City* (allowed to control its own affairs) as a reward for helping Octavian (the future Caesar Augustus) against the murderers of Julius Caesar.
Today	It is called *Salonika* with a population of 300,000+

Paul visits Thessalonica on his second missionary journey (Acts 16:8–17:10). Paul is forced out of Philippi. Silas and perhaps Timothy are with him. Paul's practice is to hit the major centers of Roman administration, Greek culture, Jewish colonies, and trade/transportation hubs. He goes to the Jew first (the synagogue), where more Gentile proselytes to Judaism respond than those born Jews.

Acts 17:1-2 mentions "three Sabbath Days" (twenty one days) in Thessalonica, but it would seem that he stays there longer than three weeks. Philippians 4:16 tells us he receives not one but two offerings from Philippi during his stay at Thessalonica. We know from 1 Thessalonians that the converts are won from paganism. To disciple them would seem to require a greater length of time. Therefore, he might have been there up to six months.

Eventually jealous Jewish leaders run him out of town. He is charged with "turning the world upside down" and "treason." A bond is taken from Jason to ensure Paul would not return. Paul does visit again on the third missionary journey (Acts 20:4) and later takes Aristarchus with him to Rome (Acts 27).

Acts 17 and 18 tell us Paul travels quickly from Thessalonica to Berea, Athens, and then to Corinth. He is worried about his young converts. He sends Timothy to check on them. Upon receiving a good report from Timothy, he writes 1 Thessalonians. In the letter, he praises their endurance though persecution, refutes slander against him, exhorts them to even greater Christian living and answers questions about death and the return of the Lord (vv. 1:10; 2:19; 3:13; 4:15; 5:23).

The first epistle is dated 51 A.D.; the second, within the next twelve months. According to Acts 18, Paul is at Corinth for eighteen months. Gallio is Proconsul at Corinth at that time. We know that proconsuls only hold office for one to two years; therefore, from Roman history we can rather accurately date Paul's stay in Corinth. This makes Thessalonians one of Paul's earliest epistles (This is about twenty years after Christ died and rose again. Paul has been saved for about eighteen years. Paul has been a missionary for about eight years).

2 Thessalonians is written in response to the reaction of 1 Thessalonians. Apparently, word comes back to Paul that some have quit their jobs, expecting the immediate return of Christ and have become a financial burden to the church. There is also confusion about the Day of the Lord, some thinking that they were already experiencing it. Each chapter addresses an area of confusion: Chapter 1, Persecution; Chapter 2, Prophecy; and Chapter 3, Practice.

1 Thessalonians 1:1-5

What is the writer saying?

How can I apply this to my life?

PRAY South Africa – Protection for believers in a land with a murder rate that is seven times that of the U.S.

Paul went by his Hebrew name, Saul, before he was saved. Living in the Roman city of Tarsus, "Paul" would have been his Roman (Gentile) name. The Hebrew name is a proud name, both because it is the name of the first king of Israel and also for what it means: *Asked for*. Paul, on the other hand, is a humble name meaning *Little*. It is also appropriate for someone whose main ministry is to Gentiles. "Silvanus" means *of the forest*. He was also called "Silas" which is a Greek variation of "Saul." He replaces Barnabas as Paul's traveling companion and is instrumental in determining how Gentile converts would be treated at the Council of Jerusalem in Acts 15. He is jailed with Paul at Philippi and ministers at Corinth. He apparently also ministers with Peter (1 Peter 5:12). We know more about "Timothy" (*He who honors God*). The little word "in" (v. 1) speaks of our sphere of blessing. Jesus is given three names. "Lord" is the Greek word for *Jehovah*, which describes His essence as deity. "Jesus" is His human name, the Greek form of "Joshua" which means *Jehovah is Salvation*. This speaks of His mission to the planet. "Christ" is a title. It is the Greek equivalent of "Messiah" (*Anointed One*) referring to His kingship. Notice the key theological terms: "Grace ... peace," which are also the Greek and Hebrew greetings of the day. What a prayer life Paul has! Paul says they were patient in their persecutions, which can be graphically defined as *optimistic fortitude in spite of indignities suffered*. "Beloved" (v. 4) is in the Greek perfect tense, indicating a past event with presently continuing results.

LIFE STEP *Election* is God setting His love on us in His past councils so that in the present we respond to the Word as convicted by the Holy Spirit. Thank God for His amazing interest in us!

1 Thessalonians 1:6-10

What is the writer saying?

How can I apply this to my life?

The believers at Thessalonica are primarily Gentiles (1:9 says they "turned to God from idols"). They apparently are undergoing social rejection because of their new faith. In verse 6, this "affliction" (*tribulation*) is a word that refers to the pressing of grapes to get the juice. Despite the pressure, they become followers (*mimics*) of Paul and "received" (*to welcome as a guest*) the Word he preached to them. They are so noble under their persecution that they became "ensamples" (examples from *tupos*, the Greek word from which we get the English word type.). Paul is saying that all believers should be that *type* of faithful follower of Christ. "Macedonia" is northern Greece, "Achaia" is southern Greece. Their good testimony *echoes* (sounds out) like a trumpet blast or thunder bouncing off distant mountains. Verses 9 and 10 amplify the three phrases of 1:3. Their "work of faith" is their past salvation. Their "labour of love" is their present service. Their "patience of hope" is their longing for the future reunion with Christ. In the midst of struggles, Paul encourages them with the blessed hope of the return of Christ. Statistically, one out of every thirteen verses in the New Testament refers to the return of Christ. When He returns, He will deliver us from the wrath to come (a future wrath). Since fire is already a punishment for the unsaved dead and Colossians 1:13 says that we are already delivered from hell, we conclude that this future wrath must refer to the judgments of the tribulation period. This deliverance is "from" (*out of*) the wrath to come. This small Greek word (*ek*) implies complete exemption from, not just protection within (see Revelation 3:10). Theologically, this wrath is described as something determined for the unsaved (earthdwellers – Revelation 3:10) and Israel (Jeremiah 30:7; Daniel 9:24).

LIFE STEP Even if Christ doesn't come back for another one hundred years, Paul still wants us to be encouraged by the fact that He could come back today. This hope motivates us to personal holiness and evangelism.

1 Thessalonians 2:1-8

What is the writer saying?

How can I apply this to my life?

In chapter 2, Paul turns to the issue of his own credibility as an apostle. They know that his message has supernatural power. The phrase "not in vain" means *not devoid of power*, that is, Holy Spirit power. He could not have had ulterior motives because of the personal price that he is paying. He suffered (physically) and was mistreated (emotionally) at Philippi (Acts 16). There is opposition at Thessalonica as well (Acts 17). Opposition is the word *agony* which is also used for the sport of wrestling (one athlete "agonizing" with the other). In his preaching, Paul exhorts (*parakaleo*) them. It means, *called alongside to help*. It is not deceitful (compare the "cunningly devised fables" of 2 Peter 1:16). It is not delivered with unclean motives (seeking personal benefit by way of manipulation). It is not preached with "guile" (from the word for *catching a fish by baiting a hook*). In fact, God continually "trieth" his heart. The word "allowed" is in the Greek perfect tense, meaning that God approved him in the past, and that approval continues right up to the present. Some of the details of that approval process are mentioned in other books. Paul is personally taught by Christ for three years in the wilderness near Damascus. He worked for seven years in Tarsus and at the church in Antioch. On the first missionary journey, he experiences disappointment with John Mark's defection, danger at Lystra, and a dispute with Peter (leading to the Council of Jerusalem in Acts 15). He concludes in verses 5-7 that his motives and behavior are pure. He is no smooth-talking religious huckster. He does not use a mask of deceit ("cloak of covetousness"). He is motivated neither by greed nor glory. He is like a professional nanny taking care of her own children (v. 7).

LIFE STEP *Approved*. What a blessed word to hear from the Lord! Determine to live today so that if Christ returned tonight He could look you in the eye and say, "Approved!"

1 Thessalonians 2:9-13

What is the writer saying?

How can I apply this to my life?

Paul is motivated by the spiritual benefit of his converts, not for personal gain. As an apostle he has the right to financial support. Often he would not ask for it, working as a tent-maker to pay his own way. As a result he labors "night and day." Part of the time is devoted to preaching, teaching, and discipling, while the other time is devoted to working to earn money. According to the Talmud (an encyclopedic collection of the beliefs and practices of Judaism), every Jewish father is obligated to do three things for his son: 1) Circumcise him (bringing him under the covenant of Judaism); 2) Teach him the Torah (Law of Moses); and 3) Teach him a trade (so he doesn't become a thief). Paul's father apparently taught Paul how to take the skins and wool of animals and sew them into tents. This is interesting because working with the skins of dead animals borders on what the Book of Leviticus refers to as ceremonially *unclean*. Interestingly, when God is getting Peter ready to take the Gospel to the Gentiles, he places Peter at the home of Simon the tanner! The words "labour" and "travail" in verse 9 both refer to agonizing activity. "Labour" comes from a word that means, *to strike* and would be comparable to our English saying, *I'm whipped*! In verse 10, Paul creates a courtroom atmosphere as he calls the Thessalonians and God to testify that indeed he is above reproach in his financial dealings with them. "Unblameably" means *not able to find fault* as in a court of law. "Exhorted" comes from *parakaleo*, meaning called alongside to help. "Comforted" is even more sensitive (*alongside to console*). In verse 13 Paul concludes with a strong statement about the self-defending nature of the Word of God (compare Hebrews 4:12, "quick, and powerful, and sharper than any twoedged sword").

LIFE STEP We are children of the King. What can we do today to live up to that position?

1 Thessalonians 2:14-20

What is the writer saying?

How can I apply this to my life?

PRAY United Kingdom – For revival in Strathclyde, Scotland's most densely populated, non–Protestant area.

Gentile converts in the first century might have felt like *Johnny-come-latelies*. The Judaizing tendency (Hebrew Christians promoting Gentile observance of the Law of Moses, as rejected at the Council of Jerusalem in Acts 15) doesn't help their feelings of second-class citizenship. Paul argues in verse 14 that they were "followers" (mimics from the Greek word *mimeo*) of the Judean Hebrew Christians in that they also are persecuted by their fellow countrymen for the faith. The New Testament in general, and Paul in particular, are accused of being anti-Semitic. Since most of the authors of the New Testament are Jews themselves, this is rather strange. If you look at the Gospel of John, his condemnation of the Jews does not refer to Jewish people but rather to the Jewish religious leaders of the day. Likewise, Paul's reference to Jewish persecutors can be accurate without also being *anti-Semitic*. Actually, even in Thessalonica, it is some in the Jewish community who run Paul out of town (Acts 17:5). Paul feels abandoned ("taken" means *orphaned*) and he lusted ("with great desire") to see them again. Satan "hindered" them. This is a military word that means *to break up the road*. Paul concludes with the happy thought that even if in this life they can't get back together, at the rapture there will be a joyous reunion. "Coming" (v. 19) is *parousia*. It means *to be alongside of* and refers to the Lord's coming/arrival. Since it is the word also used for the arrival of kings in the ancient world, it is also called, *The Royal Visit*. This is the first time in the New Testament it occurs. It is only used of Christ's return to the planet, never of His first coming.

LIFE STEP Paul longed to be with his Christian friends. If not again in this life, he certainly looked forward to the reunion when Christ came back. How many of our friends will be there?

FRIDAY 47

1 Thessalonians 3:1-5

What is the writer saying?

How can I apply this to my life?

PRAY Japan – God to reveal Himself in this land where only 10% believe in the existence of a personal God.

In 2:19 Paul uses one term for Christ's second coming. There are two others to consider. Apocalypse (*apokalupsis*) means *revealing* or *revelation*. Epiphany (*epiphaneia*) means *seeing*, especially His glory. These terms are used for both the Rapture and the return at the end of the tribulation period. This does not require that they are one and the same event. They are *qualifying terms* (descriptive of an action) not *quantifying terms* (identifying one and only one event). Having reflected on that great reunion with the saints when Christ is revealed in all His glory in His coming, Paul continues with the account of his attempts to be encouraged by them. His heart pain is so strong, that even though it means being left alone in hostile territory there in Athens (Acts 17), he nevertheless sends Timothy to see how they are doing. "Left" (v. 1) is used elsewhere of being abandoned by the death of a spouse (Mark 12:19). In verse 2, Paul identifies Timothy (*He who honors God*) as a "fellowlabourer." Fellowship has been defined as *two fellows in one ship*. What would "fellowlabourer" be? Actually, in the Greek text it says *God's fellowlabourer*, which implies that both Paul and Timothy are in the harness with God. The word "establish" is a construction term; the *buttress* used to support heavy stone walls. "Comfort" is our old friend *parakaleo* (called alongside to help). The English word actually means *with* (com) *strength* (fort). It means that God wants to strengthen us before the task, not just make us feel better when hurt in the task. The word "appointed" in verse 3 refers to careful planning and is used of the building of a city (*set*) on a specific location.

LIFE STEP Satan is alive and well on planet earth. We should encourage one another in the struggle to make sure our fellowlabourers don't slip away.

1 Thessalonians 3:6-13

What is the writer saying?

How can I apply this to my life?

Timothy's great report is a *gospel* to Paul's ears; *good news*. Even though this doesn't alter Paul's physical living conditions, the emotional support greatly improves his frame of mind. The "affliction" of verse 7 is defined as *choking care* while "distress" is *crushing trouble*. "Affliction" refers to an internal stress such as that brought on by lack of finances. "Distress" is external and, in fact, elsewhere is translated *persecution* and *tribulation*. In all this, he is *parakaleo-ed* by their love. Some English versions flip the words "distress" and "affliction." This is not a change of word order but the translators' idea of the best English word for the underlying Greek word. Since the words are so close in meaning in both languages, it is hard to say which is the superior translation. When you see the word "distress," it is not necessarily translating the word that means, *crushing trouble*. You need to check the Greek. In verse 8, Paul's happy exclamation could be phrased, *Now we really live!* The "if" doesn't mean that Paul has any doubts and could also be rendered *since*. If Paul could spend more quality time with them, he would be able to give them more instruction about the Christian faith and life. He launches into a doxology ("Now"). There is a plural subject (God the Father and our Lord Jesus Christ), but a singular verb indicating that in Paul's mind they are of equal essence (deity), authority, and purpose. As with all the chapters in 1 and 2 Thessalonians, Paul refers to the coming of Christ as a motivating hope. The "saints" (*holy ones*) of verse 13 can refer to angels or saved humans. In this case, probably both are in mind as both will be involved in the Second Coming of Christ.

LIFE STEP

Love of fellow Christians is a chief marker of a true follower of Christ. It is one thing to say we love them. What can we do to show our love to our fellow Christians today?

1 Thessalonians 4:1-8

What is the writer saying?

How can I apply this to my life?

Paul first addresses a problem and then makes practical applications. Having handled the problem of his separation from them and his desire to be assured of their spiritual well being, he now exhorts them in the area of personal holiness. In verse 1, "beseech" is a term of request that would be made between socially equal parties. In verse 2, superiors give "commandments" to subordinates. The topic is sexual purity. Paul requests it, the Lord Jesus commands it, and in verse 3, God wills it. In verse 1, "walk" refers to our whole manner of life. Paul is confident that they are already living careful lives, but he wants to reaffirm the importance of personal holiness. Jesus' command is particularly convicting because He already lived a holy life in the flesh. "Sanctification" means *to be set apart*. It is the root word for sanctify, holy, and saint. The specific issue is "fornication" (*pornea*). It refers to any type of sexual misconduct. The "vessel" (body) of verse 4 can refer to a person's own body or the body of the spouse as the appropriate object of sexual expression. Both concepts occur in Scripture (1 Cor. 9:24-27; 1 Peter 3:7). "Concupiscence" refers to greedy, self-centered satisfaction of fleshly desires. Even in marriage, romantic expression is to be for the benefit of the partner. The Gentile pagan world not only uses sex for recreation, but also religion. Therefore, this warning is especially appropriate to the culture of Thessalonica. Sexual sin defrauds or *steals from* another person. This would include both the other person and the present spouse if married, or the future spouse if currently single. In verse 8 Paul warns that to treat sexual impurity lightly is to treat God lightly. He empowers us for purity with the indwelling Holy Spirit.

LIFE STEP There is hope. What our flesh can't do the Holy Spirit can! In times of temptation be sure to call on Him for help.

1 Thessalonians 4:9-12

What is the writer saying?

How can I apply this to my life?

Beyond personal purity, Paul also urges a continuation of their noteworthy love for fellow believers. "Brotherly love" is *philadelphias*. This is not *agape*, the highest expression of love, but rather the love that binds the children of one set of parents together (*blood is thicker than water!*). Paul tells them about this, but also reminds them that God Himself has included this in His written instruction manual (Leviticus 19:18). Thessalonica is a city in northern Greece, which at that time is called Macedonia. In fact, the *classical* Greeks such as Homer, Socrates, Plato and Aristotle all come from Achaia (Southern Greece). Those in Achaia consider the Macedonians to be backward. It is Philip of Macedonia (the father of Alexander the Great) who unifies Macedonia and Achaia. He hires Aristotle to tutor Alexander. It is Alexander who not only creates the *Greek Empire*, traveling all the way to India in his conquests, but also spreads his adopted Greek culture everywhere he goes. This is three hundred years before the birth of Christ, but clearly sets the stage for the language of the New Testament and Christian missionary expansion ("But when the fullness of the time was come, God sent forth his Son" Galatians 4:4). In verse 11, Paul asks that they be distinguished in being quiet. Taking everything that Paul says about work in 1 & 2 Thessalonians, apparently a number of the believers have lost their jobs due to persecution, or quit working because they think they are in the end times. As a result, when they run out of money, they begin to bother others, and therefore become a poor testimony.

LIFE STEP Notice how working and minding your own business go hand in hand. The donkey doing all the braying is not the one out pulling the plow!

TUESDAY 48

1 Thessalonians 4:13-18

What is the writer saying?

How can I apply this to my life?

PRAY China – For the failure of all government attempts to impose false doctrine on registered churches.

This is the earliest written account of the Rapture. The Rapture is not mentioned in Matthew 24 because there has to be a church before you can have the Rapture. The doctrine of the church isn't introduced until the Book of Ephesians. Contrast Matthew 24 and 1 Thessalonians 4 to see all the differences between the Rapture and the Second Coming of Christ. Paul doesn't want the Thessalonians to think that their dead, believing loved ones would miss out on anything. "Sleep" is a kind way of referring to death. Certainly believers are *awake* in heaven after death (see 5:10; Philippians 1:23; Luke 23:43). God lovingly *put them to sleep* (passive voice). Christ will lead them back as in a triumphal military parade. In verse 13 in the Greek text, Paul uses a double negative for emphasis: *by no means no way*. Christ Himself (emphatic) will lead the way. The "shout" is a military cry of command (see John 5:28). The only archangel we know by name is Michael. He is always seen protecting Moses (Jude 9) or Israel (Daniel 10; Rev.12). In the Bible trumpets are used for the monthly new moon, the annual New Year, and as commands on a battlefield. Therefore, it signifies *assemble and go forward*. If this is the "last trump" (1 Cor. 15:52), then the first trump is the one associated with the giving of the Law (Exodus 19:13; also Hebrews 12:26) which launches Israel. It is a qualitative not a quantitative term, just like the *First Resurrection* which includes several resurrections under the concept of *believer's resurrection*. Therefore you can have a "last trump" to rapture the church but still have other trumpets later such as the seven trumpet judgments or trumpets associated with the Battle of Armageddon. The phrase, "dead in Christ" occurs forty times in the Bible, always referring to church saints. The word *rapture* ("caught up") is used elsewhere of Philip (Acts 8:39); Paul (2 Corinthians 12:2); and Jesus (Revelation 12:5).

 LIFE STEP Encourage one another with these words. Thank the Lord that we are busy waiting for the return of Christ, not the coming of the Antichrist!

WEDNESDAY 48

1 Thessalonians 5:1-8

What is the writer saying?

How can I apply this to my life?

PRAY Ghana – For the liberation of those women being forced to live in bondage to the fetish system.

It is clear from 5:1 that Paul is changing subjects. The Greek phrase, *peri de* (here translated "but") is used by Paul eight times. Each time it indicates a change of subject (see 4:9). Having covered the Rapture of the church in chapter 4, Paul now turns his attention to that which follows the Rapture, namely the tribulation period (Daniel 9:24) also called, "the day of the Lord." There is no need to discuss *timing*, because it is unknowable. Just as a thief (cat burglar) does not announce his coming, likewise the start of the day of the Lord is sign-less. The day of the Lord is an Old Testament doctrine (see Isaiah 2; Joel 2; Zephaniah 1). Thirty Old Testament passages are similar to the events in Revelation 6:12-17. Not only is a thief unexpected, but also the homeowners are unprepared. The unsaved are lulled into complacency by the peace and safety of the era. Peace is the platform that brings the Antichrist to power. Peace certainly is not a characteristic of the end of the tribulation period where some want to start the day of the Lord and a rapture of believers. Labor pains are an Old Testament illustration (Isaiah 13). They have three characteristics that apply to this event. They are sudden, intense, and inevitable (both in the eventual coming and the outcome). The day of the Lord events are the *birth pangs of the new age*. Paul argues that these events will not "overtake" or *seize* believers. Our moral alertness allows us to be taken from the earth. As we wait for this deliverance, we are to continue the attitude of alertness by putting on the whole armor of God. We do this by *putting on* Jesus Christ according to Romans 13:14.

LIFE STEP Live like children of the King in anticipation of the great position that awaits us when He returns as the King of Kings.

What is the writer saying?

How can I apply this to my life?

PRAY Austria – For the more than 45 towns of over 5,000 people without a Gospel witness.

Those who teach a *Post-Tribulational Rapture* (that the church will go through the Tribulation and be raptured at the end) argue that 1 Thessalonians 5 presents Christians persevering on earth in the midst of moral darkness. If we only had verses 5-8, we might grant their argument. However, verse 3 says "they" are saying, "Peace and safety," and the day of the Lord will come upon "them" and "they" shall not escape. Verse 4 says that day shall not overtake "you" (believers). Finally, verse 9 explains that "God hath not appointed us to wrath." We deduce, therefore, that the day of the Lord is a period of God's wrath upon earth-dwelling sinners. In order to fit the data, the Post-Tribulational Rapture theory has to argue that none of the judgments touch believers or that the day of the Lord does not begin until the Battle of Armageddon, after believers are safely removed. The easiest understanding of all the Biblical statements is to say that we miss the wrath of the day of the Lord/tribulation period because we leave earth before the seven-year period begins. Notice the Christ-centered nature of the discussion in verses 10 and 11 (not centered on the Antichrist!). In verses 12 and 13, Paul gives a *Pastoral Job Description* using three participles in the Greek text. Pastors "labour," "are over you," and "admonish you." "Admonish" means to put in mind, coming from the Greek word *noutheo*. This is the name given to a popular theory of confrontational Biblical counseling. Notice that Paul expects them to follow a chain of command even though they are all the same age in the Lord. In verse 14, the "unruly" are *soldiers not in proper rank*. "Patient" means *to go a long way before overheating*.

LIFE STEP It may be simplistic, but *be good to everyone* covers it all!

1 Thessalonians 5:16-22

What is the writer saying?

How can I apply this to my life?

PRAY Kenya – Pray that Christians within the government would provide wisdom to avert political collapse.

Verse 16 has the distinction of being the shortest verse in the Greek New Testament. (It takes fewer letters in Greek to say, "rejoice evermore" than "Jesus wept.") People say, *Praise the Lord anyway.* This is not accurate. Verse 16 is asking us to *Praise the Lord because of it!* This may be humanly hard to do, but as we learn to rest in the absolute plan and power of God, we eventually learn that "all things work together for good" (Romans 8:28). The verb used in "pray without ceasing" is used elsewhere of a repetitive, uncontrollable cough. It doesn't mean constant coughing/praying, but rather periodic, spontaneous prayer. Verse 18 indicates that the only way we can be thankful for all things is to live "in Christ Jesus." "Quench" means *to put out a fire.* The Holy Spirit is the fire of God leading us to do certain things (such as witness to a friend). We should not resist the Holy Spirit's leading and throw cold water on His plan. Elsewhere it says that our sin "grieves" the Holy Spirit. This refers to His emotional distress. We grieve the Spirit when we do what we shouldn't do, and we quench the Spirit when we don't do what we should do. Apparently, the Thessalonian church is so careful about false prophetic utterances that they completely ignore anyone with the gift of prophecy. This is the opposite problem of the Corinthian church that shows no restraint or discernment in that area. Verse 21 strikes the proper balance, namely, don't be gullible. Check the message and messenger against the standard of the Word of God. Finally, verse 22 is not saying that we should avoid appearing as though we are doing evil (although that is good advice). It is saying that we should avoid every type of evil.

LIFE STEP Our morning devotions with the Lord should set the stage for a whole day's worth of quick communications to heaven for help and guidance. Practice the conscious presence of Christ in your life today.

1 Thessalonians 5:23-28

What is the writer saying?

How can I apply this to my life?

PRAY Turkey - is the least evangelized country in the world. Pray that God would send forth laborers into the harvest.

"Sanctify" means *set apart*. It does not immediately mean *morally pure*, but because we are set apart unto God, and since He is morally pure, we should then be morally pure as well (the Greek word is also the root for "saint" – not perfect one but *set-apart one*). Paul then asks that their entire person be "preserved blameless" (*no accusations*) until Christ comes (His *Parousia*). It is certainly possible that we are tripartite beings, however, verse 23 does not prove that we are. Elsewhere, the Bible talks about our heart, mind, strength, will, and conscience. Therefore we might have more than three parts or some of these terms are synonymous. We know that in Scripture the words soul and spirit are used interchangeably, so all we can say for sure is that we have a physical part ("body") and a non-physical part ("spirit and soul"). We particularly need to avoid developing other teachings based on an assumption that indeed we have three parts. Some argue that in salvation, our dead spirit becomes alive, turning us from two-parts to three-parts. Actually, salvation affects our whole being, not just our spirit. Others argue that Christians can be demon possessed in the soul since the Holy Spirit is only related to the spirit. This is also invalid. A few argue that the unsaved go out of existence at death because only a human with a spirit lives for eternity. All of these are inappropriate applications of the make-up of man. God is faithful and will see us safely to the end of our journey (v. 24). The "holy kiss" is fulfilled in today's culture with a holy handshake or other socially acceptable forms of warm greeting. "Charge" (v. 27) means, *bind with an oath*.

LIFE STEP Of all the adjectives he could use to describe God it is interesting that he chooses "peace." Sin brings discord into every area of life, but God and His plan of salvation bring harmony – between God and us, within ourselves and between each other.

2 Thessalonians 1:1-5

What is the writer saying?

How can I apply this to my life?

PRAY Cayman Islands – For the wealth of the island to be used to extend God's kingdom.

Chapter one deals primarily with the problem of the persecution which the Thessalonians are experiencing. Paul's typical salutation occurs in the first two verses. "Paul" is a Greek name meaning *little*. Perhaps he felt it more appropriate than his old Hebrew name "Saul" which means *asked for* (such as a child who becomes the pride and joy of his family). "Silvanus" means *of the forest*. Paul sends him back to Antioch with the decision of the Jerusalem Council in Acts 15. He joins Paul on the second missionary journey after Paul's falling out with Barnabas. Later, he is Peter's secretary. "Timothy" means *he who honors God*. He is the favorite *son* of the Apostle Paul, as well as recipient of his last will and testament in 2 Timothy. This is the last time that these three appear ministering together (at this time, in Corinth). Notice both the typical Greek ("grace") and Hebrew ("peace") greetings. Notice also the way in which God the Father and God the Son are mentioned together on equal footing. In 1:3-12 we have the first major section of the outline: *Paul's Thanksgiving for the Thessalonians*. Paul is proud of his spiritual children. "Are bound" means *ought*, indicating his moral obligation to say this. The Greek word translated "groweth" (v.3) only occurs here in the Bible. It speaks of the rapid expansion of a vigorous plant. "Abounds" speaks of their love spreading with the aggressiveness of a flooding river. In verse 4 Paul claims *bragging rights!* Verse 5 is difficult. Paul seems to be saying that their patient endurance under the persecution is proof that God is working in their lives and in the situation. Since God is working, then He will eventually rescue them and punish their tormentors.

LIFE STEP Witnessing is bragging about Jesus. Paul brags about the Thessalonians for bragging about Jesus despite the great opposition they experienced.

2 Thessalonians 1:6-12

What is the writer saying?

How can I apply this to my life?

"Tribulation" refers to the persecution of believers in many passages (see also v. 4). It also refers to God's judgment on sinners, as in verse 6. Therefore, believers of all ages can expect "tribulation" from the world, the flesh, and the devil. However, there is coming a special tribulation period, when God will pour out His wrath on sinful mankind. Verse 7 speaks of Christ's Second Coming at the Battle of Armageddon to finalize this judgment. This verse does not mean that church saints, Paul or these particular saints, are on the earth when Christ returns, but that the punishment is finally executed on all sinners. Their punishment is termed *everlasting destruction*. This is not annihilation, for other passages speak of eternal conscious punishment in Hell. It does speak of the horrors of eternal separation from the only One that can make life worthwhile – the Lord God.

Verse 10 says that Christ will be glorified "in" (not by) His saints. It is not talking about what we say but what we are! In our glorified state, we will reflect His glory at His return. Paul prays that the Thessalonians would remain faithful and not crack under the immediate pressure of the persecution (vv. 11-12). This prayer is designed to empower them for further service. God desires to be glorified through our lives and accomplishments. The *secret* then is to think of and pray for things that would bring Him glory. For a third time in chapter one, God the Father and God the Son are mentioned on equal terms. Notice it is the name of God that is to be glorified. This does not refer to the letters that make up His title or the sound of His name. It speaks of character – everything that makes God, God. Therefore, to glorify His name we repeat and meditate on all of His attributes.

LIFE STEP Paul's prayer life must have been incredible when you consider the number of times he tells people that he is praying for them! How is our prayer life by comparison?

What is the writer saying?

How can I apply this to my life?

Paul now shifts to a doctrinal discussion: The return of Christ and the day of the Lord (2:1-12). In verses 1 and 2 we have the reason for Paul's instruction. Apparently someone has spread a rumor that Paul is publicly teaching that the day of the Lord has already begun. Since this upset them, they must have expected to be raptured before the day of the Lord. The "coming" of verse 1 (*parousia*) can be used of both the Rapture and the Second Coming. Context has to decide which coming is in view. In the second half of the verse, it is the coming in which we are "gathering" to Him. For the Church Age saint, this is clearly the Rapture as described in 1 Thessalonians 4, and located time-wise as Pre-Tribulational (1 Thessalonians 1:10; 5:9; and Revelation 3:10.) They are "shaken" (such as a sudden shock to a ship in a storm) and "troubled" (as in the ripple effect of the initial shock).

This rumor comes in three avenues: a prophecy, a report, and a letter claiming that the day of the Lord has begun. Verses 3 and 4 teach that before the day of the Lord can come, the *apostasy* must come first. This is a reference to the colossal departure from the faith by organized Christianity in accepting the Man of Lawlessness (the Antichrist, Beast, Little Horn, Prince that Shall Come, Willful King). Verse 4 contains the only reference to a Tribulational temple in the church epistles. Once is enough and clearly demands a restored Israel and temple worship in order to be fulfilled. Paul is a tad frustrated in verse 5. He feels that he has been perfectly clear on the scenario in his previous teachings and is disappointed that they don't realize that this rumor was false.

LIFE STEP We sometimes feel that it is *childish* to long for the return of Christ, but it was a daily consideration for Paul and the early church. Do we look forward to the return of Christ?

2 Thessalonians 2:6-12

What is the writer saying?

How can I apply this to my life?

PRAY For professors and staff at Word of Life Bible Institutes as they prepare for a new school year.

Holding back the full manifestation of evil on the earth is the function of the *Restrainer* ("he who now letteth"). Paul states that the Restrainer is known to the Thessalonians from previous teaching, that he is stronger than Satan, and that "he" is also an *it* (neuter). This points to the Holy Spirit. The Greek word *spirit* is neuter, but as a person the masculine gender would also be appropriate (v. 7). While the Holy Spirit is the restrainer, His tool of restraint is the church. Since the Book of Revelation describes people coming to the Lord during the tribulation period, the Holy Spirit cannot be permanently removed from the earth. This is simply a reversal of Pentecost, with the Holy Spirit removing the church from the earth in the rapture. Then the Holy Spirit returns with the two witnesses (Revelation 11) who spread the Gospel once again, even in the earth's darkest hour. "Mystery of iniquity" (v. 7) means that Satan already works and perhaps always has an Antichrist ready. The "spirit of his mouth" refers to His words. "Destroy" means to render inoperative. "Brightness" is the Greek word *epiphany*, another word for Christ's coming, with emphasis on the fact that we will see Him. The Antichrist mimics and counterfeits the work of Christ with his own *parousia* (v. 9). Satan is his energizer. In fact, there seems to be an unholy trinity, with Satan as God the Father, the Antichrist as God the Son, and the False Prophet as God the Spirit in Satan's *Satanocracy*. Verse 10 indicates that unbelievers will swallow *the lie*. "Them that perish" actually reads, *those who are in the process of perishing*. They are walking dead men!

LIFE STEP "Hear the Just Law, the Judgment of the Skies: He that hates truth must be the dupe of lies. And he who <u>will</u> be cheated, to the last, delusions strong as hell must bind him fast." – William Cowper

THURSDAY 49

2 Thessalonians 2:13-17

What is the writer saying?

How can I apply this to my life?

PRAY Serbia - Pray that this war-torn generation of embittered young people would be open to the church, missionaries, and the Gospel.

Paul says that there are three tenses to "salvation": 1) We were chosen in the past (2:13); 2) we are confirmed in the present (2:14); and 3) we will be continuing in the future (2:15). Verse 14 makes it clear that humans are responsible for their behavior and must respond to God's gracious call to appropriate the blessings of salvation. Once saved, we in our very person are glorious to God – we are trophies of His grace. Paul is careful to include both his oral and written communication in the "traditions" (doctrines) that they should hold. Jesus Christ is mentioned first in verse 16. This certainly would be bizarre if Christ is not indeed God, of very God. He is called "Lord." The Greek word is *kurios*. It can mean sir, master or lord. However when Jewish scholars translated the Old Testament into Greek they always used *kurios* for the Hebrew word *Jehovah*. Therefore we conclude that when Paul or the disciples refer to Jesus as "Lord" they don't mean *Mr. Jesus* but rather *Jehovah Jesus*. "Jesus" is His given name as a human. It is the Greek equivalent to Joshua and similar to Isaiah and Hosea, all of which contain the concept of *salvation*. Jesus/Joshua means *Jehovah is Salvation*. "Christ" is a title. It is the Greek equivalent of the Hebrew *Meshiach*, *Messiah*. That means that every time we speak of Jesus Christ, we are really saying *Messiah Jesus*. That also means, as Christians, we are *Messianics*. Both the Lord Jesus Christ and God our Father loved us (past tense). "Grace" is undeserved favor.

LIFE STEP "Everlasting consolation" means that this gracious gift of comfort is ours forever! How is God comforting you today?

FRIDAY 49

2 Thessalonians 3:1-5

What is the writer saying?

How can I apply this to my life?

PRAY Colombia – For the need for quality teachers to train young leaders among the 20 theological schools.

The rest of the book (chapter 3) deals with the practical application of *abstract* doctrine. In the first three verses, Paul requests prayer. Notice that with one-third of the book left, Paul (as with many preachers!?) has the audacity to say "finally." Actually "finally" doesn't mean in conclusion, but rather, *my final topic*. The "us" would be the men mentioned in 1:1, Paul, Timothy and Silvanus. "Free course" means, *spread rapidly or run*. Paul envisions the Gospel catching on like wildfire or growing profusely like a healthy vine. "The word" is the *logos*. It is the background to our English word logo (as a saying, or the insignia for an organization). It can mean the written or spoken word. It refers to Christ as the living Word (communication) from God. It also is the ancient Greeks' concept of ultimate thought, philosophical thought – the logic that controls the material and immaterial universe. Christians, therefore, possess ultimate logic, "the way, the truth and the life" (John 14:6). Paul prays that this precious gift of knowledge is recognized and prized by others. Verse 2 expresses concern about <u>the</u> (in Greek) "unreasonable and wicked men." Paul has a particular conflict in mind, perhaps the one he is enduring as he writes from Corinth (Acts 18). While the average man is faithless, God is faithful and will protect the child of God from <u>the</u> (Greek) <u>evil one</u> (namely Satan). Paul encourages the Thessalonians in 3:4-5. He is a master motivator. He uses the technique of positive reinforcement to ensure that the Thessalonians do what he requests. By stating his confidence in them, his exhortation becomes a self-fulfilling prophecy.

 LIFE STEP Patience is a virtue. It is also a command as we wait for the Lord to intervene in the affairs of men and set things straight on planet earth.

What is the writer saying?

How can I apply this to my life?

Apparently, some believers are begging instead of working. The Thessalonians are to "withdraw" from such people in order to shame them into repentance. Paul says that they "ought" (moral obligation) to follow Paul's example. "Follow" is the Greek word *mimic*. Paul does not beg (3:8). *No work, no eat* is a familiar concept to students of American history. In the early settlement at Jamestown, the governor, John Smith, had to insist on this principle to ensure that every person carried his own load in the difficult task of building a successful community in the new world. Eventually this became known as the Protestant Work Ethic. Verse 11 is a play on words. Instead of being busy (i.e., working), they were "busybodies" (using the time they had on their hands to mind other people's business). The "quietness" of verse12 means *settle down*, probably over the agitations of the rumor about the day of the Lord. "Note that man" literally means to *brand* him. He is to be shunned by other believers giving him the message that they do not approve of his behavior and will have nothing to do with him as long as he behaves that way. The goal is not punishment, but to shame him to a point of repentance and return to fellowship. In a pagan society, it would get lonely real fast. Paul says that he is to be admonished with love (3:15). "Admonish" means *to put in mind of the truth*. Sometimes it is not a matter of not knowing, but not remembering what the truth requires of us. Paul uses a secretary to dictate his letters, perhaps because of poor eyesight. He says he signs all of his epistles so that they would be able to recognize forgeries.

LIFE STEP In the past (before Christ), we were not able not to sin. In the present (in Christ) we are able not to sin. In the future (glorified with Christ) we will be not able to sin!

It has been about five years since Paul was in the area where the city of Colosse is located. During that time, a lot has happened in the apostle's life: a trip to Jerusalem, an arrest, an appeal to Caesar, a hazardous adventure at sea, and now a house-imprisonment at Rome.

In Colosse, a more dangerous enemy than Caesar has begun to wreak havoc in the local church. That enemy is heresy – false doctrine. Called the *Colossian Heresy*, it is nowhere defined specifically. All that we know about it comes from inferences Paul makes in this letter. It is generally believed that the heresy is Jewish in origin. It involves legal ordinances, circumcision, food regulations and the observance of Sabbaths and other holy days (2:16). Combined with these Jewish characteristics are several features of what later would be called Gnosticism. Gnosticism, coming from the Greek word *ginosko* meaning to know, is the belief that there is a clear separation between the physical and the spiritual realms. By denying one's physical needs, one would be able to achieve great spiritual power. Thus asceticism (denying oneself) is a natural product of such thinking.

In order to bring together sinful and physical man with a spiritual and holy God, the Gnostics invented a whole hierarchy of angelic beings. These angels become the mediators between God and man. All God's revelation is delivered by them to man, and all man's prayers are in like manner delivered to God. Thus, they hold a very important position in the Gnostics' minds and often become objects of worship.

To counter these claims, the Apostle Paul, in this rather short letter, has one overriding theme: *the preeminence of Christ.* He is sufficient to provide a complete salvation. Works are not necessary. He alone is both man and God and therefore able to be our advocate before God. Angels are created beings just as we are. He is fully God and fully man. In Him all the fullness of Deity dwells in bodily form.

This book is a companion volume to the Book of Ephesians. In that letter we see the church, Christ's body; in this book we see Christ, the church's head.

The book breaks down into two major sections. The first is doctrinal; the second, practical. The first demonstrates that Christ is preeminent in the creation; the second, that Christ should be preeminent in our lives.

The following is a brief outline of the book:

- 1:1-14   Introduction
- 1:15–3:4 Christ: His Person
            and Work are
            Sufficient
- 3:5–4:6   Christian: Live in
            Christ's Sufficiency
- 4:7-18   Personal Greetings

Colossians 1:1-8

What is the writer saying?

How can I apply this to my life?

Paul begins his letter to the Colossians reminding them of his unique authority as an apostle – he is appointed an apostle by the will of God.

He addresses the believers: they are "saints" – meaning *they are set apart for* Christ *from* the world. They are also "faithful brethren," a remarkable commendation. They are standing steadfast despite the false teachers that sought to corrupt them.

As Paul thinks of these Colossian believers, he thanks God for them as he constantly prays for them (v. 3). Paul's familiar trilogy – faith, love, hope – reveal the Colossians' maturity in Christ.

• *Faith* is a calm trust in Christ despite trials and troubles.

• *Love* is more than emotion; it is a reasoned decision and determination to love other believers.

• *Hope* is an abiding trust and patient waiting, knowing that God has determined the future and provided a rich inheritance in heaven, reserved for His own (v. 5; 1 Peter 1:4).

These Colossians are remarkable. When they heard the gospel, the word of truth, they responded to it, and that word continues to bear fruit in their lives. Paul pictures the Colossians as a tree, beginning with a small sapling that would grow into a large, sturdy tree. From the very first day they heard the word, they began to produce fruit – and continue to do so. How did it happen? Through a faithful servant, Epaphras, God's truth came to the Colossians and it bore a bumper crop of fruit. His ministry kept the Colossians from falling into false teaching and it promoted a rich, spiritual life of faith, love, and hope.

LIFE STEP As I examine my life, do I possess the tripod of maturity – faith, love, and hope? Am I exhibiting a deep-seated trust in Christ amid difficult circumstances? Do I exhibit an obvious love for believers? Do I have a calm assurance – and joy – in the prospect of heaven?

Colossians 1:9-14

What is the writer saying?

How can I apply this to my life?

When Paul hears Epaphras' good report about the Colossians, he is further encouraged to pray that the Colossians would be filled with a knowledge of God's will. The present participles "pray" and "desire" reflect the intensity of Paul's prayer for them. Why is Paul fervent in his prayer for them? Because he fears false teachers might lead them astray. To avoid this, Paul prays that they would have a full knowledge of God's will which is only found in God's Word. God reveals His will through His Word. If we follow it we will not fall into error. A proper knowledge of God's Word also results in wisdom – knowing how to apply God's Word to life's experiences. When a believer conducts himself in a way that is pleasing to the Lord (Philippians 1:27; 1 Thessalonians 2:12), four things will result:

1) He is constantly *bearing fruit* in every good work (John 15:5) while revealing the life of Christ through himself (Galatians 2:20) as he learns to glorify God in *every* realm of life.

2) He is constantly *growing in the knowledge of God* and in fellowship with Him (2 Peter 3:18).

3) He is constantly being *strengthened by God's power*. Note that the verb is passive, meaning we do not do this, but God empowers us (Ephesians 3:16; 6:10) with a supernatural result: steadfastness amid difficulties, and patience in forgiving and tolerating others.

4) He has a characteristically *thankful spirit* because God has, through His grace, qualified him to share in the glorious, heavenly inheritance in Christ. The reason we rejoice is because of His provision of redemption, Christ has delivered us from the realm of Satan's power (Ephesians 2:2) and translated us into the kingdom of Christ!

LIFE STEP The best security against deception by false teachers is feeding daily on God's Word. How much time have you spent in His Word this week?

Colossians 1:15-19

What is the writer saying?

How can I apply this to my life?

PRAY Uganda – That the nearly 2,000,000 orphans of AIDS and war would embrace true life in Christ.

The heart of Christianity is Christ. The actual, undiluted Deity of Jesus Christ is the doctrine that separates Christianity from cults and other religions. Jesus is God! In battling the false philosophy in Colosse, Paul instructs the believers concerning the supremacy of Christ. He is supreme in the universe and in the church. Just as a painting of George Washington reveals what the first president looked like, so Jesus is the exact image and likeness of God – He reveals what God is like (v. 15; Hebrews 1:3). As the second person in the Godhead, Jesus is equal with the Father. Jesus is also the "firstborn," which does not mean He was created, but rather emphasizes His uniqueness in having authority over all creation. 'Firstborn' stresses the preeminence, lofty position, dignity, and authority of Christ. He is sovereign over all creation (Psalm 89:27).

Moreover, in countering the false teachers who taught that angels created the world, Paul informs us that Christ, in His preeminence, has created *all* things (v. 16; John 1:3; Hebrews 1:2). Clearly, if Christ created all things, He is un-created and eternal. Christ created the visible and the invisible – destroying the argument of the heretics who teach that matter is evil, but spirit is good. Christ created all things for the purpose of glorifying God; all creation is to magnify the majesty of God. Christ has no beginning. He is eternal (v. 17; John 1:1; 8:58) and He is also the cohesive force of the universe (v. 17; Hebrews 1:3). The ultimate purpose of the fullness of Deity dwelling in Him is that He might have first place in the church and in believers' lives (vv. 18-19).

LIFE STEP Take some time and reflect on one of the many aspects of the doctrine of the Deity of Christ. Also, ask yourself this: *Since I am in vital connection with Christ, and Christ is God, what difference should that make in how I conduct my life today, this week, and throughout my life?*

What is the writer saying?

How can I apply this to my life?

Described here is the divine transaction that took place through the death of Jesus Christ. Jesus became our Redeemer who came to "reconcile all things unto himself" (v. 20). Reconciliation means *to exchange hostility for friendship*. Since the fall of Adam, all humanity is dead in sin (Ephesians 2:1) and hostile toward God. Man is at war with God. Fellowship with God has been broken. But through His sacrificial death, Christ has removed the barrier and brought reconciliation and peace. Christ has *provisionally* provided reconciliation for the entire world (2 Cor. 5:18-20), but it is *effective only* in those who respond to the call of the Gospel. People must believe in Christ to acquire this gift of reconciliation. Just as some marriages end in separation, so unbelieving people are alienated, estranged from God (v. 21; Ephesians 2:3). Reconciliation came "In the body of his flesh through death." Jesus did not die merely as a martyr, a hero, or as an example. He died as a *substitutionary atonement* to provide reconciliation with the Father. *Substitutionary* means *He died in my place*. *Atonement* means *He paid the full price to cover and wash away my guilt*. And what is the result? Through Christ, we stand before the Father, "holy, unblameable and unreprovable" (v. 22). Positionally, as believers we stand sanctified and holy– passed on to us through Christ. We are also blameless– sin is entirely removed from our account. And we are "unreproveable," or beyond reproach, so sin is never called against us again. All this is true if (*since*) we continue in the faith (v. 23). Salvation in Christ is complete!

LIFE STEP We who have been *reconciled* to Christ are also committed with the *ministry of reconciliation* (2 Cor. 5:18-20). Are you a faithful ambassador of reconciliation in bringing the Good News to the lost? Who will you see today that needs to hear from you about how they can be reconciled to God? Spend some time praying to God for them. Pray that God would provide you an opportunity to speak to them.

Colossians 1:24-29

What is the writer saying?

How can I apply this to my life?

PRAY India – Protection and boldness for believers facing persecution by Hindu extremists.

In bringing the gospel to the Colossians and others, Paul suffers physically. His dedication results in his imprisonment in Rome (Acts 28). But Paul counts it a privilege to suffer for the Gospel (v. 24). Of course, this does not mean that we can add anything to the saving work of Christ, as some falsely teach. We can't. Christ's work on the cross is complete (Hebrews 10:10-14). We are justified by the blood of Christ (Romans 3:24-25). Nothing remains to be done for our salvation. Paul is thinking of his service to the church (v. 25). The Lord has set Paul aside and indicated he would suffer for the Gospel (Acts 9:15-16). Christ died to save the Church; Paul suffers to preserve the Church through preaching the Gospel. Paul's service to the Church is a stewardship given to him by the Lord. As a slave is given a responsibility to serve in his master's household, so Paul receives his stewardship from his Master, the Lord Jesus, to serve the Church (v. 25).

Paul has the glorious privilege of preaching a new message, a "mystery" that has never before been revealed (v. 26)! It is Christ's permanent indwelling in every believer, whether Jew or Gentile. This is a mystery in the Old Testament, but is now revealed by Paul. He particularly speaks this astonishing truth to the Gentiles; Christ is in you Gentiles! Christ is now their "hope of glory" (v. 27). When Christ returns in His glorious splendor, Jews and Gentiles alike will have their hope realized in Him. For this reason, Paul preaches Christ, admonishing believers to avoid being led astray by false teachers. Paul's purpose is to present believers "perfect (*complete*) in Christ" (v. 28).

LIFE STEP Meditate on the phrase "Christ in you, the hope of glory." How does this bring joy to your life? What motivation do you gain from your "hope" in the coming "glory" to live a godly life now? What motivation does your "hope" give you to serve in the ministry God wants you to do?

Colossians 2:1-7

What is the writer saying?

How can I apply this to my life?

PRAY Ecuador – Praise – In 1967 only 115 Quichua people were believers and today there are nearly 200,000.

Paul's strenuous struggle reveals his love and concern for the believers in Colosse and Laodicea. Paul fights like a warrior against the false teachers for the purity of the Gospel (see Ephesians 6:10-20). His purpose is that they would be encouraged and united in love. Legalism discourages; grace encourages and unifies. Love is the cohesive force among Christians, knitting them together through the Gospel of grace. Through love, believers attain to all the wealth that comes from a full understanding of Christ – He is the believer's riches! This is experiential knowledge – being guided by the Spirit in applying the truths of Scripture to the issues of life. It means knowing Christ in fellowship and recognizing that He is the true source of wisdom and knowledge. Christ supplies a rich storehouse, a wealth of knowledge that we can apply to all the circumstances of life.

True knowledge is essential to prevent being led astray by persuasive but false arguments. Paul sees the believers' good discipline in spiritual matters. Like military soldiers, they don't break rank; they are not moved away from the Gospel of grace. Individually, they are spiritually disciplined and, corporately, they are stable. What a commendation! The Gospel of grace begins and ends our spiritual journey. We receive Christ by grace through faith and we walk with Christ by grace through faith (v. 6). In this way, we are firmly rooted in our faith. Jesus Christ is the rich soil that causes the believer to grow. Like a building under construction, in Christ we grow to maturity; faith being the cement of our spiritual building.

LIFE STEP Since Jesus Christ is the ultimate expression of wisdom and knowledge, do you seek constant fellowship with Him through His Word? How can you become mature and be firmly rooted in this spiritual life supplied by Christ?

Colossians 2:8-15

What is the writer saying?

How can I apply this to my life?

PRAY Spain – For people to be called to evangelize to the remote areas of the country.

Zealous for the *Gospel of Grace*, Paul continues to warn the believers against worldly false philosophy and deceptive traditions that would lead them astray. Truth is found in Christ – He is the complete and final revelation of God. The fullness of Deity dwells in Him. This is invariably the doctrine that divides true Christianity from the cults. Jesus is God! And the benefits that are available to the believer are numerous:

1) *Complete in Christ* (v. 10). Through Christ's redemptive work, we stand spiritually complete in God's presence.

2) *Circumcised in Christ* (v. 11). We have been united to Christ in a spiritual circumcision. This spiritual circumcision occurs at the time of one's salvation. It removes sin's power over the new believer by "putting off" (v. 11) sin's control over him.

3) *Buried with Christ* (v. 12a). At salvation, we are baptized into (or plunged into) union with Christ and one another (1 Corinthians 12:13). This is not water baptism, but water symbolizes the union.

4) *Raised with Christ* (v. 12b). As Christ was raised from the dead, sin having no power over Him, so the believer has been raised in union with Christ. Thus, sin no longer has authority over him (Romans 6:11).

5) *Alive in Christ* (v. 13). While we were dead in sin, Christ gave us spiritual life, making us *alive*, "quickened together with Him."

6) *Forgiven in Christ* (vv. 13-14). Out of His abundant grace, God forgave us all our sins – past, present, and future.

7) *Triumphant in Christ* (v. 15). As the Romans held a victory parade after battle, so we spiritually triumph in Christ. Sin is defeated!

LIFE STEP To help you remember all you have gained by your salvation through Christ, take a colored pencil and number or highlight in your Bible all these *in Christ* benefits. Then pick one that causes you to especially rejoice in Christ and return a prayer of thanksgiving to God for this blessing!

SUNDAY 51

Colossians 2:16-23

What is the writer saying?

How can I apply this to my life?

PRAY — Bahrain – For the American Mission Hospital, which is well regarded, to see fruit from the tactful witness of believers employed there.

Since the purity of the *Gospel of Grace* is at stake, it is to be anticipated that believers need to be warned concerning false teachers. Paul warns believers concerning three areas:

1) *Legalism* (vv. 16-17). "Therefore" looks back to verses 8-15. Because of the believers' glorious union with Christ, they should not again be enslaved to a legalistic system. At Colosse, it is a Jewish heresy that seeks to corrupt Christianity. They prohibit eating certain foods, probably a reference to dietary laws (Leviticus 11). "Drink" probably refers to the Nazarite vow (Numbers 6:3). "Holyday," "new moon," and "sabbath" refer to the Jewish festivals. Legitimate as they were in their time, they were only a shadow of the future, pointing to their fulfillment and completion in Christ. Christ is the reality – not the practices that foreshadowed His coming!

2) *Worship of Angels* (vv. 18-19): Legalism ultimately glorifies self. Through self-humbling in such things as fasting, the flesh is glorified. These legalists also worship angels instead of God. The modern emphasis on angels is Satan's deception in bypassing worship of the true God. These false teachers also infer they receive visions from God – thereby claiming special status before God. These things all cater to a carnal mind.

3) *Asceticism* (vv. 20-23): Since the believer has died with Christ, he is dead to the ascetic, legalistic things of the world. Legalism comes from man, not God, and it is destined to perish. Legalism has no merit before God; we come to God only through grace.

LIFE STEP Evaluate your life spiritually and ask: *Am I seeking merit or favor with God through some fleshly work or regular religious ritual? Do I recognize that everything I have and am is due to the unmerited grace of God?*

Colossians 3:1-7

What is the writer saying?

How can I apply this to my life?

PRAY Venezuela – Boldness for Bible school students getting hands-on experience ministering to the lost.

Paul provides the positive corrective to legalism in these verses. Since we have been raised with Christ, we are to constantly, habitually seek the "things which are above" (v. 1). We must control what we think about. What are *those things*?

1) We must remember the spiritual blessings of our rich inheritance in Christ (Ephesians 1:3) – we rejoice in our glorious position in Christ.

2) We are to have a mindset that concentrates on these wonderful things (v. 2; Philippians 4:8). Concentrating on worldly things will never lead to spirituality; moreover, worldly things are destined to perish. We seek the things above because this is both possible and necessary.

3) Since we died to sin and the world through our union with Christ (2:20; Romans 6:2), we live on a different level. We live in union with Christ where our life is hidden in God, suggesting fellowship and security in Christ. And when Christ ultimately comes for the church, we will be transformed into His likeness, having new glorified bodies (1 Corinthians 15:51-58; 1 John 3:2).

4) But these positive truths have practical implications. Since we have died with Christ to the world, we must consider ourselves as dead to earthly passions (v. 5). While we have positionally died with Christ, we must practically appropriate this truth in our daily lives.

5) As a result, we make daily choices to "put off" all evil tendencies. God will one day judge things like immorality and idolatry. But these things of the flesh are no longer a part of our lives. Through our union with Christ, we are called to a new life, a life of new thinking and living.

LIFE STEP How do I *set my affection on things above*? How does this affect what I watch on TV or what I read or where I go? Perhaps you need to write a note to God asking Him to help you "put off" some things from your life!

Colossians 3:8-17

What is the writer saying?

How can I apply this to my life?

PRAY   France – For an impact to be made on the core French population.

The new life in Christ is likened to *taking off* old, dirty clothes and *putting on* new clothes (vv. 8-10). The old life of sin is to be removed like dirty clothing. Not only are acts of sin to be set aside (v.5), but also attitudes reflected in deep-seated and blazing anger, hatred, slander, filthy talk and lying (vv. 8-9). Why? Because believers have laid aside the old self. *Positionally*, at salvation, the old nature was crucified with Christ; *practically*, we daily resist the old self, which is the old way of life as we used to live it, before coming to Jesus in salvation.

At salvation we put on a *new nature*, like a *new set of clothes*, that is constantly being renewed in progressive sanctification (Romans 12:2; 2 Corinthians 4:16) into the image of Jesus Christ (v. 10; Ephesians 4:23-24). In this new life, cultural and social distinctions are erased; we are one in Christ (v. 11; Galatians 3:28). Because believers are the chosen and beloved of God, we are called to put on new spiritual attributes: compassion, kindness, humility, a gentle spirit, patience, bearing with others, and especially forgiveness. These are to mark the new life.

We are to be "forgiving one another" out of grace. Even if we have a legitimate complaint, we are to forgive. The reason? Because Christ has forgiven us. "Even as" we have been forgiven, "so also" (v. 13) we must forgive. This is a critical issue for all of us. *We must forgive others, no matter what the complaint.*

The final piece of clothing to wrap around us is *love*. This is the attribute that ties us together in unity (Galatians 5:22).

Finally, the peace of Christ must direct our decisions through the Word of Christ (vv. 15,16), guiding us to honor Christ in everything we do.

LIFE STEP   Ask yourself: Am I harboring a grudge or bitterness against someone? Do I need to go to someone today and ask forgiveness? Take a minute and ask God to help you "put on" this important set of clothing!

What is the writer saying?

How can I apply this to my life?

Perhaps there is no passage in Scripture like this one as it emphasizes that Christians should not follow culture for their beliefs. For the home to survive, it is imperative that we follow the Bible's teachings. The command for wives to be subject to their husbands comes from a military term meaning, *to rank under*. While spiritually a husband and wife are equal before the Lord, in function they are different (1 Corinthians 11:3).

Man's headship is based on the order of creation, and judgment because of deception (1 Timothy 2:13-14). The woman is told to be subject to her husband because it is a duty "in the Lord." Husbands are instructed to love their wives. Love (*agapao*) is more than an emotion. It is a selfless, reasoned-out love that loves the other person regardless of the response one receives. The present tense of love emphasizes that love should be continuously expressed. Husbands are warned not to be harsh and bitter toward their wives – they are not to be dictators. Rather, husbands are to honor their wives (1 Peter 3:7).

Children are instructed to be under their parents' authority by obeying (*listening to*) them because it is honoring to the Lord. Children should not be discouraged through a father's inconsistency. They must be nurtured through discipline and instruction (Ephesians 6:4).

Finally, for an orderly, biblically directed society, there must be proper relations between slaves and masters. Employees are subject to their employers and must obey them – not superficially pleasing them when they are watching, but with undivided loyalty, out of honor to the Lord. Masters, meanwhile, must treat their servants justly and fairly, recognizing that the Lord is in authority over them.

LIFE STEP   How can you be applying the biblical instructions given above? What are some practical ways that you can be a biblical husband or wife, son or daughter, employer or employee? Be specific.

THURSDAY 51

Colossians 4:2-6

What is the writer saying?

How can I apply this to my life?

PRAY Pray for some of the missionaries that your church supports.

Why would Paul discuss prayer at this point? Having taught on crucial issues on the home and society, Paul reminds believers that prayer is the cohesive element in carrying out these commands. In difficulties relating to the previous commands, we are to "continue in prayer" (v. 2). Believers are to be busily engaged in the practice of prayer. It is to occupy our time and lives as we pray thoughtfully with vigilance ("watch," v. 2).

It is also important to be continually praying for one another. Paul requests prayer that his ministry would flourish. Only as we pray for each other, will we see the ministry succeed. Through prayer, God opens opportunities of ministry – the door of ministry. Through prayer, God has opened the door to the Gentiles, bringing them the Gospel (Acts 13:3; 14:27). And what is the message Paul wants to bring? It is the "mystery of Christ" (v. 3) – the wonderful truth that Jews and Gentiles are one in Christ. No circumcision, no works are to obstruct the grace of the Gospel.

This Gospel must be clear, not confusing; hence, Paul requests prayer for clarity in speaking (v. 4). This is essential in setting forth the pure Gospel, devoid of human works.

Connected with this is Paul's reminder to live consistently before unbelievers. It is imperative that our lives reflect the sweet aroma of Jesus Christ, being consistent with our words (2 Corinthians 2:15-16). We are to use our time wisely in our conduct with non-Christians. Our speech should be gracious, seasoned with salt. Just as salt adds flavor to food, so our speech should be attractive and tasty to unbelievers.

LIFE STEP How can you be praying so that you might *flourish* in your ministry? Along with this, ask: *Am I living consistently before unbelievers so that my witness to them is not obstructed by my walk?*

Colossians 4:7-11

What is the writer saying?

How can I apply this to my life?

PRAY United Kingdom — Wisdom for those ministering among the 900,000 college and university students.

People are important. This list of names reflects the importance Paul placed on the people around him. Here he mentions five individuals by name. As the one who delivered the epistles to the Ephesians and Colossians, *Tychicus* is particularly close to Paul. He is a reliable servant of Christ: *beloved*, *faithful*, and a *fellow bondslave* in ministry for Christ. What a wonderful commendation and example for us! Tychicus tells the Colossians about Paul and also encourages them. Perhaps there is no greater ministry that we perform to one another than that of encouragement. Every believer can use a word of encouragement.

Traveling with Tychicus is *Onesimus*, a converted slave. Onesimus serves as a reminder of the power of the Gospel in transforming wasted lives into useful people. He ran away from his master, Philemon, and came to Rome where he met Paul and was saved. Now he is returning to Philemon, his master, for restoration (see Paul's little letter to Philemon!). A remarkable change has been wrought in his life: he is now a faithful and beloved brother.

Aristarchus is a fellow prisoner with Paul. He had previously experienced persecution in a riot against Paul in Ephesus (Acts 19:29). He is willing to suffer physically for the cause of Christ. Paul's mention of *Mark* is interesting. He had previously joined Paul on a missionary journey but had deserted him (Acts 13:13; 15:37-38). Now Mark is in Rome, involved in ministry with Paul. He is restored.

These, along with *Justus*, have been an encouragement to Paul. These names show us that people from all levels of society can serve Christ with effectiveness in ministry and be a blessing to other believers.

LIFE STEP Take a few minutes and ask God who you can minister to. Who are you going to be seeing today that has a divinely prepared appointment with you, as God's ambassador?

SATURDAY 51

Colossians 4:12-18

What is the writer saying?

How can I apply this to my life?

PRAY   Brazil – Pray for a stable financial climate so that inflation will not diminish missionary support.

Concluding words in a letter are frequently significant summary statements, and so it is in this letter. Paul, a Jew, mentions *Epaphras*, a Gentile, in considerable detail. His concern for the Colossian believers is so intense that Epaphras is "labouring fervently" for them in prayer. The picture is graphic: the word is *agonize,* as a wrestler would struggle physically. Epaphras prays intensely for their spiritual welfare. His concern is that they would develop spiritual maturity, with a conviction that they understand the will of God. Epaphras's concern is pictured as strenuous labor, exerted to the depth of his soul for them (v. 13). *Luke*, the traveling companion of Paul and the 'beloved physician,' also greets them, as does *Demas*. But Demas does not remain with Paul. Later, Paul writes that Demas has forsaken him because of his love for the world (2 Timothy 4:10). Not all who start well, finish well.

Paul sends greetings to the believers in Laodicea, located across a valley ten miles northeast of Colosse. He also sends greetings to *Nymphas* (a female name), since the church meets in her home (like Lydia in Philippi from Acts 16:15, 40). Paul's love and concern for the believers is reflected in these words. Paul's final charge is for *Archippus* to be vigilant and persistent in the ministry: *don't quit, Archippus, your ministry is a lifetime commitment!* As a solemn reminder, Paul points to his own imprisonment – he has been faithful in the ministry to the point of suffering imprisonment. We are called to that kind of commitment.

LIFE STEP   What kind of an example of spiritual commitment is your life? Are you an Epaphras, wrestling with great zeal at your spiritual task? Are you a Demas, who gives up because he loved the things of the world? Or perhaps you are like Archippus, having a difficult time in your spiritual work. Ask God to help you live for His glory.

The thirty-nine books of the Old Testament can be sub-divided into three categories: the Law (Genesis through Deuteronomy), the Writings (Joshua through Song of Solomon), and the Prophets (Isaiah through Malachi). The Law and Writings are sometimes referred to as the Former Prophets (Moses, Joshua, Judges, Samuel, Kings). The Later Prophets are then Isaiah through Malachi. The Later Prophets are subdivided into the Major Prophets and the Minor Prophets. The four Major Prophets have parallel themes:

Isaiah: "Salvation of Jehovah"
Jeremiah: "Judgment of Jehovah"
Ezekiel: "Glory of Jehovah"
Daniel: "Sovereignty of Jehovah"

The Minor Prophets number twelve. They are *minor* because of their relatively small size, not due to any inferiority. The twelve Minor Prophets are divided into the Pre-exilic and Post-exilic Prophets (referring to the exile of Judea to Babylon for 70 years starting in 605 B.C.). They can also be described in relationship to the Assyrian captivity (Pre-Assyrian Exile) or grouped based on the nation addressed (Israel, Judea, Edom, or Assyria). Dr. Walter Kaiser also notes the themes of the prophets by the century in which they ministered:

900-800 (Joel)
    Day of Promise
800-700 (Isaiah)
    Servant of Promise
700-600 (Jeremiah)
    Renewal of Promise
600-500 (Daniel)
    Kingdom of Promise
530-500 (Zechariah)
    Triumph of Promise
500-400 (Malachi)
    Forerunner of Promise

The prophets had two types of messages. *Foretelling* involved predicting the future while *forthtelling* was the process of admonishing the people to live godly lives. When the Bible was written, about 25% of the material was predictive prophecy. Many prophecies were fulfilled in Christ's first coming. By studying how the New Testament applied the Old Testament prophecies to Christ we can learn how God expects us to interpret prophecy. Our system of hermeneutics (the science and art of Biblical interpretation) is called the *literal, historical, grammatical, contextual method.* Conservative scholars have developed and defended the Golden Rule of Interpretation, "When the plain sense of Scripture makes sense seek no other sense or it will become nonsense." Other features include telescopic summary, "What the Bible presents together may unroll across time in fulfillment." *Illustrative foreshadowing* refers to a phenomenon in which an earlier episode becomes a picture of a future person or event, such as Antiochus Epiphanes illustrating the Antichrist or John the Baptist coming in the role of Elijah.

The Minor Prophets also emphasize the importance of social justice and true worship. *Joel* means "Jehovah is God." Joel is the earliest writing prophet. He ministered to Judah around 835 B.C., before the Assyrian Captivity. He warns of the coming day of the Lord (judgment) illustrated by a locust plague in Joel 1:1–2:17. He promises that Judah will be restored in Joel 2:18-32 and then concludes with a prophecy of the future day of the Lord climaxing with the return of Christ, Joel 3:1-21. In the Old Testament, the day of the Lord is sometimes used of a past judgment (Zephaniah 1:14) and most of the time of a future event such as the Tribulation period (Isaiah 2), the Second Coming (Joel 2), or the millennium (Isaiah 4).

Joel 1:1-10

What is the writer saying?

How can I apply this to my life?

PRAY Portugal – For a Bible-believing church in each of the more than 300 counties that currently have none.

We know very little about Joel. His father's name means *Opening of God* and his name means *Jehovah is God*. Based on the enemies of Judah that are mentioned, it is assumed that he lived and wrote around 835 B.C. The boy king Joash took his throne about that time. This timing is reinforced by the fact that Joel does not mention a king but does refer to elders and priests. Joash's reign was marked by goodness as long as the high priest was alive, but apostasy once this influence was removed from his life. The occasion of the book was a devastating locust plague. Since locust infestations were common, this must have been a particularly large attack. Joel accurately identifies the four major stages in the life-cycle of a locust. The Hebrew word for canker worm means *ground licking*. This is the stage immediately after hatching from the egg. The next stage is the caterpillar or *completion* stage. The insect is able to move greater distances on the ground and eat more vegetation. The palmerworm or *pruner* stage indicates that the insect is able to climb up into the branches of plants and trees. In the final stage the insect has achieved adulthood, is able to fly great distances to reach food, and then lay eggs to start the cycle all over (locust means *multiplication*). Locusts are a type of grasshopper. In normal conditions they are harmless. In certain weather conditions—a dry season followed by sudden rain—they can multiply rapidly and swarm. Swarms can stretch for miles, darkening the sky and counting in the billions. Locusts are high in protein and are considered a delicacy in many countries.

LIFE STEP God is longsuffering. He desires that all His creation bow to His will. He induces us in various ways, some gentle, others abrupt. Are we paying attention to His providential tugging at our hearts and minds?

What is the writer saying?

How can I apply this to my life?

PRAY Cuba – Godly and moral men of integrity to be placed in key leadership roles of any future government.

Historians speak of the *seven species* indigenous to Israel. They include barley, wheat, grapes, figs, dates, olives, and pomegranates. All seven are mentioned in Joel plus the apple. Wheat was the *staff of life*. It was used for human consumption, primarily as bread. Barley was normally used for animal feed. Poorer people would grind it for bread. This tells us something about the boy who donated his five loaves and two fishes to Christ for the feeding of the 5,000 (John 6). The farmers are ashamed because the Law of Moses promised that God would bless their crops if they were obedient (Deuteronomy 28-30). The poor harvest was a mark of God's displeasure on their lives. The priests would mourn, not just because of the spiritual calamity, but also because they fed their own families with the sacrifices and offerings, which were greatly diminished by this judgment. We are so used to the graciousness of God in our lives that we sometimes do not think to weep, lament, and fast when our sinful behavior becomes apparent. What would happen in our church if the pastors, elders, or deacons called the prayer chain and invited every member to an all-night season of prayer, introspection, fasting, praise, confession, and intercession? Joel argues that the agricultural disaster was a sure sign from God that repentance and humble intercession were required. Many a Christian has testified that God had to put them flat on their backs in the hospital for them to look up to Him. It has been argued that there are no atheists in a foxhole. Even our post-Christian society briefly turned to God for answers in the aftermath of 9/11.

LIFE STEP It is much easier to take preventative measures to protect our health than it is to try to recover from an illness. Feed on the vitamins of the Word and exercise your faith on your knees in prayer.

Joel 2:1-11

What is the writer saying?

How can I apply this to my life?

Joel uses the recent locust plague as an illustration of the coming of another army of judgment from God. Here and in Revelation 9, God's avenging armies are said to have the appearance of horses and horsemen. An Arab proverb notices the following characteristics of the locust: it has the face of a horse, the eye of an elephant, the neck of a bull, the horns of a deer, the chest of a lion, the belly of a scorpion, the wings of an eagle, the thighs of a camel, the feet of an ostrich, and the tail of a serpent. This prophecy of a future coming of the *Day of the Lord* would apply to the 722 B.C. destruction of the northern kingdom by Assyria, the 586 B.C. destruction of the southern kingdom by Babylon, and the A.D. 70 destruction of Jerusalem by the Romans. In fact, both the first and second temples were destroyed on the very same day in the calendar. All these calamities anticipate the ultimate time of Jacob's trouble (Jeremiah 30:7) in the seven-year-long Tribulation period. Joel envisions this horrible day as a day of consuming flames, untold loss, and seemingly invincible foes. The soldiers advanced relentlessly like the masses of billions of locusts in a swarm. They are not turned aside, they don't break rank, and swords are not effective against them. Their progress is noted by the sound of their munching through the green vegetation. Nothing is left in their wake. Their activity (flying for locusts, burning for human soldiers) blocks out the sunlight. The fortunate die and escape the horror. The unfortunate live on to bury the dead, mourn the destruction, and attempt to eke out a living after the agricultural carnage.

LIFE STEP It is a fearsome thing to fall into the hands of a holy God. God is good. God is gracious. But He is holy and His holiness demands respect. Those who respect His holiness enjoy His graciousness and goodness.

What is the writer saying?

How can I apply this to my life?

Joel is filled with apprehension, but also hope. While there is breath there is life, and where there is life there is hope, hope that sinners will see themselves as they are and stand humbled in the sight of a holy God, utterly broken over the sense of their sinfulness, and vocalize a change of heart and mind. The root idea of *repent* is that of a turning or a changing of heart and mind. There is an element of sorrow and we are told that "godly sorrow worketh repentance" (2 Corinthians 7:10) but feeling sorry is not the totality of repentance. We must act on that sorrow by a determination of the will to stop going our way and to start going God's way. "Fasting" (v. 12), is the spiritual discipline of giving up food to have more time in prayer. "Weeping" (v. 12), and rending garments (v. 13) were external manifestations of a broken and contrite heart. Joel anticipates that it is easy to *go through the motions* of mourning. God demands the real thing. He is "gracious" (giving us what we don't deserve) and "merciful" (withholding the punishment we do deserve) (v. 13). "Great kindness" is perhaps the most descriptive Hebrew term for God's love for us in all the Old Testament. The root word means *covenant loyalty*. It refers to the two signers of a treaty promising each other that they will abide by the requirements of the contract. As men of their word, they will *love* each other by showing integrity. God has covenanted to save us and His *covenant loyalty* guarantees that we are safe in that kind of love.

LIFE STEP Isaiah 57:15 "For thus saith the high and lofty One that inhabiteth eternity, whose name is Holy; I dwell in the high and holy place, with him also that is of a contrite and humble spirit, to revive the spirit of the humble, and to revive the heart of the contrite ones."

Joel 2:22-32

What is the writer saying?

How can I apply this to my life?

PRAY Uruguay – For men and women committed to bringing more Christian radio programming to this region.

A classic statement of agricultural blessing in the Old Testament is that every man will *sit under the vine and fig tree* (Zechariah 3:10). Imagine a lazy summer afternoon with a glass of Welch's grape juice and a pack of Fig Newtons! The Old Testament promised physical blessings for obedience. If Israel repents at Joel's preaching, she will experience agricultural blessing even after the massive destruction. An earlier example of this was the recovery of the whole world after the universal flood of Noah's day. The *former* and *latter* rains (v. 23) are the fall and spring rains. All summer long there is no rain in Jerusalem. The local farming fields bake rock-hard. In the fall of the year the sheep and goats are grazed in these fields, eating the stubble from the previous harvest, dropping their fertilizer into the soil, and breaking up the clods with their hooves. During the Feast of Tabernacles, the people pray for the fall rains. When they come, the soil is ready to receive the winter wheat. Winter wheat has to grow several inches in the fall and then lie dormant all winter or it will not produce heads of grain. In the spring, the latter rains get it growing again. "Oil" (v. 24) refers to olive oil. The promise that they shall "never be ashamed" (v. 27) has not been fulfilled yet. It awaits fulfillment when Christ returns to so bless Israel. Verse 28 looks forward to the spiritual blessing that will accompany this revival and outpouring of physical blessing. Peter quotes this passage in Acts 2 after the baptism of the Spirit in the upper room. Verses 30-32 await fulfillment in the Tribulation period.

LIFE STEP There is power in the blood—for the cleansing of sin. There is power in the Spirit—for daily victory and service. Sensitive believers seek both.

FRIDAY 52

Joel 3:1-13

What is the writer saying?

How can I apply this to my life?

Joel is normally dated to 835 B.C. Since Joel 3 refers to a return from captivity, some would argue for a later date for Joel (around 586 B.C.). On the other hand, Deuteronomy 28-30 predicts that Israel will go into exile if she disobeys, so a reference to returning from exile in this chapter does not require that she has already gone into captivity. Notice the universal scope of this section. "All nations" (plural!) will be summoned to the valley of Jehoshaphat (v. 2). Jehoshaphat means *Jehovah judges.* It is another name for the Kidron Valley which runs north and south between the eastern wall of Jerusalem and the Mount of Olives. All three of the great monotheistic faiths (Judaism, Christianity, and Islam) refer to this valley to the east of Jerusalem as the place of the final judgment. Tyre and Zidon (or Sidon) were the chief cities of Phoenicia to the north of Israel today in the country of Lebanon (v. 4). The coast of Palestine was the home of the Philistines (v. 4). Slavery was a standard result of war. Ever since 722 B.C. there have been more Jewish people living outside of the land of Israel than inside. The Sabeans were aggressive traders from 1200 miles away in the southern Arabian peninsula. The Queen of Sheba was a Sabean. These curses on Israel's enemies fell on them in the fourth century B.C. as the Persians and then Alexander the Great came through the region, defeated them, and sold many into slavery. Micah 4:3 and Isaiah 2:4 anticipate taking weapons of war and turning them into implements of peace. Here the process is reversed. Israel will be empowered to defend herself against her enemies. God's final harvest and the crushing of grapes to release their *blood* is a theme in Revelation 14.

LIFE STEP — God's payday is coming some day. God's patience has limits. Today is the day of salvation. Now is the time to bow the knee to God.

Joel 3:14-21

What is the writer saying?

How can I apply this to my life?

PRAY Bolivia – For missionaries willing to serve in the remote villages of the Quechua and Aymara people.

Comparing all the passages that refer to the return of Christ to establish His kingdom (such as Zechariah 14, Isaiah 63, Joel 3, and Revelation 19) we construct this scenario: Christ returns in the sky over the Valley of Armageddon and speaks the destruction of the armies of the world. He touches down on the planet at the same spot from where He left—the Mount of Olives (Acts 1:12). He will pursue the attackers of His people down to Bozrah (*Grape Gatherers*) in the territory of Edom where He will crush them (Isaiah 63:1). Cosmic signs are associated with the return of the Lord in Matthew 24 and Revelation 6. The ancients were fascinated with the heavenly bodies, ascribing deity to them. Even we moderns stop to marvel at an eclipse. God will get the whole world's attention. There will be no doubt in anyone's mind that God is working for Israel from her undivided capital of Jerusalem. The promise that "no strangers pass through her any more" indicates that this is the final conflict (v. 17). The curse will be lifted off of the earth so that the desert will blossom like the rose (Isaiah 35). Ezekiel 48 and Revelation 21 envision refreshing waters flowing from the Temple of God. The Valley of Shittim is the dry wilderness by the Dead Sea (v. 18). *Shittim* means "acacias," a tree that grows in dry regions and provided the wood used to make the Ark of the Covenant. The classic enemies of Israel, such as Egypt (400-years of enslavement) and Edom (country founded by Jacob's twin, Esau), will be judged. Judah and Jerusalem will finally and eternally be blessed.

LIFE STEP What prayer has been prayed more than any other in human history? Could it be the Lord's Prayer with the plea, "Thy kingdom come, Thy will be done in earth, as it is in heaven" Maranatha! Even so come Lord Jesus!

THE FOLLOWING CHART IS PROVIDED TO ENABLE EVERYONE USING WORD OF LIFE QUIET TIMES TO STAY ON THE SAME PASSAGES. THIS LIST ALSO ALIGNS WITH THE DAILY RADIO BROADCASTS.

week 1	Aug 28 - Sep 3	Psalms 120:1-126:6
week 2	Sep 4 - Sep 10	Psalms 127:1-134:3
week 3	Sep 11 - Sep 17	Psalms 135:1-139:12
week 4	Sep 18 - Sep 24	Psalms 139:13-145:9
week 5	Sep 25 - Oct 1	Psalms 145:10-150:6
week 6	Oct 2 - Oct 8	1 Timothy 1:1-4:8
week 7	Oct 9 - Oct 15	1 Timothy 4:9-6:21
week 8	Oct 16 - Oct 22	Proverbs 26:1-28:28
week 9	Oct 23 - Oct 29	Proverbs 29:1-31:31
week 10	Oct 30 - Nov 5	Galatians 1:1-3:9
week 11	Nov 6 - Nov 12	Galatians 3:10-5:1
week 12	Nov 13 - Nov 19	Galatians 5:2-6:18
week 13	Nov 20 - Nov 26	Daniel 1:1-2:49
week 14	Nov 27 - Dec 3	Daniel 3:1-5:16
week 15	Dec 4 - Dec 10	Daniel 5:17-8:27
week 16	Dec 11 - Dec 17	Daniel 9:1-12:13
week 17	Dec 18 - Dec 24	2 Peter 1:1-2:22
week 18	Dec 25 - Dec 31	2 Peter 3:1-Jude 25
week 19	Jan 1 - Jan 7	Jeremiah 1:1-5:31
week 20	Jan 8 - Jan 14	Jeremiah 6:10-10:23
week 21	Jan 15 - Jan 21	Jeremiah 12:1-20:18
week 22	Jan 22 - Jan 28	Jeremiah 21:1-27:15
week 23	Jan 29 - Feb 4	Jeremiah 28:1-32:27
week 24	Feb 5 - Feb 11	Jeremiah 32:28-50:20

week 25	Feb 12 - Feb 18	Acts 1:1-3:11
week 26	Feb 19 - Feb 25	Acts 3:12-5:32
week 27	Feb 26 - Mar 3	Acts 5:33-8:13
week 28	Mar 4 - Mar 10	Acts 8:14-10:8
week 29	Mar 11 - Mar 17	Acts 10:9-12:25
week 30	Mar 18 - Mar 24	Acts 13:1-15:12
week 31	Mar 25 - Mar 31	Acts 15:13-17:21
week 32	Apr 1 - Apr 7	Acts 17:22-20:12
week 33	Apr 8 - Apr 14	Acts 20:13-22:30
week 34	Apr 15 - Apr 21	Acts 23:1-25:27
week 35	Apr 22 - Apr 28	Acts 26:1-28:31
week 36	Apr 29 - May 5	Hab. 1:1-Zeph. 3:20
week 37	May 6 - May 12	Deuteronomy 1:1-4:40
week 38	May 13 - May 19	Deuteronomy 5:1-9:12
week 39	May 20 - May 26	Deuteronomy 9:13-16:17
week 40	May 27 - June 2	Deuteronomy 18:9-34:12
week 41	Jun 3 - Jun 9	Job 1:1-10:22
week 42	Jun 10- Jun 16	Job 12:1-23:12
week 43	Jun 17 - Jun 23	Job 26:1-42:17
week 44	Jun 24 - Jun 30	1 John 1:1-2:27
week 45	Jul 1 - Jul 7	1 John 2:28-4:21
week 46	Jul 8 - Jul 14	1 John 5:1-3 John 14
week 47	Jul 15 - Jul 21	1 Thessalonians 1:1-3:13
week 48	Jul 22 - Jul 28	1 Thessalonians 4:1-5:28
week 49	Jul 29- Aug 4	2 Thessalonians 1:1-3:18
week 50	Aug 5 - Aug 11	Colossians 1:1-2:15
week 51	Aug 12 - Aug 18	Colossians 2:16-4:18
week 52	Aug 19 - Aug 25	Joel 1:1-3:21